Lavish **P9-CBD-719**

ROSALYNN CARTER
FIRST LADY FROM PLAINS

❧❦❧❦

"A resourceful and determined woman ... the apron strings of Plains, as it turned out, were her liberation, providing her with a dignified and invaluable role at which she clearly excelled.... The common characterization of her as a 'steel magnolia' probably is more malicious than factual, but by her own account she is a tough, even cold-blooded, politician. The shy girl from Plains grew into a determined campaigner and a ruthless strategist."

Washington Post

"Because she kept extensive diaries, because she has a disarming ability to describe the daily bits of life in rural Georgia, on the campaign trail, in the White House, we have what may be the most readable, insightful, entertaining and thoughtful look at Jimmy Carter's presidency."

Chicago Sun-Times

"A highly personal account of an extraordinary personal—and political—odyssey ... Truly an American success story."

Boston Globe

"The Carters were the closest working partnership ever to live in the White House.... If it were twenty years from now, Rosalynn Carter would have run for the Presidency herself."

Vogue

❧❦❧❦

❧❧❧❧

"Mrs. Carter is tough, emotional, ambitious, strongwilled and fiercely dedicated to her husband. ... At the White House, Mrs. Carter rattled more than teacups. And she gives us an idea of what Scarlett O'Hara might have been like as a First Lady. She was determined to be involved in her husband's Presidency, despite occasional criticism that she was overstepping her place, and this is one reason why her memoirs are more interesting than most."

New York Times

"Rosalynn Carter fills her memoirs with juicy tidbits. ... an insider's view of one of recent history's more unlikely presidential campaign ... The tone is chatty and seemingly constantly wide-eyed."

Los Angeles Times

"Engagingly candid ... sheds at least as much light on how Carter's Oval Office functioned as it does on the First Family's private life ... *First Lady from Plains* is the work of an unabashedly political animal; for good or ill, it is unimaginable that Nancy Reagan would ever come up with anything like it."

Newsweek

❧❧❧❧

FIRST LADY FROM PLAINS

"What makes her so interesting and her memoir so compelling is her awareness that she is part of a long and distinguished historical tradition: the Southern lady in politics. . . . What ought to be a continuing legacy . . . is Rosalynn's success in breaking new ground as a First Lady without uprooting the traditions of the past. Her sense of being in the midst of generations of strong women is powerfully expressed."

Minneapolis Tribune

"Readable and revealing . . . Mrs. Carter manages to come across as Everywoman, the universal woman-wife-mother who frets about the fate of the Earth and at the same time the comfort of children and guests. . . . *First Lady from Plains* includes many funny anecdotes."

Philadelphia Inquirer

"The voice in this book is forthright. . . . She is outspoken and eloquent in her disapproval of our current government's human rights policies and its activities in Latin America. . . . Tactful, deft, humorous, always entertaining, she comes across as a likable and gracious woman—once again, letting nobody down."

Anne Tyler
USA Today

ROSALYNN CARTER

FIRST LADY FROM PLAINS

❧❧❧

ROSALYNN CARTER

FAWCETT GOLD MEDAL • NEW YORK

A Fawcett Gold Medal Book
Published by Ballantine Books
Copyright © 1984 by Rosalynn Carter

All rights reserved under International and Pan-American Copyright Conventions. Published in the United States by Ballantine Books, a division of Random House, Inc., New York, and simultaneously in Canada by Random House of Canada Limited, Toronto.

Library of Congress Catalog Card Number: 84-548

ISBN 0-449-12828-8

This edition published by arrangement with Houghton Mifflin Company

Manufactured in the United States of America

First Ballantine Books Edition: May 1985

For Jimmy

Contents

Acknowledgments

"*I am grateful* to many people for their contributions to this book. It was not easy for me to write about my life. But I began by interviewing old friends and relatives and by reading my personal diary, in which I had recorded so many experiences. This brought back a rush of memories, some that were painful and some that made me laugh aloud. My long conversations with Jimmy and our children, my White House staff and our special friends, added a sense of balance—and humor.

After I had finished typing more than a thousand pages, I turned to Linda Bird Francke, without whose help the final version would not have appeared in this form. Having bravely waded through my document, she made two trips to Plains. Her hundreds of probing questions clarified my thoughts and on occasion revealed some that I would otherwise have preferred to keep buried. I am deeply grateful to her.

I would also like to thank Nan A. Talese, my editor, who became my friend as well as my adviser; Judy Carter for her help with research and suggestions, and even a word or a paragraph when I needed one; the late Rita Merthan, who typed all of my White House diary notes, coming to Georgia after we moved home to finish them for me; Madeline MacBean for her invaluable assistance; and Jimmy for his help and his patience over the past three years.

Thanks also to Bob Pastor, Mary Hoyt, Dr. Tom Bryant,

Gretchen Poston, Kathy Cade, Hamilton Jordan, and Steve Hochman for reading the manuscript; and to members of my White House staff for their help—Carol Benefield, Barbara Block, Andrena Brown, Rhonda Burnette, Jane Cabot, Faith Collins, Paul Costello, Kit Dobelle, Carol Durst, Marilyn Funderburk, Ellen Kelley, Nancy Konigsmark, Barbara Langhoff, Wanda Lewis, Vikki Lovett, Carroll Ann Rambo, Amy Ryan and Jake Sullivan.

I am deeply grateful to all those at Houghton Mifflin who worked so hard, especially Helena Bentz and Luise M. Erdmann.

Thank you, and thanks also to the many others who helped but are not mentioned by name.

FIRST LADY FROM PLAINS

❧ *Prologue* ❧

It is early, too early, when we wake up on January 20, 1977, in Blair House the morning Jimmy is to be sworn in as the thirty-ninth President of the United States. It's dark outside and bone-chilling cold, so cold that the outdoor concert on the Mall last night had to be canceled for fear the mouthpieces of the instruments would stick to the musicians' mouths. In Union Station, the doors on a train filled with people coming to the inauguration froze shut and couldn't be thawed open for several hours.

Now, at 5:30 A.M., Jimmy and I can see the White House dimly across the street, a few lights twinkling in the morning dawn. Already two hundred soldiers are at work along Pennsylvania Avenue, using jackhammers to break up the ice on the sidewalks in preparation for the inaugural parade.

I look at Jimmy, the President-elect, the man for whom the Kennedy Center was filled just last night with some of America's greatest artists performing for him, the one person who would command all the world's attention today. He is still the same person who spent yesterday morning with me, mopping up the garage in Plains after the hot water pipes burst from the cold, the same son who had called Miss Lillian later to admit the motorcade had forgotten to pick her up on the way to the airport. "Stay right there," he told her. "We'll send someone for you."

This morning we are all safely in Washington somewhere, even Misty Malarky Ying Yang, Amy's cat, who had crawled all over the plane on the flight from Plains. Jimmy, Amy, and I have an

1

early breakfast in our bathrobes in the Blair House bedroom. While Jimmy works on his inaugural address, listening to it for the last time on his tape recorder, I fuss over my hair. I had a haircut and a permanent just before we came to Washington, and my hair feels strange . . . and much too short and curly. In a futile attempt to make it look longer, I roll it on big curlers, but it still comes out just as short. It seems incredible that the day my husband is to be sworn in as President, what worries me most is my hair!

And the cold. Jimmy asked me a few days ago what I thought about walking instead of riding from the Capitol to the White House after the inauguration. The Secret Service, he told me, had cleared it if there was no publicity and absolutely no one knew about it ahead of time. Thomas Jefferson had walked to the Capitol for his inauguration, and I thought it was a wonderful idea, a symbol of the open and accessible atmosphere Jimmy hoped to return to the presidency. Now, suddenly, I'm not so sure. Will Amy, at age nine, be able to make it all the way in the cold? Will I have to get in the car and let Jimmy walk without me? And what about Chip's wife, Caron, who is eight months pregnant? But it's too late for second thoughts. It's time to dress, and warmly. For good luck, I put three small crosses on the gold chain around my neck, one each for Amy, our grandson, Jason, and the new grandbaby yet to be born. For warmth, I put on my boots and my knee-length knit underwear. It doesn't seem like the most stylish way to dress for your husband's inauguration, and I laugh at myself a little as I bundle up, but I'm determined to enjoy this day, which may be the most important one in my life, without my teeth chattering.

As the day begins to unfold, I soon forget completely about my hair and almost about the cold. The significance of the events becomes far more important and humbling. Chip, who had been working with the inaugural committee in Washington since the election, had been to several churches in the city and had picked the First Baptist Church as the one he thought we would like to join. Now we assemble there with our family, the Mondales, and several of the Cabinet and staff members for a private prayer service. The Reverend Nelson Price, a special friend from Georgia, invokes the words of President John Adams, words that are inscribed on a White House mantel: "I pray Heaven to bestow the best of blessings on this house and on all that shall hereafter inhabit it. May none but honest and wise men ever rule under this roof." The thoughts Nelson borrowed from Thomas Jefferson are just as pertinent to what Jimmy hopes to bring to his presidency: "Our generation needs persons with hearts like unto that of James Monroe, who was so honest that if you turned his soul inside out, there would not be a spot on it."

It's now Jimmy's turn to live "wisely" under the White House roof, to try to keep his soul as spotless as James Monroe's, to become one of the leaders children will read about in history books. How I wish his father could have been here to see him take the oath of office—my father as well. All these thoughts and more are milling around in my head as I ride in the limousine from the White House, where we all gathered briefly, to the Capitol. Jimmy rides with President Ford and I follow with Mrs. Ford. I'm sure her thoughts are as deep and varied as mine, but like most people, we do not express them. Instead we chat, mostly about Camp David, where the Fords had just spent their last weekend. The food is so delicious there, Mrs. Ford tells me, that she is going to have to go on a diet.

We are met at the Capitol and taken to a small waiting room, where I talk with Happy Rockefeller, Betty Ford, and Joan Mondale. I feel numb. All that Jimmy and I have worked for so hard is about to become a reality. Then it is time, and Joan Mondale and I walk down the aisle between the dignitaries and our families to take our positions on the presidential platform. Dimly I hear applause from the crowd. This is the moment I have anticipated so long, but all I can do is go through the motions. Then it is President Ford's turn to make his way down the aisle, and I tremble slightly as the Marine Band strikes up "Ruffles and Flourishes" and "Hail to the Chief." The next time they play it, it will be for Jimmy.

As the sound of the brass, the vastness of the crowd, and the American flags snapping in the cold wind contribute to the overwhelming sense of pageantry, Amy slips over onto my lap. She is used to big crowds and had been to Jimmy's inauguration as governor of Georgia, but she seems awed by the scene. She is old enough to know what is going on, though, and I am thankful for her presence. She comforts me at this moment as much as I comfort her.

The band plays the Navy Hymn, one of Jimmy's favorites from his days at the Naval Academy, and more memories stir . . . of our Navy days and my sentimental visits with Jimmy to the chapel at Annapolis, when I was young and filled with the anticipation of an exciting and unknown future. The hymn also reminds me of John Kennedy, not only of the excitement and promise he brought to our country, but of his funeral as well, when that excitement was extinguished too soon. I look out at the sea of faces on all sides, as far as the eye can see, and feel the air of expectancy and hope and promise in the crowd. I also feel an awesome responsibility now that Jimmy is about to be President. All these people. And we are responsible to them, and for them.

Jimmy appears, and a sudden hush falls over the crowd before an explosion of applause and cheers. "We love you, Jimmy," someone yells. Then another: "God be with you, Jimmy." I stand to join him at the front of the platform and hold the Bible his mother gave him a few years ago while he takes the oath of office. It is a moment I will never forget. I look right at him, the same person I've looked at so long, and smile, thinking what a wonderful thing this is for our country, what a good, honest, and capable man we are getting for our President, a man who is going to work hard and wisely for all the people of the country, not just the elite few. I have never felt so proud.

Even the words of his inaugural address, one of the shortest in American history, sound fresh and new to me, though I have heard and read them many times before. We studied all the inaugural addresses of past presidents in our den in Plains, and I read the drafts over and over as Jimmy was writing them, surrounded by bits and scraps of paper. I even made a small contribution, suggesting that he add the strengthening of the American family as one of his goals for the presidency. Now these words, so familiar and yet so new, bring tears not only to my eyes, but to the eyes of many around us as well. And the applause of the crowd takes the frost out of the air as he finishes.

Jimmy Carter has been inaugurated, and the celebration begins.

With Jimmy's inaugural, we hoped to set a tone for an open, inclusive administration, one that would focus on all kinds of people, and to revive some of the older, simpler traditions of the presidency that had gotten lost in more recent administrations. We knew that George Washington, a farmer and surveyor, had discouraged royal trappings and customs for the American presidency from the very beginning. And other presidents gave us glimpses of a basic plainness of style that fit closely our American character: Thomas Jefferson waiting his turn for lunch on his inauguration day; Eleanor Roosevelt serving hot dogs to the king and queen of England; Harry Truman washing out his own socks; and Abraham Lincoln's letter to a child who wanted him to grow a beard.

We planned a simple inauguration, a "people's" inauguration, so that everyone who came would find something fun or meaningful to do. We had met and spoken to and spent the night with and shaken hands with so many friends from one end of the country to the other, and we wanted them all to join in the celebration and to share the victory. We wanted all 216 million Americans to feel comfortable in Washington. But not all at once! And not at all in the style of Andrew Jackson's famous inaugural, when people had to sleep on pool tables after all the hotel rooms were full, often with five to a bed. One journalist noted that at Jackson's inauguration in 1829, "orange punch by barrels full was made, but as the waiters opened the door to bring it out, a rush would be made, the glasses broken, the pails of liquor upset, and the most painful confusion prevailed . . . it was mortifying to see men, with boots heavy with mud standing on the damask covered chairs, from their eagerness to get a sight of the President."

Though we felt a kinship with Andrew Jackson, who saw himself as a direct representative of the people, we did not want to repeat the story of his inauguration!

So we planned all kinds of activities in different places around Washington: Some two hundred different musical events were scheduled—brass concerts, classical music, jazz festivals, organ recitals, country and western music, and folk music from all over the world. There were prayer meetings and poetry readings, parades and plays, films and fireworks. There were twelve events especially for children, a half-dozen free tours of the city, and countless parties and receptions. And that was only the official list. Unofficially, there was everything from the first public showing of the art of George Meany to a quiet little reception, instigated by Jimmy, for all living recipients of the Congressional Medal of Honor.

The biggest event of all was the inaugural parade. After a light lunch at the Capitol following the inauguration, we climb into the waiting limousines and drive outside the grounds in perfect formation. Then the cars stop, to the great surprise of everyone but the Secret Service and our family. The word spreads down the parade route. "He's out of the car!" people yell. "They're out of the car!" And we are out of the cars and start to walk, Jeff and

Annette, Jack carrying Jason on his shoulders and his wife, Judy, Chip and Caron, Amy skipping along sometimes with Jimmy and me, sometimes with the boys, bringing the whole parade to a halt when she stops for Chip to tie her dangling shoelaces.

And we keep walking and waving, smiling and laughing, warm as we go through the snow and ice in the subfreezing temperature. All along Pennsylvania Avenue are people wearing green and white woolen Carter hats, left over from the primaries in New Hampshire and Wisconsin, people bundled up with scarves or hats or blankets, people holding signs and cheering. There are many familiar faces in the crowd: some who had ridden the "Peanut Special" train from home, many who had campaigned for us everywhere. I didn't realize the impact the walk would have until we stepped onto the street and began to hear all those voices. Just as we want to be close to the people, they want to be close to us. "Hello, Jimmy. Hello, Rosalynn," they call again and again. "Good luck, God bless you." Some are crying, standing in the cold with tears rolling down their cheeks. I can't feel the cold at all!

We reach the reviewing stand, and we discover that the cold is still with us. Though it is supposedly a solar booth, something has happened to the sun this day and the booth's heater doesn't work. As the parade begins to pass, we forget the cold again, and I feel especially warmed by Senator Hubert Humphrey, the grand marshal of the parade and someone I love. Entry after entry reminds us of the vastness and diversity of our country, from the bands from every state to the enormous, helium-filled peanut carried by members of the "Peanut Brigade" at the end. We don't realize how long we've been sitting or how chilled we really are until it's time for us to make our way officially up the frozen driveway of Pennsylvania Avenue for the first time.

It is an overwhelming experience to walk through the front door of the White House and know it is going to be your home for the next four years. I had been to the White House several times before, as a tourist with the children; for dinner during a Governors' Conference, when President Nixon advised me to always keep a diary; and for a short visit with Betty Ford after the election. As is customary, I had been given a book of photographs of the family living quarters, so I could plan which rooms should go to each child, and had had one quick tour, also customary, of the upstairs when the Fords were skiing in Vail during Christmas. I also know that by the time we walk into the White House, all our things will have been unpacked and put away by the staff, even to my dresses being hung in the closet. It is a tradition at the White House that until the outgoing President leaves the house to go to the inauguration of the incoming President, nothing is disturbed. During the inauguration, the old President's things are removed and the new President's put in place, so when the new family arrives they're already settled. But right now, even with all those preparations, I am hardly feeling settled.

I am still numb from the whole experience of the day and what it really means. It is a heady feeling to hold the Bible while your husband takes the oath of office, to receive applause and cheers from the huge crowds, and to know that history will record everything you did that day.

I suddenly think about all the obligations and responsibilities we have just assumed. I am now in the White House as First Lady; I will live in the same rooms where Dolley Madison, Mary Todd Lincoln, and Eleanor Roosevelt lived. We are answerable to all the people—and indebted to so many whom we will try forever and never be able to repay.

As we walk through the White House door, fires are burning in the fireplaces and hot spiced tea is being served. And we are met, not by ambassadors or Cabinet members, but by homefolks, members of the Garden Club of Georgia who have come and filled the White House with flowers trucked in from home.

Here greeting us are the people who know us best, who have confidence that we will do whatever needs to be done. I try to thank them for being here, for caring about us, and for the beautiful flowers in every room. But I don't think they grasp the significance of what their presence here at this moment means. For in spite of the cheers of the crowd, in spite of the fact that Jimmy is now officially President of the United States and I am now First Lady, they remind us of who we really are and where we come from. And though we face extraordinary responsibilities and will live a life we never even dreamed of, we are first and always Rosalynn and Jimmy Carter from Plains, Georgia.

❧ 1 ❧
The Early Years

Jimmy and I grew up three years and three miles apart, he on a farm in the "country," and I, along with my two younger brothers, Jerry and Murray, and my much younger sister, Allethea, in a simple white frame house in the middle of Plains. The red clay soil is very fertile in southern Georgia, and my mother grew zinnias, petunias, hollyhocks, crepe myrtle, and what seemed like hundreds of other flowers in carefully tended beds on the street side of our house; the back yard held our vegetable garden and lots of trees—fig, pear, pecan and wild cherry, and pomegranate bushes and a scuppernong arbor. I remember very well that we had rosebushes too, because once I fell out of the sitting room window and landed in one of them. I still have the scar on my chin to remind me.

Our back yard seemed enormous. At its edge was a woodpile for the cook stove and coal for burning in the fireplaces. There was a smokehouse, a chicken house filled with chickens, and at one time a rabbit pen, though we finally had to get rid of the rabbits because they kept multiplying and we ran out of room for them. We also had a barn for the milk cow and a few pigs, and another barn for the mules my father used on our nearby farm. Behind the barns was someone else's field. Every spring the rains formed a pond in it, and we could hear the loud chirping of the frogs from our porch at night.

Dust was a prominent part of our life. Billows of red dust

engulfed us every time a car passed or the wind blew. The only paved road in town was the main highway that went to Americus. We lived on a heavily traveled dirt road, and the dust would settle on the front porch and seep into the house. There was no way to keep it out. The doors and windows had to be open in the spring, summer, and fall because of the heat and humidity.

Plains was very small, only one square mile with a population of about 600. Everyone in town knew everyone else, which was very nice when there was trouble or someone was sick, or when there was a death in the family. There was no such thing as privacy, though; everyone knew everyone else's business. But it was a good place and a good spirit to grow up in. We grieved with one another over the sad things and rejoiced together over the happy things. Collectively, we were secure and isolated from the outside world.

We had no movie theater, no library, no recreation center, in Plains. Occasionally someone would open a restaurant, but it would never last very long. The social life of the community revolved around the churches. My grandmother Murray was Lutheran, my grandfather Baptist, and my parents Methodist. I went to all three churches—almost every time the doors opened, it seemed—to Sunday school and regular Sunday church service, to prayer meeting, Methodist League, Baptist Girls Auxiliary, and Bible school. We regularly went to family nights at the church and sometimes ate dinner outdoors on the church grounds, and looked forward eagerly to one of the big events of the year, the revival meeting. For a whole week during the summer there would be preaching morning and night, and we never missed a service. We sang and prayed, and the preachers always came to our house for a meal.

God was a real presence in my life, especially in those revival times. We were taught to love Him and felt very much the necessity and desire to live the kind of life He would have us live, to love one another and be kind to and help those who needed help, and to be good. But we were also taught to fear God, and though I loved Him, I was afraid of displeasing Him all my young life. I didn't think about Him as a forgiving God but as a punishing God, and I was afraid even to have a bad thought. I thought that if we were good He would love us, but if we weren't, He wouldn't.

The other focal point of our community was our school. We were very proud of our school, which had less than a hundred and fifty students in eleven grades, and the parents participated in all school activities. Like other southern towns then, we had a school for blacks and a separate school for whites; an invisible barrier separated the white community from the black community, and few people crossed it. Miss Lillian, Jimmy's mother, was one of the exceptions. She was a registered nurse, and no matter who was sick, black or white, she was there. Always. People didn't have money for nurses or even doctors much of the time, and this was before we had penicillin or other antibiotics. People got sick at home and died at home. And Miss Lillian was always there. She was a wonderful person, and the whole community had great respect for her. My parents even named my sister, Lillian Allethea, after her.

My father, Wilburn Edgar Smith, was a tall, handsome man with dark, curly hair. He drove the school bus, worked in one of the mercantile stores in town on weekends, owned an auto repair shop, and ran his farm on the outskirts of town. When I was a child we felt very fortunate because we always had a car. It was never a new one, but my father had a reputation of being able to fix any car so it would run like new. My mother, Frances Allethea Murray, whom everyone called "Allie," was beautiful, with wavy brown hair and dark brown eyes to match. She met my father, who was nine years older, when she was in high school and he was driving the school bus. They didn't marry, though, until she had finished college, graduating with a teacher's diploma. The next year, on August 18, 1927, I was born and named Eleanor Rosalynn Smith after my mother's mother, whose name was Rosa.

Times were hard then, not only for us but for everybody. My father lost his nest egg, $1000, when the Plains bank failed in 1926. And soon after my first brother was born in 1929, the stock market crashed in New York. As children, however, we were unaware of any hardship. We grew our own food and had good clothes. In school I often drew pictures of a dress I wanted, or I'd go to Americus, ten miles away, and copy dresses from the store windows (I'd never dare go inside) and my mother would make them for me. I thought I had the prettiest dresses in town, and my clothes were the envy of all my friends. When Ruth Carter, Jimmy's sister, who was two years younger than I, became my best friend, I gave her the ones I had outgrown. Our family didn't have much money but neither did anyone else, so as far as we knew, we were well off.

There were literally no other girls in town my age. Ruth lived in the country, and I didn't really know her until she started to school. So I played with my two brothers, Murray and Jerry, and the other boys who lived on our street. We played kick the can and cops and robbers and set up a play store in our barn, where somebody would clerk and others would buy things. We "played out" at night under the street lights, and climbed on the bales of cotton that lined the streets in the summer waiting to be shipped out on the railroad. When it got really hot, we hiked to Magnolia Springs, two miles out of town, and swam there in a cool, spring-water pool. One of our favorite places was the railroad depot, which was close to my father's garage. There were passengers arriving and others departing for unknown places away from Plains, and there were always freight trains switching boxcars and being loaded with watermelons, peanuts, cotton, or whatever produce the farmers had brought to town. Often the farmers would give us a watermelon from the huge piles of them on the ground. I never thought it was odd to be playing with boys. There just weren't any girls, and I never had any trouble with the boys because I was always the oldest.

I also played by myself much of the time. I loved dolls, and my mother made clothes for them and taught me how to sew. I liked paper dolls too, and often I'd cut them out of old Sears, Roebuck catalogues. I made quilt squares out of the scraps from Mother's sewing, and she would stitch them together and make quilts. But more than anything, I liked to read. I read *Heidi* and *Hans Brinker* and *Robinson Crusoe* and dreamed about faraway places.

We all had chores to do around the house. I helped make the beds, churn, sweep the porch, and wash and dry the dishes. My brothers milked, took care of the cow and pigs, and brought in the wood and coal for the stove and fireplaces. Our father was very strict about our responsibilities and we did our best to please him. One day, when it was Murray's turn to take the cow to graze by the side of Daddy's garage, a car passed, frightening the cow. It ran the whole long block home, dragging Murray the last part of the way, badly bruising and scratching him. When Mother asked him why he didn't just turn the rope loose, he said, "I couldn't. Daddy told me not to!"

Though my father was strict, I remember many warm and wonderful times together. He did tricks for us, told us stories, and turned cartwheels and stood on his hands for us in the front yard.

One night when Mother went to her missionary circle, he even baked a cake to entertain us. He didn't drink and had no patience with those who did. He did like to hunt and fish and would take time off occasionally to go. And he smoked a pipe. I can see him puffing away, listening through the earphones to our battery radio, laughing over "Amos 'n' Andy" or tapping his foot to the Grand Ole Opry.

When Daddy came home from work, he always rushed into the kitchen, picked up my mother, whirled her around the room, and gave her a kiss. My friends' parents didn't act this way in front of their children, so I thought my house was very special. We followed a daily routine that rarely varied. My father got up early, very early, and went into the kitchen to build a fire in the wood stove. After my mother had made the coffee, he would drink a cup of it, black, and so hot that we always marveled at him. He kept a little mirror and a razor strap in the kitchen so he could shave where it was warm. The stove was in front of the window, and often I would wedge myself onto the windowsill and watch while he shaved, more than once burning my knees on the side of the stove. After he shaved, my father would leave to drive the school bus, coming home later for a big breakfast of grits, side meat or sausage, eggs, and hot biscuits before going to work in his garage or on the farm.

We were brought up to mind our parents, and we did, most of the time. My worst behavior was always "running away" from home. I crossed the street to play with my friends, but crossing the street was dangerous for one so small, and thus forbidden to me. My father always spanked me for this, and afterward he would tell me not to cry. And I wouldn't. But later I would go to the outdoor privy and cry and cry there all alone. I thought my mother always took up for him. She'd say that we needed the punishment, but she didn't like to watch us being punished. She always left the room, sometimes with tears in her eyes. But after all, we had done something wrong to deserve it. We were brought up to believe that you did what your mother or father told you to do or you took the consequences. Often we took the consequences.

I don't know why my father wouldn't let me cry. I thought it was very unfair that I couldn't, that I had to keep it all inside. Maybe he was teaching me to be strong. But often I would think that he was mean and imagine that he didn't love me. Just having these thoughts troubled me and gave me a guilty conscience for years.

When I started school I studied hard and was very conscientious about my work. It soon paid off. I made all A's on my first report card and ran all the way home to show it to my parents. They were just as proud. Mother said, "I knew you could do it," and Daddy gave me a dollar! I continued to make good grades, and when I was in the third grade, I helped teach arithmetic to those second-graders who were slow learners. I took great pride in pleasing my parents, and I loved school as a young child. My teachers, all women, were my idols.

Even at that age, the burden I put on myself of always having to do well began to be heavy. I knew I wasn't perfect, but I didn't want my daddy to know. He thought I was really smart and that I could do everything just right, which made it very painful whenever I failed. Our house was a couple of blocks from the school, and every day I walked by my father's garage, which was halfway between. At school we had a midmorning recess and later a brief lunch period, when I walked home to eat. One day I was walking past the garage when my father called out to me, "Sister, where are you going?" I told him I was going home for lunch and he began to laugh and laugh. "It's not lunchtime yet," he said. "It's recess." I was so embarrassed to have made such a stupid mistake that I cried and begged him to let me just go on home and stay there until after lunch. But he made me go back to school, where everybody laughed at me all over again. I have never felt so humiliated; I felt I had lost everyone's respect.

I set very high standards, and although I sometimes found it difficult to live up to them, I could not let up on myself. When I was in the seventh grade, a merchant in town who had failed the seventh grade offered a $5 reward to the student who had the highest yearly average. I had to win it. Everyone expected me to—my mother, my father, my teachers, and my classmates. I don't remember working so hard before or since, unless it was in a presidential campaign, but I finally won the prize. That kind of pressure is intense when you're twelve years old. But I also began to see that the satisfaction of accomplishment sometimes compensates for the hard work.

It was in the seventh grade that I began to realize that the boundaries of the world extended beyond our sheltered and isolated community of Plains, Georgia. We had a young teacher who was beautiful and who I thought knew more than anyone I had ever met. She was extremely interested in current events and prodded us to read the newspapers and listen to the radio, to stretch our minds about our country and the world. One day Miss MacArthur brought a map of the world to school and told us that there was a war in Europe and that it was important we know about it. Each day she assigned a different student the task of bringing the class up-to-date on the war news. For the first time in my life, I began searching newspapers to discover a world of interesting people and faraway places, but also a menacing and ominous world. I worried about all the terrible things that were happening as war approached, and lay in bed at night, hoping it would just go away somehow. The year was 1939, however, and that was not to happen.

That summer was the first time I went away from home. For months I had been badgering my parents to let me go to summer camp with a group of girls from our church, but they had expressed little enthusiasm. So I was startled when one morning in June my mother called me in and said, "How would you like to go to Camp Dooley?" Would I! I immediately began to get ready, making myself some shorts and a couple of cotton skirts. Off I went, suffering only a twinge of homesickness but a very nice feeling of independence.

When I returned home, I understood their sudden change of mind. My father was sick—very, very sick. When I had been at camp and my brothers and little sister were visiting my mother's parents, Daddy had been in the hospital for tests. The adults had known about his illness for some time, and they assured us that he would soon be all right.

But he wasn't. Several weeks passed, and although Daddy didn't stay in bed all the time, we knew something was very wrong. He'd always been a strong man who worked on automobiles, who could do anything, but now he wasn't even going to work every day. He kept reassuring me that he was doing exactly what the doctors had told him and that he was going to get well, but I began to worry. And I began to pray.

In August I knew I was right. One day Daddy started having trouble breathing and Mother told me to call the doctor quickly. I was so frightened that instead of telephoning, I ran all the way to the doctor's house and got so out of breath, I couldn't tell him why I had come. But he understood. He bundled me into his car and we went to my house. From then on nothing did any good, and my father became steadily worse. He stayed in bed all the time and would often call the family to gather around, asking each one of us what we had done during the day. He seemed genuinely proud of our reports, and we did everything to make sure he would be. He often talked about the future and his expectations for us when we grew up. And he always wanted us to read the Bible together.

I don't think I have ever felt so sad. I thought he was suffering because of the mean thoughts I'd had about him in the past, that somehow I was part of the cause of his illness. I felt so guilty that I tried to do everything I possibly could to erase those bad thoughts and to let him know how much I loved him. I waited on him hand and foot, brushed his hair for him, and read to him for hours—detective stories were his favorites. I thought I would never forgive myself if anything happened to him, and I didn't dare tell anyone how I felt. Especially my mother. I didn't want to add to her hurt.

His face, once ruddy under his black hair, grew whiter and whiter, and when we played in his room or read to him, I noticed he often had tears in his eyes. Finally, one day in October, Mother called all of us in around his bed and he began to talk to us. "I want you all to listen very carefully to what I have to say and be very brave," he said. "The time has come to tell you that I can't get well and you're going to have to look after Mother for me. You are good children and I'm depending on you to be strong." I wanted to cry out "It can't be true. It can't be true." But of course it was, and my heart was broken. I began to cry, sobbing uncontrollably, and tears rolled down my father's cheeks as well. He soon contained his emotions and told us to stop crying, but one of my brothers kept sobbing and sobbing. My father kept talking, telling us many things that day he had never told us before. He explained that he had always wanted to go to college but could not, and that no matter what happened, we were to go to college, to have the opportunities he hadn't had. He told my mother to sell even the farm if she needed the money for our educations. His greatest sorrow, he said, was that he was not going to be here to make sure we all got good educations and had good lives. I was devastated. I ran from the house to be alone with my grief in my usual crying place. My childhood really ended at that moment.

After that, someone was always at our house to help. Miss

Lillian, who had been there from the beginning, now came every day to give my father shots and help my mother care for him. Men from the community, Daddy's friends, took turns staying with him, keeping him company and helping to turn him in his bed. Other friends brought food, ran errands, and helped Mother with the housework and the smaller children. Everyone in our community was concerned, and though our world was falling apart, we knew we were cared for. There were times I resented all the attention and the people, but I couldn't let anyone see my feelings. I wanted to be by myself or just with my mother or father.

The night it was clear that Daddy was going to die, Jimmy's mother came to take me to her house to spend the night with Ruth. I don't remember seeing Jimmy that night—I wasn't interested in him then—but I remember that I was relieved to get away from home. We had waited and waited for the end, and too many people had been crowding around the house. When I went to bed that night, I never wanted to wake up. I wanted to stay asleep and believe it was all a bad dream. But in the middle of the night Miss Lillian woke me and took me home. My father was dead of leukemia at the age of forty-four. My mother was thirty-four. The youngest of the four children, my sister, was only four. I was thirteen.

The next few years were very difficult for all of us, and we were not spared from further loss. After Daddy died, our maternal grandparents, Mama and Papa Murray, helped us a lot. My grandfather rented the farm and collected Daddy's bills. Our grandmother stayed with us sometimes to help my mother, and we in turn stayed with her. One morning less than a year after Daddy died the phone rang, and suddenly I heard Mother crying. Mama Murray, the caller told her, had died. That morning Papa had gotten up and gone out to milk the cows. When he left, Mama had been getting dressed, but when he came back from the barn, he found her leaning over in her chair, as though she had been tying her shoes when it happened. Once again, our house was filled with neighbors helping in our new loss. And another funeral. It was many years before I could bring myself to attend yet another funeral.

After Mama Murray died there were many changes. At seventy, Papa left the farm, which had been the only home he had ever known, to move in with us. Now he leaned on Mother for strength, as did we. And my mother, an only child who had always been special and secure and dependent, now had the responsibility, not only of managing the meager finances of our family, but also of raising four children and caring for her father. She did what had to be done—she took charge. Since we only had the income from the farm and my father's insurance, $18.25 a month, to live on, Mother went to work. She "took in" sewing for others, and I helped her. One of her first jobs was making an entire trousseau for a local bride: suits, dresses, slacks, even gowns. She sold the milk and butter from our one cow. She worked for a while in the school lunchroom and in a grocery store and finally, when I was still in high school, she went to work in the post office, part-time at first, but later it became a full-time job.

Mother depended on me even at that early age. She asked my advice about the smaller children, about which job she should take, about what she would wear or what we could afford. She expected me to be responsible. I felt very sorry for myself at times, always having to be so grown up. And Mother never laid down any rules for me, like not smoking or drinking or staying out late. She just expected me to be good, which made me better than I would have been otherwise. She put me on my best behavior because I was the one she depended on to make all the right decisions. I had to be very strong . . . or appear to be strong.

But I wasn't. Underneath I felt very weak and vulnerable. I had lost much of my childhood enthusiasm and confidence. I had always thought I could do anything I set out to do, like getting all A's, winning the seventh-grade prize, living up to what my father expected of me. I could do anything except the most important thing: I couldn't keep my father alive. I had prayed and prayed for him to get better, and because of those prayers, I'd expected him to get better. But he hadn't. And now my grandmother had died too. I felt very sorry for myself and didn't understand why this had to happen to me. Had I been so bad? Didn't God love me anymore? I had doubts about God, and I was afraid because I doubted. That was long before I knew that God is a loving God who cares for us and loves us, who suffers when we suffer and who knows that we are going to have doubts and that we're not always going to do what is right, but He loves us anyway. At that time I thought He was going to punish me more for my thoughts. I didn't share these thoughts with my mother, either, with all her burdens. I didn't want her to worry about me, and I wouldn't tell other people how sorry I was feeling for myself. I believed doubts were shortcomings, and I didn't want anyone to know about them.

In a curious way, my father affected me even more after he died than while he was alive. It seemed more important than ever to do what he had expected me to do. Whenever I was faced with a decision or even a temptation, I would think about whether Daddy would like it or not. The things he had talked about when I was little loomed large in my mind. I had heard him say many times how ugly women looked when they smoked cigarettes, so I never smoked. And I didn't dare take a drink. I had heard too much at home and in church about the "wicked" things that could happen to you if you drank. Curiously, we did have a bottle of whiskey in our house. My father bought it the day I was born because, he said, his father had always kept one in the house for medication. At Christmas he'd use it to make eggnog, and when a friend or relative got sick, he would give them a small drink. The year after my daddy died our uncle Will got sick and Mother gave him the last drink from the same bottle . . . fourteen years later!

To avoid my unhappiness after my father and my grandmother died, I buried myself in books and in my schoolwork. At night Mother read to us from the Bible, assuring us over and over that God loved us and would take care of us. Slowly I began to regain my confidence. At school, where everybody played basketball, I was thrilled when I made the first team. I visited my friends and spent more and more time with Jimmy's sister Ruth, though our relationship was always "delicate." If opposites attract, our friendship was a good example. She was beautiful. I was ordinary. She was popular, and though I wasn't a wallflower, my prom card wasn't always full. She was warm and friendly, an extrovert, while I was painfully shy, an introvert. She could dive and I couldn't. But we were still friends. In high school we double-dated together. I had a couple of boyfriends whom I could count on to ask me out on weekends, but I was always afraid something would happen and one wouldn't call. Ruth never had to worry. She had one steady boyfriend and what seemed like flocks of others just begging her to go out with them. As if that weren't enough, Ruth intimidated me more than she knew. She would say things like, "You look worse with your hair on top of your head than anybody I have ever seen."

Still, we stayed close friends and shared everything, including the moment America joined World War II. We were double-dating at a movie on December 7, 1941, when the screen suddenly went blank and the announcement was made that Pearl Harbor had been attacked by the Japanese. Overnight our lives changed. There was sugar rationing, shoe rationing, and gas rationing, which made us give up our class trip and almost all our parties my senior year in high school. We formed a Victory Corps at school and wore uniforms: straight khaki skirts, long-sleeved khaki shirts with black ties, and khaki hats like those Army privates wear. We marched and drilled like soldiers. There were daily chapel services at school, and the names of all our hometown boys who were off fighting would be read aloud and we would say a prayer for them. When someone was killed or reported missing in action, there was a special chapel service for the whole community.

We were all, more than ever, encouraged to make something of our lives. Miss Julia Coleman, our very special school superintendent, let us know that nothing less than the best in our schoolwork was sufficient. We had to be prepared for the outside world, she told us, reminding us that in a country as great as ours, "any schoolboy, even one of ours, might grow up to be President of the United States." The only realistic future for girls at that time was as housewives or schoolteachers. But Miss Julia's ambitions for us fired my imagination. I liked math and science, and I loved machines and the feeling of mastery that comes from operating them. I had visions of becoming an architect, a stewardess, an interior decorator, even a famous artist. I drew everything from building plans to airplanes (the most exciting). One of my teachers had a boyfriend who was a pilot, and he would fly over the school and drop notes to her in handkerchief parachutes. Whenever we heard a plane, all the students would be let out of class to see it.

In the ninth grade, my love of machines brought me face to face for the first time with the startling inequity in the education of black and white members of our community. Knowing that I had a typewriter and loved to type, Annie B. Floyd, a black woman who had grown up on Papa's farm, came to our back door one day (all blacks came to the back doors of the whites then) and asked me to help type the thesis she needed to graduate from a nearby black college. When I looked at her paper, I was amazed to find it was grammar school level. I did the best I could to correct the spelling, grammar, and punctuation, and we were both proud when Annie B. made a passing grade. It was a shocking experience, to discover how low the standards were in our black schools; they were supposed to be "separate but equal." It had a great impact on me as a young teenager. But this was the south in the forties, and challenging the status quo was inconceivable.

During these years, I continued to build my self-confidence. I worked for a while in the beauty parlor, giving shampoos, and Mother let me keep my small salary for spending money. I studied hard at school, and when it was time to graduate, I was the class valedictorian. I practiced my speech until I knew it by heart, managing to deliver it with my knees trembling but without missing a word. I wore a beautiful store-bought evening gown, my first one, made of white eyelet and organdy, with ruffles and a billowing long full skirt. Mother and my aunt had cut roses for several days, just as the buds were ready, and saved them in the refrigerator so I could have a beautiful bouquet for my moment on the stage. It was a happy time for me and my classmates. The spotlight was ours with congratulations and gifts, and we stayed up until dawn and parted with sadness. The year was 1944, and we knew that many of our classmates would soon be leaving for the war.

I fulfilled my daddy's wish and went to college, but not very far away. I had wanted to leave Plains, to see more of the world, but with the war going on and four children for my mother to educate, I had no choice but to attend Georgia Southwestern, a junior college in nearby Americus. I lived at home and commuted, driving to school with a neighbor who worked in a drugstore in Americus, coming back in the afternoon by Greyhound bus. I had an allowance of $4.50 a week, which covered bus fare and lunch. I quickly discovered that if I skipped lunch I could go to a movie, and I went often with my girlfriends, swooning and squealing over a new singing idol, Frank Sinatra. There were few boys around during my college days—only three in my sophomore class. All the rest had enlisted or been drafted. The ones at home were either 4F or still in high school. Our social life was bleak, our adolescent fantasies about love and romance high.

That was the year I fell in love with Jimmy's picture.

Ruth was still in high school in Plains, and we continued to spend a lot of time together. I couldn't keep my eyes off the photograph of her idolized, older brother pinned up on her bedroom wall. I thought he was the most handsome young man I had ever seen. I had known him as long as I could remember, the way everyone in a small town knows everyone else, but he was three years older than I and had been away at school for four years. I don't remember ever having said a word to him except when we bought ice cream cones from him one summer in the old bank building on the main street in town. He seemed so glamorous and out of reach.

Plotting a fantasy romance with him became a great game between Ruth and me. Whenever he was home at Christmas or on summer leave, she would call me to come to see her—and him. Every time she called I panicked. After looking at his picture so much and becoming so attached to it, I didn't know whether I could face the real Jimmy or not. And if I saw him in person, I didn't know whether I could say a single word to him. During the summer of 1945, Ruth and I kept trying to arrange a time for me to appear at their house when he was home, but each time he had plans to be somewhere else. In a way it was a relief. I knew this was the person I would fall in love with, the person I wanted to have fall in love with me, but I never thought it would happen.

That summer, just before his leave was over, Ruth called. She and Jimmy were going to the Pond House for a picnic and to clean up the yard and would like me to go with them. The Pond House was a special place a few miles from town that Jimmy's father, Mr. Earl, built when Jimmy was in the sixth grade. Many people used it for church picnics, for junior-senior proms, for club meetings and other parties. Occasionally Ruth and I cleaned it up after the latest events, which was what we planned to do that day. I went, of course, with great excitement and anticipation.

This time Jimmy paid attention to me, teasing me all day about everything, especially about the way I made my sandwich, with salad dressing instead of mayonnaise, and with the pieces of bread not matching. But I didn't mind. While we swept the house and raked the yards I discovered I could talk, actually talk, to him. I'd always been shy and quiet, and I was worried that I'd be speechless. But I wasn't. We had a very good time, although I was sure he was looking at me that day as much younger, as the age of his little sister Ruth. And when they took me home after lunch, I thought, That's that.

Later in the afternoon I went to a youth meeting at the church. It was a beautiful evening, and as I was standing outside with friends, suddenly a car drove up—and Jimmy got out. I couldn't believe it when he walked over and asked if I'd like to go to a movie with Ruth and her boyfriend—and him! While everyone watched, I left the church, forgot about the youth meeting altogether, and went off with Jimmy Carter. He was twenty. I was seventeen.

I have no idea what movie we saw that night. My mind was somewhere else. After dreaming about him for so long, I was actually with him, and it couldn't have been more wonderful. We rode in the rumble seat of the car, the moon was full in the sky, conversation came easy, and I was in love with a real person now, not just a photograph. And on the way home, he kissed me! I couldn't believe it happened. I had never let any boy kiss me on a first date. My mother told me she hadn't even held hands with Daddy until they were engaged! But I was completely swept off my feet.

I resigned myself to not seeing him again until Christmas. Jimmy already had a date with a girlfriend in Buena Vista the next night, his last night at home, but Ruth insisted that I come with her family to the train station at midnight to see him off. I resisted for a while, but Ruth always managed to talk me into doing things I didn't feel comfortable with, like going on a date with somebody I didn't want to go with or going to a movie on a Saturday afternoon when I should have been studying. But this was turning into a family conspiracy. Jimmy, I later learned, had told his mother before breakfast that morning that he was going to marry me someday, and now she, too, urged me to come with them to the station.

I went. And Jimmy was very surprised to see me there. It wasn't the proper thing to do, but I didn't really care. I just wanted to see him again. He soon put me at ease. "Come with me," he said, and walked me over to the edge of the station platform. "I'm sorry about tonight," he said. "I would much rather have been with you. Will you write to me?" I promised I would and he kissed me good-bye—only a little kiss because his parents were there. And then he was gone, off on a midshipman cruise before returning to the Naval Academy for his first-class year.

A few weeks after he left, we were stunned by the news that our country had dropped a new and powerful bomb, the atomic bomb, on Hiroshima and, two days later, on Nagasaki. Jimmy was at sea. The announcement of Japan's surrender within days came as a double blessing to me. While the church bells in Plains tolled the good news and we gathered to thank God that at last peace had come, I said a special prayer of thanksgiving because Jimmy wouldn't have to go to war.

We wrote regularly to each other during the next few months, months that seemed to creep by. It's a long time from July to Christmas when you're in love, but we got to know each other very well by mail. Jimmy continued to tease me, writing one long letter about a beautiful girl he was going out with, only to tell me at the end of the letter that she was the eight-year-old daughter of the commandant! He also kept telling me to go out with other people and not just stay at home and wait for him, which made me angry. I finally wrote him about all the boys at school I was seeing, even those I only played Ping-Pong with in the afternoons. It worked. He wrote me a furious letter back, asking me not to go out anymore with anybody else!

When Christmas finally came, it was worth the pain of being separated. We listened to "White Christmas" and "Silent Night" in front of roaring fires we built; we went to movies and took long drives and went to Christmas parties together. Jimmy teased me about falling in love with his uniform, and I'll have to admit he took my breath away in his dress blues. On Christmas morning he gave me a beautiful compact, engraved in its silver center "ILYTG," a Carter family endearment that stands for "I love you the goodest." On one of his last nights at home, he proposed to me. And I turned him down.

It was all too quick. I wasn't ready to get married so soon. I had promised my father to get a college education, and I planned to get a degree at Georgia State College for Women, my mother's alma mater. Mother had assured me we would find the money. Jimmy's proposal was too sudden and such a shock. I felt very young and naive next to his worldly manner. Though I had regained a lot of the confidence I'd lost when my father died, I still didn't feel confident enough for such an eligible bachelor. And I think I was afraid of risking the loss of another love. I tried to explain all of this to him and, thank goodness, he seemed to understand. We decided to wait, and I didn't tell anyone, not a soul, that he had asked me to marry him.

After Christmas we wrote almost daily, and just as I had fallen in love with his photograph, I now fell in love with his letters, and my indecision slowly faded. When he proposed to me again on my first visit to Annapolis, during George Washington's Birthday weekend, I accepted. We agreed to tell absolutely no one of our plans, to keep it all to ourselves, even though his parents were also there visiting him. We spent the weekend in a happy fog, learning later that Mr. Earl was furious because Jimmy had spent too much time with me instead of entertaining them. As soon as I got home, Jimmy sent me a copy of *The Navy Wife*, a guidebook, which I studied to the last detail. And we both prepared for our graduations and wondered about Jimmy's first assignment of duty.

I think I had always secretly wanted to get out of Plains, and now I couldn't wait. Jimmy teased me about it, saying that was the only reason I was marrying him.

When I finally told my mother of our plans, she asked me just a few questions. Did I know what I was doing? Did I realize I was just eighteen and could afford to wait awhile? "Yes," I answered to all her questions. She did not seem surprised, and though I would be leaving home, I believe she was happy for me.

The Carters, however, were not so happy for Jimmy. Mr. Earl was very disappointed. He was ambitious for Jimmy, had great plans for him, and being married to an eighteen-year-old girl from Plains was not one of them. I was glad he never showed those feelings to me and was always very nice. Ruth tried to be, but she and Jimmy had a very special relationship, and even though we had plotted to get us together, when it became serious she didn't like it. She was very jealous, and it would be years before we were comfortable together again and could discuss these old feelings. Jimmy's mother was my only champion. Miss Lillian was always for the underdog.

We were married on July 7, 1946, in a small, private ceremony with only our families and friends who wanted to come. We sent no invitations and had no attendants. Jimmy picked me up at my house, and we drove to the church together. As we got out of the car, we could hear the wedding march being played (later, we found out, for the second time!). Jimmy grabbed my hand and literally pulled me up the church steps. We paused at the door, looked around to see a church packed with people, took a few deep breaths, and walked as calmly as we could down the aisle. And so I became Rosalynn Smith Carter. Mrs. Jimmy Carter.

Our married life began in Norfolk, Virginia, and we both looked forward to Jimmy's career in the Navy. When we arrived in Norfolk, however, Jimmy had to be gone most of the time. His work was interesting, testing new navigation, radar, communications, and gunnery equipment that had been installed on the old U.S.S. *Wyoming*, but for newlyweds in love, the duty was horrible. He was at sea from Monday until Thursday or Friday every week, then had duty on the ship one of the nights he was in port. That left him at home only one or two nights a week. I was nineteen years old, had never been out of the rural South, and was entirely on my own. I felt overwhelmed, but Jimmy never seemed to worry about me. He assumed that I could manage well and always made me feel he was proud of me. So I was forced to discover that I could do the things that had to be done, even though at the beginning I often felt inadequate and very lonely.

I learned to deal with the landlord, the plumber, and the electrician. I opened our first bank account and handled our bills. I learned to cook, though I had trouble planning the menus. When we were first married, I could cook breakfast, chocolate fudge, and brownies! I had helped Mother by shelling the peas, snapping the beans, and by cleaning up after meals, but she had always done the cooking. Now Jimmy helped me, although I don't know where he learned. One of the big differences between us then was that I was so afraid I wasn't going to do things just right that I usually didn't try. He went ahead and did them anyway.

I was constantly faced with new challenges. After we had been in Norfolk for three months, Jimmy was sent to radar school in Philadelphia for several weeks. I went with him, and the morning of our second day there, the manager of the hotel called to say we would have to check out by 3:00 P.M. because they needed our room for a convention. Jimmy had left for the Navy base and I didn't know how to get in touch with him. The manager assured me I wouldn't have any problem getting a room in another hotel. He was wrong.

I began calling hotels, but there wasn't a room in the city! I looked in the newspapers for rooms to rent, and finally a pleasant-sounding woman said, "Just bring your bags and move in." She gave me directions that terrified me. I had never seen a subway and didn't even know what an "elevated" was, which she said I needed to take after the subway. But I mustered up my courage and set out, actually finding the house, much to my surprise. I even managed to get back to the hotel to meet Jimmy when he returned. With great pride, I led him to our new address.

Soon after we returned to Norfolk, I discovered I was pregnant. Although we were elated about the baby, I was miserable, sick not only in the morning, but afternoon and night as well. Jimmy put a big box of crackers, some sliced lemon, and a pot of tea on the table by the bed before he left on Monday mornings, and somehow I survived until he came home on the weekends. This lasted the first few months, but once they were past I had no more problems. John William Carter, named after my grandfather Murray, was born on July 3, 1947. I spent our first anniversary in the hospital with our new baby son.

When I came home Jimmy took two weeks' leave, helping with the baby, cooking, and washing the clothes. But all too soon I was alone again except for a day or so on weekends. Only now I had a tiny baby, whom I loved taking care of. He was adorable. I loved the smell and feel of him, his helplessness and total dependence on me. I loved him so much (as happened later with all my babies) that I thought my heart would burst. But it wasn't always easy. "Jack," as we nicknamed him, slept little and cried a lot. And sometimes, out of exhaustion and loneliness, I cried with him, though I didn't let Jimmy know. Tears, I had learned, instead of being persuasive or eliciting sympathy, had quite the opposite effect on Jimmy. He had, and still has, no patience with tears, thinking instead that one makes the best of whatever situation—and with a smile.

It was difficult adjusting, however, to being totally tied down, being totally responsible for someone else twenty-four hours a day. At home, there was always someone to help with newborns—grandmothers and other family members. But in Norfolk I had no one. Just going to the grocery store became a logistical nightmare. There were no collapsible strollers then; I had to carry the baby two blocks to the streetcar, ride several miles to the store, put the baby in the grocery cart, do my shopping, and then start the incredible journey back. At the store, while I juggled the baby and the grocery bags in my arms, I would ask the clerk to put the streetcar fare in my hand. Then I'd ride back to my corner, with Jack almost always crying by that time. I couldn't carry everything home at once, so I'd leave the groceries on the curb, run home to put the baby in the crib, race back to pick up the groceries, then hurry home again as fast as I could, praying the baby would be all right. This went on for six exhausting months until a shopping center opened within baby carriage distance of our apartment.

As the total wife and mother, I washed and ironed, I cooked and cleaned, mopped floors, even listened to Ma Perkins on the radio. I bought women's magazines and clipped recipes and household tips, bought how-to books and learned to crochet and knit and make curtains. We had bought a new record player so Jimmy could listen to the collection of classical records he had accumulated at the Naval Academy. Then we added a sewing machine for me so I could make my clothes and the baby's. I paid the bills and saved money. And I knitted argyle socks for my husband while I waited for him to come home on weekends. I was living the totally conventional life of a young Navy wife in the forties, and was more content than I had been in years.

In the spring of 1948, we learned that Jimmy had been selected for submarine school in New London, Connecticut, a very difficult and prestigious appointment. The requirements were stringent. Besides being in perfect physical condition, one had to be sharp, dependable, calm, and capable of making split-second decisions that were right the first time. As *The Navy Wife* pointed out, the submariner was "preferably a quiet but cheerful fellow, without mannerisms that will get on the nerves of his shipmates in the crowded, close quarters of the submarine." We were both thrilled.

We moved into quarters on the submarine base a few months later. For the first time in our two years of marriage, Jimmy kept regular hours and was home at night. All the students and their families were housed close together, and while the men went to school and studied at night, the wives visited back and forth, swapping recipes and baby stories. All of us, husbands and wives, gathered in the back yard late in the afternoon for refreshments and to watch the children play. We ate navy beans together on the night before payday. We baby-sat for each other. We could walk to the officers' club, which we did frequently, or go to the movie on the base, which cost 10 cents! It was wonderful. I felt free for the first time since Jack was born, and no longer lonely.

Jimmy and I made good use of our free time together in New London. We took a commercial art course that Jimmy had ordered for a sailor in Norfolk who was studying for his high school degree but who had been transferred before the course arrived. We learned to use the charcoals, water colors, and oil paints and studied *Treasury of Art Masterpieces*, which came with the course. And we practiced our Spanish with a young Peruvian couple, Manolo and Maria Piqueras, who had come to New London for submarine training. Manolo could speak little English and Jimmy, who had learned Spanish at the Naval Academy, interpreted for him and helped him with his schoolwork. I had studied Spanish at college and knew some grammar, but had never tried to carry on a conversation.

We also waited anxiously for Jimmy's new orders as sub school drew to a close. They could not have been better: He was assigned to the U.S.S. *Pomfret* in Hawaii. His duties began with a three-month cruise to China, so we packed the baby and our belongings in our brand-new Studebaker (our first car) and drove home to Plains, where I was going to stay while he was at sea. Then I would join him in Pearl Harbor.

While I was waiting in Plains, a heavy storm came up in the Pacific. Jimmy's submarine was on the surface charging its batteries and he was standing night watch on the bridge when an enormous wave swept over the ship, taking him with it! He found himself swimming underwater, completely separated from the submarine, and then, just as suddenly, deposited back on the top of a gun thirty feet aft of where he had been standing. Clinging desperately to the gun barrel, he was finally able to lower himself to the deck and scramble back up to his post. It was a close call, and luckily I knew nothing about it until it was over and he was safe.

I also didn't know that the same storm knocked out the ship's radio. They could receive messages but not send them, and after a few days of not being able to respond to any urgent messages, they were assumed lost at sea. The wives waiting in Hawaii were notified that the submarine might have sunk; on board, the men themselves heard the message: "To all ships in the Pacific: Be on the lookout for floating debris left by submarine U.S.S. *Pomfret*, believed to have been sunk approximately seven hundred miles south of Midway Island." I was mercifully unaware of all this back in Plains, and when I heard about it later I was grateful for the isolation of rural Georgia. It was terrifying enough to hear the news when it was all over. So much for my *Navy Wife* manual, which reassured me that a submarine was "the safest type of vessel afloat" because "in case of hurricane or typhoon [a submariner] can submerge below the swirling waters and find peace in the quiet sea one hundred feet below the surface."

Although the seas were rough, Jack and I made our voyage to

Hawaii safely on top of the water, and I saw the deep, deep blue of the Pacific Ocean for the first time. We were very excited to be met by Jimmy on the pier, leis in hand to place around our necks with a kiss, in the Hawaiian tradition. He took us to our apartment, which he had filled with the most beautiful tropical flowers I had ever seen, with champagne chilling in the refrigerator. We were very happy in Hawaii for the next year and a half. We enjoyed the tropical climate, which thrust the hibiscus plants in front of the house to the upstairs bedroom window in only three months' time, and we liked the tropical hours as well. Jimmy was home soon after lunch each day and we toured the island, saw the pineapple fields, counted the rainbows, took Jack swimming in the sea, and took pictures of him among the wild orchids.

We quickly went "native." I made matching aloha shirts for Jimmy and Jack, muumuus and holomuus for me. Jimmy learned to play the ukulele, and I did the hula to songs like "Lovely Hula Hands" and "In a Little Grass Shack" while he strummed away. Our second son, James Earl Carter III, was born on April 12, 1950, and named after Jimmy and his father. We called him "Chip" and fed him papaya and poi instead of orange juice and cereal. In the midst of all this fun, Jimmy passed his examinations and qualified in submarines, getting his dolphins, which submariners wear on their uniforms the way flyers wear their wings. We never wanted to leave, and decided that we would come back to Hawaii for good when Jimmy retired.

However, with the suddenness that often goes with Navy life, the *Pomfret* was ordered to New London for overhaul, but just as quickly the orders were canceled. War had broken out in Korea, and the *Pomfret* was instead being sent to a shipyard in San Diego, closer to the war theater.

Dutifully Jack, then three, Chip, four months old, and I flew to Los Angeles in a drafty, cold Navy transport plane with bucket seats, little knowing what lay before us. I got to a hotel, exhausted, and took Chip's bonnet off. All his beautiful brown curls were in the hat! His little round head was bare. I was heartbroken. (I still don't know what caused it to happen.) Our car was arriving from Hawaii at Treasure Island Navy Base off the coast of San Francisco, so two weeks later Jack and I traveled by bus, train, and ferry to pick it up, then drove back to Los Angeles, picked up Chip, whom we had left with a friend, and continued on to San

Diego, our new home. It was an exhausting drive with two babies, and I had to stop constantly along the way to check the map and study the routes.

When I reached San Diego, it seemed that everybody in the U.S. armed forces had been sent there; the city was overrun with military personnel. Jimmy had been lucky to find us any house at all, but the one we had was in a terrible section of town, a few blocks from a row of bars. Not only was he not there to meet us, but the house was locked. I finally found the unpleasant landlady next door and rushed back to make baby formula for Chip, who by then was screaming. But there were no pots or pans. I had to bundle the children back into the car, find a store, buy supplies, go home, and make the formula. When I finally sat down to feed the baby, I hit a hard board in the bottom of the sofa. The cushions had no stuffing! I was jolted all the way through, and it was probably just as well Jimmy wasn't there because I sat on that bone-hard couch and cried and cried—and both babies cried with me.

It was an appropriate start, because this tour of duty didn't get much better. Jimmy was gone all week long the five months we were in San Diego, only home on weekends. I was so afraid in that neighborhood that I locked the doors to be sure the children were safe when I went out in the back yard to hang up the clothes. At night I put empty ice trays on the windowsills, so if anyone tried to break in the trays would fall with a clatter and wake me up. But often I was too scared to sleep anyway and stayed awake until dawn.

Our landlady, Mrs. Johnson, would go into our house every time I left it, and I left often because I looked for another place to live all the time we were there. Then she'd tell me when I got home that I hadn't cleaned the house properly. I had to put my garbage in her garbage can, and one day I threw away a whole pound of bacon that had black mold all the way through every slice. She took it out of the garbage can and immediately came over to lecture me on the wastefulness of young people. I couldn't talk back to her; I was afraid she would put me and my two babies out in the street.

Along one side of the house were fig trees growing by the curb. Figs would drop on the sidewalk, and the little Mexican and black children in the neighborhood would come and eat them. Mrs. Johnson didn't want the children to have the figs, and every day she would scold me, again on the wastefulness of young people, for she believed I should pick them up and make fig preserves. One day she knocked on the door with a dishpan full of figs, jars, and a recipe. I made fig preserves for a week.

Living upstairs over Mrs. Johnson was another Navy wife, who one day asked me if our landlady had brought me figs. Mrs. Johnson was bringing them to her as well, and since she couldn't put them in the shared garbage can, every day she mashed them up and flushed them down the john. I had found the solution!

I was still on my futile search for another place to live when orders came to go to New London again. We were delighted to move. Jimmy had asked for and been assigned to the first new ship built by the Navy after World War II, the U.S.S. *K-1*. It was a very small submarine, designed to fight other submarines at great depths. Since it was still being built in the shipyard, Jimmy was home at night. In his spare time he worked in the carpentry shop on the base and made a beautiful cabinet for our record player. We bought our first television set and became Yankee fans. I ironed while I watched the games, cheering for Mickey Mantle and Joe DiMaggio. In the evenings, we often fished for striped bass from the rocks by the water close to our house. And we had our third son, Donnel Jeffrey, born in 1952 on my birthday, August 18.

Connecticut is beautiful in the fall. I used to put the boys in the car while Jimmy was at work and just ride, soaking up the beauty of the autumn leaves. One fall Jimmy's submarine was sent to Provincetown, Massachusetts, at the tip of Cape Cod, for builder's trials. We rented an upstairs apartment in a big old house, and there the children and I could sit at the breakfast room table and watch the *K-1* operate and dive just offshore. In the winter I found the town library and finally got around to reading *War and Peace*. And we bought the boys their first sleds—even though they had to compete with us to use them.

Back in New London, Jimmy qualified to command submarines after writing a thesis on a new range-finding technique he had developed, a technique the Navy later used extensively. Jimmy was rising rapidly in the Navy and, always looking for a bigger challenge, he next applied for the nuclear submarine program, headed by the formidable Admiral Hyman Rickover. Admiral Rickover interviewed every applicant personally, and Jimmy went off to his interview with equal parts of confidence and trepidation. He was right on both counts.

Admiral Rickover sat at a small table across from him and grilled him for more than two hours. He started the interview by asking Jimmy if he'd read *The Caine Mutiny*, which he had, then questioned him about the details of the story. Then it was Jimmy's turn to choose the topics, and naturally he chose the subjects he knew best. But no matter what subject he introduced—current events, seamanship, literature, music, electronics—Rickover would one-up him. "He would ask me questions until he proved I didn't know much about anything," Jimmy told me when he got home, convinced he'd blown the interview. In talking about classical music, for instance, Rickover not only wanted to know Jimmy's favorite composers and music, but then would press him about the nuances of the particular pieces he had named, such as the "Liebestod" from Wagner's *Tristan and Isolde*. And most of the time when Jimmy gave an answer, Rickover would dispute it, just for the sake of argument.

But it was Admiral Rickover's last question that disturbed Jimmy most. After questioning him about his record at the Naval Academy, Rickover leaned forward in his chair, looked Jimmy full in the eye, and asked, "Did you always do your best?" Jimmy almost answered yes, but knowing in all honesty that he hadn't, he was forced to say no. The interview made a lasting impression on him, especially having to say no to the crucial question. And Rickover himself haunted him. (Even after he was governor, when the telephone operator would announce that Admiral Rickover was on the line, Jimmy would break out in a cold sweat.) But as impressed as Jimmy was with Rickover, so also must Rickover have been impressed with him. Jimmy made it into the nuclear submarine program and was assigned to the precommissioning detail of the *Sea Wolf*, the second nuclear submarine to be built. We made our last move in the Navy to Schenectady, New York, where the sub's reactor was being built. Jimmy was the senior officer for the *Sea Wolf*, working with the crew, while he also studied nuclear physics and reactor technology at Union College. His work was challenging and exciting, and he thought he had the best and most promising job in the Navy. So did I.

Then came the telephone call. Jimmy's father had cancer and was dying. Jimmy left immediately for Plains.

The next few weeks were heartbreaking—and fateful as well.

Jimmy had been away from home for eleven years and now felt very guilty about having spent so much time away from his father. Mr. Earl had always been active in the community, serving on the school board, the hospital authority, and in the Lions Club, and he had recently been elected to the state legislature. But when Jimmy returned, he learned much about his father that he'd never known. Mr. Earl had quietly bought graduation clothes for children who couldn't afford new outfits; he had loaned money to the farmers who bought his seed and fertilizer; he had helped support a widow in town for years after her husband died so she could make ends meet. Yet no one, not even his family, ever knew it except those he had helped. With Mr. Earl on his deathbed, many of his neighbors came to tell Jimmy about how much his father's life had meant to them. These revelations gave Jimmy a whole new perspective on life in small-town Georgia and made his glamorous success in the Navy seem very small.

It was not too long before I realized the handwriting was on the wall. And I couldn't bear it. After his father's funeral, Jimmy told me that he had decided to leave the Navy and return home. His only brother, Billy, was still in high school, the harvest season would soon begin, and there was no one to take over the business that his father had worked hard to build and that meant so much to so many people. Besides, Jimmy pointed out, no matter how high he rose in the Navy, he would always be working for someone else. And there was no way his life could ever have the significance his father's life had had.

I argued. I cried. I even screamed at him. I loved our life in the Navy and the independence I had finally achieved. I knew it would be gone if we went home to live in the same community with my mother and Jimmy's mother. Plains had too many ghosts for me. And what about the children? Jack had been to kindergarten. The others wouldn't have a chance because there was no kindergarten in Plains. There was no swimming pool, no beach nearby. Surely we would never travel anymore, and they would miss those adventures and experiences, too. But Jimmy would have none of it. His mind was made up, and he is a very stubborn man. It was the most serious argument of our marriage, and I wondered how or if I could hide the way I felt or the tension between us from our families.

I had a long time to think about it as we packed all our things, loaded the children into the car, and began the drive south. And

I became more and more dejected the closer we got. I didn't want to live in Plains. I had left there, moved on, changed. But Jimmy was determined—and happy. I stared straight ahead in sullen silence as we drove into town. He was grinning from ear to ear. Never had we been at such cross-purposes. I thought the best part of my life had ended. But Jimmy turned to me with a smile and said cheerfully, "We're home!"

2

The Return to Plains

I was miserable.

There is always a housing shortage in Plains, so we moved into a new government project that was home for about ten families. We qualified easily: We had no income. The back door of our apartment opened onto a courtyard with clotheslines and a grassy area, where most of the mothers sat during the day, chatting and watching the children. But I didn't join them often. Besides doing the everyday chores, I was busy sewing, making curtains, slipcovers for the sofa, and clothes for the children, and reading when I got a chance—the stereotypical 1953 housewife.

And I clung stubbornly to my new "old" ways. The boys and I had been happy with a sandwich or a bowl of soup for lunch in the Navy. But in Plains, the big meal was traditionally served in the middle of the day. The farmers who bought fertilizer and seed from us and sold us their crops in the fall went to work in the fields before daybreak, and by lunchtime they were starving. And now Jimmy came home for lunch each day, and most of the time, since we had no restaurant in town, he brought some customer with him from the warehouse. I didn't want to cook in the middle of the day and was determined to have our main meal at night. But Jimmy strongly objected to my serving a small bowl of chicken noodle soup to a very large farmer, knowing full well his wife probably had meat, vegetables, and potatoes ready for him at home.

35

"How do you expect me to take care of three small children, have the house cleaned up, and cook dinner for company every day?" I asked.

"The house doesn't have to be perfect," he told me again and again. "If I went to his house, it wouldn't be perfectly clean. And it doesn't matter what we have for lunch. If it's good enough for me, it's good enough for him."

But regardless of my feelings about coming home to Plains, there was so much that had to be taken care of—the business, the farms, Jimmy's father's estate, and his mother, who was devastated by the loss of her husband—and there was no one to do it but him. During those early months at home, Jimmy humored me but never sympathized with me. He wanted me to accept the situation and not give in to my displeasure. And he always thought it was good to be home and that we would both be glad someday. I couldn't stand to hear that one more time. "I will not ever be glad! Don't say that anymore," I said at the top of my voice, sometimes with a smile but most often not.

My fears about life in a small community were realized several months after we had been home. Mother came to see me and said a neighbor was worried because I was spending so much time in the house. That was her polite way of letting me know that people were saying I was being aloof. I had turned down all invitations, particularly those to play bridge. I didn't want to play, and I have never been able to sit and chat over a cup of coffee for very long. I'd rather be making a dress or reading a book. And I knew my neighbors disapproved of the way I handled my children, putting them to bed early so Jimmy and I could have time alone together, while the other children in the back yard stayed up until their parents went to bed.

But I just didn't care. I made myself miserable, and probably everyone around me, for months. But finally Mother's words sank in, and I began to make a conscious effort to linger over the clothesline and be more sociable. Many of my fears proved to be unfounded. My mother was a great help, often looking after the children for me. I could call her for advice about a recipe or a dress pattern, a pleasure I never had in our Navy days. I began to relax and to get involved with the community. We were going to church again, which we had often neglected during our Navy days, and not only did it soothe our conscience, it renewed old friendships. Jimmy was studying new farming techniques, already thinking big about the business. He brought home descriptions of new peanut warehouses, peanut seed cleaners and dryers that he had designed and wanted to build, and slowly he began to draw me into his enthusiasm. The boys had a full-time father, a great-grandfather, grandmothers, and cousins. I was getting to know my sister, Allethea, who had only been nine when I left home. Maybe, just maybe, it was going to be all right—in the future.

The first year, 1954, though, we were living on a shoestring; we didn't have money to do anything. Before, we had been saving $75 a month out of Jimmy's $300 Navy salary, and we had put almost all these savings into buying equipment and keeping Mr. Earl's business going in partnership with Miss Lillian. As luck would have it, 1954 proved to be one of the worst drought years in Georgia's history. The peanut crop was a failure, as were the cotton and corn crops, and no one could pay back the credit Jimmy had extended them. Our annual income was less than $200.

Then, in the spring of 1955, Jimmy called me one afternoon to ask if I could come and answer the telephone for him so he could get out of the office and visit some customers. Jimmy was doing everything—buying and selling seed and fertilizer, loading it on the farmers' trucks, visiting farmers, keeping the books, making out the bills, keeping the office clean; there was no money to hire helpers. I went that afternoon, taking the children with me, and soon I was going one day a week, then two. Before long I began making out bills for the customers, posting sales to the farmers' accounts, and paying the bills. It was a pleasant change for me. I felt I was doing something more important than cooking and washing dirty blue jeans, and the children couldn't wait to climb on the bags of fertilizer and seed in the back of the office and ride in the big trucks with their father. They also began to pitch in, doing little chores Jimmy found for them.

The one for whom our return was the most difficult, though, was Jimmy's brother, Billy. He had been working in the warehouse after school when Mr. Earl was sick and taking more and more responsibility the summer before he died. Billy had been expected to have the business, but no one had anticipated that his father would die when he was just a sixteen-year-old student. When Billy got out of high school, he married Sybil Spires and joined the Marine Corps.

The drought of '54 gave way to the rains of '55, and the atmosphere in our farming community suddenly changed from despair and depression to excitement and anticipation. The crops would be good, so the farmers laughed, slapped each other on the back, and went ahead with plans for a new freezer, a new TV, a vacation for the family, or just a chance to pay their bills. There is no way for people who haven't depended for their very existence on the weather to understand the sense of relief and renewal that comes with the rain. Even now, no matter where I am, in Plains, Atlanta, or Washington, I still have a happy feeling when it rains.

From mid-August to mid-October that year, peanuts poured into our warehouse by the truckload, ton after ton after ton. We weighed them, determined their quality and value, bought them from the farmers, and stored them in our warehouses or loaded them onto tractor-trailer trucks to be shipped out of Plains; then they would be roasted and made into peanut butter or candy or peanut oil. "Peanut season" involved hard, hard work. Days stretched into evenings without a break; all of us, including the seasonal workers we hired, often worked around the clock.

As soon as possible, we rented a big, old house on the outskirts of Plains that stood high off the ground on brick pillars. It was a hundred and four years old, with barns in the back yard and wonderful open spaces where the boys could play. Years before, the house had been a handsome antebellum plantation home settled in the midst of a large peach farm, with magnolia trees and camellias that still bloomed in the front yard. To add to the fascination, it had a legacy of being haunted, and the little boys were always looking and listening for the ghosts!

There was one drawback to our convenience and comfort: There was no central heat, only open fireplaces. It was cool in the summer, but it was *cold* in the winter. Even after the owner, at our urging, installed gas space heaters, most of the house was cold, with only the kitchen and adjoining den being comfortable, so we essentially lived in those two rooms in the winter. We would turn on our electric blankets to warm the beds, put on our pajamas in the den, and then dash across the hall and jump under the covers. Getting up in the morning was painful.

Since the house was up off the ground, all the pipes were exposed, and every time it got cold they would freeze and burst. We wrapped them with old newspapers, but that didn't help in the really cold weather, and turning the water off didn't always help, either. One cold winter night we were comfortable in bed under our warm blankets when we heard a loud crash in the bathroom. We had to go out on the back porch to get to the bathroom, so Jimmy, after some hesitation because it was freezing, got up to see what had happened. Lo and behold, the sink had fallen off the wall! The water in the pipes had frozen and expanded, forcing the sink up until it broke away from the wall and toppled onto the floor.

Despite the inconveniences, which could have been remedied, we loved the house. It was in the country, yet only a mile from our office. The boys thought it great fun, for they had room for animals: a pony, and bird dogs and a little Chihuahua, frogs and bugs and pigeons, lizards and even a snake in a box one time. And it had an attic that went across the top of the house, with windows in each end and two chimneys with fireplaces. It was floored with open rafters and was a perfect place for playing cowboys and Indians and good guys and bad guys. One day Jack found a loose brick in the hearth of one of the fireplaces. As he lifted it up, a few more moved, and soon he had discovered a ladder and a secret room suspended between the ceiling of the bedroom and the attic floor. We dreamed up all kinds of tall tales about what that room could have been used for and decided there had to be spooks in our house. They even had a room of their own.

Soon after we came home, Miss Lillian decided to go away. She was alone and restless without her husband and with Billy gone. When she heard there was an opening for a housemother at the Kappa Alpha fraternity house at Auburn University, in Alabama, she jumped at the chance. And there she stayed for the next seven years, being mother, friend, and confidante to a houseful of partying boys.

Jimmy was energetic with our business, which was expanding after our first bad year and even promising to be in the black. We were always adding on—a new warehouse, a new office building, a new service for the farmers—and we were always experimenting, trying new things. As soon as we got one part of the business paid for, or before (which always worried me, because I was paying the bills and didn't like to be in debt), Jimmy was already dreaming up something else he wanted to do. I don't know how many times I said to him, "Can't you ever be satisfied? Can't we relax and leave well enough alone for a while?" But it has never been his nature to relax, not when there is something else that can be done, and there's always something else that can be done.

Jimmy also picked up where his father had left off in community service. He became project chairman of the Lions Club, the only civic club in town, and that year our town was transformed! It was the year of a Georgia Better Home Towns contest, and under the leadership of the Lions Club, the whole community got together to "better" our home town. Funds were available for small communities to pave their streets, but until then, no one in Plains had applied for them, even though paving was badly needed. The paving was done, and as the dust settled, literally, everyone began to "freshen up" their houses—every house in town was painted and every business, too. And in a new rush of community spirit, we raised money for other projects, such as a community swimming pool that Jimmy designed and helped build. We held bake sales, barbecues, car washes, and picnics. One night I helped cook spaghetti for four hundred people in the school lunchroom. And we were successful. We entered four categories of the Better Home Towns contest and won two first places and two seconds.

Jimmy soon was a director of the county Chamber of Commerce and a member of the Library Board, the Hospital Authority, and the county School Board. He also became a scoutmaster and a deacon in our church.

I joined the Baptist church with him, and we both taught Sunday school on Sunday mornings and at the Baptist Training Union at night. Jimmy was the leader of the Royal Ambassadors, a club for young boys in our church, and helped build a camp for them, designing the buildings and joining other churchmen in clearing the land and nailing the cabins and assembly hall together. He worked with the mayor of Plains to secure a doctor for the town, and when we finally found a prospect, Jimmy helped organize the Plains Development Corporation, to finance a health clinic where the new doctor could work.

Not satisfied, Jimmy soon began taking on responsibilities outside Plains: organizing a seven-county planning commission, becoming state president of the Georgia Crop Improvement Association and state chairman for the March of Dimes. He became district governor of Lions International and chairman of Georgia's district governors, the highest position in the state.

At the same time, I joined the PTA and the Garden Club (even though after my first flower-arranging class the instructor advised me to grow the flowers and let someone else arrange them), became a member of the board of a little theater group and den mother for the boys' Cub Scout pack. There were swimming lessons and basketball games with the children, and Jimmy was still bringing everyone home for lunch!

Jimmy has always said that you can find time to do the things you want to do, but I've learned that there are times when you're so busy, you can't do everything. But we seemed to be doing everything. As each new project developed, our minds and our lives seemed to expand with them, and our "ordinary" lives in Plains became more exciting. We grew together—as full partners.

Simultaneously, I took on more and more responsibility at the warehouse. A friend who taught accounting at the nearby state technical and vocational school gave me a set of accounting books, which I studied and studied. The more I learned, the greater satisfaction I got out of balancing columns and pages and financial statements. And I still do. I have always written all our checks and kept our personal books, even in the White House.

Besides the work and the new responsibilities, we were having fun. We played golf, we took dancing lessons, and we went to the college in Americus to take a speed reading course. We broke Plains tradition and closed our warehouse on Saturday afternoons so we could go camping and spend more time with the boys. Every year we went fishing in Florida with our friends and all the children, and we also went to Sebring to the automobile races. Once we flew to Cuba with reservations for one night and stayed two, leaving at 5:00 A.M. the second morning after staying up the whole night long! We saved $300 for a trip to New Orleans with friends, but instead of budgeting this time, we decided to do anything we wanted until the money ran out. It lasted for four days! We stayed up all night every night, slept every morning, ate pompano *en papillote* (having no idea what to do when the fish arrived in a paper bag), drank wine with lunch for the first time and much, much chicory coffee. We also went to the horse races, spent hours listening to good jazz, and even got special permission to listen to the New Orleans Symphony Orchestra practice one afternoon. Jimmy couldn't resist saying "See? If we were still in the Navy we couldn't pick up and go whenever we wanted to. Now aren't you glad we're home, and aren't you glad I'm my own boss?"

And I had to admit yes, I was enjoying this life.

* * *

For all our fun, there was trouble brewing at home that would directly affect Jimmy and me. The Supreme Court had ruled in 1954 that public schools should be integrated, and the news immediately swept through Plains. Jimmy was listening to the radio when the boys and I walked into the office the day of the decision. He was worried about the reaction among our neighbors. "I don't know what's going to happen around here," he said. Then we watched as little knots of people began to congregate on the sidewalks, in the stores. And for some time—not only in Plains, but across the South—wherever two or more were gathered together, integration was the primary and, more often than not, heated topic of conversation.

The situation was enflamed by Georgia's governor, Herman Talmadge, who pointed out that such an adverse decision would abolish Georgia public schools altogether, for the state constitution prohibited the collection of state or county taxes for unsegregated schools. By 1958, the issue was just as inflammatory. Our newly elected governor, Ernie Vandiver, whose campaign slogan had been "No, not one!", promised flatly that "come hell or high water, there will be no mixing of the races in Georgia's schools." Further, he said, he would see to it that Georgia would prevent any mixing of the races anywhere, in schools or out.

There were few people with whom Jimmy and I could talk openly about the issue. I could count them on two hands—the "liberals" in the community. We didn't consider ourselves liberal; rather they, and we, were "realists" who knew that desegregation was a foregone conclusion; the issue was not defiance but, rather, how to go about integrating the public schools in a way that would be least harmful to our children.

Though we were both raised in the South and had accepted segregation as children, Jimmy and I had traveled enough to see a different way of life. In the Navy, Jimmy had lived and worked on an equal basis with blacks and could not go home and support the same old status quo. The racial issue had always been a sore subject with Jimmy and his father, who believed sincerely that segregation was best for everyone. The two had a mutual agreement to avoid the issue completely during the brief times Jimmy was home on leave. But Miss Lillian had nursed whoever needed her, black or white, and Jimmy was very influenced by her. And I in turn was influenced by him. So there was an unspoken difference between Jimmy's parents as well. Miss Lillian had even encouraged one very bright black teenage boy to go on to college, which he did, and when he came home from school, he called on her at home. But he did the unspeakable in Plains in those days—he always went to the front door. If Mr. Earl was at home, he would either leave or stay in the back room of the house, refusing to acknowledge the black man's presence. These sentiments were deeply engrained in the South, and they would not easily go away.

After the Supreme Court decision, we were quickly thrust into the middle of the controversy. Jimmy was invited to join the White Citizens Council by the chief of police and the depot agent, who also happened to be a Baptist preacher. He refused, but they persisted, even offering to pay the $5 dues for him if that was holding him back. He still refused, even when they claimed that he was the only white adult male in the community who had not joined. Then they threatened to boycott our business, which frightened me. We couldn't afford to lose customers at that point. But the boycott failed to materialize, with one or two minor exceptions—one being my cousin, who never came back to our office again.

Jimmy's appointment to the school board brought us further into the thick of the segregation issue. In anticipation of the Supreme Court decision, there was a rush in public school systems across the South to catch up at least with the "equal" part of the prevailing "separate but equal" ruling. In Plains, a handsome new school for black children had just been built, but when Jimmy went on the board, he learned that most of the old inequalities remained. The black children had no school buses and still walked to school. Their textbooks and typewriters were old, discards from the white schools, and the quality of education overall for the blacks was far inferior.

The events of the fifties were sad eye-openers for both of us. One day a black farmer and customer asked Jimmy if he could borrow some money to buy shoes for his little girl, who was just starting to school. He said she was going to school barefoot but that he would have to keep her out when the weather got cold. He would pay Jimmy back when he gathered his crop. A few days later, Jimmy rode down to the farmer's house. The whole family lived in a shack without heat or electricity, indoor water or plumbing. There was a garden in the yard with collard greens and sweet potatoes, and Jimmy learned that that plus corn bread was the family's food. A house full of children, and none of them could remember when they had had any kind of meat to eat, even chicken. This image remained in Jimmy's mind long after we bought shoes for all the children and as he worked to help our customer improve his farming operation.

By 1959, we had added new storage warehouses, a peanut cleaner, a peanut dryer, and a shelling plant to our business operation. Jimmy designed the shelling plant himself, and before long we were shelling breeder and foundation seed—extremely pure high-quality seed—for the Agriculture Experiment Stations of Georgia. We then went into the liquid nitrogen business and built a corn mill. We took in partners in two of the businesses and, as our reputation grew, started growing certified seed peanuts on our farms and selling them throughout the South.

We all worked very hard, including the boys, especially during peanut season, and they would trade hard-luck stories back and forth: "Where were you when we had about sixty farmers' trucks and trailers full of peanuts on the yard, and it came a big downpour, and we got drenched trying to cover them up or get them under sheds?" "You never had seven flat tires in one day." "You never turned over three trailers in the same ditch the same day!" "You never had the front end of a trailer break and have to shovel all four tons of peanuts off by hand!" There was always something breaking down around a peanut plant. It didn't matter how good the equipment or how much you had prepared for the harvest season. One day it was the cleaner, and there was a long line of trucks waiting while Jimmy was in the pit trying to get it fixed. Chip went to tell him about something else that had broken down and came back wide-eyed. "He cursed!" Chip reported. "That's the first time I ever heard him say that!"

Jimmy expected those of us who helped him to figure out how to do things on our own. He thought we were capable, and he certainly didn't want to hear "I can't" or "I don't know how." If he told one of the boys to go to Mr. Tanner's farm and pull in two trailer-loads of peanuts, even if the tires blew out and the tractor broke down, that boy wouldn't come back without the peanuts. The job was taken care of, as far as Jimmy was concerned, and he had gone on to something else. He was kind and patient, but he let us know that if he had to explain all the details of a job to us, he might just as well do it himself.

After a few years I was explaining some things to him. I knew more about the books and more about the business on paper than

Jimmy did. I knew which parts of the business were profitabl
which were not, how much money we had, how much credit, an
how much we owed on our debts. When the corn mill proved t
be disappointing, I suggested that it would be better to buy th
corn from the farmers and resell it without grinding it. We soc
phased out the corn mill operation.

By 1962, one of Jimmy's chief concerns was in his capacity as
member of the School Board. He was determined to improve th
quality of education for all our children. There were three whi
high schools in our county with enough students for one goc
one, about five hundred in all. Jimmy had read the reports of th
James Bryant Conant and John Gardner commissions, and he mac
plans, along with a majority of the School Board, for a mod
high school, one that would consolidate the three existing schoo
and provide a diversity of courses that could not be offered
three small schools. We would be able to have language classe
science labs, special education classes for slow learners, advanc
studies for the gifted, music instruction and a school band, a
an expanded sports program. In addition to the bare minimu
required for graduation, there would be a variety of courses
match the needs of individual students.

Jimmy made speeches throughout the county, trying to sell th
plan to skeptical audiences, while I and other supporters mac
telephone calls, wrote letters, and raised money for newspap
and radio advertisements. It was our first venture into politics-
and we lost. Every time we had a vote on the consolidation issu
which was a prerequisite for building the new school, we lost.

The school would have been in the county seat, ten miles awa
and merchants in the smaller towns voted against it, certain th
they would lose the business the schools generated. Other town
people voted against it because they would lose their local schoc
and "we wouldn't even have a basketball team." And some peop
voted against it because they thought it was a prelude to integr
tion. Integration was not the issue in the beginning, but as t
race issue grew in people's minds, a few vocal opponents accus
us of using consolidation as an excuse to integrate the school
At church on Sundays some of our friends wouldn't speak to u
and again we lost a few customers.

Racial tensions continued to build. The University of Georg
and the public schools in Atlanta had been integrated without a

serious incident in 1961, but the city of Atlanta was racked by sit-ins, demonstrations, and boycotts as other barriers—segregation in waiting rooms and restrooms, at lunch counters and drinking fountains—were challenged. The issue was getting closer and closer to rural Georgia, where the attitude was still "No, not one!"

Private academies for whites only were springing up everywhere, including three or four within a short distance of Plains. We were opposed to them because they weakened the public schools, in many instances taking away the students who could afford the tuition and leaving behind those who were poor.

John Sibley, an Atlanta lawyer appointed by the legislature to assay the sentiment of Georgians throughout the state, came to Americus to speak. Jimmy and I crowded into the courthouse with hundreds of others as he quietly said we could either abide by the law or close the schools. The crowd was polite and well mannered, but the sentiment remained uncompromising.

In this atmosphere another school consolidation vote was scheduled. To counter the "integrationist" attacks, the School Board suggested separate schools for boys and girls, thinking this might ease the fears of parents concerned with possible integration in the future. On the night of the vote, we went to a high school basketball game in which Jack was playing, knowing we would face people who were bitterly opposed to what we were trying to do. The results were announced in the gymnasium, and the crowd burst into loud applause. We had lost again, but this time by only a few votes. Many had quietly supported us while those opposed were outspoken. It was small comfort. I sat there at the ball game with my chin up while everyone gloated over our loss, but I was crying inside. On the way home from the game, we passed our office and noticed something on the door. It was a homemade sign: COONS AND CARTERS GO TOGETHER. I was devastated. I knew how some people felt, but it was a shock to have it right there in front of me. We tore the sign down and I took it home and hid it in my closet, where it stayed for years; we never told a soul about it.

Jimmy was never one to take defeat lying down, and instead of being discouraged by the school votes, he decided to take on a bigger challenge. On the morning of his thirty-eighth birthday he got up and announced to me that he was going to run for the state senate. He had talked about running for office occasionally before, but there had been little opportunity. When his father had died during his first term as a state representative, his mother was offered the seat, and when she declined, an old family friend had taken it. Jimmy didn't want to run against him, and there was no incentive to run for the state senate. At that time senators served only two years on a rotating basis in our three-county district and they were usually hand-picked by a small group of political bosses, county by county.

But Georgia had recently been reapportioned to comply with the U.S. Supreme Court "one man, one vote" ruling, and a special election had been called. Our district had been expanded to include seven counties, and the race was wide open. Jimmy's opponent, Homer Moore, from nearby Stewart County, had the sympathy of many people because he had already won the seat under the old rules and was now being forced to run again. But Jimmy thought he had an edge with the farmers he had visited often in most of the counties as we expanded our business. And we lived in Sumter County, the largest in the new district.

I was thrilled at the idea. I had met our state representative, but I had never met a state senator. And maybe Jimmy could improve our schools from the state level. We had been trying to get a four-year status for the college in Americus. Maybe he could do that too. Then I thought about the business. Jimmy would be in Atlanta almost three months of the year except for weekends, and I would be totally in charge of the warehouse. He would be gone in the winter, though, our slow season, and I decided I was more nervous about the political race than I was about the business. With only two weeks before the election, I couldn't imagine how he could do it. But that is one of the fundamental differences between Jimmy and me. I don't like to take a chance on losing. I always want to win! Jimmy wants to win as much as I do, but he is more philosophical about it. He says you must accept that you might fail; then, if you do your best and still don't win, at least you can be satisfied that you've tried. If you don't accept failure as a possibility, you don't set high goals, you don't branch out, you don't try—you don't take the risk. But I have always had difficulty accepting failure in anything, and in this race, the odds were certainly against us.

It was a brutal introduction into the world of politics. Jimmy campaigned from county to county while I ran the warehouse. In my spare time I tried to call everyone on the voters list in Sumter County. I introduced myself as Rosalynn Carter to the people I knew, Mrs. Jimmy Carter to the people I didn't because I wanted them to remember his name. It was sheer drudgery calling one number after another, and my ear got sore and my mouth hurt from talking. But I kept calling and soon I had help. Jimmy's sister Gloria and I, along with other friends, addressed thousands of letters and divided the voters list for other volunteers to call. I took an afternoon off and went door to door, to every house in town, to tell people that Jimmy was going to run for the senate, asking them to vote for him. It was difficult at first, because I knew many of the people hadn't supported us on the school issue; but they were all courteous. One said, "What in the world is Jimmy Carter going to do next?"

On primary day, Jimmy went from one polling place to another and quickly discovered why elections in Quitman County always went the way of county boss Joe Hurst. There were no voting booths, and everyone was marking ballots in public while Mr. Hurst watched. Jimmy's protests were completely ignored, and he called a friend to come watch the polls for him. That didn't help either. On election night, when the returns came in from every county except Quitman, we were leading by 70 votes. The political bosses in Quitman County decided to change the results, and when their returns finally came in, 330 people had voted, but 430 votes were counted. We had lost the election.

But Jimmy didn't give up. He challenged the election results, traveling to Quitman County every day to collect affidavits from voters pointing out voting irregularities. He was followed from the moment he crossed the county line, and when he got out of the car to talk to anyone, two men followed not more than ten feet away, listening to his conversation and making notes. There were threats on his life, and one day in the peanut warehouse, one of our customers told me that the last time anyone had crossed Joe Hurst his businesses had burned down.

I was scared all the time. I think Jimmy was frightened too, but we didn't talk about it much. And I never asked him to withdraw. I never thought about it, and neither did he. He had run for office, this was the result, and we were determined to see it through. These were crooks! And they had cheated the Quitman County people long enough. No one had ever prevailed against Joe Hurst, but we intended to this time.

In the six weeks before the general election, there were hearings, appeals, and counterappeals. A neutral judge examined the

Quitman County ballot box, an Old Crow whiskey carton that had been found under the bed of Joe Hurst's daughter. It was sealed at the top, but not at the bottom. When he opened it, the judge discovered that not only was the list of voters gone, but the ballot stubs as well! He declared Jimmy the winner. Homer Moore appealed to the local Democratic Executive Committee, controlled by none other than Joe Hurst, and Homer Moore was declared the winner. With the help of Charlie Kirbo, whom we met for the first time and who became our lawyer, we were able to obtain a directive from the secretary of state of Georgia to substitute Jimmy's name for Moore's on the ballot. Hurriedly, on election eve we went to the courthouses of all seven counties, and everyone—Jimmy, me, our children, Gloria, Billy and Sybil, Miss Lillian, and other volunteers—hand-stamped Jimmy's name on all the ballots, thousands of them. We were scarcely finished when a Superior Court judge ordered that both names be struck from the ballots and a completely new write-in election be held. We couldn't believe it. It was after midnight, seven hours before the polls opened. But when the results came in that night, Jimmy had won by 851 votes. It was over, and we all went home to bed, sick and exhausted.

But I was totally disillusioned with the whole political process. I had been naive enough to think that politics was straight, and that sheriffs were straight, and that judges were straight, and that county officials and political figures really had the best interests of the people at heart. What I witnessed at first had contradicted all I had believed in. Jimmy had won and I was pleased about that, and I never thought about giving up or getting out or living an easy life away from all the ugliness. But I hated the dirty politics we had exposed. And it wasn't over yet.

The legislative sessions lasted about two and a half months each year. As soon as Jimmy left for the session in Atlanta, Joe Hurst sent me a message that the last time anyone had crossed him, their liquor stores had burned down. So these were the businesses I had already heard about! Two legal liquor stores someone had built in competition with Hurst's moonshine business had both burned on the same night. It was not an idle threat. I worried that our warehouses and our house would meet the same fate. During that first year Jimmy was in office, 1963, I was afraid the whole time he was away. The boys were older now—Jack was fifteen—

and they teased me to ease my fears, possibly dampening theirs in the process. But I took the threat seriously.

The boys stayed with me after school at the warehouse because I didn't want them at the house alone. And when we got home after work, I looked under the beds and climbed the outside stairway to the attic to make sure nobody was there. I locked all the windows and even nailed some of them shut. I never liked to stay by myself, even in the Navy, and now I was more afraid than ever. I left lights burning on the porches and in the halls. I barricaded doors with chairs, and a few times—when I was really frightened—I pushed the sofa against the door to the den, locked the doors, and slept there with the boys. I often stayed up late, sewing and doing the washing and ironing to take my mind off my fears. Nothing happened, however, and when Jimmy came home, everything was all right again. When he went back to the senate the next year, my fear was gone.

I liked being a political wife. A number of the other senate wives went with their husbands to Atlanta during the session to enjoy the social activities; others stayed home to take care of the children. Some felt burdened with all the responsibilities while their husbands were away. I stayed at home and took care of the children, but I never felt burdened. I had an important task. I had to keep the business running while Jimmy was gone. I liked the feeling that I was contributing to our life and making it possible for him to pursue a political career. I was more a political partner than a political wife, and I never felt put upon. During the next four years (Jimmy was re-elected in 1964) I only had to call him home once, when one of our old brick warehouses collapsed, dumping several hundred tons of peanuts into the street!

The hard part, however, was learning to cope with the criticisms that seemed to go along with political life. I fluctuated between being very hurt and very mad when I heard them. Local politics, I have found, is the worst. At the state or national level, you don't expect everyone to be for you, and you accept the fact that you'll have enemies. But at home you expect everyone to like you, and it hurts to hear untrue, unfair, and unwarranted accusations from people you know personally. You just have to live with it, though it took me a very long time to learn that lesson. Jimmy soothed me by saying, "If you don't think I'm doing the best job I can possibly do, then worry about the criticisms. But if you think I am doing my best, then just relax."

* * *

The race issue continued to change the age-old tradition of politics in the South. The South had always been solidly Democratic, but now a Democratic President, John F. Kennedy, was trying to persuade Congress to pass vast social and civil rights programs. On television we were watching confrontations in Mississippi and Alabama, where federal troops were marching in to calm the rioting. SNCC and the NAACP and Martin Luther King, Jr., became household words and objects of intense hatred for many in the South. The President was becoming increasingly unpopular, too.

The morning John Kennedy was shot, I was at the beauty parlor when Jimmy called me with the news. I ran back to the office, my hair half up and half down, to be with him and listen to the reports. We felt such sorrow for the President whom we had admired and loved and for his family. But not everyone shared our sadness. When the news was announced in Chip's classroom, the teacher said "Good!" and the students applauded. Chip, who has a quick temper like mine, picked up a chair and threw it at the teacher—and spent the next few days in the principal's office. It was not a proper thing for him to do, but we never blamed him.

The lines were now redrawn between Democrats and Republicans. The national Democrats had become the party of civil rights while the Republicans were for states' rights, then a euphemism for continued segregation. In the 1964 election between Goldwater and Johnson, it was Goldwater and his stand on states' rights that made him a hero in Georgia and several other Deep South states. When the time came to open an election headquarters for Lyndon Johnson in Americus, no one could be found to run it. So Miss Lillian stepped in. She had never been afraid of controversy—in fact, I think she thrived on it. And she certainly had it now! Frequently, when she left the Johnson headquarters at the end of the day, she found her automobile smeared with soap and her radio antenna tied in knots. She just smiled and worked even harder.

Our whole family became politicized, and at no small cost. Chip, who was fourteen, bravely wore an LBJ campaign button to school, pinned on his shirt pocket, and pasted an I'M A DEMOCRAT sticker on his notebook. Often he came home with his pocket torn by one of his belligerent classmates, but he persisted. He only wavered once, when he had taken an overload of abuse and had been dumped on the floor during Glee Club practice by a boy who pulled his chair out from under him. I found him crying in his room after school. "I went out in the tall weeds and took off my button and tore the sticker off my notebook," he sobbed, "and I'm not going to be a Democrat anymore." But the next morning he put his pin back on and left for school with a brand-new Democratic sticker on his notebook.

After voting for every Democrat for almost a century, and after having given John Kennedy a bigger margin of victory than he got in his home state of Massachusetts in 1960, our state voted Republican in 1964. The voting rights bill passed the next year, and the race issue escalated. Our own county was now the target of demonstrations. Fieldworkers from civil rights organizations came in to help organize, and tensions rose. For twenty years there had been a commune six miles south of Plains called Koinonia Farms, where blacks and whites lived and worked together. Few local people approved, but they had grudgingly accepted it. Now many turned solidly against the farm. Shots were fired at the living quarters from passing automobiles, and the farm's roadside vegetable stands were dynamited. In Americus, a white boy was shot and killed during a demonstration. Trying to defuse the situation, our good friend and attorney Warren Fortson suggested setting up a biracial committee to work things out. The suggestion brought such an intense wave of hatred against Warren that his children's lives were threatened, and he had to send them out of town for a while for their own safety.

Our children were becoming increasingly concerned. There was threatening talk both at the warehouse from the farmers and from the children at school, such as: "If one tries to go to our school, I'll stand behind a bush with a baseball bat and knock him in the head." We had long talks with our boys about it, explaining that these people were wrong, that integration was going to come because it was the law and because it was the right thing to do. But they became more and more disillusioned, especially with the church. While Jimmy was speaking at another church one Sunday, the other deacons voted unanimously to propose to the congregation at the next monthly conference that no blacks be allowed to enter our church. We had to attend the wedding of one of Jimmy's cousins in north Georgia the day before the vote came up, and I pleaded with him to spend the night in Atlanta and not go to church in Plains the next day. I was tired of confrontations and the threat of boycotts against our business. Furthermore, Jimmy quietly was preparing to run for Congress, and I didn't think we needed any more controversy. I was not very courageous and didn't want to take the risk, but Jimmy insisted on being there.

The church conference was packed. Ordinarily we would have around fifty members present. That morning there were more than two hundred. When the resolution was read, Jimmy rose to urge the pastor and the congregation to reject the deacons' recommendation and allow blacks to enter the church as long as their motives seemed peaceful and they were there to worship, not to provoke a deliberate racial confrontation. We lost. Six people voted to keep the services open to all worshipers: Jimmy, me, Miss Lillian, Chip, Jeff, and one elderly man who may not have understood the issue. (Jack was not there.) But, encouragingly, only about fifty voted for the resolution, and when we got home the telephone was ringing. Many of the church members told Jimmy they agreed with him but couldn't face the consequences of voting publicly to integrate the services. And many of our boys' friends told them that they also believed the church was wrong but were afraid of their parents' displeasure. This was the first indication we had that a majority of our people felt as we did and were ready to end the long struggle against integration. Nevertheless, the resolution to keep blacks out of the church was passed, and it was an experience our boys have never forgotten. Or forgiven.

Surprisingly enough, although there was a series of threats and a few lost customers because of our family's relatively liberal stand on the race issue, it never seriously affected our business—except once. The summer Jack was graduated from high school, we took the children to Mexico on a three-week vacation, thinking it might be the last chance we would have to be together for some time. We got home just in time for peanut season. But no one came into the office. After a few bewildering days, one of our loyal customers came by to tell us that no one was going to bring us peanuts that year because, he said, "everybody knows where you've been." We told him we had been to Mexico, but he would have none of it. "No need for you to tell me that," he insisted. "Everybody knows you've been to a camp run by communists in Alabama to train integration workers." We were dumbfounded!

"Everybody" turned out to be one prominent businessman who hated the federal government for trying to force integration on us. In fact, his hatred was so deep that he asked the postmistress to put any government letters he received on top of his stack of mail so he wouldn't have to touch them. He had spread the integrationist camp rumor after he had called Miss Lillian to find out how to get in touch with us and she had told him she didn't know because we were traveling in Mexico. That did it. If Jimmy's own mother wouldn't tell him how to reach us, he knew where we really must be! So he spread the word, and before we got home, everybody "knew."

We spent the next few days working hard, visiting all our customers to convince them that we had indeed been to Mexico with our children, and Jimmy confronted the gentleman, who finally admitted starting the rumor. Our customers slowly returned, but it was a harrowing experience, not only emotionally but as a potential disaster for our business. Peanut season makes or breaks a peanut warehouse operation, and we could see our total livelihood and our life's investment slipping away.

The crisis was short-lived, and soon everything returned to normal; I worked days at the warehouse, handled Jimmy's state senate correspondence at night, and somewhere in between did the housework with the help of Jimmy and the boys. I was struck by how much my life had changed, how frivolous some things seemed that had once been so important. I no longer spent days worrying over what I would wear on certain occasions but went to the store, bought what they had, and looked just as good as when I had worried about it. I spent a day or two doing all my Christmas shopping, and everyone liked their gifts just as much as when I had spent weeks pondering over them. I wasn't trying to be perfect anymore. I was doing my best to survive and enjoying my varied duties. And as Jimmy so often advised, I no longer cared as much what people thought about me.

In the spring of 1966, Jimmy announced his plans to run for Congress. He had been very successful in the state senate and in 1965 was named one of the five most influential and respected senators in a poll of his peers and journalists in the capital. He wanted very much to replace the incumbent Republican, Bo Callaway, a wealthy textile heir who had switched parties, from Democrat to Republican, in the heat of the Goldwater mania. He was the favorite of a very active John Birch Society in our county and not one of our favorite public servants.

During this campaign, we had more help at the warehouse.

Billy was now working with us, and Sybil was helping during peanut season. After Billy had left the Marines, he had not wanted to return to Plains. Instead he attended college and then went to work in Macon, Georgia. He and Sybil soon had a baby, and Jimmy finally had talked him into coming home and working with him as a partner. Billy was perfect with the farmers, talking and joking with them in the warehouse and in the fields, and he and Jimmy worked well as a team.

We had learned a lot in our previous campaigns, and we started this one off better organized. Each day Jimmy drove around the district, meeting people and seeking support, and after each visit, when he got back in the car, he used a small tape recorder to list the names of the people he'd met, plus something personal about each one. That night, Jimmy, Gloria, and I laboriously wrote letters to each person on his list. In preparation for the campaign, Jimmy had taken a memory course to help him remember names and information. He and I both practiced thinking about something outrageous to associate with individuals whom we met. For instance, if a name started with *B*, we would think of a bee landing on a person's nose. It got to be a game when we went into crowds of people, to receptions and parties; afterward we had a lot of fun comparing notes and seeing who could remember the most names. And we wrote letters to all of them without making many serious mistakes!

The campaign suddenly switched in midstream. The leading Democratic candidate for governor had a mild heart attack and withdrew from the race. Bo Callaway immediately forgot about the congressional race and announced that he would run for governor instead. The Republicans were riding the crest of the states' rights wave, and a poll had found Callaway the overwhelming favorite for the top seat in the state. I was delighted. It left us with only token opposition—what better way to run for office! But Jimmy was appalled. He went to Atlanta to try to persuade two of our most popular state Democratic officials to run for governor, but neither they nor any other potentially successful Democrat wanted to face the formidable Republican opposition. Suddenly Jimmy was being mentioned by a few people as the only Democrat both willing and perhaps able to stop Callaway.

It seemed unbelievable to me. It meant giving up the congressional seat, which would surely be easy now. The governor's primary was only three months away, and no one knew Jimmy outside our district. Also, there were several other dark horse Democratic candidates already in the race. Ellis Arnall, who had been governor twenty years before and was considered honest and effective, was now considered by many as having been away from the political scene too long to be taken seriously. He was described in the press as "Rip Van Winkle re-emerged after two decades of political retirement." Also running was Lester Maddox, a fiery segregationist and former restaurant proprietor, who had made his reputation by waving a pistol and brandishing an ax handle at blacks who tried to eat at his establishment. He had become a folk hero to many Georgians when the law told him he either had to serve blacks or quit the business and he had chosen to close his doors.

Jimmy couldn't let Lester Maddox walk away with the party nomination, and he wouldn't back away from a fight with Callaway. Thus we launched our first family campaign. Billy ran the warehouse, Sybil filled in for me, and the rest of us traveled across the state. Jimmy, Jack, Chip and I all had separate schedules. Jeff, who was fourteen, traveled with me, as did Miss Lillian much of the time. We had a big map of Georgia with different-colored pins for each member of the family. Every week we mapped out our separate routes, coming home on Saturdays to collapse for one evening, going to church on Sunday morning, then heading back in the afternoon to state headquarters in Atlanta, three hours away, to start all over again.

It was exciting, exhausting, and discouraging at the same time. We were all doing things we never thought we could do, which was a challenge. In every community we looked up the newspaper office and the radio and television stations and said, "I'm here, interview me." And they did. We shook hands with every person we could find, gave them a brochure, and went on to the next town, where few people if any had ever heard of us. This was a brief and rushed campaign, but we all learned many things that were helpful to us later.

One painful lesson was how dedicated supporters of one candidate are sometimes willing to hurt the others. The worst political experience of my life came in that first gubernatorial campaign. I handed a brochure to a man standing in the doorway of a shoe shop in Washington, Georgia, and asked him to vote for my husband. He was chewing tobacco, and it was drooling down his beard of several days' growth. "I'm for Bo Callaway, lady," he said. Then he spat on me.

We never stopped, no matter what happened, driving through every town in Georgia with posters of Jimmy taped on both sides of our borrowed cars. Despite our late entry and apparently hopeless prospect at the beginning, our standing in the public opinion polls was rising rapidly as the campaign came to a close. By primary day we were $66,000 in debt and Jimmy had lost twenty-two pounds. At midnight we were certain that we were one of the two top vote getters who had made the primary runoff. I was so confident that I went to bed, but at four-thirty Jimmy woke me to say we had missed by 20,000 votes out of a million cast. We called the children together to tell them; we all felt sick.

In the runoff between Arnall and Maddox, many Republicans crossed over to vote for Maddox, believing that he would be a pushover for Callaway in the general election. However, because of many write-in votes cast by Georgians unwilling to support the nominees, neither Maddox nor Callaway received a majority. An antiquated Georgia law required the state legislature to choose the winner. The General Assembly in 1966 was made up almost entirely of Democrats, and thus Lester Maddox, an arch-conservative segregationist, was chosen governor of Georgia.

We went home, to our house and our community, which has always been a refuge, and picked up our old lives, out of the spotlight of politics. The disappointment of the campaign stayed with me; I felt horrible. I don't take defeat easily, and for the first time since my father died I hadn't wanted to wake up in the morning. Lester Maddox had defeated us. Jimmy and I took a couple of days off, driving to the east coast of Georgia. When we went through the town of Waycross, where I had campaigned especially hard—once standing all night at a gospel singing—only to have the town vote solidly for Maddox, I put my head in my arms and refused to look out the window. (I believe Jimmy felt the same way, but he was driving.)

A month later Jimmy started campaigning again, though he didn't officially announce his candidacy for four years. The morning after the defeat, he had told our handful of original supporters that he would run again in 1970 and he didn't intend to lose. This time we knew what to expect and made great preparations. We bought an automatic typewriter that would also record the names, addresses, and descriptions of people as we wrote letters to them. We coded everyone by occupation, political philosophy, and potential as a financial contributor and campaign worker. Jimmy still tape-recorded the names of everyone he met. We obtained copies of every telephone book for Georgia (more than a hundred and fifty), looked up the addresses and telephone numbers of the names on his recordings, and sent letters to everyone. We wrote standard letters and coded them so we also knew which letter each person had received—grass-roots politics, but with scientific sophistication! Jimmy started coding his speeches too, using words to indicate the issues he wanted to talk about, and he even coded his jokes by number. His speech notes were small slips of paper with a few words and a couple of numbers on them, which I filed. That way, when he went back to the same community, he wouldn't repeat himself.

As the campaign progressed, I kept files for him and clipped news articles on education, health care, agriculture, the environment—any subject I thought might be helpful. Jimmy wrote his own speeches, and though he had always been a worker, I had never seen him study so hard. He read several books on a subject, consulted with experts, and reviewed my clipping files until he knew each issue well and knew exactly what he wanted to say about it. He developed standard speeches on the major topics. The last two years of the campaign he was hardly ever home at night, and I took to the campaign trail the last year myself. But in the interim, there was much going on at home.

In quick order: Miss Lillian decided at the age of sixty-eight to join the Peace Corps, I discovered I was pregnant at the age of forty, Jack dropped out of college to join the Navy, and the first black students enrolled in Chip's class in school. The 1960s were turbulent all over the country, and our family was as caught up in the turmoil as everyone else's.

Some of these events caught us by surprise. Miss Lillian had already sent for the application forms and filled them out, requesting service in either Africa or India, before she told anyone of her plans for the Peace Corps. One day she walked into the warehouse and announced: "I'm going to join the Peace Corps!" She admitted later, only half in jest, that her spirits fell a little when Jimmy responded, "That's great, Mama," and Billy made a similar statement. She said she thought surely they would try to talk her out of it. In any case her mind was made up, influenced by a television commercial that said: "Is your glass half empty or is it half full? Join the Peace Corps and help others. Age is no barrier." She had decided that her glass could be fuller, and she couldn't think of any other exciting challenge where age was no barrier.

In 1966 she was sent to India to assist in a family planning program in Vikhroli, a small town about thirty miles from Bombay. Because of her training as a registered nurse, she was asked to help part of the time in a small clinic. She became indispensable in her work with the doctor and soon was working there full-time.

Like many Westerners visiting India for the first time, Miss Lillian was totally unprepared for the degree of poverty, disease, and starvation she saw. And leprosy. How do you prepare for leprosy? She was often hungry herself but didn't know how to let us know. She had heard that a former member of the Peace Corps had written a postcard home with some unkind remarks about his host country, creating a short-lived international incident, which she didn't want to repeat. We wondered why she kept referring to food and poverty in her letters and only woke up to reality when she asked us if we were "reading between the lines." Immediately, we started sending her food and money regularly, but she gave the food away to people who were hungrier than she and spent the money on medicine for the clinic. She lost more than thirty pounds during her two years in India, and came home not only skin and bones, but unable to eat much for a long time. She claimed it was because her stomach had shrunk, which was probably true, but we also knew that she felt guilty because her friends in India were still hungry.

Once she was back home, Miss Lillian's experiences in India made her a celebrity, and she began to make speeches and to appear on television. She enjoyed it, but it puzzled her. She didn't feel different or unique. This was the way she had always lived, as a strong southern individualist, and she had always had a weak spot for the poor and needy and for anyone who was the object of discrimination. She was, she told me one day, "the only young person in Richland, Georgia, who would admit that Abraham Lincoln was a hero." She was a great baseball fan and became an avid follower of the Brooklyn Dodgers when they signed on Jackie Robinson. She was there when he became the first black to play in the major leagues. She got her "tolerance," she said, from her father, Jim Jack Gordy, who was the only man she knew when she was young who treated blacks with kindness and a degree of equality. As postmaster, he and the local black leaders would often eat meals together in the back room of the post office, where Miss Lillian worked as an assistant.

Besides the stir Miss Lillian created, there was another cause for excitement—a new child in the Carter family. Jimmy and I had wanted another baby for years, with no luck. But I had recently had a large uterine tumor removed, which may have helped. So I was happily pregnant again after twenty-one years of marriage, with three grown sons—twenty, seventeen, and fifteen. Although Jimmy and I were nervous at first about their reaction to the news, the boys were just as pleased as we were; and luckily for me, I wasn't sick during this pregnancy and continued to work every day at the warehouse.

I hoped the baby would be a girl, and all of us talked about the new baby sister. Maybe I wanted a girl so much because I had lived all my adult life surrounded by men both at home and work. Jimmy and I suggested several names, but the boys didn't like any of them. So one Sunday afternoon, the whole family gathered on the back porch and each of us wrote down five names; there was only one name that appeared on the combined lists even twice! Jimmy then started to read the list of girls' names out loud from the dictionary, and he never got further than "Amy." For the first time, there was no objection from the boys, and "Amy" sounded right to all of us. We added Lynn from my own name, and "she" became Amy Lynn Carter.

Our baby was born October 19, 1967. If I had known then what I know now about the risk of having a baby so late in life, I would have been anxious. But I was blissfully ignorant as I lay in my hospital bed, luxuriating in an indescribable feeling of satisfaction. Jimmy was out of town, about eighty miles away, when I knew it was time to go to the hospital; he was being interviewed on a radio show when I reached him. He left the audience dangling about the impending birth to race home. After we got to the hospital Jimmy called the boys, and when I was rolled out of the delivery room with the baby in my arms, they were waiting for me. I told them myself that we had a baby sister, and they burst into tears of joy. They were so happy that when they returned to Plains after midnight, the boys knocked on doors telling everyone the good news about our baby girl.

The next six months were one of the most pleasant interlude in my life. For the first time in years I stayed home and cared fo this tiny baby while working on the warehouse books. I woul spread the books out on the breakfast room table, the baby besid me. We had a bird feeder in the tree right outside the window and I bought a field guide to help me identify the mockingbirds sparrows, cardinals, and other birds that came by for a meal. I was a wonderful, wonderful time.

Then Jack dropped a bombshell. One morning after I'd gon back to work, he called to tell us he was dropping out of college Nothing seemed to be going right for him. He had transferre from Georgia Tech to Emory University in Atlanta, hoping : wouldn't be so technical and would give him more time to read But he was still dissatisfied and having great difficulty with hi studies, and in the atmosphere of the 1960s, he was disillusione with the political process. Lester Maddox, the symbol of racisr to Jack, was still governor of Georgia. Jack was also disillusione about the war in Vietnam and the unfairness of the draft. The onl young men being drafted were those too poor to go to college, h said, and he wasn't going to take advantage of his privileged statu as a student any longer.

He joined the U.S. Navy and was soon assigned to a sma buoy tender just off the coast of Vietnam, where instead of watch ing bombs drop on television, he saw them drop in person. thought I had failed him as a mother; even though he was alread twenty, I still thought of him as a child. He wasn't, and now can see that his decision was probably right. After he got out c the Navy, he finished Georgia Tech with a degree in physics, the went on to law school at the University of Georgia and subse quently passed his state bar exams with flying colors. So muc for the guilt of motherhood.

As soon as Jack had gone, I worried about Chip. He had entere his junior year in high school in 1966, and we had learned tha for the first time, black students would enroll in our previousl all-white school. The school was not far from the warehouse, an we had watched as state patrol and police cars arrived for th opening day. And every time anyone came into the warehous they would ask, "What's happening?" or "Has anything hap pened?" By some sort of miracle, nothing "happened." Two blac children had shown up and just walked into the schoolhouse. Ther was no violence, no trouble of any kind, and not only we bu almost everyone in Plains had been relieved and proud that the long-awaited and dread happening had come to pass so peacefully. It was twelve years after the Supreme Court decision that integration had come to our community. But even those who had had such harsh things to say were courageous and took it in stride. In a way I think it was easier for us in the South. We knew the blacks in our communities. We had grown up with them. So it was not the same as having strangers come into the schools, as often happened in the North.

But old sentiments die hard. When Martin Luther King, Jr., was shot in Memphis in 1968, the proprietor of the local tavern passed out beer on the house in celebration. And George Wallace, whose demagogic reaction at that time to the race problems appealed to our people, carried the State of Georgia in the presidential election that same year, which brought Richard Nixon to the White House. There were few supporters of Hubert Humphrey in our town that year; the only political poster for him hung on our warehouse door.

Jimmy's sister Ruth came for a visit during this time. After all the years since she had married and moved to North Carolina, we were finally friends again. She had "forgiven" me for marrying her older brother! She was now doing Christian work full-time, and we listened carefully as she described her close personal relationship with God and what it meant to her life. One day she and Jimmy went to see the pine trees he had planted on her farm. Jimmy talked to her about his life, telling her that he had accomplished a lot for himself but felt he hadn't done enough for anyone else, that he wanted to be a better Christian. He had been struck, he told Ruth, by a recent sermon in our church entitled, "If you were arrested for being a Christian, would there be enough evidence to convict you?" Would there be? The question had haunted him. And he had decided to put God first in his life, to search for and always try to do His will. He and Ruth had a long and intimate discussion, and he learned that her much deeper religious life and convictions were what he wanted and needed.

This was Jimmy's famous "born again" experience—no flashing lights, no weeping, no trauma or emotional scene, just a quiet acceptance of God and God's will for his life. In a speech later, Ruth said that tears had come into Jimmy's eyes while they were talking about his reaffirmation of faith; in the campaign of 1976,

the story got blown out of all proportion by news reporters, mo:
of whom have never been quite sure what "born again" means.

On April 3, 1970, Jimmy formally announced his second car
didacy for governor, one of twelve Democratic hopefuls. Every
thing was in place. Billy and Sybil would run the business; Jei
was going off to boarding school in Atlanta, where our stat
headquarters would be. Chip took the year off from Georgia Soutl
western College to campaign, and, like Jack's service in Vietnan
it turned out to be a blessing. He was running with a questionabl
crowd at college, some of whom were involved with drugs, an
more than once we were called to get him out of a certain friend'
home or a dormitory that was suspect. Working on the campaigr
in which he proved to be invaluable, saved him from this trouble
and when it was time for him to go back to college, he settle
down and made the Dean's List.

Then it was time for me to leave home. The worst part wa
saying good-bye to Amy. She was only two, and so depender
on me. I didn't want to miss a single day of her life. But I als
knew I had to campaign. Our major opponent was a young an
very attractive former governor, Carl Sanders, whom the publi
opinion polls showed as having 85 percent of the support of th
people. (The governor of Georgia could not succeed himself, s
Maddox was not eligible.) The only way Jimmy could possibl
win was for everybody in our family to work. While I was gone
my mother stayed in our house with Amy and I called hom
regularly. But every time I came home she had changed, and
was always sad to go off again and leave her. I have sympathize
ever since with working mothers who have to leave young childre
at home, and so has Jimmy, which is one reason good day car
centers became very important to him.

We added new members to our original, small group of sup
porters—Charles Kirbo, Bill Gunter, David Gambrell, Beverl
Langford, Ford Spinks, Philip Alston—who had encouraged u
in 1966 and who stuck with us through this campaign and int
the presidency. Young people began coming to Jimmy to see ho\
they could help. Hamilton Jordan, our student coordinator in 196(
arranged a meeting at the Pond House in Plains for these nev
campaign workers. I had come home that day to prepare food fc
everybody when a young man named Jody Powell knocked on th
door, looking for Senator Carter. He said he was going to writ
about a political campaign for his doctoral thesis at Emory, an

he wanted to be involved with ours to get first-hand information. I sent him to the Pond House.

In Atlanta, a young attorney named Stuart Eizenstat had organized a superb group of volunteers to help with the analysis of issues; we met with them every Sunday afternoon for strategy sessions when we were in Atlanta. Frank Moore, who was working with Jimmy on our regional planning commission at home, was always there, too. And Jerry Rafshoon signed on to do our campaign advertising. Our neighbors and supporters offered to travel across the state for us and so the Peanut Brigade was born, though in that campaign they called themselves the "Hi-Neighbor" group. Once more we got out our big map of Georgia, and soon everyone had his or her own colored pins and schedule, including Jeff after he graduated from high school and Miss Lillian, who campaigned tirelessly and almost every day at the age of seventy-two.

The whole year was grueling. Up before dawn, we went to factories, then in and out of every establishment in town, approaching each person we saw to ask them to vote for Jimmy Carter for governor. We searched for crowds at sporting events, livestock sales, tobacco barns, rodeos and horse shows, dog shows, county fairs, and any other kind of local festival. We stood in front of swinging doors at major shopping centers, meeting every customer going in and coming out, until those coming out had the brochures we had given them going in! At the insistence of a campaign supporter I even got up at 3:30 A.M., after campaigning until midnight, to drive across the state to be at a special factory to shake hands with workers entering the plant—only to have that supporter, one week later, endorse our most formidable opponent, former Governor Sanders. Each day the first person I approached in the morning was always the hardest. Sometimes I felt that I just couldn't possibly smile and be nice and beg and plead for support and say the same things over and over for another day, but usually once I got started I was all right. I tried to choose the easiest-looking person to begin with, but it didn't always work. Early one morning I saw a stout, middle-aged woman approaching. She looked safe, so I handed her a brochure, which she smilingly accepted. "Good morning! I want you to vote for my husband, Jimmy Carter—"At his name she screamed, "No, God, no! Not Jimmy Carter!" and dropped the brochure as though it would contaminate her. And I watched as she fled into a store to get

away from the sight of me. I waited a few moments before tryin
again that day!

We learned that the best places to begin the day were whe
the policemen, firemen, maintenance crews, and garbage collec
tors gathered before work. Every city has such places, and then
is always great camaraderie at dawn. My favorite place turned ou
to be the fire stations. Firemen cook the best side meat and biscui
I have ever eaten, and if I got there at the right time they woul
share them with me. My least favorite places became the K-Marts
which didn't allow soliciting. I have been thrown out of or ordere
away from the front door of nearly every one in Georgia. W
should have respected their policy, of course, but they always ha
such crowds of people, I couldn't resist them. I would go to th
back of the store and pass out brochures until someone asked m
to leave.

We often found ourselves in the most unlikely places. I wer
to sea in a shrimp boat, for instance, and up in a hot-air balloor
I saw my first tobacco auction and even witnessed a rattlesnak
roundup. One day Miss Lillian and I campaigned in a north Geor
gia community, stopping at a poultry processing plant to shak
hands with the workers. Cold, wet, plucked chickens passed over
head on conveyor belts while the women sitting at rows of table
below cut off their wings or their feet or other parts. Miss Lillia
and I had been given plastic kerchiefs to keep our heads from
getting wet as we walked under the chickens, but as we ducke
under the last row, a part of one fell from the belt, hit Miss Lillia
who was looking down, on the back of her neck, and slipped dow
inside her dress. She screamed so loud you could have heard he
all the way to Plains: "Get the chicken guts out of my clothes!"

Jimmy traveled separately from me most of the time and ha
just as exotic destinations. In the mountains of north Georgia, h
joined the crowds to watch Karl Wallenda walk across Tallula
Gorge on a tightrope. Carl Sanders, our opponent, arrived dra
matically in a helicopter, and when he stepped out, not a hair c
his head moved in the strong wind. "Carl Sanders wears hair spray
was reported by the press the next day—unfair, but good for us
It fit right in with Sanders's image as a wealthy Atlanta lawye
out of touch with the average citizen. Jimmy took a real blow o
another campaign stop. Approaching a young man on the stree
who had his head turned to the wall, Jimmy touched him lightl
on the arm, saying, "I'm Jimmy Carter and I'm running for gov

ernor." Immediately, the young man, whom we learned later was a battle-fatigued ex-Marine, turned and swung at Jimmy, hitting him so hard on the chin that he landed flat on his back in the middle of the street. This time it was Jimmy who made the headlines, but far more painfully than Governor Sanders.

I took some blows, too, but mine were self-induced. I had gone through the whole last campaign without making a speech, and I thought I might get away with it this time, too. The idea of standing up in front of people absolutely terrified me, even though I had had no difficulty speaking before my class in high school and actually enjoyed one-on-one political conversations at luncheons or receptions—even interviews with reporters. Though interviews made me nervous, I could always carry on a conversation when someone was asking me questions. But speeches were impersonal, and I was certain I would be struck dumb if I ever had to make one.

Then it happened. I was at a luncheon in Gainesville, Georgia, and was very pleased by the large crowd that had turned out. I was talking with my luncheon partner when suddenly I heard someone saying, "And now Mrs. Carter will say a few words." I couldn't believe it. I knew it had to come sooner or later, but I'd never thought about being called on to speak on the spur of the moment. Stand up, I ordered myself. Just tell them about Jimmy and his qualifications. But all I could think of standing there was how scared I was and what they were going to think of me. All of my poised calm and self-confidence left me. I finally stammered out something about my husband running for governor and needing their help, then sat down, trembling. I was miserable, not only about the speech but about the realization that it was going to happen again and again.

I spent that night with friends in a neighboring town, and as soon as I could get away, I went straight to my room to sit down and write a speech—something, anything—to say the next time I was called on. I wrote and wrote and cried, fearful of humiliating Jimmy and also myself in public. I finally got something down on paper and went to bed. But I couldn't sleep. The words kept whirling around in my head and I felt so alone. I couldn't even call Jimmy because I didn't know where he was. I wanted to see Amy and cuddle her and feel necessary and competent again. I had always managed to do what I had set as a goal, but this seemed beyond me. I couldn't do it. But I had to.

I started practicing at small coffees and receptions, making deliberate decision to say a few words at each. I always arrive very nervous and headed straight for the bathroom, locked myse in, and said my lines (which couldn't have been more than tw minutes long) over and over. Then I would reappear, supposed refreshed, glad to see everyone and eager to speak to them. F a long time it was torture for me. I never knew when I opene my mouth whether any words would come out or not. My kne shook. I was always afraid I would go blank in the middle of m remarks and not know what I was going to say next. My mou would get dry, and I learned to ask for a glass of water in ca my voice cracked. Then I could make an excuse and drink t water. I always asked for a podium so I would have somethin to hang on to. And I never used notes: I was too proud. I wante everyone to think I knew what I was talking about and was since It was a dumb thing to do, bringing back my old determinatic to be perfect. But I wanted people to think I was more sophist cated, more experienced, more blasé and capable than I real was. They never saw me behind the scenes.

During one of the Sunday afternoon strategy sessions, I dre the short straw when the subject of local political rallies came u It was a waste of Jimmy's time to go to these rallies, because w knew that few people would come other than the sponsoring group Suddenly everyone was looking at me, and I was too proud to te them I was too scared to speak. So off I went, the first time speak for Jimmy on the same dais as representatives of all t other twelve candidates. On the way to the rally, where I had take my turn with all of them—all men, including Lester Maddo who was running for lieutenant governor—the pressure and ne vousness got the better of me. As we reached the city limits I sa to Jeff, who was driving, "Stop the car. I'm going to be sick And I was. It got much easier for me, though, and before t campaign was over I was making brief speeches often.

It was a long, long campaign, and we never had enough money— our biggest worry. We drove around in cars borrowed from su porters. Not one of our family ever spent the night in a hotel motel. We and our campaign workers always stayed with t friends Jimmy had made through our business and the years political work. Our campaign headquarters had a list of all t people we knew in each community, and they would call ahea saying, "Rosalynn Carter is coming to town. Can she stay wi you?" But still we ran out of brochures, posters, and bumper stickers and learned early to pick up the pamphlets people threw down so we could use them again. We quickly discovered a pattern to this. In a crowd, if one person dropped a brochure others would follow, so we always tried to have someone pick up any discards.

Passing out literature at the doors of department stores or supermarkets had a pattern of its own. When the time came to move on, we went into the store and found the place—a shelf, a counter, or more often than not a telephone stand—where someone had put down the first brochure and others had added to the stack. We could always pick up handfuls to use again; brochures were expensive!

After a whole year's campaign, money became more and more worrisome. One Saturday when Jimmy and I were taking a breather, walking on the farm with Amy, he asked me if I would be willing to sell our land if we had to pay for the campaign. We both agreed we'd do it. It's sobering when I look back on it now. If we had lost the election, we probably would have lost our farms as well. But in the heat of a campaign, there is a life-or-death tendency to do whatever is necessary to win.

In the meantime, we had good luck when a stranger offered us his airplane and practically gave up his business to fly Jimmy from one appearance to another. We were warned that our new friend was "controversial," but we had never shunned controversy; to us, his looks were the most controversial thing about him. He wore only blue jumpsuits and shaved his head, a problem when he wanted to ride in parades with Jimmy or accompany him to church. He didn't exactly fit the image of a south Georgia peanut farmer!

The stranger (whose name should remain anonymous because at the time of this writing he is in prison in Iran, falsely accused of being a CIA agent, and to let the Ayatollah Khomeini know how close he was to my husband might endanger him) became a very good friend, and one day, when Jimmy was feeling particularly grateful for his help, he asked what he could ever do to repay him. "Just do what you can about the race question," our friend replied. Jimmy thought for a moment and then wrote these few words on the back of an air navigation chart: "The time for racial discrimination is over." "I'm going to say this in my inaugural speech," Jimmy said. "Sign it, and give it to me," our friend replied. Jimmy did and handed it over, sealing the bargain.

These words put Jimmy on the cover of *Time* magazine, giving him national exposure. And our friend never asked for anything else. A few years later he came to visit us in the Governor's Mansion, then vanished from our lives altogether. We have never seen our benefactor again.

You always come in contact with extraordinary people during political campaigns, and often you hear their innermost secrets. I began to recognize the people who had something personal and very important to tell me: They would stand patiently at the side of the crowd or just wait next to me. Usually they needed money, but they always wanted to make sure I knew why: a loved one in trouble with the law or in prison; a sick parent or child, often with a terminal illness. Over and over again the subject would be mental illness, and "I have a mentally retarded child at home" became a constant refrain. "What will your husband do to help me if he's elected governor?"

The issue of mental illness began to prey on my mind. One morning when I was standing at the door of a cotton mill at four-thirty, a woman emerged, lint in her hair and on her sweater after a long night's work. I asked her if she were going home to sleep. She said yes, she would nap some during the day, but she had a retarded child at home. The child's expenses were more than her husband's income, so she had to work nights to make ends meet.

By chance, later that day I discovered that Jimmy would be coming to the same town I was campaigning in for a big afternoon reception. I never saw him during the week, so I decided to stay and be with him for a little while. I stood in the back of the hall while he was speaking, then joined the line with everyone else to file by and shake his hand. He reached for my hand before realizing who I was, but I didn't care. I had an important question to ask him: "I want to know what you are going to do about mental health when you are governor." He replied immediately, "We're going to have the best mental health system in the country, and I'm going to put you in charge of it."

We approached primary day with nervous confidence. Carl Sanders had been endorsed by most of the major newspapers and public officials in the state and had the weight of the establishment behind him. Our support came from the rural areas and from the voters who recognized Jimmy as hard-working, knowledgeable about the issues, and with no ties to the establishment. Which credentials would prove to be more persuasive?

Election day began well. Jimmy and I voted at home, then drove to Atlanta, stopping in the communities along the way to greet people as they were going to the polls. We stopped for lunch; I couldn't eat. And once in Atlanta I couldn't sit still. In midafternoon I went with Chip and Jeff to the Ford Motor plant in a suburb and stood in the middle of the street outside the factory gate, handing brochures to the people in their cars as they drove away from work and reminding them, "Don't forget to go to the polls, and vote for my husband."

The last car rolled by; we had done all we could do in this campaign. We headed back to the hotel to await the election returns. Stopping for a traffic light, we pulled up alongside a beat-up pickup truck with a wheelbarrow in the back.

"Ah," I said to myself. "A working man. A typical Jimmy Carter supporter," and on impulse, feeling a need for the reassurance I would surely get, I rolled down the car window and shouted to him, "Who're you going to vote for today?" "I'm a Carl Sanders man, myself," came the devastating reply. We're finished, was all I could think as we continued on to the hotel.

Election days are no fun. My stomach stays in knots, the tension almost unbearable. The worst time is from the hour the polls close until the returns start coming in. I always go to my room at home—or to our suite if we're waiting in a hotel—and on the exact hour that the polls close I get in the tub, leisurely bathe and dress as though it were any other day, and then join family and friends. At least that gives me something to do during the agonized waiting. By that time usually a few scattered returns are coming in, and almost always a trend, so we can know where we stand.

On this election night when I came downstairs everyone was excited. The figures were promising. We were going to be in the runoff. In fact, we almost won without a runoff. Jimmy's credentials had proved the most persuasive and we were jubilant!

With this good showing we went on to defeat Carl Sanders in the runoff and then Hal Suit, the Republican candidate, in the general election.

Jimmy Carter had become the seventy-sixth governor of Georgia.

✣ 3 ✣

The Governor's Mansion

I had never been inside the new Governor's Mansion in Atlanta and had not had time in the hectic months of campaigning even to consider what my responsibilities as the governor's wife might be. So before the inauguration, while Jimmy was working on the state budget for the next year and preparing his program to present to the new legislature, I went to visit Mrs. Lester Maddox.

The Governor's Mansion was only three years old, built in the same style as the original Governor's Mansion was in the 1830s, but at the mid-twentieth-century cost of $2 million, an appropriation Jimmy had voted against as a state senator. He thought it should be built for much less, but I'm glad he lost on that issue. It's a beautiful, massive, classical building, with columns on all four sides, standing behind a tall wrought-iron fence on eighteen acres of rolling lawns and gardens and great oak trees, hickories, magnolias, and dogwoods. I was nervous that first day as I drove up to the entrance gates and was stopped by state patrolmen. I associated state patrolmen with traffic accidents and speeding tickets, but these men were cordial and directed me up the circular driveway to the front door, where I was met by more state patrolmen. They seemed to be everywhere. They escorted me into the house and through the beautiful marble foyers. They were intimidating. But what Virginia Maddox had to tell me was more so.

We met in a small parlor, and I immediately felt at ease with her. She was nice and comfortable, a kind of mother figure. But her duties as the wife of the governor were definitely not what I had in mind. I asked her who did the cooking, and she said, "I do." She had had several cooks but had been unable to find one she could depend on, the last being a man who was inclined to big weekends and who had never showed up on Monday mornings, so she just did the cooking herself.

I asked her who served dinner when she had small groups to entertain, and she said, "I do." I asked her where her office was in the house; she said she didn't have one. All her mail went to the governor's office in the capitol and she saw little of it. Her secretary there turned down all the requests for her to speak because she didn't like making speeches, although the governor's mother stood in for her sometimes, particularly at church events. That was the first thing she said that appealed to me!

The mansion was open to the public six days of the week, she told me. And who greeted the tourists at the front door, shaking hands with each one? She did. I had been shaking hands for as long as I could remember, and I didn't plan to do it every day for the next four years. She admitted she was very tired of it. And there was another problem. The mansion was always in great demand. "Everyone wants to use the mansion for everything—club meetings, benefits, even private parties and weddings," she said. "I've never been able to work out a satisfactory system for handling it." I was getting more and more uncomfortable.

The state patrolmen were there as guards and were very necessary, she went on, because tourists would pick up everything they could as souvenirs. They had even taken the handles off the fixtures in the downstairs bathrooms. But the patrolmen were very helpful, she said, as were the rest of the staff, all prisoners. Having "trusties" for servants in the Governor's Mansion was a long-standing custom in Georgia. Although some had committed serious crimes, they were not habitual criminals, and all had been carefully selected by prison officials. Some were good household workers and some not so good, but "they get the work done," Mrs. Maddox said, then added firmly, "with supervision." Who did the supervising? "I do," she said.

I didn't know what I was going to do when I left her that day. I didn't want to spend all my time taking care of that big house. That's not what I had campaigned for. By the time Jimmy was elected, I had become very involved in the issues and had projects of my own lined up. I didn't see how I could ever do the things I wanted to do if I was so completely tied down. Mrs. Maddox was a traditional southern wife, taking care of her husband and family. She ran the Governor's Mansion the way she ran her home; that's the way the governor wanted it and I admired her for it. But just the thought of it overwhelmed me, and it didn't help when she said as I was leaving, "You're probably like me. If your husband wants you to do it, you'll do it!"

I learned more about my future at a conference for newly elected governors, held that year in North Carolina. This traditional get-together of a few current governors and the governors-elect was helpful in many ways, and for newcomers like me it was a blessing. But I was apprehensive the first evening, when we attended a formal dinner party given by Governor Robert W. Scott and his wife, Jessie Ray, at their Governor's Mansion. I had a new evening gown, and Jimmy, I thought, looked especially handsome in his tuxedo. A long, sleek limousine arrived at the golf resort where we were staying to take us to the mansion, and as we drove in comfort, a thought flickered through my mind of a particularly frustrating campaign day when our car wouldn't start. We were all exhausted and Jeffrey finally said, "I give up. I'm just going to quit." Chip's reply had been quick: "And we'll lose and you'll be having trouble with this car for four more years. Wouldn't you rather ride in a limousine?"

We arrived at the North Carolina mansion to be greeted by a flourish of trumpets and splendid men in uniforms with much gold braid, who I later learned were National Guardsmen. Music was playing inside the lovely old home as we were greeted by Governor and Mrs. Scott. Soon we were at ease with friends we had made earlier in the day, other governors-elect and their wives. The new responsibilities we were about to assume were a common bond, and we all had similar questions that needed answers.

Dinner was served at round tables by waiters dressed in tuxedos and wearing white gloves. Our names were written on place cards in elegant script, and there were engraved menu cards at each place along with a centerpiece of beautiful flowers. I looked carefully at everything, absorbing it for the time when I would be the one entertaining. It made me nervous just to think about it. And when the bowl of warm water with flower petals arrived, I had no idea what to do with it. My instincts told me it was a finger bowl, but this was my first experience with one. I waited, carefully watching the governor next to me. Nonchalantly I followed suit, lifting the bowl and the small doily underneath from my plate and setting them aside as though I had been using finger bowls all my life.

Over the next few days, we had many practical sessions with the governors and their wives on ways to handle telephone calls, correspondence, invitations, and projects. We would need someone to screen telephone calls. We had already gotten an unlisted number at home for the first time because the telephone never stopped ringing, day or night. Even in the wee hours of the morning our inebriated friends would call—as well as those who were inebriated and not so friendly. And now we were warned that we would be deluged with calls from people who would claim to be relatives or close friends.

I wanted to know how the other wives handled the use of the mansion, having been warned of the problem by Mrs. Maddox. Some of them let their favorite organizations come at any time, some never, while others, like our hostess, Jessie Ray Scott, let each organization use the mansion once during the term. All of the wives had outside projects: Some were very active; others lent their name to good causes without otherwise becoming involved.

I was pleased to learn that our new mansion in Georgia, with its ballroom that would seat four hundred for dinner, was the envy of almost everyone, especially those from outside the South. Southern states are more lavish in their provisions for governors and their families than many other states. In Massachusetts, for instance, there is no mansion at all; the governor lives in his own home. The wife of the governor of Arizona told me that they lived in a high-rise apartment building and did all their entertaining in hotels. And Mrs. Kneip, the wife of the governor of South Dakota, said they were provided with a nice house, but she had eight little boys, the oldest about thirteen. She was aware that "the people of South Dakota are worried about their governor's house!"

I left the conference feeling much better. I was not alone in being overwhelmed by my new circumstances; the other new governors' wives shared my feelings. And best of all, we had learned there were no set rules. I felt more confident as the time for Jimmy's inauguration grew closer and I was officially to become the First Lady of Georgia.

Inauguration day dawned, cold and cloudy. When the ceremony began, rain was threatening, but just as Jimmy started his inaugural address, the clouds moved away and the sun broke through. It was an omen. Thousands of people spilled across the capitol grounds and filled the streets as far as one could see. "It's a long way from Plains to Atlanta," Jimmy began his inaugural address. "I started the trip four and a half years ago, and with a four-year detour, I finally made it." And he kept his promise to our anonymous friend: "The time for racial discrimination is over. No poor, rural, weak, or black person should ever have to bear the additional burden of being deprived of the opportunity of an education, a job, or simple justice," he said to the crowds. And on the stroke of noon, as nearby church bells pealed, Jimmy Carter was sworn in as governor.

After the ceremony we went home to the Governor's Mansion on West Paces Ferry Road, opened the doors, and let the streams of guests pour in for a public reception. We shook hands with them all—young and old, black and white, large and small, friends and a few foes. And still they came. We were pleased even though our hands, toughened we thought by the campaign, were limp before the day was over—from firm handshakes, limp handshakes, and some that hurt so much that I tried not to wince as I smiled and said hello. One person pumped my hand so hard that one of my earrings flew across the room! At dusk the line still stretched down the long driveway, and Jimmy and I went out of the house to greet the people there. He went in one direction and I the other until we had shaken hands with everyone who had come.

When the reception was finally over, we hurriedly changed clothes and were off to the four inaugural balls, I in a beautiful new blue chiffon gown. A friend and supporter in Americus, from whom I had bought clothes for years, had had it designed for me in New York—yards and yards of pale blue chiffon with gold embroidery. And Jimmy wore white tie and tails.

The balls were a crush of people, but we danced for a few moments at each one after the state patrolmen formed a small circle around us to give us space. We loved to dance, but there was no room or time to do much dancing this night. It was once around the patrolmen's circle, up to the stage to say a few words, and on to the next ball.

We settled quickly into our new home. Jack, fresh out of the Navy and back at Georgia Tech, and Jeff, who had transferred to Georgia

State University, shared the second-floor living quarters with us. Chip, who was also at Georgia State, chose a small apartment in the basement with an outside entrance, which had originally been planned for live-in help. It now became the children's headquarters, where they could turn up their music as loud as they wanted without our ever hearing it. They could entertain their friends and come and go as they pleased without being involved with official activities or the tourists. After all, they were twenty-four, twenty-one, and nineteen, not children anymore.

Amy got the choice room in the house, the large and sunny first lady's bedroom, which adjoined ours, the governor's bedroom. Her room had a giant closet that became a perfect toy room for a three-year-old.

For the first time in four years, the whole family was together again. A few nights after we moved in, we were eating dinner in the family dining room on the State Floor, enjoying the attention and being waited on, when one of the maids came into the room and said, "If anybody has shoes that need shining, if you'll just set them outside your room door we'll do them for you." We just looked at each other, and finally Jack with his usual nonchalance said, "I think we can get used to this in a hurry."

So much happened those first days after the inauguration, there was only time to act, no time to plan ahead.

Georgia's elder statesman, Senator Richard Russell, died nine days after Jimmy became governor, and President and Mrs. Nixon came to his funeral. It was the first time I had ever seen a President and the first time Jimmy had ever met one. I remember the limousine pulling up to the curb and our walking down the steps of the capitol to meet them, arriving just as they stepped out of the car, not a moment earlier. I smiled and pretended not to be nervous. What do you say to the President of the United States, especially to one you had worked very hard to defeat? "Hello, Mr. President. We're sorry about the purpose of your visit, but very glad to have you in our state." Nothing to it! But after his visit came my first critical mail: I hadn't worn a hat to meet the President. How I wish all criticism could be so trivial.

We also had to learn quickly how to manage the mansion's entertaining. Jimmy was inaugurated on January 12, and on January 30 we had a formal "after the concert" reception for Van Cliburn, who was performing in Atlanta at the invitation of the Atlanta Music Club. I called Jimmy's Aunt Sissy for help with the refreshments and flowers, ordered tuxedos for the prisoners who served as butlers, and with the help of the Music Club, invited prominent people in Atlanta who were interested in music and the arts. It was an exciting and beautiful evening for us. Van Cliburn was our first "celebrity" guest, and he couldn't have been nicer. Everyone had told me to be prepared for him to be temperamental, but he was not at all. He called in the afternoon before his performance to tell me how pleased he was to be coming to the Governor's Mansion, and that evening when he arrived we whisked him upstairs to the guest suite and served him a big steak, at his request, before he came downstairs to be with our guests. He was charming to everyone, and every year since then he has sent us flowers at Christmastime.

As lovely as our first big event was, it convinced me that we had a long way to go before we could do things right on a regular basis. We had to get a competent staff together. I hired a housekeeper with experience in food preparation and managing a kitchen who, in turn, trained one of the prisoners to be the cook. We served special dishes to the family over and over until they were perfected before serving them to guests. Together we trained the prisoners to wait on tables, serving from the left and taking away from the right, lifting a water glass to fill it rather than reaching across. They practiced on the family—some serving us breakfast, some lunch, others dinner at night—which was as new to us as it was to them.

We all enjoyed it. The servants got satisfaction out of learning the professional way of doing things, and they also enjoyed pleasing us. They were even capable of doing their work too well. Though they could never master the art of cutting a tomato properly to hold chicken or shrimp salad, they became expert at cutting the crusts off bread for tea sandwiches. Once we invited the press for an informal get-together and planned to serve them beer and submarine sandwiches on French bread. When the trays came out of the kitchen, all the crusts were neatly sliced off the French bread!

As the servants and schedules were being coordinated, Jimmy informed me that he planned to get up at six-thirty and leave for the office at seven, with no breakfast. After twenty-five years of my getting up to cook for him, he now told me that the best thing about the campaign was that he didn't have to eat breakfast. He could have told me a few years sooner! He did without except on weekends.

After breakfast every morning with Amy, I embarked on a day that was very different from that of Mrs. Maddox. I had taken care of my correspondence and schedule of activities for so long that I decided to have an office and secretary in the house. (The governor's office and staff was in the capitol, in the heart of downtown Atlanta, seven miles away, too far for immediate access.) I chose a corner room on the second floor. It had a single entrance next to the guest suite and could be reached without going through any of the living quarters.

Within weeks I hired Madeline MacBean. She was young, petite, and striking, with long, strawberry blond hair. I liked her immediately, and she answered the description of the type of secretary I would need, someone who was competent and could do my correspondence but who was also attractive and could meet people well. Madeline became indispensable as my personal social secretary as well as manager of the mansion, press secretary, and even keeper of Amy's schedule. She quickly learned all of my friends, foibles, habits, my strengths and weaknesses.

One of our biggest problems was settling into a house that was so big and unfamiliar. At first, I never knew where anybody was. On more than one occasion I found myself standing in the middle of the foyer, calling at the top of my voice to anyone who could hear me: "Dinner is ready" or "Come to the telephone." It was frustrating. We finally settled on a sign-up sheet for meals, set seven o'clock as dinnertime, and whoever was going to eat showed up in the dining room.

The telephones were more frustrating. The phone would ring in one room and before anyone reached it, it would stop and be ringing in another room. We devised a system for answering the phone that involved installing bells in several places in the house so that no matter where you were, you could hear one of them. Then we worked out a code for answering: If one bell sounded, the call was for Jimmy; two was for me, three for Jack, and on down the line for the other children. When your bell rang, you picked up the nearest telephone and the call was put through. It worked perfectly.

Another issue was the constant presence of state patrolmen in the house, which didn't make the mansion as inviting as I thought it should feel to guests. The patrolmen had to be there for security, and they had always stood at the doors of the public rooms during tours. We made it less threatening by putting stanchions with velvet ropes in the doorways and at the foot of the stairs leading to the family quarters, so that we only needed one or two patrolmen on the floor. And to make it easier for me when I went out, I asked the patrolmen who accompanied me to wear plain clothes. At that point, few people recognized me; with them in ordinary suits, I could travel incognito, even go shopping without attracting attention.

The governorship was our first experience with security. It was alarming to think that we needed protection, but it was good for Jimmy to have someone to drive him wherever he needed to go, and I thought it was good for Amy too. It meant I didn't have to worry about her. She was just past three, and we had been warned that she would be especially vulnerable as a target for anyone wanting to hurt the governor. There was always a guard with her, even when she was out in the back yard, where we had built a little dollhouse for her. But I didn't really believe that any of us were in danger.

Then one Saturday morning, soon after we moved in, we were eating breakfast in the family dining room when a state patrolman walked past the French doors that opened onto the porch. It was very unusual. When there were no guests in the house, the patrolmen always stayed out of sight to give us as much privacy as possible. When he appeared again, we realized he was patrolling the porch. Jimmy went to the door to question him and learned that there had been a serious threat on his life, therefore the extra caution. I was frightened. I asked Jimmy to stay at home and not go to the office, but he would have none of it. When he left, there were extra guards in the back seat of the car. After that, if I noticed security men patrolling the porch or extra men in the car, I knew there had been more threats than usual, but I never asked questions. I didn't want to know the details, which made me feel easier about it.

I soon set out to tackle the public aspect of the mansion and luckily found eager and willing help wherever I looked. Jimmy's Aunt Sissy, who had been active in the campaign and who lived in a suburb of Atlanta, organized volunteer hostesses to greet tourists at the door, and we made plans to train them as docents to conduct tours and give visitors some of the history and background of the furnishings and artwork. It seemed to me much better for a tourist to be met by a warm welcome from a cheerful hostess than by an intimidating state patrolman in uniform.

The house had been furnished with a museum-quality collection of Federal American furniture selected by a Fine Arts Committee that was inspired, I think, by Jackie Kennedy. It was in vogue at the time to collect Federal antiques, and the collection in the Georgia mansion is one of the finest anywhere in the United States. The committee had also obtained a beautiful selection of sculptures, paintings, and Chinese export porcelain. It included bronze busts of George Washington and Benjamin Franklin cast by the French sculptor Jean Antoine Houdon in 1778; a portrait of Andrew Jackson by Ralph E. W. Earle; other portraits by the American artist John Neagle, a leading portrait painter in Philadelphia in the early nineteenth century; a landscape by Martin J. Heade; paintings by Benjamin West and Severin Roesen; and *View of the Berkshires* by Thomas Doughty, which became one of my favorites. We were always told that the single most outstanding piece in the house was a very large, rare French porcelain vase with a medallion portrait of Benjamin Franklin painted on one side. Most of the valuable pieces were in the rooms behind the ropes, but the Franklin vase sat on a Lannuier marbletop pier table in the center hall, where visitors walked past it every day. I posted a state patrolman, in uniform, close by to guard it every time we had crowds in the house. And one or two times when I found Amy crawling underneath the table, my heart almost stopped! I worried about the vase from the day we moved in and breathed a sigh of relief when our four years were up and it was still intact.

We were living in a museum, and though Jimmy and I had studied art books for years, I knew very little about porcelains, sculptures, or antique furniture, so I asked two members of the original Fine Arts Committee to teach the volunteer docents and me the history of these treasures. We conducted many tours for special groups over the next four years, and our knowledge and appreciation of the collection made our tours, I think, especially meaningful to the public.

We had open house for all kinds of groups—senior citizens, schoolchildren, mentally retarded children, garden clubs. We also divided the state by congressional districts, and on Sunday afternoons we had open house for everyone from that district. We made announcements on the radio and put notices in the newspapers inviting them to come.

It was always amazing to me to see what people liked about the house. The docents gave details about the art and furnishings, but the questions would be: "Are the windows bulletproof?" "Does the family ever sit in these rooms?" "Where does the baby eat?" One day Amy had dropped a small stuffed animal under the table, creating a near stampede to the family dining room when someone saw it and called out, "There's the baby's toy."

People would also ask how it felt to live in a house with so many treasures. How did we relax? Did we always feel as though we were living in a museum? The answer was that the Governor's Mansion became home immediately, treasures and all, because our family was together. Not only were the upstairs living quarters very comfortable, with a den and small kitchenette that we used for snacks, but the first floor had a warm feeling about it, too. As soon as the tourists left every day we took the ropes down, and we were "home."

Outdoors, the grounds and gardens were a pleasure to look at and walk in. They were carefully tended by trusties who pruned and watered and nurtured the acres of giant hardwood trees and dogwoods, azaleas, crepe myrtle, and jasmine, two formal gardens, and a spring garden whose flowers changed with the season. There was a wisteria arbor with tables beneath for outdoor parties, and one whole acre of the grounds was given over to native flowers, plants, and woods, made even more wonderful by the small natural stream that ran through it. And we didn't have to do anything but enjoy it.

What I did have to do was arrange flowers every day to decorate the mansion. There was no budget for flowers, but they seemed essential to me. For big events such as legislative dinners, volunteers from the Garden Club helped out or I bought arrangements from a florist. But we opened the house for tours four days a week, and despite my feelings of inadequacy and the experience in the flower arranging class years before in Plains, I had to do them. I bought books on flower arranging, studied the pictures, and had the flowers I needed for the arrangements planted in the beds. I soon learned that I liked flowers in profusion in the vases I found at the mansion—spring flowers or roses or whatever happened to be blooming in the yard, or even greenery when there were no flowers. And I could do them without the difficult lines I had struggled with in my one flower arranging class.

Besides the formal gardens, I had my own rock garden just

outside the garage doors. I planted it with candytuft and pansies, or crocuses in the springtime, and tulips, begonias, and geraniums. And I could work in it even when the tourists were there; they never expected to see me in my jeans and they'd walk right by without recognizing me. In the spring of our first year in the mansion, a gentleman visiting Atlanta for a flower growers convention called and asked to see the grounds. I was at home that day and said I would be glad to give him a tour. It happened that he grew roses in California, and that fall he sent me a hundred and twenty rosebushes of different varieties that bloomed from very early in the spring until November. It was one of the most wonderful things that happened to me, and when we moved to the White House, the few roses in the Rose Garden were disappointing in comparison. At the edge of the garden Jimmy planted a row of peanuts, and each year he pulled them up, picked them off the vines, and we had our very own roasted peanuts to eat in the Governor's Mansion.

Organizing events was harder than dealing with furniture and flowers. Through trial and error, Madeline and I soon developed our own set of rules that became a guide for the use of the Georgia mansion, not only for ourselves but for outside groups and organizations. From the hundreds of requests we received, we had to turn people down every day. We decided to allow no fund-raising events and no events that I could not attend. This limited the activities considerably because I had a busy schedule. We revised our rules as time went by. When one group used the mansion and served refreshments that were not only inadequate, but unattractive as well, I was very embarrassed. The quality of the food served was a reflection on me, even when I had no responsibility for it. One of our first rules was that an acceptable caterer be chosen from a list we provided.

There had been a tradition that no alcohol other than wine and beer was served in the State Rooms of the house, and we didn't change it. Word was passed that the liquor companies would provide free "refreshments" for our parties, but I didn't want to be indebted to them. The tradition stood.

We also learned, after one disastrous experience, to audition whatever entertainment we had selected before the actual performance. One of our worst blunders occurred the night we combined a dinner for the racing car drivers in town for races at the

Atlanta Speedway and a singer who sounded very good on paper. Jimmy had always been a racing fan; he knew the drivers by name and was really looking forward to entertaining them. We had a barbecue and everybody was having a great time until the entertainer started singing—not very good light opera! Our guests, who were expecting country and western music, sat there with their mouths open, but he went on and on. I kept praying he'd just quit, but he didn't. I sank lower and lower in my chair—I couldn't decide whether I wanted to hold Jimmy down or have him get up and go stop it. It was terrible. The drivers came back for more the next year, however, and then we had great entertainment.

During this time Jimmy was working hard to make Atlanta an international city and to attract foreign business to our state. I was excited as we traveled abroad—to Europe, to Central and South America, and to Israel—and invited many foreign officials and diplomats to the mansion. The number of consulates expanded to eight, with twenty-one honorary consulates, and trade offices were opened in Brussels, Bonn, São Paulo, Toronto, and Tokyo. Most important, authorization was passed in the legislature to build a World Congress Center, which is now a reality.

Soon after we moved into the mansion, we were invited to dinner at the home of the German consul-general, Roland Gottlieb. I learned that evening that Mrs. Gottlieb had written a book called *Gracious Entertaining*. She was an authority on food and wines and, having been in the foreign service for twenty-five years, was knowledgeable about the protocol of entertaining.

As we began to entertain foreign diplomats and officials, Ruth Gottlieb proved very helpful with ideas and advice. One evening we invited the British ambassador and his wife, Lord and Lady Cromer, to dinner and had everything planned to the last elegant detail. We had a menu topped off with Grand Marnier soufflé for dessert, hand-written menu cards by each place, our best silver, china, and linens, and beautiful flowers on the table and throughout the house. Our best caterer, Stig Jorgensen, would prepare the food. Ruth stopped by the mansion in the afternoon to see if we needed any help. Noticing a wrinkle in the tablecloth, she asked the maid for an iron and, since the places were already set, pressed the cloth still on the table. The evening was perfect, but trouble started the next day, when we had scheduled a large party for members of the legislature.

I was upstairs when one of the maids rushed in, saying, "Mrs. Carter, oh, Mrs. Carter, come quick, something awful's happened." And something awful had happened. The pad underneath the tablecloth had been glued to the antique tabletop by the heat from Ruth's iron. We peeled it off, leaving a coat of white fuzz stuck to the melted wax and in the finish of the table. I panicked, not only because of the party, but because I thought the table was ruined for good. Fortunately, we had an overnight guest in the house, a state senator and old friend, who came to the rescue. He spent the entire morning working on the table, rubbing, polishing, even sanding it lightly, and finally applying shoe polish and everything else he could find. And it worked. By the time the party started, the table was as good as new!

Though it was wonderful to have someone prepare our meals in the mansion, I soon yearned to get back into the kitchen myself. Although I planned the meals, making out the menus a week in advance, it wasn't the same. I started letting the servants go home on Saturdays and Sundays after lunch, a practice I continued in the White House. But even then I didn't do much cooking. I was not familiar with the kitchen, and every time I started to cook I had to search all the cabinets to find what I needed. The pots and pans were huge, big enough to cook for at least twenty-five people a day, counting the help. It was too frustrating, so usually the cook left enough food already prepared so that all I had to do was take it out of the refrigerator—and I went to a class at Ursula's Cooking School once a week to satisfy my yearning.

There was a tremendous ballroom downstairs in the mansion, designed to seat five hundred people and serve four hundred comfortably for dinner. The space was marvelous, but when we arrived it was big and cold and empty, with a terrazzo floor and stacks of chairs at one end. Even when we entertained, filling it with plants and flowers, it still wasn't very attractive. One morning during Jimmy's first year in office, I was visiting the High Museum of Art in downtown Atlanta, walking through and enjoying the paintings, when I thought, "Why not ask the museum for paintings for the walls of the ballroom?" We were about to serve as host for the Southern Governors' Conference and had planned a big, gala evening at the mansion, and the paintings would make the ballroom very special. Our tight security at the mansion would serve the art as well. The museum was enthusiastic. They had many paintings in storage, from which the curator made a selection to bring to the mansion and hang. The room was transformed!

The morning of the governors' dinner, I started down the stairs to see the last of the paintings being hung. Suddenly the sound of beautiful music filled the house. Robert Shaw and the Atlanta Symphony Orchestra were going to perform that evening, and they had arrived early to rehearse. I stopped, poised in my steps, with the strangest feeling of wonder, as though I were in a dream. First, an exquisite collection of paintings on permanent loan to the Governor's Mansion. Now, the sound of a symphony filling the house. It was all so beautiful that it was breathtaking. The "fantasy" lasted through the entire evening, and I couldn't help remembering the panic I'd felt at the governors-elect conference at the prospect of holding such grand entertainments myself.

The social schedule at the mansion quickly became almost a full-time business. One week, for instance, we had dinner for 144 people one night, 44 the next, and 86 the next. This was typical when Jimmy had a big project going. When he was working on government reorganization, we invited to the mansion large groups of county commissioners and mayors, corporate executives, legislative committees, and all kinds of special study groups. And since my entertainment budget was only $25,000 a year, we learned to economize. It was actually much easier to have large functions on successive days. The same flowers could be used, the menus could be coordinated, and it saved taking down tables and putting them back up again.

We also had dinners and receptions for groups involved with my projects—my mental health committee, the committee for the Special Olympics for Retarded Citizens, a Foster Grandparents Recognition group, transportation officials, and the Georgia Garden Club women when we were working on a highway beautification program. We entertained the Georgia Press Association, the Board of Regents, the Democratic Charter Commission, and when they came back from Vietnam, the Georgia Prisoners of War. We had dinners auctioned off to raise money for the Savannah Symphony, and we held our high school reunions and big family get-togethers there, too.

Needless to say, all of this entertaining required a huge wardrobe, and the women in our family worked out a highly successful arrangement for long dresses. It seemed very wasteful for everyone to have to buy so many new ones for special occasions. But by a stroke of good luck, we were all the same size. Jack and Chip both married while we were in the mansion, so there was Jack's wife, Judy; her mother, Edna Langford, who was at the mansion often and helped me with the entertaining; Chip's wife, Caron; Jeff's girlfriend, Annette; and I. We all wore size 6 or 8, so we pooled our clothes. We had one large closet on the second floor that we called the "gown room," filled with an impressive collection of cocktail dresses, long gowns, evening wraps, shoes, and bags. I didn't mind buying clothes so much when I knew the others could wear them, too, and we were always prepared with something special to wear. (And according to protocol, I got first choice.)

But even with my making great progress toward being the kind of First Lady I wanted to be, all the strains and challenges began to take their toll. There had been no precedents to follow when we moved into the mansion, no staff in place to carry on the routine while we adjusted to it. With little background, I had to start from scratch, and because I still had very high standards, I wanted everything to be perfect. Overnight, it seemed, we had become "public" persons, living in a fishbowl at the mercy of the press and sometimes the public. The transition from the simpler life of being a wife and mother in Plains and working in the peanut warehouse to being the First Lady of Georgia was a difficult one. The move to the White House later was much easier for me compared to this initial move.

I had long since acknowledged that there would always be people in the house—servants, security men, and tour groups four days a week. And there was no way to get downstairs to the kitchen without going through the tourists. At first I thought that Amy and I both had to be perfectly groomed, with every hair in place, every time we went downstairs, even when there were no tourists in the house. I often remembered when Jimmy was a state senator and I had seen the governor's wife at a football game: Everybody craned their necks to see what she had on, including me. In the beginning I imagined that everyone was looking at my hair, my fingernails, my clothes, and my shoes and looking to see a spotless baby girl in ruffles and bows.

I couldn't live that way very long. I had to be able to brush out my hair and let it fly and put on my jeans if I wanted to. That's what I would have done at home—but I *was* at home; this was home for four years. After a couple of months I began to go downstairs to breakfast in my robe. Why not? There was no one in the house but the servants until nine o'clock, when the tours began. And how do you keep a three-year-old perfect and spotless all the time? I began to let Amy be a normal child, and we all felt better.

My whole attitude changed. I would never be perfect, and I had decided to relax and do the best I could and not worry about it, as Jimmy had tried to tell me forever. I made myself at home. I dressed properly, but casually, and began to enjoy my new clothes rather than feel enslaved by them. I was neat and well groomed, but I didn't put my makeup on every single morning before I stepped out of my bedroom door.

Even with these adjustments, after we had been in the mansion for almost a year I found myself very unhappy. The first excitement of being in the Governor's Mansion had worn thin in the midst of all the work and all the pressure, and I was tired. Not just tired—I was exhausted. I couldn't remember when I had ever rested. And I couldn't even cry. If I shut myself in the bathroom for too long, one of the maids would knock on the door and say, "Are you all right, Mrs. Carter?"

I snapped at the children, at the maids and the security men. And I found myself in long and continuous arguments with Jimmy over everything, especially my discontent.

I missed my friends. I missed walking up and down the street at home, and I missed the contact with neighbors. Now if I ever saw a friend it was in a receiving line: "Hello! How are you?" and they were gone.

I felt trapped—by my schedule and by the security.

I wanted to do something that wasn't on a schedule. I wanted to drive a car myself, not have somebody drive me, wherever I wanted to go—not just where my schedule said I should be next.

I couldn't leave the house, even to walk in the yard, without someone following me. But I didn't want to be constantly watched. I wanted to buy a blond wig and go shopping incognito. I wanted to push a grocery cart up and down the aisles without everybody looking at every item I put in it. It used to be so much fun to go to the store with Amy and put her in the basket and let her pick out the cereal and cookies. No more. And it used to be fun to look through the clothes in a store and pick out the ones I wanted to try on rather than being shut in a room with someone who didn't know me bringing me "things." I longed to be alone and lost in the crowd.

Finally, after months of hearing my threats about buying a blond wig, Jimmy began to pay attention. One day he said, "Why don't you get in the car and go for a ride?" "Alone?" I asked. "Alone," he said. "I'll tell the state patrolmen to fix the radio in the car so you can call them if necessary, and you just drive around for a while. Maybe it'll make you feel better."

I scrambled to get dressed and rushed downstairs to the car. Jimmy had forgotten to tell the patrolmen to let me go, but that didn't stop me. I told them. They showed me how to work the car radio; I got in the car and drove out of the yard. What a feeling of freedom! I was alone. I was driving myself with no destination in mind, much less written on a schedule. I turned on the car radio and sang aloud with it as I drove all the way to Calhoun, Georgia, sixty miles north of Atlanta. I went to see Edna Langford, who by now was a very close friend. I knocked on her back door, and when she came to open it I took one look at her and burst into tears. "What in the world is the matter?" she asked with concern. "Nothing. Everything," I managed to say. And she immediately understood.

We spent a lovely afternoon chatting about our children and other womanly things. I even spent some time weeding the flower beds in her back yard. After a while, I called the Governor's Mansion to tell the state patrolmen where I was because I had told them I wouldn't get out of the car. They already knew. "We watched you and alerted the state patrol offices along the way," they told me. Oh no, I thought, I still can't get away. But I drove home feeling much better.

I joined a Bible class, thinking it would be just the thing to help me. A few days later I learned from the teacher that a well-known evangelist would be in town; I paid $60 to hear him teach a course on Christian living. It was the wrong thing to do. I argued in my mind with almost everything he said. He taught subservience by the wife and mother and children, with no acknowledgment or thought of mutual respect and sharing and love within a family. Subservience and discipline. There's more to life than that, I thought, and there's more to living the life Jesus wants us to live than being punishing and rigid and afraid.

The evangelist said that if a mother told her child to do something and the father came along and told the child something else, the child should always mind the father. I didn't believe that. I believed there must be mutual respect between a husband and wife in their actions with the children. Then he told us that if a child was put in jail for using drugs, the child should be left there to teach him a lesson. The child had committed a crime and he should pay for it. I got up and left.

Then I felt very guilty about walking out on an evangelist whom people came from everywhere to hear. Something must have been wrong with me, or maybe I was reading interpretations into what he was saying that he didn't intend. I went back the second night and managed to stay twenty minutes.

Soon afterward, a friend from the Bible class asked me if she could come to the mansion and speak to the prisoners about Jesus. I was glad to have her come. The prisoners might need Jesus, and I needed Him, too. I especially needed to be reassured after my conflict with the evangelist. Had she sensed that? I'll never know. "Jesus loves you. You are precious to Him," my friend said to the prisoners, and me, assembled in the ballroom. "It doesn't matter who you are or where you are or what you have done, He loves you. Everyone in this room is precious to Him. I am precious. Mrs. Carter is precious, every one of you is precious to Him. He wants all of us to be happy. He wants to take away our problems and our cares, and He will—if we'll only let Him."

If we'll let Him. There it was. That's what was wrong. I'd clung to all my problems and not let them go. I ran from the ballroom to my bedroom upstairs to look for a little booklet Jimmy's sister Ruth had written. And she had said the same thing. When problems come, when you are burdened down, when you have tried everything and nothing works, release it to God. That was the key. Release! Release! And I had forgotten to do that. I prayed that day: "Oh, God, I have been trying to solve all my problems alone. I can't do that. There are too many pressures, too many tasks, too many demands. I release them all to you. They're yours. Take them, and just let me know what to do."

It was a burden lifted. Things didn't change suddenly. It took awhile for me to work through all the problems I'd saved for myself, and each day I'd find something else I had to give to Jesus. Sometimes I'd have to say, "Here, take this one again," when I couldn't seem to let go.

But that experience and that lesson saved my life. I have been in many situations since that were difficult, that could have been very lonely and defeating, but I am constantly aware that God is with me to help me through the difficult times.

As soon as things had become organized a little during that first year of Jimmy's governorship, I began to follow up on my commitment to work for projects I thought were important in Georgia. I had worked as long as I could remember, and when we moved to the Governor's Mansion, I knew I would want something to do in addition to the daily routine of housekeeping supervision and entertaining. I hadn't planned to spend all my time pouring tea.

A First Lady can pick and choose her projects and do almost anything she wants because her name is a drawing card, she is influential, and although legislators may not always support her, she can always get their attention, as well as the attention of other powerful people. She also has access to the press.

The problem is sorting out priorities: which causes to be involved in, what to do, and how much to do. I was approached by many organizations and many good causes, but my first choice was mental health. We knew from Jimmy's senate years that much needed to be done, and I had learned at first hand in the campaign that services were not adequate. I had asked Jimmy myself for a commitment that he would do all he could for mental health programs, so I had to be willing to work on them too.

Jimmy kept his word, and very soon after the inauguration, he formed the Governor's Commission to Improve Services to the Mentally and Emotionally Handicapped. He did not, however, put me in charge, but appointed mental health professionals, laymen, parents, and concerned citizens along with me. I didn't have sufficient knowledge of the problems to help in a substantive way; I had a lot to learn. I went to all the meetings of the commission, worked one day a week as a volunteer at Georgia Regional Hospital, and toured the other state hospitals, reporting back to the commission members what I found in an effort to determine the needs. I listened and I learned. At Georgia Regional Hospital in Atlanta, one of our newest and most advanced facilities, I worked in every area of care. I found the work with the children rewarding but very frustrating when I wanted the progress to be more rapid; I planted flower beds with the elderly men and women from the geriatrics ward; and I did follow-up work with alcoholics who had come to the hospital to dry out. I fed some of those who needed help and read stories to them and watched them respond to attention.

One of my very first visits was to our main state hospital for children. It was a devastating experience. These were mentally retarded children, some profoundly retarded; I had to hold back tears all morning long and could hardly ask a question. At the end of the tour, the superintendent asked me to come into his office for a few minutes. As he closed the door, he said, "Mrs. Carter, I've watched you this morning and I have to say one thing. Most mentally retarded people are happy. They do not know that they should be sad. If you are going to help at all, you've got to accept that and get over your tears. Don't let it get the best of you. We need you."

He was right, of course, but it was a struggle. It didn't come naturally to me not to feel sorry for every retarded child I saw, and for every adult, many of whom had been in institutions most of their lives. And it was frustrating not to be able just to unlock whatever it was inside the emotionally disturbed persons that kept them from functioning properly and leading normal lives. But over a period of time I developed a sense of acceptance and with it a determination to do everything I could to help. One thing I had learned for sure was how totally dependent these people are on others, including me, to care for them. They cannot care for themselves, and their families aren't always influential enough to be heard.

I also had learned that there were some very good helpers in our state, as there are in other states throughout our country: laypeople, volunteers, parents, and professionals who are totally dedicated to do what is best for the mentally afflicted. These good people steered me through the early days of my "education" with patience and understanding.

The Governor's Commission worked for months to formulate a comprehensive report, in which we outlined a plan for the care of the mentally afflicted in Georgia. The thrust of the plan was to shift the emphasis away from the large institutions to the smaller, more intimate community mental health centers. This would allow some of those who were afflicted to live at home, surrounded by loved ones, yet have somewhere to go during the day to learn and be cared for. We wanted a center within reach of every person who needed help, and we almost accomplished that. Our mental health system changed completely in the next three years. From twenty-three community mental health centers when Jimmy was elected, the number jumped to one hundred thirty-four! And there were twenty-three group homes for the mildly retarded, those people who should not be in institutions but who have no place to go. We were treating 56 percent more mental patients, and the number of resident hospital patients during the last three years of Jimmy's term decreased by about 30 percent.

One weekend I drove to Ocilla, in a rural area of our state, to visit the community mental health center and saw the real, human results of our commission: A three-year-old child whose parents were both deaf-mutes, and who was always thought to have the same affliction, had now begun to talk. A teenage girl who had spent her lifetime in a wheelchair had recently become an excellent swimmer. An elderly man who stuttered so badly that it was painful to listen to him told me, "I-I-I was the t-t-town crazy unt-t-til th-th-they opened th-th-this place." He had spent his life on the streets, taking handouts and causing trouble. But he had not missed a day at the center since it opened. He kept the yards spotless and helped inside the building, and everyone told me that they didn't know what they would do without him. During the program, when he was called on to sing, he opened his mouth and the words of "How Great Thou Art" poured forth, clear and beautiful, without a stutter. I cried.

Jimmy implemented much of the plan outlined by the commission, and people came from all over the country to see what we had done. When people ask, "What was the most rewarding thing you did as First Lady of Georgia?" I always answer, "My work with the mentally ill."

One of my favorite programs was the Special Olympics, competitive games specifically tailored to retarded children. Started by Eunice Kennedy Shriver, it is one of the most exciting things that has been done for the retarded. Not only does the competition provide an opportunity for these children to develop physically, it also instills a sense of pride and a feeling of belonging that is so important to their lives. We made sure that all our centers had active Special Olympics programs, and by the last year of Jimmy's term, we had twelve thousand children participating in them.

Some of the results were miraculous. I worked very hard with one little twelve-year-old boy who spent his time sitting in a chair, rocking and staring into space. For months we taught him that you put one foot in front of the other to walk, a long, slow,

painstaking process. The one day he walked! Not far, but h
walked. And soon, with a lot of love and encouragement fro
the people at the hospital, he was ready to enter a race in th
Special Olympics. We worked and worked and he practiced an
practiced, and when the day came, we all held our breath. He wa
so excited that we didn't know whether he would be able to ru
or not, but he did, and he won the race! Can you imagine the joy
And it wasn't long before this child was functioning in a publi
school.

As time went by, I also became involved in other projects. Wit
the help of Lady Bird Johnson and the Texas Highway Departmen
we started our own Georgia Highway Wildflower Program. Th
Texas program is famous, and I wanted to know more about it
With an offer of funds from an anonymous donor toward a highwa
beautification project, I joined other members from our state Gar
den Club on a trip to see Mrs. Johnson at the LBJ Ranch. W
flew to Texas in a small state plane and landed on the strip jus
behind her house, where she welcomed us in her friendly, charm
ing way. One of the keys to a successful wildflower program, sh
explained, was to provide an incentive to the highway foreme
who did the best job of maintaining the roadsides. The idea wa
not only to plant wildflowers but to locate areas where they gre
in abundance by the roadside and have the Highway Departmen
agree not to mow them till the proper time for the flowers t
reseed. The Georgia Highway Department was enthusiastic, an
together with the Garden Club, we developed a thriving progra
in our state. We now have horticulturists in the Department o
Transportation and an annual awards program. And our roadside
in Georgia will get more and more beautiful every year as th
wildflowers multiply into masses of color along the way.

I met Betty Ford, the wife of the newly selected Vice Presiden
while working on another project. A special train had been con
verted into a six-car museum to take works of art, including pain
ings, sculpture, and even a medieval suit of armor, into rural area
of the country that had no access to museums. Called "Artrain,
the movable museum originated in Mrs. Ford's home state o
Michigan. Most of the exhibits were constant, but the last tw
cars were reserved for art from the particular region the train wa
touring and for artists at work, painting or making pottery o

jewelry. I was the chairperson of the southeastern tour of Artrain and spent many months in preparation, along with the wives of the other southern governors, making arrangements with the railroad companies to pull the train, getting together paintings and items to fill our cars, and working with the communities to be visited. Most of the old depots in the towns on the tour were no longer in use and had become eyesores in the community; they were renovated and painted to welcome Artrain. Many became permanently improved locations for community activities, or, in some instances, museums that continue to function as cultural centers.

In the tiny community of Parrott, just twelve miles from Plains, where the train stopped for its customary two or three days, a platform was erected in the middle of the street and there were continuous performances by dancers—ballet dancers, square dancers, modern dancers—as well as one-act plays and trios playing classical music. There were also banjos and guitars and country music singers.

Artrain was fun and very successful, made more so by our special visitor from Washington. Mrs. Ford wanted to be involved in the arts, and Nixon's White House thought a perfect opportunity for her debut would be at the first stop of Artrain on its southeastern tour.

I was anxious to meet her, for I had heard that Mrs. Ford and I had many things in common, families that were an important part of our lives as well as political husbands. I also quickly learned how differently our political lives had developed. She had lived in Washington for many years and had had little experience campaigning alone. We rode together in a parade before the opening ceremonies, and I was waving to everyone, as usual, calling, "Hello," "Hello," and "Hey, how are you?" It's always embarrassing to have someone listen to me when I'm riding in a parade, even the driver of the car, as I call out over and over again. That day was no exception. After listening to me for a while, Mrs. Ford said, "You must know all of these people." I turned to her in astonishment and said no, that I didn't know them at all, and soon she was waving and saying in her slow and very distinct way of speaking, "Hello, how are you?"

We were late everywhere we went that day. When we finally got to the press conference in the caboose of the train, the first question she was asked was: "Mrs. Ford, are you on something?"

to which she frankly answered yes, that she took Valium every day. Pencils began writing, though I don't think she realized she had created a stir. Later, when she was back in Washington, the White House explained that Mrs. Ford had a pinched nerve in her neck and had to take Valium to relieve the pain. Her admission that day was the beginning of a public awakening to the pressures put on political spouses. Because any blemish on the public's image of a candidate's or an elected official's perfect wife, children, and idyllic family life can be a detriment, most suffer in polite silence. In the caboose of the Artrain, there was no way to know how significant Betty Ford's openness would be. She began to make it possible for other spouses not to have to be quite so perfect.

Another one of my projects caused a confrontation with Jimmy. The Equal Rights Amendment was to come to a vote in the Georgia House of Representatives in January 1974. This was before the ERA became a big national issue, and it didn't stand a chance of passing in Georgia. Just like the Supreme Court decision on integration in 1954, Georgia was not ready to accept the ERA in 1974. Our people were exhausted from the long civil rights turmoil, which had forced so many changes in the way we lived and thought about each other. More change, instigated by what seemed to be strident, militant women from outside the South, was just too much for our legislators to accept. I had made a few calls, but had done very little else for the futile cause.

The television news had been full of bra burnings and strong statements by ERA supporters such as Bella Abzug and Gloria Steinem. When Jimmy and I were watching all this one night, we heard that Gloria Steinem had been invited to lead an ERA march on the capitol in Atlanta. I told Jimmy I thought it was the worst possible thing to do to get the ERA passed because the people in Georgia were not sympathetic to Gloria at the time. They considered her radical and threatening, and I thought having her here would have an adverse reaction on the legislators.

A few days before the ERA was to come to a vote, Jimmy invited the huge crowd of anti-ERA demonstrators who were swarming all over the capitol into the large reception room of his office. As many as could crowded in, spilling over into the hall; Jimmy was barely able to make his way to a desk and climb up on it to be seen. Then he dropped his bombshell. "I respect your right to oppose the ERA, but my mind is made up," Jimmy told the excited crowd. "I am for it—but my wife is against it!"

"My wife is against it!" I couldn't believe it later when I heard what he'd said. That evening we went to a concert and a friend approached me in the foyer of the concert hall. "Rosalynn," he said. "I'm surprised that you're against the ERA." I shook my head. "I'm not against it," I told him, but he persisted. "That's not what your husband said this morning." I turned to Jimmy, but all I could say in such a public place was: "How could you?" He just grinned. I can't believe he seriously thought I opposed it, although to this day he says he did. The truth, I think, is that he vaguely heard me opposing Gloria Steinem's trip the evening we were watching television, and with his mind on something else, he just thought I was opposing the ERA.

The next day I arranged to go to the capitol to have lunch with him, giving me a chance to wear my big I'M FOR ERA button past the demonstrators. When I arrived they were there—waving placards, sitting on the stairways and on the floor, and standing everywhere. They were camped all over the capitol, lobbying legislators very effectively. I walked through them, wearing my button proudly. I didn't want them to believe mistakenly that I agreed with them. I was booed all the way in, and as we left to go to lunch (Jeff was with us and he wore a button, too), we were booed all the way out. Needless to say, the legislature soundly voted down the ERA the next day.

I soon learned at first hand about the inadequacies and inequality in our judicial system from the prisioners who worked in the mansion. Mary Fitzpatrick, a young trusty at the mansion who took care of Amy and me as if we were her own family, had been convicted of manslaughter after becoming involved in a shooting accident in Lumpkin, Georgia. She had not even seen her court-appointed lawyer until she was in the courtroom, where he had persuaded her to plead guilty to a murder she hadn't committed. Pleading guilty, he told her, would get her a lighter sentence; pleading not guilty would just make everybody mad. She was young, black, and penniless, so she did as he told her and got a life sentence in return. Pearl, another of the prisoners and the mother of six, had also been given a life sentence for killing her husband. He had only come home on her paydays, always drunk, to take the money she earned as a dental technician. Her court-appointed lawyer and the judge together decided either to fine her $750 or to give her life imprisonment, thinking she would just pay the fine and be out of the way. She could only raise $500, so she went to jail. By the time we knew her, she had already served several years of her sentence. One day she came to us and asked to borrow $250. She was worried about her children because her mother, who was keeping them, was seriously ill. She said that if she had $250 she could get out of jail. "Pearl, you know you can't buy your way out of jail," I said. "Yes, I can," she replied. "I've got a letter that says so." She was right. She brought us the letter, which was from her parole officer, and Jimmy turned it over to his legal aide to investigate immediately. Whether or not her crime justified more punishment is arguable, but within days she was free, on the ground of an illegal sentence.

Other prisoners who worked for us were being fleeced for $50 a month by their lawyers the year before they were due to be paroled. It was common practice for these lawyers to convince the prisoners that without help, they wouldn't get out. I'm sure the lawyers obtained lists and approached all the prisoners in this manner, knowing that because our prisons were so crowded, almost anyone who was eligible would be automatically paroled. There was no question about it, especially for the ones who worked at the mansion, who were all trusties. We had one woman whose elderly parents had paid a lawyer out of their meager welfare check for almost a year before we found out about it, and others were borrowing money in order to pay. As soon as we became aware of the situation, we got the names of the lawyers and gave records of their calls to the Georgia Bar Association. They were not disbarred (which they should have been), but were only warned. Being exposed made an impact, but that didn't satisfy my anger, and I picked up the telephone one day on impulse and called one of the lawyers, personally telling him exactly how I felt about his underhanded practice. The prisoners who worked for us were never approached again.

I visited the Fulton County prison where many of our servants, including Mary, slept at night, then went to the large state facility for women in Milledgeville. The conditions in both were deplorable. Because Mary was a trusty, she shared nicer arrangements with nine or ten other prisoners, each with her own cot and one cardboard box for personal belongings that fit under the bed. Their bathroom, in one corner of the room, at least had a folding screen across it. The other women were not so fortunate and lived thirty or forty in a room or in "cages," with iron bars on all four sides. Tin pans of food were handed to them through a window in the door, and the two bathrooms in the center of the cell had no doors at all. They lived and slept with no privacy whatsoever, and though the inmates were just supposed to stay in these cells temporarily, while awaiting trial or serving thirty- to sixty-day sentences, many had been there for months and months.

I couldn't sleep for many nights after my visit, and I began to work with the Women's Prison Committee of the Commission on the Status of Women, newly activated by Jimmy, to secure a decent place where some of the women could live and work. We located a suitable old house, which had at one time been used as a Carter campaign headquarters, and painted and scrubbed while working out the necessary arrangements with the prison authorities to create a Work Release Center. We were very proud of it and had a big opening when it was ready for occupancy. It wasn't the best place in the world, but it was a mansion compared to the jail. Approximately sixty-five women were transferred to the new center, and this is where Mary lived after we left the Governor's Mansion and before she came to the White House to be with us. The women were happy there—as happy as they could be in any place where they were detained—working "on the outside" during the day.

Working with the new corrections director and with the Committee on the Status of Women, we were also able to get the women in our big state prison moved into better quarters. My conscience was salved to some extent, though I will always be concerned for those who suffer the indignities of prison life.

With so much to do, my old nemesis, making speeches, returned quickly. All during the campaign I had longed for the day it would be over because then, "I'm not ever going to make another speech!" I didn't like to make speeches, I didn't want to make speeches, and when the campaign was over, I thought I wouldn't have to make speeches. But the invitations poured in. I said no to my friends all over the state. I said no to every mental health organization. I said no so many times that after a while it became embarrassing.

It was Jimmy, combined with my own shame at avoiding the issue, that put me back up on the podium. Six months after we had been in the mansion, I was invited to speak to the Georgia

Association for Retarded Children, and Jimmy thought this was an opportune time for me to outline his plans for mental health programs in the state. I reluctantly agreed, and he helped me write the speech. I went over and over it; I studied and studied it; I even memorized it. I made it through the speech all right—my voice only cracked once or twice—but it was a horrible experience. I knew that everyone realized how nervous I was. It was even worse now that I was the governor's wife because I was expected to do a good job and not to be afraid. I went home and cried. "That's it," I said to Jimmy. "I just can't do it."

Jimmy tried to console me, but I knew he didn't have much patience with my problem. He had always thought I could do anything, and he never accepted "no" or "I can't" as an answer or excuse from anyone. The sweeter he was to me, the worse I felt. I had failed. I had failed him . . . and myself.

I didn't speak in public again for months, and once again it was Jimmy who encouraged me. One day, when I was feeling particularly inadequate, he said, "Why don't you do what I do? Write down a few words that will remind you of the things you want to say and then just get up and talk about them." I realized I had been talking to the tourists who came to the mansion, describing the house and its furnishings as I guided them through with no problem at all. So when an invitation came from the Atlanta Women's Chamber of Commerce and they wanted to hear about the Governor's Mansion, I mustered my courage and said yes. This time I would try Jimmy's way.

I went to the luncheon at a downtown hotel armed with my card with six or eight words on it. I tried to appear nonchalant as though I did this every day with great ease. I carried on conversation with my hostesses in a conscious effort to keep the speech out of my mind. I even ate my lunch. Finally I was introduced, I stood up to speak and looked out over the crowd and pretended they were all tourists. Suddenly they all looked like tourists—all strangers, all looking at me, just as they did at the mansion—and while I was enjoying the thought because that made it easier, I began to talk about the Governor's Mansion . . . and was easy. They were listening attentively, and when I got through they wanted to hear more. So I answered questions with no problem, no problem at all.

The speech over, I said my good-byes, walked calmly from the room, then ran to find a telephone. I couldn't wait to tell

Jimmy. I called him at his office: "I did it! I did it!" And Madeline, my secretary, still remembers that day when I got back home: She was in the ballroom looking over the tables being set for a big dinner party that evening when my car drove up, the door opened, and I burst in, saying, "I did it! I did it!"

I had done it. It was a wonderful feeling and quite a break-through for me. Although I have never gotten completely over my nervousness, I have been making speeches regularly ever since.

After that, most of the problems I had while speaking were circumstantial, like microphones that didn't work or a podium that was too high or too low. Once the problem was more bizarre and I almost didn't make it to the speech at all.

I went to a high school to talk about the subject "Life in the Governor's Mansion." I was met at the front door and presented with a large corsage, which I pinned on my suit. Then I excused myself to go to the ladies' room. When I was ready to return, the door of the bathroom stall wouldn't unlock. I shook and shook the door. I thought about screaming, but I was too embarrassed. There was no room at the bottom of the door, so I couldn't crawl out. The only exit was over the top. After hesitating a few moments I put one foot on the commode, the other on the toilet tissue rack, and hoisted myself up and over the top—corsage and all—scared to death that someone would come in and find me suspended five feet off the floor. No one did, and I walked calmly out to deliver the speech as though nothing had happened.

It was in the Governor's Mansion that I realized that people are just people, no matter who they are or how famous or powerful or influential. They have simply had more experience or more opportunities or a special talent, and I was not as intimidated by them as I thought I would be.

One night the famous evangelist Oral Roberts stayed up until 3:00 A.M. in our kitchen, eating a bowl of cereal and discussing religion with the boys and Jimmy. Another day, when I came home from a mental health meeting, the guards told me that Jimmy was at home, in the presidential suite with a guest. I went upstairs to find him, two of our boys, and Senator Hubert Humphrey with Amy in his lap. They had served him lemonade and brownies and he had crumbs all over his face. Amy was feeding him. Another time Ethel Kennedy came for the Special Olympics and we had great fun, sitting on the floor in the Red Room and talking.

Margaret Mead came to the mansion, and we talked about mental health problems. Film stars also became regular guests, particularly since Jimmy was successfully encouraging the movie industry to film on location in Georgia.

One of the most interesting events we had in the mansion was an evening with Georgia authors. The library on the State Floor was my favorite room: It was small and intimate, with cherry paneling and an open fireplace, and the shelves were filled with books that were either by Georgia authors or related to Georgia. We invited our authors to donate signed first editions of their books, and collected others by such famous Georgians as Joel Chandler Harris, Erskine Caldwell, Flannery O'Connor, and Carson McCullers.

We had many political guests also, including most of the Democratic candidates for the presidency in 1972. Senators Muskie, Jackson, and McGovern each came, as well as Senator Humphrey. I sat in on some of the conversations with the candidates as Jimmy explained to them how federal programs and grants worked at the state level. We had been thinking privately that Jimmy might run for President in 1976, and I was overwhelmed by the thought, but listening to these men, I realized that he probably knew more about how government worked at the point where it served people than they did. The senators, however, were eager listeners and made themselves at home. When Senator Muskie started for bed, he asked me for a nightcap of whiskey and milk. I walked partway down the hall, turned, and went back. "Mixed?" I asked him. "Mixed," he said.

One year Jimmy was able to attract the Organization of American States to hold their meeting in Atlanta. It was the only time I recall that we might have seemed inhospitable. Henry Kissinger was then secretary of state, and we invited him and his new wife, Nancy, to stay at the mansion for the duration of the meeting. Our feelings changed a few days before their visit, however, when a crew arrived to install special telephones for Dr. Kissinger, announcing that they would have to drill as many as twenty-three holes in the house, most of them in the guest suite's parquet floor, to accommodate the wiring. I said no. I still don't understand it. Having lived with a President and been in situations where telephones and security were essential, I still don't understand twenty-three holes. We had the Kissingers stay in the hotel, reserving a whole floor for them. I took Nancy sightseeing when the men were busy, and she told me how disappointed she was that so many of her personal wedding gifts from foreign officials would have to be turned over to the government. At that time, any gift from a foreign official valued at more than $50 was the property of the government, and Nancy said she envisioned her presents as well as those of others piled under every building in Washington.

In the spring of 1974, Ted Kennedy was invited to be the keynote speaker at the Law Day ceremonies at the University of Georgia, and as was our custom with visiting dignitaries, we invited him to spend the night at the Governor's Mansion before the festivities. Jimmy was to be a Law Day speaker, too, at the luncheon following the ceremonies to which only top lawyers, Supreme Court justices, and special guests were invited.

When the day came, Ted spoke first and said almost everything Jimmy had been going to say, so Jimmy, forced to discard his prepared text, made some impromptu remarks about our system of justice as he saw it working in Georgia. He described several cases in which people had been cheated or sent to prison just because they were poor and lacked influence, and he criticized the legal establishment soundly for looking the other way while those things were occurring in front of them. In a quiet voice, he compared the deprivation of blacks under forced segregation with the continuing deprivation of the poor and helpless in the courtroom.

It was, by all accounts, an extraordinary speech. It was received with a moment of shocked silence and then a standing, cheering ovation. When the group returned to the mansion, even Ted Kennedy's staff told us that Jimmy had outdone himself that day, and the Law Day speech later became famous in the 1976 presidential campaign. What we did not know at the time was that the writer Hunter Thompson, who was visiting that day, was captivated by what Jimmy said. He had been sitting in the back of the audience, quietly sipping Wild Turkey bourbon disguised as iced tea. When Jimmy began speaking, Thompson began to ease toward the exit for a refill, but when he heard the names Reinhold Niebuhr and Bob Dylan he stayed to listen. He immediately asked the university to send him a taped copy of the speech, and for months afterward he played the tape over and over for anyone he could force to listen. Later, he came to Plains to visit us, and wrote a long article in *Rolling Stone* with the Law Day speech as the focal point.

The Law Day speech was one of the interesting moments of history in Jimmy's term as governor, but I was proudest of his everyday work that resulted in good government.

Jimmy's major goal as governor was to reorganize the government, and he persuaded some of the larger businesses in Georgia to lend him some of their top personnel for a year. I made some of the calls myself to businessmen, and everyone was eager to help. A team of a hundred people was put together to study the tangle of some three hundred state agencies, bureaus, and commissions that often duplicated each other's work, and to draw up recommendations to make the government work more efficiently and economically. Everything and everyone came under review and the battle was bitter. My heart skipped a beat the day the Senate took final action on reorganization; it passed by one vote!

The results were gratifying. Gone was the practice of depositing the state's money in the banks of "friends" without requiring interest or accepting interest at half the going rate. With a new provision requiring banks to bid actively for these deposits, the yield in interest rose from $8.2 million a year to a whopping $28.2 million, which Jimmy told me was enough money to finance the five smallest departments of the state government. Gone also was the inefficiency of overlapping bureaucracy: The number of state agencies, boards, and commissions was reduced from three hundred to twenty-two. Umbrella departments were created, like the new Department of Human Resources, which not only streamlined but greatly improved services. Before the reorganization there were sometimes five or six different caseworkers going into one home, with no coordination of a family's separate problems. Now, the programs for mental and physical health, retardation, vocational rehabilitation, welfare, alcoholism, drugs, juvenile offenders, and the elderly were all merged under the responsibility of this department, and one or at the most two caseworkers dealt with the varied problems of each particular family.

"Zero-based budgeting" became a household word, at least to me, as we had one dinner after another at the mansion for Jimmy to explain it to different groups. Government departments, instead of routinely asking for, and getting, a yearly increase in their funding, now had to re-evaluate all their programs and start again from scratch. Many programs were changed or eliminated, saving the state millions of dollars each year.

There had been so many racial incidents in the years before Jimmy became governor that we worried about real trouble, but Jimmy formed a biracial Civil Disorder Unit, and the number of racial incidents dropped dramatically during his term. The unit was trained to enter any community where there was tension and mediate the problems rather than force a confrontation. The CDU was so successful that the State Patrol's time spent on civil disorders was reduced from 45,910 man-hours the year before Jimmy took office to only 177 by his second year. In one tense situation, the CDU team even managed to calm down two groups, one black and the other white, armed with machine guns. After two days of negotiation, they returned to Atlanta with the machine guns safely stashed in the trunks of their cars.

One of my favorite programs was the Heritage Trust, which was set up to preserve Georgia's natural and cultural resources. I enjoyed visiting sites with Jimmy that were identified as unique and endangered. Nineteen of these sites were acquired while he was governor, including Lewis Island, which has the only known stand of virgin cypress trees in our state and is a habitat for certain rare species of birds such as the limpkin and the swallow-tailed kite; 142 acres in Atlanta along the Chattahoochee River, the most unspoiled and scenic river remaining in any metropolitan area; Wormsloe Plantation, which depicts Georgia's colonial history; and Pickett's Mill, one of the best-preserved Civil War battle sites. There were others identified, and I'm pleased that our state is still acquiring these sites as funds become available.

Though this may all sound like some sort of magic, it was not. It was hard work, accomplished despite great opposition from the lieutenant governor, "just ole Lester Maddox," as Amy called him. Jimmy had to fight for almost everything, but the hard struggles made the victories even sweeter. And he managed to win the battles that mattered.

In 1971, when we went to the Governor's Mansion, I had thought we would be going home to Plains in 1975 because the governor of Georgia could not succeed himself. But we weren't. Since early 1972, Jimmy had been quietly planning to run for President. His success as governor had brought him national recognition, and two assignments helped put him on the road to the White House. At the 1972 Democratic National Convention, Jimmy nominated Senator Henry Jackson for President (at the senator's request), and, along with a few other governors, was mentioned as a possible vice-presidential candidate. Several weeks later he told our family and a few close friends that he had definitely decided to make the race for President in 1976, and the detailed planning for such a campaign proceeded for the next two years among these close advisers.

Then in 1974 Bob Strauss, the chairman of the Democratic National Committee, asked Jimmy to head a committee to recruit and train candidates for state and national offices during the 1974 midterm elections. In this capacity he traveled from state to state, working with Democratic party officials and candidates. Our political world was moving beyond Georgia.

❦ 4 ❧
The '76 Campaign

"*I'm Mrs. Jimmy Carter*. My husband's running for President."
  "President of what?"
  "President of the United States."
  "You've got to be kidding!"
  The reaction was always the same—astonishment, disbelief:
  "I never thought I'd see anyone who even knew a presidential candidate, much less his wife."
  "I didn't know this was an election year."
  "You mean he's really running for President? That's wonderful!"
  Edna Langford, the mother of my daughter-in-law Judy, and I had driven across the state line into Florida for our first venture into presidential politics. We were nervous or, rather, I was nervous. I had never campaigned outside Georgia, but Edna and I both considered ourselves seasoned campaigners. She had worked in all of Jimmy's campaigns and in those of her husband, a state senator, and since Florida was close to home, maybe people wouldn't be too different. I worried, though, about what they would expect me to know and what kinds of questions they would ask. We planned to stay two weeks and see what we could do. The date was April 14, 1975—and the election was eighteen months away!
  Beginning with a few contacts, Edna and I had been planning our trip for weeks. In Tallahassee I knew Eleanor Ketchum, who

had taught school in Plains when Jimmy and I both were in gram
mar school. I hadn't seen her in years, but her sister married m
cousin. Edna had recently met a young couple, Doug and Jud
Henderson, who also lived in Tallahassee, and she had a friend
Judy Neal, from Chipley. Then there were Al and Shirley Seck
inger in Tampa—Al's father had been the Lutheran preacher i
Plains for many years and Al and Jimmy had gone from the firs
through the ninth grades together, so I was sure we could spen
one night with them. Richard Swann, another friend of Edna's
lived in Orlando and would probably help. Her mother and fathe
lived in Sun City, just below Tampa; that would be another "hotel.

And so it went. With a few planned destinations we set ou
campaigning, stopping in every community, shaking hands an
passing out brochures, and getting all the press we could by knock
ing on the doors of radio and television stations and newspape
offices and saying, "I'm Mrs. Jimmy Carter and I thought yo
might want to interview me."

Armed with a 1974 *Florida Almanac of Democratic Par*
Officials, we searched out these people every place we went. W
found Mr. J. D. Henry, for example, in his garden in Live Oal
and walked up and down the rows with him, admiring his veg
tables, and came away with his valuable lists of statewide par
workers and contributors accumulated over the previous four de
cades.

My nervousness began to disappear when I realized peop
seemed pleased to meet me, though I still had trouble with a dr
throat and sometimes a trembling voice when I approached a
interview or a speech. But I learned that a presidential candida
(or a member of his family)—and one from the South at that—
was news. And I shouldn't have worried about people's question
After their initial surprise at seeing me, the questions on this fir
trip were simply about where we were from and who Jimmy Cart
was and about his experience. "What has he ever done before
I've never heard of him!" Even reporters were sometimes at a lo
for questions when I appeared suddenly, "out of the blue," at the
newspaper offices or especially at rural radio stations, where the
was often only one employee who did everything, mostly pla
records. "Why sure," they would say, "I guess I could intervie
you, but I don't even know what to ask."

Before the first day was over, I had made a list of five or s
questions that would focus on the points I wanted to make abo

Jimmy, and for the rest of the trip, as I approached an interview I would say, "And these are some questions if you want to ask me something." Nine times out of ten they used them, over and over again, day after day. I was getting my message across.

Since my purpose on this trip was to get Jimmy's name before the public and to tell them something about him, the questions were as basic as "Who is Jimmy Carter?" My answer: "governor of Georgia until three months ago, now running for President of the United States." The other questions were about his background, and I would go on to describe him as a farmer who knew what it was to work for a living; a businessman who started from scratch and scrimped and saved to make his business a success; a fiscal conservative who balanced the budget every year as governor, leaving the state with a surplus, making him an economical man who knew how to cut the waste and extravagance from government. Jimmy was also a community leader, I would add, pointing out his service on the Hospital Authority, the library board, the School Board, and on the Chamber of Commerce and as a scoutmaster and a leader in the church. And there was not a hint of scandal in his background. He could restore honesty and integrity and openness to government—an important point thanks to Watergate. Finally I would point out that Jimmy would be an outsider in Washington, "a man who can look at government with fresh eyes and an open mind," and one who would go to the people for support rather than bear obligations to the wealthy and powerful special interest groups.

Soon it was like our old campaigning in Georgia, and Edna and I felt very much at home with the people we were meeting. For two weeks we toured Florida: Up early every morning, working into the evenings, we covered the Panhandle and went as far down the west coast as Tampa.

By the time we drove home, we had left a trail of newspaper headlines with the name of Jimmy Carter prominently displayed, and we had learned the tremendous value of radio interviews from the frequent response: "I heard you on the radio this morning and hoped I would get to see you. Is your husband really running for President?"

We also had the names of several hundred people on 3-by-5 cards who had said they would help in the campaign—some very influential, others who had never been involved in politics but were ready to go to work. We had a summary of where we had been and what we had done every day—Edna had kept good records. While I shook hands or made my way through a courthouse or city hall or any kind of crowd, she would take down names and make notes about the people we met. Then, as we rode between stops and at night, we would go over her notes and add my comments. We were good working partners, and Edna traveled constantly with me throughout the campaign.

Coming home from that first trip, we had some valuable hints for our next forays:

• Stop at courthouses. They are a good source of information. From the sheriff or the clerk of court or the ordinary we could learn who the influential people in the community were and who were the best politicians. (We would then call on them.) And we could learn all the political gossip.

• Insist on the front page of the newspaper, and if that's not possible, at least the news section. Don't let the newspaper receptionist send you to the society editor or the women's page writer.

• Look for large radio antennas. Before the trip was over it had become a game with us to head toward large antennas, looking for radio stations. Occasionally we happened upon police stations. Oh, well, they vote too.

• Stay in people's homes. It works. We could learn about the people and their problems and the issues that bothered them; but also, our hosts would feel personally involved in the campaign and want to go out and work even harder for us. This soon proved a valuable campaign asset. With Jimmy and all of the family and the staff traveling, there was no way we could have paid for hotel rooms and still had brochures and television advertisements and campaign offices, eventually in every state. Staying in private homes was a naturally evolving strategy based on our experience in the governor's race. We also had no other choice.

• Muster up the courage and intrude—on meetings, events, carnivals, any place where people gather. This was difficult at first, but I soon discovered that no one cares; in fact, they may welcome it. At a motel where Edna and I had stopped for lunch, I noticed a car in the parking lot with a press sticker. "What's happening? Why is the press here?" we asked the manager. The Rotary Club was having its weekly meeting. Getting up our courage, we opened the door and peeked in. Someone mentioned to us, out of curiosity, to come in. Quickly Edna said her husband was a Rotarian and I said my husband was running for President. "President of what?" came the familiar response, whereupon Edna introduced me and I proceeded to say a few words; I could have spoken longer. When I got through, I was thanked profusely for the intrusion, and learned that the program planned for that day had fallen through. Despite the brevity, a whole new group of community leaders was now talking about Jimmy Carter.

Another day when we had been driving in the Panhandle, we saw a large crowd by the side of the road. Stopping, we learned that we had come upon the weekly cattle sale. What luck! We already knew from the courthouse crowd that Buddy Neal, who ran the sale, was the President of the Cattlemen's Association of Florida and an astute and influential politician. And besides, there were farmers everywhere and Jimmy was a farmer. We spoke to everyone on the grounds, then walked into the barn and found Mr. Neal, and right there, with a lift of the hand, Mr. Neal stopped the auctioneer, and while the cow waited, I spoke to the crowd about Jimmy Carter. As I stepped away, the auctioneer took up where he had left off, hardly missing a beat!

When we got home from the trip, I couldn't wait to tell Jimmy: "I know we can do it. If I hadn't been looking at a map I would have thought I was in Georgia. The people are the same!"

It was just the beginning.

For the next eighteen months we were on the go constantly. I stayed home for one week and was off again, this time to Iowa. From Iowa it was back to Florida, then to New Hampshire, to Iowa again, and back to Florida. I traveled and traveled and traveled in that campaign. At first I was gone three days, then four, and then five days a week. Before it was over, I had spent seventy-five days in Florida alone. Tim Kraft, a campaign coordinator, said I had covered 105 communities in Iowa alone. And though I didn't count, I spent days and days on end, weeks and weeks, in New Hampshire and Maine, with side trips into Vermont and Massachusetts. I campaigned in Pennsylvania, Ohio, Illinois, Wisconsin, Mississippi; at the end I had been in forty-two states in our country.

It was like a job, a very demanding job, with pressures and deadlines (more than thirty primaries with one general election); a job that required constant studying and cramming to stay current and being able to stay cool under fire; and it was a traveling job.

On the weekends I tried to come home to be with Jimmy, who was on the campaign trail all week too, and with Amy. And to head for the grocery store to buy some green vegetables, for I was always starved for a square meal. It was not a vocation I would want to pursue for life.

But it was essential. More and more Democratic candidates were entering the race, and our opposition went far beyond George Wallace to finally include Morris Udall, Frank Church, Henry Jackson, Birch Bayh, Sargent Shriver, Jerry Brown, Ellen McCormack, Lloyd Bentsen, Milton Shapp, Terry Sanford, Fred Harris, and other "favorite sons" in individual states. We had to beat them all.

Looking back, the first months were the best. I had time to visit and talk and enjoy being with people and to learn what was on their minds. There were coffees and teas and receptions, luncheons and dinners in private homes, more often than not with only a handful of people—ten or twelve was a crowd. In an hour spent at a coffee in a farmhouse in Iowa with eight people, I could learn a lot about farming and people's problems as well as all their complaints about Washington, which I would then pass on to Jimmy.

There was no way to avoid issues. In these early sessions I answered questions about health, mental health, education, prison reform, the reorganization of government—the things I knew from our time in Atlanta. And I became familiar with other issues.

After my first week in Iowa, for instance, I came home and told Jimmy that I had had a long discussion about the price of fertilizer, which had almost doubled in the short time since I had kept the books at the warehouse. I had also learned that the farmers saw the Ford and Nixon embargo on grain sales to Russia as a federal ruse for controlling grain prices. This would become an important campaign issue, and Jimmy pledged never to use a grain embargo for the purpose of influencing the economy.

In Pennsylvania I talked with a young coal miner who had black lung disease. He was only thirty-six years old and had six children, and he said to me with tears in his eyes, "I'm too far gone to help, but tell your husband to do something to keep others from getting in my shape." After his election, Jimmy's bill was passed that provided for a new trust fund supported by an excise tax on coal to pay for black lung disabilities.

I visited convalescent homes, nursing homes, and other senior centers in every community, seeing and talking with elderly citizens about their problems. I visited day care and mental health centers, rehabilitation programs for the handicapped, schools, shoe factories and steel mills, listening and learning and answering questions.

When I didn't know the answer to a question, I would make a note to ask Jimmy about it. Would he guarantee appointing a woman in his Cabinet? What was his position on revenue sharing, on the Displaced Homemakers Bill? Often the campaign headquarters had the answers ready, so I didn't have to bother Jimmy. With one telephone call, for example, I learned that he thought states should be excluded from revenue sharing and that he had endorsed the Displaced Homemakers Bill introduced in the House of Representatives by Yvonne Burke. "I will continue to be deeply concerned about those women who choose to stay at home and devote themselves to their families," Jimmy had written. "These women, faced with a rising divorce rate and the possibility of early widowhood, and often having no marketable job skills, are among the most vulnerable members of our society."

Researching the answers to these questions, and cramming every night to keep up to date with issues of particular importance to different areas of the country and to special interest groups, was a great educational exercise for me.

And just as much understanding came from the actual traveling through the country, staying in people's homes, wandering in and out of communities, seeing the sights, and talking to anybody and everybody: stopping in the orange groves in Florida and spending the night in a fishing camp; speaking Spanish in Miami; sleeping in an A-frame house with glass windows overlooking a beautiful lake on the edge of an apple orchard in Maine (and the moon was full that night); visiting with the lobster fishermen on the wharves; taking a look at a prize-winning sow on an Iowa farm; riding through corn and wheat fields as far as the eye could see; going into the steel mills in Pennsylvania and seeing the red-hot metal pouring into huge vats; eating salmon fresh out of the stream in Washington State and kringels in Kenosha, Wisconsin; visiting the San Joaquin Valley in California, lush with the most beautiful fruits and vegetables I have ever seen; and even flying low over the carved figures of Mount Rushmore.

Later I was thankful for those early months when there were no large crowds, although I wanted them at the time, and when there was no press with me to record every slipup or misstatement. I was soon able to anticipate questions and to answer them, falteringly at times, but I learned. I also developed a standard stump speech and learned to get my message across in the often small time allotted no matter what questions were asked.

Jimmy had told me that often interviewers would spend most of the time asking questions about George Wallace, then give him one minute to say all he planned to do if he were elected President. After a few similar frustrating experiences, I learned to twist the questions to make the points I wanted to about my candidate. It bothered me at first because I had always been impatient with politicians who, when asked a question, would go off on a tangent rather than give a straight answer. I always thought they were "beating around the bush," trying to play both sides of an issue. I soon found myself doing the same thing, not trying to ease out of a question, but I had more important things to talk about than the answers to the questions I was being asked, such as: "Mrs. Carter, do you like to cook?" "Yes, I like to cook," I would respond, "but I'm not doing much of it this year. I'm trying to help get Jimmy Carter elected President. As a housewife, I know our country needs him because . . ." Or, "Mrs. Carter, would you rather be vacationing in Europe than campaigning every day?" "Yes, but what I'm doing is more important to Europeans than my visit would be. They also need for Jimmy Carter to be our President because . . ." Jimmy and the children were having similar experiences all over the country, listening, learning, and answering questions.

Chip began by helping to raise money in various states, first by telephone from the Atlanta headquarters, then on the road in one-on-one conversations with potential donors. Jimmy sent him to Texas and said, "Don't come back until you raise $5,000." He did such a good job that he was sent into state after state. Late in the summer of 1975 he and Caron, with twenty-two other young campaign workers, moved into a big house in Concord, New Hampshire, which they named Camp Carter, and with that as headquarters, they traveled to other states. From the time they arrived until the primary, we estimated that they worked day in and day out in New Hampshire for a total of six solid months, besides campaigning in Florida, spending November and December of 1975 in Iowa, and campaigning in Vermont, Maine, and Massachusetts. After the New Hampshire primary, Chip was in every state that had a primary except Alaska. He and Caron had their own separate schedules, meeting as often as possible along the way.

Jeff and Annette always campaigned together; they spent the early months in the Atlanta headquarters making telephone calls, working on voter lists, and helping raise money. They later moved into an apartment, a fifth-floor cold-water flat, in Manchester, New Hampshire, and worked there for seven and a half weeks before the primary. The two of them campaigned in seventy-three towns in New Hampshire alone—that's a lot of local newspaper headlines and radio talk shows. They left New Hampshire the day after the primary and started to work in Florida. They also campaigned in Illinois, Indiana, Kentucky, and Pennsylvania, among other states, and were on the road constantly until after the Democratic Convention, when we took a break before starting all over again in the general election.

When Jack graduated from law school in June of '75, he joined us on the campaign trail. He had already been traveling into South Carolina and making telephone calls in the Atlanta headquarters before graduation, and now he and Judy traveled continuously with separate schedules. Judy took time out to have a baby in August (Jason, our first grandson!); Jimmy was at a television station in Boston, about to go on an early morning talk show, and the host of the program announced the birth to the world by presenting him with a cigar on the air. Jack and Judy moved into a condominium in Pompano Beach, Florida, and traveled around the state from there. Their separate schedules ensured that one of them could always be with the baby. After a few weeks, my mother moved in to care for the baby so they could both get out. They went to Iowa the week before the caucuses in January of '76 and campaigned in New Hampshire the last week before the primary there. After these early elections they went everywhere, spending a lot of time in New Jersey and Illinois. They traveled all over upstate New York, Pennsylvania, Ohio, and went to California, Washington, and Oregon, among other states.

We stayed in touch with each other as much as possible; the children usually called us each weekend to report on what they were doing and to get an update on our thoughts about the progress we were making.

Once again Billy and Sybil were taking care of the warehouse, and this time, instead of campaigning, Miss Lillian was keeping

Amy for us. Occasionally she would go on a campaign trip and Amy would stay with my mother. Since this was a national campaign, we had schedulers and advisers who told us which states we should visit; it was all too complicated for the old colored-pins-on-the-map organization.

In those early days we did some amazing things to get media coverage. In Iowa, Jimmy appeared on a television talk show, but he had to promise not to talk politics since the station didn't want to have to give equal time to the other candidates. Instead, he cooked fish, giving his favorite recipe. It was one he had liked at a fishing camp in south Georgia. (Cut catfish or bass into strips like french fries; marinate in Heinz 57 or A-1 sauce for several hours or overnight; coat the fish with Bisquick or pancake mix by putting it all into a paper bag and shaking; fry in hot oil. The fish are delicious, either hot or cold.)

The worst part of campaigning for me was asking for money. And we always needed money.

"Jimmy Carter? Running for President? President of what?" Still? It seemed that no one had ever heard of him when I was calling to ask for money. In the summer of '75, months after we began, I had to leave the campaign trail and spend several weeks in the Atlanta headquarters raising money. It was crucial: If we could raise $5000 in each of twenty states in contributions of $250 or less, we could qualify for federal matching funds. We not only desperately needed the money, we needed the impetus and recognition our campaign would surely get if we were successful in qualifying. The new campaign financing law was a great advantage to us; in fact, if it had not been for the 1974 Federal Elections Act, Jimmy would not have been able to run for President at all. We were not personally wealthy and did not have access to large corporate or private funds. However, under the new law, no other candidate had access to them either. No one person could contribute more than $1000 to a presidential candidate. No corporation could contribute any money at all. But the best part was that the federal government would match individual contributions up to $250, dollar for dollar, for every candidate who qualified.

I spent hours and hours on the telephone, from early morning until late in the evening—the three-hour time difference between Atlanta and California gave me the extra time. It was not easy, but I did it. Some calls drew the promise of a contribution that never came; some ended in misunderstanding. One day I spoke with Roger Horchow, the owner of a large mail order business in Dallas, Texas. He was originally from Georgia, and though I didn't know him, we had mutual friends in Atlanta and I thought he might be willing to help us. I called, explained the "two-fifty" limit, and he said he would be more than happy to help. I was delighted until his contribution arrived—$2.50! In spite of the misunderstanding and the disappointments (Roger did send us $250, and more), our hard work paid off, and in August 1975, Jimmy qualified for the matching government funds.

All our family knew that this campaign for the presidency was an awesome undertaking, but Jimmy thought he could do it, and we were all convinced . . . although I have to admit that occasionally I had twinges of doubt. Flying over Chicago one day, looking down at row after row of houses spreading as far as the eye could see in all directions, the thought came to me, Every single person in every one of those houses has to know who Jimmy Carter is if we're gong to win this election. How will we ever do it?

But we had a lot of things going for us, and soon help came from an unexpected source—unexpected and underestimated by opponents and political prognosticators. It was the Peanut Brigade, and I'm not sure we could have won without them. Patterned after the Hi Neighbor effort in the gubernatorial campaign and organized by Hamilton Jordan, the Peanut Brigade was made up originally of fellow Georgians who traveled all over the country, meeting people and telling them about Jimmy Carter. I bumped into them in factories in New Hampshire, in shopping centers in Florida, and in Wisconsin, Kansas, Pennsylvania, and Ohio. They were everywhere—passing out brochures in shopping malls, making speeches to groups of Democrats, appearing on local radio and television programs, and making headlines wherever they went. Paying their own way, they did the hard, tedious jobs that are necessary to any campaign, such as making telephone calls for hours on end from voting lists in local campaign headquarters and motivating, sometimes even organizing, the local workers.

The Peanut Brigade made a great impact on the first primary in New Hampshire, setting an example for the balance of the campaign. Almost a hundred Georgians chartered a plane and flew to New Hampshire in January 1976, a month before the crucial vote. Dividing up into teams each group was assigned a street route in Manchester and Nashua and given cards arranged by street address for every registered Democrat in the area. They wasted no time, and the day they arrived they were on the streets, knocking on doors, handing out literature, telling people how they knew Jimmy Carter and could vouch for his record and capability. They stayed in the state for a whole week, talking personally with at least half of the twenty thousand Democrats on their lists, leaving personal notes on the doors or in the mailboxes of those who weren't home. When our friends returned to Georgia, they sent handwritten letters to each New Hampshire voter they had met who seemed at all favorable to Jimmy, including personal messages such as: "The hot bread you baked was delicious" or "I liked your cute little dog" or "I hope you are feeling much better." They made a difference.

Meanwhile, Edna and I were moving through state after state, sometimes two or three in one day. And I was doing things I had never thought I would or could do.

"Aaron Copland's *A Lincoln Portrait*? I'll try." I would try anything. The campaign depended on it—or that's the way I felt. But performing on the stage at Constitution Hall in Washington was more than I had anticipated. I couldn't believe I had been asked to do it, nor could I believe I had accepted. I had never done anything even similar before, but I had been assured that "it won't be hard, since all you have to do is read." When I arrived for the rehearsal on the morning of the performance, Leonard Bernstein, who would be conducting the music, was surprised when he learned that I had seen neither the score nor the text. He said he had mailed them to me, but I was hard to catch up with in those days. One the spot I read my lines, practiced my part—which was interwoven with the music, not read between selections as I had been told—and that evening, before an audience of two thousand, in Constitution Hall, with Leonard Bernstein conducting a full symphony orchestra and with my knees shaking, I narrated Aaron Copland's *A Lincoln Portrait*. And no one recorded it for posterity or, indeed, proof to me that I had done it.

"Tim Kraft, where are we going?"

"Well, you and Edna said you headed for every antenna you saw, looking for radio stations, and there's a big one!"

Tim, our coordinator in Iowa, had turned off the highway onto a very short road that climbed steeply and ended at railroad tracks. The front of the car was perched atop the tracks, and there in front of us was indeed an antenna, beyond a barbed-wire fence and across a pasture. We had been riding through Iowa for a week, campaigning furiously, never stopping between events, and now I began to laugh. Tim and Edna started laughing too; in fact, we giggled hysterically and couldn't stop. We had been so tired and so tense about what we were doing, trying to make every minute count, and suddenly we had relaxed. Then we were ready to go on again, and on and on.

Other hazards of campaigning involved clothes. One day I arrived in a community in Tennessee for my second visit, and when I checked the press clippings from my previous visit, there I was, wearing the same dress!

At least I had a dress in Tennessee. The first day of a twelve-day trip with Edna through Massachusetts, Pennsylvania, California, Texas, and Louisiana did not start well. I had already made appearances in three cities in Georgia before flying to Boston, where I had attended three fund-raising receptions, and I was tired. I couldn't wait to relax at the home of our Boston hosts, the Scallis, but when we arrived at their townhouse, I couldn't get out of the car. My seat belt was jammed. I should have known that the struggle with the seat belt was an omen of things to come. I pulled and tugged, but nothing happened. Everyone pulled and tugged to no avail. I sat pinned in until someone could fetch the scissors, cut the seat belt, and let me out. I went into the house to find that many of the downtown guests had stopped by to say goodnight. After speaking to them all and leaving Edna (who was wonderful with hosts and required little sleep) to entertain them, I made my way upstairs to go to bed only to learn that our luggage was gone. It had been stolen out of the car. I sat down on the bed in despair. I had the clothes on my back, my briefcase (which luckily had my makeup in it), and my coat. Nothing else.

And I had lost my wig.

My wig was my security—against wind, against rain, and if I was just absolutely too tired at night to wash my hair, my security against worry. It was the one and only wig I ever had that was perfect. Even my mother didn't know when I had it on, and now it was gone. Edna and I made a list of the things that had been stolen for the police, and since I had to be up at five o'clock the next morning, I decided to take a bath and go to bed. I reached to turn the water on and the faucet fell into the tub.

The search for our luggage was futile, and we campaigned all the next day in Pittsburgh in the same clothes. Late in the afternoon, on the way to the airport to fly to California, we spotted a shopping mall. With ten minutes to spare, we ran into a dress shop only to discover that they carried junior clothes. There was one, just one, longer skirt hanging on the rack among all the short skirts. I grabbed it, along with a short-sleeved blue sweater, a scarf, and a half-slip; the whole bill was $28.91. I arrived in Hollywood that evening in my new outfit, looking a little like a cheerleader. During the remainder of the trip I washed out my clothes every night, and my hosts were very understanding, lending me nightgowns and robes for the evening. One set I shall never forget was the red chiffon in size 20 with red plumes around the neck of the robe. But I wasn't in a position to be choosy.

My most embarrassing moment came in Dallas, Texas. I had been campaigning there for two days, and just before leaving, I stopped by the county fair because I had been told that "my cake" had won a prize. I arrived to find a very unattractive pound cake, with no icing and unshelled, raw peanuts filling the center, with a blue ribbon on it! I was supposed to cut the cake with the cameras rolling and pass it out to the crowd. It looked so unappetizing that I was embarrassed to be associated with it, and when I tried to cut it, the knife would hardly go through. I finally handed out one piece and made my getaway as quickly as I could. Someone in a campaign headquarters somewhere had evidently seen a peanut butter pound cake recipe and attributed it to me. I never did find a way to keep that sort of thing from happening.

Aroostook County, the largest county in Maine, which includes all of the top of the state, is isolated and beautiful potato country and was one of my favorite places of the whole campaign. I have been there several times, always in the winter, when it is a fairyland in the snow. (I've been invited to the annual potato festival, and someday I'm going back.) There, on a Saturday night after all our scheduled activities were over, Edna and I and State Senator Floyd Hardin and his wife, Jean, went to a dance at the Knights of Columbus Hall. I danced and danced and danced, abandoning all thought of the campaign for the first time in those many long months, and it was fun, pure fun.

And then New Hampshire. I would introduce myself: "I'm Mrs. Jimmy Carter."

"Who?"

"Mrs. Jimmy Carter."

"Who?"

"My husband's running for President."

"Oh, you're Mrs. Jimmy *Cah*tuh!" I overcame my southern accent and learned to say it just like the natives: "I'm Mrs. Jimmy Cahtuh."

"Oh, your husband's running for President."

"You're exactly right!"

And the posters held by the people in the crowds that greeted us were wonderful.

WIN WITH A GRIN—HEAL THE NATION WITH PEANUT OIL—PUT AMY'S DADDY IN THE WHITE HOUSE—LET'S CARTERIZE THE COUNTRY—WE LOVE YOU JIMMY AND ROSALYNN

I loved them too, everyone who held up a sign!

One day in Pennsylvania, Edna and I took off from an airport on a short hop between communities, but we seemed to be flying forever. We were in a small plane that belonged to a friend of one of Jimmy's Naval Academy classmates, and I kept thinking that we were taking much too much time and would be late for my next appearance. Finally the pilot turned to his friend in the front seat and said, "See if you can find the airport on this map. I know you go over a mountain range and the airport's just on the other side, but we've already been over several and I haven't seen it yet." As we flew back and forth, I was scared to death. And it didn't help when we finally flew over the right mountain range and saw the airport beneath us to hear the pilot say, "How am I going to land? I guess I can fly way over and come in from the other side." I closed my eyes and prayed.

A serious problem in our campaign strategy developed in Illinois several months before the primary. Illinois had an early filing date, and we were already in a delicate position there. Jimmy, George Wallace, Sargent Shriver, and Fred Harris were the only candidates to challenge Richard Daley, the influential mayor of Chicago, who was supporting Senator Adlai Stevenson as a favorite son. In deference to the mayor, every other candidate had decided not to run in Illinois. We had compromised by not challenging Daley in Chicago but running in the rest of the state.

Not only did we have the temerity to take on Mayor Daley, we took on the entire Illinois Board of Elections as well. Jimmy wanted to appear on the ballot as "Jimmy Carter," not "James

Earl Carter, Jr.," but the election officials said the law required full names. Jim Wall, our state campaign chairman, finally resolved the issue by getting an affidavit from Georgia's secretary of state, Ben Fortson. The official document was sent to the Illinois Board of Elections, stating that for election purposes in the State of Georgia, Jimmy had always been "Jimmy Carter" and therefore, for any election purpose, his legal name was "Jimmy Carter." Illinois gave in, and after that precedent, there were no further serious challenges to the use of "Jimmy Carter."

Then there was the day in Maryland, when, in our best campaign style, Edna and I raced in to meet the early shift at the first factory and began to hand out brochures. The first worker threw his down and, looking me in the face, said, "Lady, we make the B-1 bombers." Jimmy had come out against the B-1 bomber the day before!

The first official political event of the season, the Iowa caucuses, took place on January 19, 1976, nine months after I had started campaigning. These caucuses were very important, which is why we had all been in Iowa so many times in the past year. We knew people in almost every community on a first-name basis. If we could win in Iowa, the heavy media coverage would project Jimmy into the national consciousness as a serious candidate. As a result of our grass-roots organization and hard work, plus Jimmy's personal touch, we swept the caucuses with 27 percent of the vote. Birch Bayh came in second with 13 percent; Fred Harris, 10 percent; Morris Udall, 5 percent; Sargent Shriver, 3 percent; Scoop Jackson, 1 percent. Jimmy Carter was on the political map, taking a lot of Democrats in the country by surprise. And that was just the beginning.

A little more than a month later, on February 24, 1976, was the long-awaited and eagerly anticipated New Hampshire primary. We had made many friends there, and it seemed Jimmy and I, in addition to our children, had been in and out of the state all year. It paid off. When the returns came in, Carter was the winner, with 30 percent of the vote. This time it was Udall who followed, with 24 percent, then Bayh, Harris, and Shriver. There was pandemonium in the Carter headquarters that night. Someone said it was "like New Year's Eve in Times Square for the hugging, kissing, dancing, and hollering." And it was, with Peanut Brigaders mixed in with our New Hampshire friends. We spent the evening watching the returns at the home of a supporter in Concord with our boys, their wives, Jody Powell, and Pat Caddell. On the way to the headquarters for the victory celebration, Jimmy got carried away and held up his hand in a *V* sign. Though I don't remember it, someone wrote that, concerned about the Nixonian imagery of it all, I said, "Jimmy, please don't make that sign— and especially, please don't use both hands!"

We had won in Iowa. We had won in New Hampshire. We were confident. We smiled smugly to ourselves when we learned that rumor had it that the Washington pros thought we were going to muddy the waters so that none of the announced candidates would have a chance to win and that Hubert Humphrey would be the nominee, with possibly Ted Kennedy on his ticket.

Vermont and Massachusetts . . . March 2, our first disappointment. We hadn't invested the money or the time in Massachusetts that we had in some other states. The original date of its primary had been much later in the year, and we had spent our time in the early states, depending on our momentum and victories there to carry us over in the later ones. When the date of the Massachusetts primary was moved up, we had to depend to a great extent on the victory in New Hampshire for momentum, but it didn't work. Though we won in Vermont, we lost in Massachusetts, and we lost big. Scoop Jackson finished first with 22.7 percent, followed by Udall with 18 percent. Wallace was third with 17.1 percent, and Carter in fourth place with a bare 14.2 percent.

Though Massachusetts had never been big in our game plan, we hadn't expected this kind of loss. I was campaigning in Florida the day of the primaries in the North and had to appear on a television panel in Pensacola that night with representatives of all the candidates. I was so nervous about Massachusetts that I couldn't think. The Vermont results came in during the program and I was temporarily elated, but even then the announcer said, "But the real story will be in Massachusetts." Massachusetts had 104 delegates; Vermont, 12. I left Pensacola still not knowing the results and flew with Edna to another community on a small mail plane. We crawled over the bags of mail, sat on a hard seat in the rear of the plane, and were not very talkative. We knew we were in trouble in Massachusetts, but we didn't know how much until we landed and learned the results. I thought it was all over for us then, that Jimmy now had no chance of winning the nomination. I called him the moment I could get to a phone, and his spirits were low too. I don't think I slept a wink that night.

The all-important Florida primary was one week after Massachusetts, on March 9, and our early start there came back to reward us. Every member of the family felt at home in Florida, just as we had in Iowa and New Hampshire. We had spent so much time there and had so many friends working for us and pulling for us. The Peanut Brigade had been in Florida in full force, and I even saw our friends the Landrys, from New Hampshire, working with them in Florida. (That became the norm as supporters traveled from state to state to help us.) Although George Wallace had long been considered unbeatable in Florida and our hopes had always been to come in a strong second, ahead of the other major candidates, the loss in Massachusetts had given us a scare. But when the returns were in, we had swept the Sunshine State, beating George Wallace and Scoop Jackson, who, buoyed by his Massachusetts win, had made an all-out last-minute effort in Florida. The election returns gave Carter 34.3 percent, Wallace, 30.6 percent, and Jackson, 23.9 percent. We were back in the contest!

Illinois...March 16. We won overwhelmingly! Udall and Jackson both passed in Illinois, but Wallace campaigned hard, trying to overcome his loss in Florida. Results: Carter, 48 percent; Wallace, 28 percent; Shriver, 16 percent; and Harris received only 8 percent of the vote.

North Carolina...March 23, another southern state coming early and giving us an impressive victory. We won with 53 percent to Wallace's 34.7 percent, and Wallace was considered to be out of the race.

New York and Wisconsin...April 6. This was one of the worst-best days of the campaign. We had written off New York, not by choice, but while we had been campaigning in every state, Scoop Jackson had concentrated on a few big ones. New York was one of them, and he was well known and predictable to New Yorkers. Our main problem, though, was that the names of the candidates originally were not going to be on the ballots, just the names of the delegates, and Scoop had been successful in lining up an impressive slate of prominent Democrats as delegates. Our strategy was to "avoid disaster," as Pat Caddell said, and pick up as many delegates as possible. Jackson did win, as anticipated, but he had projected a landslide 2 to 1 victory, and his 38 percent share of the vote fell remarkably short.

But there could be no excuses in Wisconsin. We had to win.

Two defeats in one night would have been disastrous. And that evening when the returns began to come in, that's what we thought was happening. Udall was not only being projected as the winner by most of the television networks but was claiming victory as well. It was one of those times I wanted to go to sleep and not wake up, as though it would go away and I wouldn't have to face it. I went upstairs in the hotel and lay down on the bed, but couldn't sleep. I was too tense and too miserable. We were supposed to win this primary; we had counted on it. I felt sick, and so tired. Then Jimmy, who was with Pat Caddell and Jody monitoring the election returns at the campaign control center, called on the house phone. The rural vote, which is always late, was coming in, and he said it was tilted in our direction. I jumped out of bed, trying not to be too optimistic. "Keep your chin up," he told me, "and go downstairs and tell everyone what is happening."

Straightening my rumpled clothes, I headed for the ballroom, which had emptied when the returns were not good. But the rumor of a change in the predictions swept through the hotel, and in five minutes everyone had gathered again. "This election is not over yet!" I said to the cheering crowd, and the music began to play. But we waited and waited until after midnight, when Jimmy appeared waving a newspaper headlined UDALL WINS to announce that Udall had *not* won. *We* won! Jimmy Carter had won the Wisconsin primary by 5000 votes out of the 670,000 cast.

The Pennsylvania primary was three weeks later, on April 27. CARTER WINS had replaced the false headlines in Wisconsin, and the good news influenced Pennsylvania. We beat Scoop Jackson, a real coup since he was supposed to have solid labor support in the northern industrial states.

After Wisconsin, Udall was essentially defeated, though he persisted to the very end out of loyalty to his fellow liberals. After Pennsylvania, Jackson seemed unlikely to prevail, and everybody knew it. That evening as Jimmy and I came down the stairway in the hotel in Philadelphia with our children to celebrate the victory, with all the press there and our friends applauding, we knew we had reached a turning point in the campaign. We walked through a maze of camera flashes, television cables, and microphones, and my feet hardly touched the floor. It was heady, heady. Winning is more fun than losing!

Jimmy appeared now to have a clear field, even though there continued to be talk of Humphrey entering the race to save the establishment Democratic party. Many regular Democrats were hoping for a deadlocked convention in which Humphrey would emerge as a nominee. There was even speculation about a Humphrey-Carter ticket now, since our good showing, but the Humphrey people had supported Jackson in Pennsylvania and we had beaten Scoop in spite of them. Soon after the Pennsylvania primary, Humphrey called a press conference in Washington and announced that he was not going to enter the race. He had decided Jimmy was unstoppable.

Nothing in politics is ever certain, however, until the polls close, and now two fresh faces, Frank Church and Jerry Brown, entered the race, and a movement known as "ABC" (Anybody But Carter) was launched. The chief supporters of these candidates and this movement were the other active candidates and the Democratic party liberals, still bent on securing the nomination for Humphrey. All those opposed to or threatened by a Carter victory joined to stop him, and they almost succeeded. Jimmy had been campaigning with all the resulting publicity for a long time, an impossible momentum to sustain, and people were tired of the campaign. His front-runner position also made him a target for all the candidates, old and new. He was attacked for everything from being too conservative to being too liberal, and Mo Udall had labeled him "wishy-washy," which stuck and hurt. Being a middle-of-the-roader is not easy. You catch it from the right and from the left, but what Mo and many others could never understand is that one can be sincerely conservative on fiscal matters and sincerely compassionate in dealing with the poor and weak. The two are not incompatible.

By then it was the first of May and the last big primary day was the eighth of June, so there was little time left. May started well and ended in anxiety. There were twenty primaries left and we had to make an effort in all of them. That was our strategy, but also, as the leading candidate, Jimmy was expected to win. We had to make a good showing, if not in all the primaries, in most of them. The new candidates, on the other hand, could go into one state, spend a lot of money, gather all the opposition, and defeat us. And when you're defeated in one primary, then in another, you begin to slide in the polls. In early May we still had momentum and swept Texas, winning 122 delegates to 8 for the favorite son, Lloyd Bentsen; we carried our home state of Georgia with 83.9 percent of the vote. We won in Indiana with a large majority and in the District of Columbia. In Wallace's home state of Alabama we finished a respectable second, 27.4 percent to Wallace's 50.8. Then the ABC movement went into action, and on May 11, Frank Church squeaked through to win Nebraska by only 1 percentage point, and though Jimmy had spent only one day in the state, according to press reports it was a major defeat for us. Senator Robert Byrd ran unchallenged in West Virginia the same day, the only primary we didn't enter. The next week Brown won in Maryland, and we won by less than 1 percent in Michigan, but we won. On May 25 we lost in Oregon, Idaho, and Nevada but had decisive victories in Tennessee, Kentucky, and Arkansas.

The last few weeks of the primary campaign were unnerving and lonely. I never saw Jimmy or the children anymore. We just kept working without going home, and nothing seemed to be going right no matter what we did. The only thing I knew to do was to keep smiling in public and try to call Jimmy every night if I could find him, hoping to hear an encouraging word, and it usually came. He felt as bad as I did over the losses but always said to me, "Don't be too discouraged. Count the delegates we're getting, not the losses." And the delegates were adding up.

June 1 . . . Rhode Island, Montana, South Dakota, two honorable and small losses, one important win. At the end of May, I had been campaigning in Rhode Island and South Dakota, states we hadn't counted on winning, and sensed that we could be wrong. "Jimmy, you need to come to Rhode Island," I said to him on the telephone. "The people here are going to vote for you in November, but if you come now and create some enthusiasm, they might vote for you in the primary." I called him with a similar message from South Dakota. "We've got great support here, but the people have never seen you," I told him. "If you could just touch down once or twice, it could make a difference." The number of delegates was small from these three states, but the psychological effect of three losses just one week before the last big primary day could have been very damaging. Jimmy changed his schedule to allow last-minute stops in Rhode Island and South Dakota, and it paid off. The turnout in Rhode Island was small, but our loss was even smaller. Jerry Brown's uncommitted slate beat us by only 798 votes. Montana, as we knew it would, went for Church, a native son. But we won in South Dakota, defeating Udall, who had made a last-ditch effort, and it was an important psychological victory.

June 8 . . . California, New Jersey, Ohio, three big states with many delegates and the last of the primaries. Jimmy, the children, and I all came in from the campaign trail to be together in Atlanta and await the returns. We had done all we could, for better or worse; I was worried about the "worse." And that night when the returns came in we had lost in New Jersey and lost in California, but we won in Ohio! Ohio had come through for us, and Ohio was what we needed. I was numb, and I think I cried from sheer exhaustion and relief. It was over. This part of it was over. We had broken our losing streak with the one victory we had to have. When Ohio came in, Jimmy kissed me and said, "We did it, and we'll win the nomination now on the first ballot!"

Our victory celebrations that evening at the Regency Hotel in Atlanta and later in Plains were made even sweeter by the telephone calls Jimmy got from the other candidates. With the win in Ohio, we had gained a total of 1260 of the 1505 delegates we needed to secure the nomination. One by one, our former opponents—George Wallace, Mayor Daley, and Scoop Jackson—called to pledge their delegates, which put us over the top. The Democratic convention was still a month away, but Jimmy already had the nomination sewed up.

It was three o'clock in the morning when we arrived in Plains, but in spite of the hour, cheering crowds of homefolks and other supporters were waiting for us. What a moment it was! And how good to share it with the people who meant the most to us, in the place to which we always returned—Jimmy Carter, peanut farmer, community leader, state senator, governor of Georgia, and soon to be the Democratic candidate for the President of the United States!

Very soon after the last primaries, when our victory was assured, Teddy White, the chronicler of presidential campaigns, came to Plains to see Jimmy. For hours they sat in our living room, talking about Jimmy's life, his decision to run for President, the campaign, and what he wanted to do for the country if he were elected. When they had exhausted these subjects and most of the afternoon, Teddy White reached down for his rather large tape recorder, which he had placed on the floor by his chair. But something had gone wrong, and the tape was curled all over the floor. I saw it when

I came in to say good-bye, but Mr. White assured us that the tape was fine, that he hadn't lost any of the interview. And off he went to his car, with Jimmy walking behind him carrying the tape recorder and the wiry bundle of tapes. I'm sure he lost the interview, for he never wrote a book about "the making of the president" in 1976. I was sorry because surely his book would have been a notable addition to the other books written about this fascinating race.

The next few weeks were a happy and busy time. We went with our family to Sea Island, Georgia, to relax for a few days; our main topic of conversation was naturally who the vice-presidential candidate would be. Everybody in the family had a favorite, and one day while we were sitting around a table playing Scrabble we decided to take a poll. The winner? Frank Church. Amy was disappointed that her choice, John Glenn, was outvoted.

Back in Plains, Jimmy interviewed most of the prospective candidates. Each arrived with his wife and we would chat for a while, then Jimmy would take the man into his study for further conversation. I liked all of the wives immediately and was glad I didn't have to make the choice.

Needless to say, Frank Church did not become the nominee, nor did John Glenn, Scoop Jackson, Ed Muskie, Peter Rodino, or Adlai Stevenson, all of whom were considered. No one knew Jimmy's choice, not the nominee and not even me, until the day he announced it at the convention. In fact, I don't think Jimmy actually decided himself until the night before he made the call . . . to Walter ("Fritz") Mondale.

It was a difficult decision. Jimmy had always felt that Mondale was too liberal for him, but changed his mind when they met. Not only did they get along very well personally, but during their three-hour discussion, they seemed to agree on a variety of domestic and foreign issues. Mondale was not as liberal as his reputation suggested. He was strong on defense and reducing the budget deficit, and Jimmy was impressed by his straightforward and crisp way of presenting his positions, having carefully prepared for the interview. Of course, there were political considerations in the choice of Mondale as well. Jimmy, being a Washington "outsider," needed someone who knew Washington well. Mondale's Minnesota constituency was a geographical plus, and Mondale as a running mate would assuage the Humphrey wing of the party. Jimmy never regretted his choice.

The Democratic National Convention in the mid-July heat of New York was a love feast once everyone accepted that Jimmy was going to receive the nomination with ease and they got on the bandwagon. There were receptions, parties, and meetings with delegates. I was still making speeches—several to different state delegations, one to the Women's Caucus at the Metropolitan Opera House—and also giving interview after interview. And we did some entertaining ourselves. One evening we invited the five thousand delegates to a party on the Hudson River's Pier 88, an old-fashioned picnic with fried chicken, coleslaw, peanuts, and beer; Jimmy and I stood for hours and hours and shook hands with everyone who came. I was numb before it was over, and burning up from the hot television lights constantly on us. My mouth got so dry that for the last hour I couldn't speak to the guests, only nod at them.

One night before the convention activities started we took the family to Mamma Leone's, an Italian restaurant, for dinner. After a wonderful dinner Chip made a toast and announced that he and Caron were going to present us with our second grandchild.

Our lives had changed completely. Though we had had security agents before Jimmy won the nomination, now security was so tight at the Americana Hotel that even Edna Langford and Madeline MacBean sometimes couldn't get though to see us. We moved about at will, with agents surrounding us, naturally, but soon learned that it was easier to stay on our floor. When I tried to take Amy to Central Park, there was such a crush of press and spectators that after she climbed on the statue of Hans Christian Andersen for a few minutes with cameras clicking, we turned and went back to the hotel. Jack and Judy had a similar experience when they took Jason to the zoo. Such crowds formed that Edna, who was with them, later said, "We suddenly realized we were the zoo! Jack had to set one-year-old Jason inside the fence with the ducks to keep him from being crushed."

When I suggested to my press secretary, Mary Hoyt, that I wanted to go shopping, you could have predicted her exclamation: "Can you imagine the fuss if you went into a department store!" Instead, she arranged to have clothes sent to the hotel. They arrived in big boxes from Saks, and quite a scene developed in our bedroom. Mary was there and Madeline MacBean; Ruth, Jimmy's sister, came in and started trying on clothes too. There were dresses spread on every piece of furniture. My curlers were plugged in, sitting on the floor. Amy and baby Jason kept running through the room, and the telephone never stopped ringing. It was bedlam. In the midst of the confusion, I not only found several things I liked, but a dress that would do perfectly that very night for Jimmy's acceptance speech. Ruth found one, too, and we charged them on the credit card of a friend of Mary's.

The night of the nomination I sat in the balcony at Madison Square Garden with Muriel Humphrey; Bob Strauss, the national chairman of the Democratic party, and his wife, Helen; and my family. There on the floor below us were all our friends, waving and shouting to us. People kept coming over to my seat, congratulating me, and I wished Jimmy were there. But according to custom, nominees do not come to the convention until the night after the nominations, so he had stayed in the hotel suite. Jason, Amy, and Miss Lillian were with him, along with a dozen or so television cameras and many reporters.

There were butterflies in my stomach when the countdown of the states began, even though I knew Jimmy was going to win. Which state would put us over the top? It was Massachusetts's turn. "Massachusetts passes." Next was Ohio. "Ohio casts 132 votes for Carter!" Ohio had done it again.

It was one of the most thrilling moments of my life. We had worked for it, planned for it, and knew it would come, but when Ohio gave us enough delegates to reach 1505, it was magic—and I couldn't wait to get back to the hotel. I wanted to be with Jimmy. I knew he was celebrating with Miss Lillian, and I wanted to be there too. When the television announcer came to my seat and asked if I had a message for Jimmy, the only thing I could think to say was: "Tell him we won!"

We had won the nomination, but the general election was still three months away, and by Labor Day, Jimmy and I were on the campaign trail again, going our separate ways. Now our opponent was Gerald Ford, the incumbent President and Republican nominee, and we had dropped considerably in the polls. After the Republican convention in August, our lead plummeted from a high of 25 points to 8 or 9 points, by Pat Caddell's figures. It was understandable, everyone assured me. Ford was the familiar figure; Carter, the unknown. But it made me uneasy. It made us

all uneasy, and Pat said later that it did wonders f
"It brought everyone back from thinking about w
were going to be in the White House!"

This time it was different for me. Instead of
Edna, I traveled with my press secretary, Mary Hoyt, and my
secretary, Madeline MacBean, and most of the time in my own
chartered aircraft. We were going for broke, and there was no
time to wait in airports and try to make connections. And we
covered sometimes three, four, five, even six states a day, flying
into the largest media markets and out again, making headlines.
It was states now, not just communities, as when Edna and I were
campaigning, but the pace was the same, and the reporters' questions kept coming:

"What do you think of Betty Ford?"

"She's going to be hard to follow."

"What issue do you find is most on people's minds?"

"Distrust of government. People don't believe anything they
hear from Washington anymore."

"I campaign separately because the country is so big, and if I
go with Jimmy I just sit there. I can use my time better than that."

"I say, 'Jimmy, don't go into so much detail and use such big
words. Just explain it to them the way you do to me.'"

*"What do you think of the polls that show your husband trailing,
as the Field poll did by a tiny margin in California?"*

"The polls are wrong."

And sometimes I got tired: After a brief confrontation with a
group carrying signs that read: WE DEMAND JOBS, NOT HOT AIR, I
didn't care anymore: "If you feel better with Gerald Ford, vote
for him!"

For all my campaigning, and that of our family and organization, it was the candidate who would win or lose the election,
and Jimmy knew it. In three debates with Gerald Ford, the first
presidential debates since the 1960 contests between John Kennedy
and Richard Nixon, Jimmy had a chance to reassure the people
about his qualifications for the presidency. We welcomed the
opportunity. Jimmy could let them know that he was well acquainted with the issues facing the country, that he was not "fuzzy"
about them; perhaps that would stop his slide in the polls. We
looked forward to the debates with great anticipation.

In every instance I was more nervous than Jimmy, and naturally, in my unbiased frame of mind, I thought he won all of them.

all uneasy, and Pat said later that it did wonders f
"It brought everyone back from thinking about w
were going to be in the White House!"

This time it was different for me. Instead of
Edna, I traveled with my press secretary, Mary Hoyt, and my
secretary, Madeline MacBean, and most of the time in my own
chartered aircraft. We were going for broke, and there was no
time to wait in airports and try to make connections. And we
covered sometimes three, four, five, even six states a day, flying
into the largest media markets and out again, making headlines.
It was states now, not just communities, as when Edna and I were
campaigning, but the pace was the same, and the reporters' questions kept coming:

"What do you think of Betty Ford?"

"She's going to be hard to follow."

"What issue do you find is most on people's minds?"

"Distrust of government. People don't believe anything they
hear from Washington anymore."

"I campaign separately because the country is so big, and if I
go with Jimmy I just sit there. I can use my time better than that."

"I say, 'Jimmy, don't go into so much detail and use such big
words. Just explain it to them the way you do to me.'"

*"What do you think of the polls that show your husband trailing,
as the Field poll did by a tiny margin in California?"*

"The polls are wrong."

And sometimes I got tired: After a brief confrontation with a
group carrying signs that read: WE DEMAND JOBS, NOT HOT AIR, I
didn't care anymore: "If you feel better with Gerald Ford, vote
for him!"

For all my campaigning, and that of our family and organization, it was the candidate who would win or lose the election,
and Jimmy knew it. In three debates with Gerald Ford, the first
presidential debates since the 1960 contests between John Kennedy
and Richard Nixon, Jimmy had a chance to reassure the people
about his qualifications for the presidency. We welcomed the
opportunity. Jimmy could let them know that he was well acquainted with the issues facing the country, that he was not "fuzzy"
about them; perhaps that would stop his slide in the polls. We
looked forward to the debates with great anticipation.

In every instance I was more nervous than Jimmy, and naturally, in my unbiased frame of mind, I thought he won all of them.

prognosticators disagreed with me, and possibly so did the American people, on the first, which was on domestic policy and should have been Jimmy's best; but whether or not he won, everyone agreed that he had scored well. The second, on foreign policy, was clearly a victory for Jimmy, for Gerald Ford made a political error that haunted him for the rest of the campaign. He said that the Eastern European countries did not consider themselves dominated by the Soviet Union; neither did the Yogoslavians, the Rumanians, nor the Poles. It was surely not an accurate assessment, and the Carter campaign didn't let the voters forget it. Opinions on the third debate were mixed.

We were still sliding in the polls, and what we didn't need was a faux pas of our own that would haunt us until election day, but that's what happened.

In an interview for *Playboy* magazine, Jimmy confessed to "lusting in my heart" for other women. Instantly, the interview became hot news, overshadowing all the other issues in the campaign and becoming the first question everyone asked me. "Jimmy talks too much, but at least people know he's honest and doesn't mind answering questions" became my standard response. No, it didn't occur to me to worry about his "lust." The only lust I worried about was that of the press and our opponents, who were out to get us because of the blooper. I was never angry with Jimmy about it, though I did experience a sinking feeling about the campaign, which was already not going well. I was angry with the *Playboy* writer, however, who had ended the interview and supposedly turned the tape recorder off and gone halfway out the door before asking the final question. In words the young man would understand, Jimmy was trying to explain his religion, but it wasn't reported that way. The *Playboy* interview hurt us, according to Pat Caddell's polls, and the "lust" issue continued to be an irritant, with questions persisting till the end. In Shreveport, Louisiana, one television reporter even asked me on camera whether I had ever committed adultery. Fighting my displeasure, I answered him firmly, "If I had, I wouldn't tell you!"

The campaign wore on and on. It seemed as though it would never end. Every day I was telling people what Jimmy was going to do for them when he became President. And a few things *I* could do: "It has been fifteen years since anyone has even done a report on mental health care, and the programs have become so splintered that it's time we look at all of them and give some direction to national health care for the mentally ill. When my husband is elected President I want him to establish a President's Commission on Mental Health. . . ."

I also wanted to work with the elderly and on issues of concern to women, especially to get the ERA ratified.

I think what made the greatest impression on me as I traveled over the country is that people are the same everywhere. They may live in different regions, they may make their living a different way, but people are the same. They have the same needs and desires. They have the same worries and concerns. They want to make ends meet and to give their children better things than they had for themselves. They care about their schools and churches, and they want their communities to be good places to live. They want to be able to provide for themselves in their old age and to have some security and joy in life.

We had come to the finale.

On November 2, 1976 we paced and laughed nervously and talked too loud and prayed silently. Jimmy was there, as was all our family, including my mother and sister and Jimmy's sister Ruth. Edna Langford was there with her husband, Beverly. Hamilton Jordan, who had managed the campaign and been part of our team for ten years, was constantly on the telephone, checking the returns in different states. So was Jody Powell, who had traveled with Jimmy for the entire campaign as his press secretary and who now alternated between chain-smoking cigarettes and drinking Cokes. Charlie Kirbo, our friend from Atlanta who had been one of the first to urge Jimmy to run for President, was in and out. So was Jerry Rafshoon, who had done much to promote Jimmy's image nationwide, Frank Moore, who managed our campaign in the Southeast, and Pat Caddell, who had read the polls and trends so well. Madeline and Mary Hoyt from my staff were there, along with a few other close friends from Georgia.

We waited in a large suite at the Omni Hotel in Atlanta—two television sets going, telephones ringing, and friends and aides wandering in and out. It was chaotic, as all election nights are, but this evening was particularly tense. This was not just another primary election night, this was *the* night. The night in which all our work, all our hopes and dreams, would either be realized or shattered. And it was too close to call. The vote kept shifting back and forth between Ford and Carter as precinct after precinct closed throughout the states and night wore on. When it got too late for Amy I put her to bed, then went back into the sitting room again to pace with everyone else.

It was after three o'clock in the morning when the telephone call came from the governor of Mississippi, and I heard Jimmy saying, "We won. We won Mississippi! Thank you, Governor. That puts us over the top!"

The room erupted in cheers, tears, and embraces. Jimmy gathered me and all the children into the bedroom and talked to us quietly. He was feeling very humble with the responsibility he had asked for and gotten, and he said, "We've done it. It was a long, hard fight and I couldn't have done it without you. I'm proud of all of you. We have a big task ahead, but we can do that too. Just wait. We'll make the whole country proud. But now let's go home and rest."

Dawn was breaking when we finally reached Plains, and just as Jimmy stood to speak to the crowd gathered at the depot campaign headquarters, the sun peeked over the horizon. I saw the sun, looked at Jimmy, and tears rolled down both our cheeks. It was a new day and a new beginning both for us and for our country. I had never felt so proud. My husband had been elected President of the United States.

✎ 5 ✎
The White House

"*Mr. President!*"

"Who? Me?"

"Yes. You. come with me to see our bedroom." It was our first day in the White House, and though we should have been exhausted by the inauguration, the parade, and the thought of attending all seven inaugural balls still to come that night, the excitement of the day and exploring our new home made us tireless. The whole family was there: brothers and sisters, nieces and nephews, all our children, and of course, our mothers. Miss Lillian was going to sleep in the Queen's Bedroom tonight, my mother in the Lincoln Bedroom, and they were thrilled. We were all thrilled, and awed, to be in this beautiful place.

None of the family had seen the upstairs living quarters before except Chip and Caron, who had come with me on my second tour while President Ford and his family were away for the Christmas holidays. My first visit had not been as fruitful.

Early in December, the Fords had invited us to meet with them at the White House. Jimmy was to see the President in the Oval Office, and I was to visit with Mrs. Ford in the family living area. Jimmy and I were staying at Blair House when the White House called to say that Mrs. Ford was ill and had to cancel her appointment with me. I was crushed; I had been counting on this day to ask Mrs. Ford about living in and running the White House, and I didn't think I would be back in Washington before the inauguration. Then the telephone rang again. "Everyone thinks it would be better if you came this afternoon" was the new message. "Maybe Mrs. Ford will be feeling all right." It was not too much later that the next phone call came: Mrs. Ford was still not feeling well and the meeting was off. But the next call was from Jimmy, who was at the White House by then with Jerry Ford: "If you don't come the press will make a big story out of it, and they don't want anyone to know Mrs. Ford is sick, so just come on over and she'll see you for a few minutes."

Hurriedly, I put on the new brown and blue wool jersey dress I had brought for the occasion only to discover that the fabric must have caught some of the confusion of the day. The skirt clung to my half-slip no matter what I did, from dampening it to spraying it with hair spray, which was all I had. Finally, in desperation I ran to Mary Schneck, the director of Blair House, for help. "Try my slip," said Mary. "It's supposed to be static-resistant." She took it off, I put it on, and it worked. I was off to the White House.

Mrs. Ford wasn't well that afternoon and our visit was brief, but cordial. We met in the Yellow Oval Room upstairs, a very formal sitting room which Nancy Kissinger reportedly called "the most beautiful room in America" but which Betty Ford that afternoon called the "leg room." Used by Harry Truman as his private office, the Yellow Oval Room is filled with art masterpieces and authentic Federal furniture. It is beautiful, but there are no overstuffed pieces to soften it. Mrs. Ford said there were about a hundred and twenty-seven chair and table legs in the room; she said the maids knew because they had to dust them. If she had stayed in the White House, she told me, she would have changed the room to make it more comfortable.

While we talked, my apprehension lessened. I didn't sense any bitterness from Mrs. Ford toward me or toward leaving the White House; she wanted to be helpful. Four years later, when I met Nancy Reagan, I felt the same way and remembered my own first visit. I didn't get to see many of the rooms that day, and it was Rex Scouten, the longtime chief usher of the White House, who answered many of my questions about the staff, entertaining, and finding someone to look after Amy. I learned that the main house is called the mansion, the West Wing houses the Oval Office and the offices of the President's staff, and the East Wing has offices for the First Lady's staff, security, the military, and the visitors office. I left that afternoon feeling reassured because I had also learned that, unlike the situation at the Governor's Mansion, there was an experienced staff already in place.

On our first afternoon in the White House, the photographs I had taken home from my first visit were becoming a reality. Our family roamed from one end to the other of the second-floor hall, which runs the entire length of the house, with beautiful semi-circular windows at each end. It is an art gallery, with masterpieces on the walls, comfortable sitting areas, and many bookshelves. We had read about the secret stairway that connects the presidential living quarters on the second floor to the third floor, and the children quickly found it, pushing a portion of the wall that opens to reveal the stairway. We were surrounded by history, evoking both recent and past memories of American presidencies. We explored the Lincoln Bedroom and the Queen's Bedroom, on the east end of the hall, and found Nixon's favorite room, the Lincoln Sitting Room, which adjoins the Lincoln Bedroom. It's a small, cozy room with a corner fireplace, and Julie Nixon Eisenhower once said that her father liked a fire so much that he would build one here even in warm weather and turn on the air conditioning. Tucked away behind a stairway was a little room that Pat Nixon had made into a beauty parlor.

Originally, when the White House was built, the President's offices were also on the second floor, and Jimmy's favorite room became the Treaty Room, which had been the Cabinet room for ten administrations. It looked solid and masculine and was decorated in deep green and maroon; when I saw it I thought a man would feel comfortable smoking a cigar in this room. Most of its furniture was bought by Ulysses S. Grant, including a walnut table on which the peace treaty ending the Spanish-American War was signed. Later, we took this same table out onto the front lawn for the signing of another historic peace treaty, that between Egypt and Israel.

Our excitement mounted that first evening as we explored the third floor and found other rooms that would become very important to our family life in the White House. There were two guest bedrooms, a billiard room, laundry and ironing rooms, and the Solarium with a magnificent view of the Washington Monument. The Solarium had served as a kindergarten for the Kennedy children and as a courting place for the Johnson girls. The Johnsons had put in a soda fountain for the young people. It became the favorite hangout for our children and their friends, the lovely setting for my Spanish lessons with Gay Vance, and a favorite spot to watch Saturday afternoon football games on television with the children.

We even went out on the rooftop that first night, something we would do often during the next four years. One can walk almost all around the house just behind the façade that is part of the familiar picture of the White House, and the view of the heavens is wondrous. Jeffrey, who is a keen amateur astonomer, used his own telescope on the roof to view the stars and planets and occasionally would borrow a larger one from the Naval Observatory. Jeffrey and Amy used to call the Dial-a-Phenomenon recording at the Smithsonian to learn what was happening in the sky, and on special nights we would all go out and view the phenomena. There was also a nice wide open space on the roof just outside the Solarium, where we could put the playpen for Chip and Caron's new baby as well as sunbathe in privacy.

Back inside the long hall, we took a quick look at the extensive library. Bookshelves lined the hall on the third floor as well as on the second floor, and the variety of books looked wonderful to this family of avid readers. Amy could do her homework from the sets of encyclopedias, collections of U.S. histories, and books on the presidency as well as American novels, nonfiction, and picture books. These volumes were almost exclusively written by or about people in the United States. One night Jimmy was looking for a quotation from *Macbeth* and, amazingly, we could find no Shakespeare in the White House. There were plenty of other books to choose from. Many authors send personalized copies of their works to the President, and the American Booksellers Association gives every President two hundred and fifty new volumes at the beginning of his term. It's a wonderful gift, and we asked for a portion of them each year, instead of getting them all in one batch, so we would always have a supply of current issues; for the first time the ABA added selections of children's stories as well for Amy. But even with all these books and bookshelves, we needed space for Jimmy's personal volumes, so we had the carpenters make a bookcase to cover most of one wall in Jimmy's second-floor study. A beautiful piece, it was made of mahogany, with doors at the bottom that locked for the notebooks that contained his daily diary notes. The day the carpenters installed the bookcase,

I overheard one say to the other: "We haven't had a President who read this much in a long time."

The living arrangements we had chosen were perfect for our family. Amy was on the second floor with us; Jeff and Chip and their wives, on the third floor, with a nursery all ready for the new baby. Jeff was going to attend George Washington University, and Chip would be working for the Democratic National Committee in Washington. We would miss Judy and Jack, but Jack was practicing law with his father-in-law in Calhoun, Georgia, and they could only come to Washington for visits. We delighted in the children and enjoyed their comings and goings and their friends. The third floor had not been completed until the Truman renovation, and I wondered how Benjamin Harrison had fitted his large family—which included his wife, her ninety-year-old father, her sister and niece; their son Russell and his wife and daughter; and their daughter Mary McKee and two infants—into five rooms on the second floor. No wonder Mrs. Harrison began the campaign for enlarging the White House.

We hadn't finished the tour that first afternoon before we lost Jimmy. He had been anxious not only to visit the Oval Office for the first time as President, but to keep an appointment with Max Cleland, a Vietnam veteran and triple amputee whom he was going to ask to become head of the Veterans' Administration. After a while, the children and I walked over to the West Wing ourselves, laughing happily and talking about the excitement of the day. All of a sudden, as we entered the Oval Office, no one was saying anything. We were just standing there, looking at the room and at Jimmy, sitting behind the President's desk, framed by the President's flag and the flag of the United States. It was an unforgettable moment.

I had to catch my breath to believe I was really there, to absorb the reality that my husband was actually President of the United States and that I was First Lady. The Oval Office is filled with the history of our country. It is where presidents have struggled with decisions that affected the whole world. Jimmy grinned, and I smiled back at him. He looked just right sitting there.

The time for touring was over, and we were soon off to the inaugural balls. Jimmy looked handsome in his tuxedo, Amy, adorable in her blue velveteen gown and cape, with *The Mixed-up Files of Mrs. Basil E. Frankenwelier* under her arm (she didn't intend to be bored). I was dressed sentimentally, in the gown I'd worn at the balls in Atlanta when Jimmy was elected governor. All the ballrooms were packed. There was virtually no breathing room, much less dancing room, and a human wall had to be formed down the aisle to hold back the cheering crowd as we made our way to the platforms.

"Are you having a good time?" the new President asked. "Yes!" came back the cheers. "Do you believe in America?" The cheers grew louder. "Are you going to help me?" The response was a roar!

There is no way to describe how I felt that evening. Everywhere I looked there were familiar faces, and I loved them all for working with us, for voting for us, for believing in us, for celebrating with us. In return, I have never felt so loved. All of these people, I thought, loved me, loved Jimmy, loved our children, and were filled with expectations and dreams about the good things Jimmy Carter would do for our country. I wanted to laugh, I wanted to cry. I wanted to hug everyone in sight. My heart was overflowing. At each party, Jimmy and I waltzed a turn under the spotlights while the band played a romantic piece; then it was time to move on to the next ball and the next and the next. It was a night of pure magic, and someone wrote after it was all over: "They could have danced all night, but even Cinderella had to go home." And so did the Carters—home to 1600 Pennsylvania Avenue!

My euphoria began to wane during the next two days of receptions in the White House when everyone in the country, it seemed, filed down the receiving line in the Cross Hall on the State Floor to shake the hands of the newly inaugurated Carters and Mondales. There were beautiful bouquets of spring flowers in the rooms, fires crackling in the fireplaces, and music from the Marine Band and string ensembles filling the air, and one by one the people came in endless lines. First were our "hosts," those we had spent the night with during the campaign and to whom we now gave small bronze plaques inscribed with the words: "A member of the Carter family stayed in this house during the campaign of 1976." Then came the governors, the members of the Democratic National Committee and leaders of the Democratic party from across the country, and in midafternoon the Georgians, almost two thousand of them! "Ya'll come," Jimmy had said, and they came!

It was wonderful, but it was also exhausting. Between groups that afternoon and the next, which ranged from all the members of Congress and the diplomatic corps to members of the military, I would go upstairs to our bedroom and sprawl across the bed for a very few minutes until it was time to get up and do it all over again. My hand throbbed; my feet hurt. I had looked and looked for just the right shoes to go with the outfits I had chosen for the receptions but ended up wearing the oldest, most stretched ones I could find, and finally slipped those off while still standing in the receiving line. When the last person filed by, I was so tired I went to bed and slept.

The rest of the family, however, went off exploring again, this time on the ground floor, which holds the public rooms: the Library; the Map Room, where Franklin Roosevelt followed the course of World War II; the China and Vermeil rooms, where some of the White House treasures are on display; and the Diplomatic Reception Room, our usual entry route into the house. Their greatest discovery that afternoon was another White House treasure, down one of the twisting corridors past the kitchen: the bowling alley. Jimmy was pleased that we would be able to get plenty of exercise even in the winter, and although I hadn't bowled since high school days, it wasn't long before I was right in there rolling balls with the rest of the family.

We also soon found the movie theater, which became one of our favorite places, one we escaped to often. Ironically, the first film we saw, on our third night in the White House, was *All the President's Men*, which brought back all the bitter memories of Watergate. It also reminded us that we were the ones in the White House now, who had to make sure nothing like that ever happened again. But mostly we went to the movies to relax and get away from the responsibilities of the day. Sometimes we made popcorn upstairs and took it down with us to the theater, or we would take a bottle of wine and hors d'oeuvres. Occasionally, when the schedule was crowded, the butlers would bring us our dinner on trays, and Jimmy and I would eat while we watched a movie. The theater was small and personal, unlike a public theater, though we could set up forty or fifty chairs, and the front row had comfortable lounge chairs and ottomans so we could prop up our feet. Often we invited the staff and other people to join us, and Amy had frequent movie parties there with her friends.

We watched old movies, new movies, good ones, bad ones. They were all available to us, any we wanted to see. The projectionist gave Jimmy a book listing all the old Academy Award—winning movies, and we ordered such classics as *Citizen Kane*, *Casablanca*, and *High Noon*. We often had screenings of movies before they were released, which were fun because sometimes the director or one of the stars would come too. We didn't always know what we were going to see, and I was a little concerned the evening after the Pope's visit to the White House. We had a big celebration on the South Lawn, which was attended by the governor of Louisiana, Edwin Edwards, and his wife, mother, and mother-in-law. They stayed for the night, and after dinner we went down to the theater and saw *10*, a good movie but not very appropriate for the day. Another night, when we had invited the staff to join us, the movie started and after a few minutes, Amy turned to Jimmy and said, "I'm going upstairs to do my homework, Dad, because I don't think I'm supposed to be seeing this."

It didn't take us long to find our way around the White House, but there were some obstacles, literally, on the way. Shortly after we moved in, I walked over to the Oval Office with Jimmy to pick up some papers he wanted. When we returned, instead of taking the elevator we walked up the stairs to the second floor—and found ourselves locked out. We walked up to the third floor; that door was locked too. We learned from the usher's office (which is inconspicuously located on the State Floor beside the elevator, with someone always on duty) that we were expected to use the elevator and that all the doors leading to the living quarters were permanently locked. I didn't like the feeling of being locked in or of being locked out on the stairwell, especially since all of us were accustomed to running up and down the stairs. The next day Jimmy arranged with the Secret Service to unlock all of the doors except during tour hours—and I felt more at home.

Getting back and forth to my own office in the East Wing proved to be a problem of another sort. Although most first ladies had had their offices in the living quarters, on the second or third floor, I wanted our quarters to be home, a place to escape from the work and the staff. I always need a place to go that is private, where I don't have to dress and don't have to put on makeup. The offices of the staff of the First Lady were always in the East Wing, and it seemed a perfect place for my office too.

Tourists were in the house from 8:00 A.M. until after noon, and they walked along the same corridor that was the route to my office. I couldn't just walk through without stopping to say hello, which took so much time. In order to stay on any kind of schedule, I had to go outside through a side door and then come back into the East Wing, which was fine when the weather was good. But the weather was often so bad that the route was inconvenient. One cold, rainy morning I was all bundled up to go outside when the doorman, a wonderful, sweet, elderly man who had been at the White House for many years, came up with the solution: "Mrs. Carter, why don't you just go downstairs and through the basement?" Gratefully I followed him down into a labyrinth of rooms through which we made our way under the mansion and up the stairway into the East Wing and my offices. We passed large laundry rooms, the machine shop, went through the plumber's shop, past the bomb shelter and emergency security rooms for the President and his staff, and passed other rooms I hadn't known about. This became my passageway to and from work and I liked it, especially on cold, cold days. With Jimmy's energy conservation program, it was the only really warm place in the White House, with the large steam pipes running overhead.

Our first breakfast in the White House was a feast of strawberries and grapefruit, of scrambled eggs, fried eggs, poached eggs, sausage and bacon, ham and even grits. It was delicious, and the splendid service was a welcome relief from my recent tour of duty in the kitchen at home.

Between the election and the inauguration our house had been liked Grand Central Station as Jimmy held meetings with the Democratic leadership in Congress, potential Cabinet members and other appointees, experts in every area of government, and advisers on every subject imaginable, domestic and foreign. Jimmy chose his Cabinet members during those days. They complemented his own knowledge and experience and were from all parts of our country. Three of them came from the academic world, four from the field of law, two from Congress, one from business, and one had been governor of Idaho. All but two had worked in Washington in previous administrations. And just as in our old warehouse days, Jimmy invited everyone to stay for meals.

I had never had a cook in Plains, but during this transition period I always had friends and neighbors to help. Usually my mother, my secretary, Madeline, and Sybil, Billy's wife, and I made stacks of sandwiches—hamburgers, barbecue sandwiches, and ham, cheese, and tomato—and put them on the breakfast room table for whoever happened to be there along with gallons of lemonade, iced tea, and coffee. The neighbors sent food in too—fried chicken, baked hams, cakes, and casseroles—but the Secret Service disapproved of this "unsecured" food and put a stop to it, or thought they did. My mother had "clearance," so our neighbors started delivering the food to her instead, and she would bring it to us. Even though we bypassed the Secret Service, all of the food was from friends, and no danger was involved in eating it. It was a busy time and I tried not to worry about things not being perfect, but can you imagine my chagrin to look up one day and see Henry Kissinger sipping iced tea from a Tweety-Bird jelly glass? Oh, well, I thought, I'll have plenty of time to serve him from crystal.

It was rather fun during that time to be in the kitchen preparing the food, but Jimmy teased me, saying I enjoyed doing it only because I knew I wouldn't have to do it for long.

After cooking for the crowds at home, the luxury of the White House was wonderful. It was a pleasure to have someone shop and cook and serve, but a shock when we got our food bill for the last ten days of January and it was over $600! I went to see Rex Scouten, the chief usher, about it, but he wasn't surprised. "Mrs. Carter," he said gently, "it's not cheap to live in the White House." He was right. I had little control over the shopping. The food had to come from special places because of security, so I met with the chef regularly to plan the meals until he learned what we liked to eat. After that, he sent weekly menus for my approval. The First Family pays for all the food served upstairs unless it is for an official visit, and we always had a houseful of company— guests of the children, family from home, or friends from around the country. Our food bill was always astronomical!

The First Family also pays for all personal items and incidentals such as toiletries, dry cleaning, tennis balls, the hairdresser, and clothes, of course. At Camp David we were charged by the meal, and if Amy brought a friend along on the helicopter, we paid for it. All of the family, except Jimmy, paid their way on *Air Force One*. If we flew home for Christmas, for instance, we all paid the full first-class fare plus one dollar (a long-standing rule of the White House military office), even the grandbabies.

The White House policy on transportation had not always been so strict, but President Nixon's misuse of public funds had caused the Internal Revenue Service to re-examine the guidelines for the presidency. I objected at first to the travel expenses—if the plane was going to Georgia anyway, why couldn't I ride along?—but Jimmy wouldn't consider requesting any exceptions to the rules.

There were many decisions I had to discuss with Jimmy, not only during the first weeks in the White House, but throughout the entire term of office—decisions about personal matters, quite often financial or involving the children. I still kept our books and wrote all the checks and sometimes needed to discuss bills I had to pay or income taxes and bank accounts. We reviewed invitations, White House entertainment, guest lists for state dinners, correspondence of interest, and the issues we were both working on. I made as many of these decisions as I could to relieve Jimmy of the responsibility, but the things I took to him involved priorities, suggestions, and advice, decisions that took some thought. When he came home at night he didn't want to talk about them. After a day of decision-making in the Oval Office those first few months, he obviously began to dread getting off the elevator on the second floor to find me waiting there with my list of more things to decide. Finally, one day he said, "Why don't you plan to have lunch with me once a week, like the Vice President does, and save these routine things so we can do them all in one day." After that, Monday lunch was with Fritz Mondale, Wednesday lunch with me.

On my desk in the bedroom I kept a brown leather folder with "Monsieur le Président Jimmy Carter" engraved on it (it had been given to Jimmy in France), and anything I needed to talk to him about at our luncheons, I put in that folder. I made lists of subjects so that when I went to the Oval Office, I had an agenda. Inevitably, questions arose that had to be dealt with between luncheons, but in general our new arrangement worked well.

Adjacent to the Oval Office is a small private study, where Jimmy spent much of his time working. It opened onto a secluded flagstone terrace that was dreary when we moved in, but I had the gardeners plant tulips and bulbs and flowers in season, and it became a beautiful little hideaway where we often ate our lunches.

One of the things we discussed early was his decision, after the first two days of receptions, to do away with most of the "Ruffles and Flourishes" and honors to the President, including "Hail to the Chief" every time he entered a room. He wanted the simple announcement: "Ladies and gentlemen, the President of the United States." I argued especially in favor of "Hail to the Chief." It shows respect and also means so much to those who hear it. I never fail to be thrilled when it is played. I agreed with him that it can be overdone, and had been overdone in the past, but his mind was made up. He thought the office of the President had too many trappings already, and after that, "Hail to the Chief" was played only on special occasions: state functions, military functions, sometimes when he traveled, and at other selected appearances.

I was worried at first that Amy would have a hard time adjusting to life in Washington. We had always tried to make life as normal as possible for her, but that would be a real challenge in the White House. We had taken her from Plains to Atlanta, back to Plains and now here. Each time she had friends who were special and whom she had to leave, and now, though she wasn't happy about it, she had to start a new school again only four days after we got to the White House. There was a lot of press interest because we had decided that she would go to a public rather than a private school. Jimmy had struggled with the problem of good students leaving the public schools when he had served on the School Board all those years at home, and we didn't want to be part of the problem now.

On Amy's first day of school, we stepped from the car into a barrage of news reporters, television and flash cameras, and spectators who crowded around her as she trudged with her books toward the door. We made it through, Amy having learned already just to look straight ahead, smile, and keep walking. But this morning she wasn't smiling.

At first her new classmates were curious about "the President's daughter" and the Secret Service agents accompanying her, but after a few days of staring, the children accepted Amy and began to make friends. It took longer for the other children in the school, who would crowd around when she went out to the playground. During the first week it created so much confusion that one day the teacher made Amy stay by herself in the classroom with the Secret Service agents instead of going out to play. When she came home that day she was very unhappy. I think the teacher realized that she didn't like to be set apart, and after that, she went out with the other children no matter how much they crowded around. Once everyone had seen her and become accustomed to the Secret Service agents, the children forgot about who she was and the playground returned to normal.

As usual, Amy made friends quickly. Her school was interesting, with children from twenty-eight countries, and the first week she brought home a little girl from Chile, Claudia Sanchez, whose father was a cook in the Chilean Embassy. Soon she was bringing home other friends, too, often to spend the night. One of their favorite adventures was to sleep in the huge bed in the Lincoln Bedroom and stay awake half the night listening for Lincoln's ghost. They always claimed, of course, to have heard him. We built a tree house for her on the South Lawn, and in the summer Amy and her friends would occasionally sleep there while the Secret Service agents kept watchful eyes on them.

When we began to settle into the living quarters of the White House, we made another wonderful discovery: the warehouse that is a repository for the furnishings of former presidents. Rex Scouten said that we should take a look and bring anything back we wanted for our rooms. It was fascinating to browse in this "museum" of White House history, which held everything from a rocking chair that had belonged to President McKinley and a room full of andirons that Truman had purchased and Jackie Kennedy later moved out, to memorabilia from Luci Baines and Lynda Bird Johnson's weddings. We chose a coffee table for our bedroom and an adorable little sofa and chair set for Amy, which had been given to Caroline Kennedy while her father was President; it was still covered with muslin and had never been used. Chip and Caron brought back a Truman chiffonier and a little chest that had been painted white for Caroline Kennedy to be ready for their new baby, soon to come. Jeff and Annette chose the greatest treasure of all: a chair that Mary Todd Lincoln had purchased. We found three large Oriental carpets to put in the hall of the third floor to replace the long, bright red carpeting that made it look more like a hotel than a home. The carpets just fit, and what a difference! They made the hall, with its crystal chandeliers and groupings of furniture, look elegant.

I didn't make any major changes in the White House while we were there, only bringing a few pieces of furniture from the warehouse, moving a painting or two, replacing drapes, and painting walls a different color. The family rooms were comfortable, with the finest furnishings, paintings, and objets d'art, decorated under the supervision of the curator, Clem Conger.

I liked our bedroom, called the First Lady's Bedroom, with paintings by Childe Hassam, Winslow Homer, and Paul Cézanne on the walls. Its four-poster canopy bed, high off the floor, was almost a replica of the one I had loved so much in the Governor's Mansion, and in one corner was a glass cabinet I filled with treasures that Amy brought home—a small pottery bowl she made at school, a fan made of lollipop sticks—even though it had green velvet-covered shelves and was obviously meant to display grander objects.

We used the adjoining President's Bedroom as a study, and spent more leisure time there than anywhere else. To make it comfortable, we put two overstuffed chairs with one large matching footstool in front of the fireplace, and we talked and read in this cozy room many evenings. Later, when Jimmy was urging people to use wood-burning stoves and energy-efficient fireplaces because of the oil crisis, we added a new fireplace insert with glass doors. Inconspicuously on the side of the marble mantelpiece was an inscription: "This room was occupied by John Fitzgerald Kennedy during the two years, ten months and two days he was President of the United States. January 20, 1961–November 22, 1963."

There were reminders everywhere of the families who used to live in the house. In a closet connecting our bedroom and the study was an old built-in hi-fi set, on which I was told that Jackie Kennedy played *Camelot* during her White House years. I think it was the same record player. Jimmy replaced it with a good stereo system with individually controlled speakers in the bedroom, the dining room, the West Hall, and even in my dressing room.

On the wall over the lavatory in Jimmy's bathroom was a long row of electrical outlets, which I learned had been put in one day after Lyndon Johnson, in a fit of temper that there weren't enough, shouted, ". . . and I want sockets here and here and here and here!"

Amy slept in the room that had been Caroline Kennedy's, Luci Johnson's, and Tricia Nixon's and did her homework on the same desk that Eleanor Roosevelt had used, surrounded by paintings by Grandma Moses, Thomas Scully, John Opie, and others.

In the dining room there was a mahogany sideboard that had belonged to Daniel Webster—an important statesman though not President—which bore his initials inside an unusual front pullout desk section. When we moved in, the walls in this room were painted yellow, but I remembered looking at pictures and seeing lovely wallpaper with scenes from the American Revolution. I found the wallpaper in the warehouse and had it rehung.

We had the Kennedys to thank for the upstairs dining room and kitchen. Previous families had had to go downstairs to the State Floor for meals. But there is no privacy on the State Floor. People are always there: visitors, security guards, ushers, doormen, butlers, flower staff, cleaning persons. I learned that President and Mrs. Hoover dressed in formal clothes every evening to go downstairs for their meal. But the Eisenhowers often ate at TV tables in the West Hall upstairs, a comfortable sitting area at the end of the hall between our bedroom and the kitchen and dining area. We ate dinner there occasionally on trays, too, if we wanted to watch a special television program, but we used it more to gather before meals with the children, and Amy could often be found lying on the floor in front of the TV, doing her homework.

We had many overnight guests while we were in the White House, and we used the Queen's Bedroom and the Lincoln Bedroom, where Abraham Lincoln signed the Emancipation Proclamation, as guest rooms. We soon learned from our friends that the mattress in the Queen's Bedroom was too soft and the one in the Lincoln Bedroom too hard. The Lincoln bed was massive— more than eight feet long and almost six feet wide—large enough for Lincoln, for sure. We discovered a board under the mattress, which we removed, but the mattress was thin and still not very comfortable. We didn't change either bed, though. We thought the mattresses would give the people who spent the night something to talk about!

My favorite place in the White House was the Truman balcony, with the most beautiful view in all of Washington. It looks out over the South Lawn to the Ellipse across the street, the Washington Monument, and the Jefferson Memorial. It opens off the Yellow Oval Room, and we brought rocking chairs from Georgia like the ones we had had on the back porch of the Governor's Mansion. Many late afternoons or at night after dinner, we sat on the balcony and talked about what had happened during the day. In the summertime we ate lunch there on a glass-topped table. The gardeners kept large tubs of tulips, daffodils, and geraniums always blooming and beautiful. It was a wonderful retreat.

Most of the redecorating I did was on the third floor. We converted the Billiard Room, with its dark green carpet and walls and shaded light, into a cheerful room with grasscloth on the walls, blue shutters at the windows, and a new blue and beige carpet. I replaced the worn green felt on the pool table with blue felt and lined the walls with family photographs. The Solarium became a light, airy room when we removed the heavy old yellow and orange flowered drapes and put up lightweight, off-white unlined curtains and decorated with yellows and blues. With the television set, Jeff's stereo, and a kitchenette well-stocked with snacks, Cokes, and beer, it became a popular place to gather. We enjoyed the living quarters and left a little bit of Georgia on the third floor, paneling a wall in one of the guest rooms with wood from a barn on Papa Murray's farm.

The State Floor of the White House, where tourists visit, is also where official functions were held. It is under the supervision of the Committee for the Preservation of the White House, with permanent members that include the curator of the White House, the chief usher, and the heads of the Smithsonian Institution and the National Gallery. Other members serve at the pleasure of the President in office. I knew about the committee before I came to the White House because when Jimmy was governor, I had been concerned about protecting the furnishings in our mansion. After visiting a historic, colonial Governor's Mansion in which antique furnishings had been replaced by modern department store furniture, I formed a committee fashioned after the Committee for the Preservation of the White House to protect the valuable furnishings and art in Georgia's Governor's Mansion.

One evening, when everyone had gone home except the guards and an usher on duty and the State Floor was deserted and quiet, Amy and I went downstairs with a White House guidebook and walked through all of the rooms—the East Room, the Green, Blue and Red rooms, the State Dining Room, and the smaller, original Family Dining Room—reading the interesting stories about each one and making notes in our book, adding the names of the paintings in the photographs.

We learned some wonderfully odd things about the house that night: Abigail Adams hung the presidential laundry in the East Room; Thomas Jefferson used the same space for his secretary, who had to find better quarters when the ceiling literally fell in; the portrait of George Washington in the East Room is the only object known to have *always* been in the White House, except when Dolley Madison had it torn from its frame as she fled when the British were coming in 1814; Andrew Jackson once placed a fourteen-hundred-pound cheese in the Cross Hall and invited the public in to eat it. They came in droves, eating and treading crumbs into the carpets, and the smell lingered for weeks. Thomas Jefferson had a pet mockingbird that he taught to peck food from his lips and to hop up the stairs after him; the Garfield children rode large, three-wheeled velocipedes while they carried on pillow fights in the East Room; and the five children of Theodore Roosevelt slid down the staircases on trays stolen from the pantry, stalked the halls on stilts, and when one of the children had the measles, his brothers took a pony into his second-floor bedroom after riding up in the President's elevator. Guests at Lincoln's inaugural cut souvenirs of floral designs from the brocaded window draperies and lace curtains. That didn't happen while we were there, but guests did take away silverware and crystal. Wine glasses evidently are easy to slip into pockets or purses, as are pieces of silverware, so sometimes, when we had large crowds, we didn't use the fine silverware and crystal. Once a very respected member of one of the presidential commissions took a silver ashtray (which he returned anonymously after being chastised by someone who had seen him take it). I was amazed that this could happen, but the residence staff, though abhoring it, had learned to expect it.

The aura of history and the elegant, comfortable surroundings of the White House were not the only advantages of living there. Virtually every service is at your fingertips. The huge house accommodates a flower room, where fresh flowers are brought in and arranged every day, the carpenter's shop, the paint shop, and even a dentist's office among the rooms one floor down.

The dentist comes from nearby Bethesda at the request of the First Family, but the White House doctor is always by the President's side. His office is on the ground floor, but wherever the President goes, so goes the doctor. Bill Lukash, a Navy admiral, was the White House doctor while we were there and became one of our closest friends. He respected our need for privacy and kept his distance unless we invited him to join us. We always found him to be a willing participant in any sport—jogging, fishing, playing tennis, swimming. He had been at the White House since the Lyndon Johnsons were there, and I'm sure he missed some of the hobbies he became accustomed to with other presidents. I saw a set of golf clubs one day languishing in an out-of-the-way corner of his office.

Another of the great pleasures of the White House was the telephone system. One could reach virtually any spot on the globe in moments simply by picking up the telephone and saying the word—no dialing, no looking up numbers, and usually no waiting; the President can always get through. I seldom called Jimmy "the President" when referring to him, but I learned to do so when talking with the White House operators. One day soon after we moved in I picked up the telephone and said to the operator, "I would like to speak with Jimmy, please." "Jimmy who?"

After our first few weeks in the White House, we fell into a daily routine that began with Jimmy awakening every morning at six o'clock. The stewards had already put two glasses of orange juice on a table in his dressing room; he drank one while he dressed, and on his way to the Oval Office at six-thirty, he put the second one on my bedside table as he said good-bye. Reluctantly I got up and awakened Amy and then returned to my bathroom to watch the seven o'clock news while I bathed and dressed. I never had to worry about Amy not getting up. I turned on the water for her bath, put on the Suzuki violin tape of the songs she was learning and left. Not once did she let the tub overflow. At seven-thirty she and I ate breakfast together and she was off to school. I lingered over another cup of coffee and the newspaper or planned my day's work. (I need time to wake up in the morning. Jimmy is just the opposite: He sits straight up in the bed, ready for another day. At the Naval Academy he was forced to say, every Monday morning upon arising, "Another week in which to excel!" Sometimes he teases me when I am gloomy early in the mornings with: "Just think, another day in which to excel!" But I don't want to excel, not at that hour.)

Several months after we moved in, Jimmy decided to begin his day at five-thirty; he moved his workday up so he wouldn't have to go back to his office after dinner. I stopped scheduling anything for myself after four-thirty in the afternoons so we could swim, play tennis, or jog around the South Lawn or bowl if the weather was bad. It was wonderful to get away from the pressures for a while and clear our minds, sit on the Truman balcony and talk for a while, have dinner, and see a movie.

Unlike Jimmy, I do my best work at night, a habit left over from the years of working in the warehouse, which left only the time after the children were in bed to do the chores, write letters, and read. During the campaign I also had to catch up on correspondence and write speeches late in the evening. There was no time in the mornings if I had to be at a factory gate before daylight. At the White House I didn't work much at night, though, because when Jimmy wasn't working, he didn't want me to be working. The one thing that took precedence over all was writing speeches. I can never write a speech ahead of time no matter how free my schedule. Sometimes, the night before a speech, I would work until the wee hours of the morning getting it just right. It frustrated Jimmy sometimes, but that's the way I work, and it never interfered with our afternoon rendezvous or the frequent evening movies.

The first months were hectic for all of us, but we learned a lot and enjoyed it all. No matter what happened, the euphoria of that first inaugural evening lingered.

❧ 6 ❧

Conservation,
Controversy, Protection,
and the Press

One night soon after we moved into the White House, Jimmy asked us to guess how many television sets were there, including those in the East and West wings. He had received a report that morning from his task force advising on ways to cut federal waste and mismanagement. I guessed forty, someone else, fifty, and Chip chimed in with "maybe a hundred." Jimmy shook his head. We hadn't come close. There were 325 television sets in the White House and 220 FM radios. And the federal tab for magazine and newspaper subscriptions came to $85,000 a year. It was not long before these numbers were drastically reduced.

The large pool of cars and drivers for staff members was soon to go, too. Jimmy insisted that the staff drive their own cars to work since there had been abuses of this privilege in the past, at great expense to the taxpayer. I argued against such a total cutback. When I traveled, I often returned to the White House after midnight, and anyone with me had to drive home. Not only were we all exhausted at that hour, but I thought it was dangerous for them to be driving in Washington alone in the middle of the night; they should at least have the use of a car and driver when it was late.

It was the topic of conversation on more than one occasion, but Jimmy made no exceptions.

In the White House my relationship with Jimmy was the same as it had always been. We discussed business and strategy when we were working together in the warehouse, or campaigning, and when he was serving as governor, the way most husbands and wives do when they take an interest in each other's work. I often acted as a sounding board for him. While explaining a particular issue to me, he could think it through himself; and I and the rest of the family often argued with him more strenuously than his advisers or staff did. To us he was the same participant in our nightly dinner table discussions that he had always been. I soon discovered that it was easier for me to learn about people's needs as I traveled than it was for him. He always had such an entourage that he could seldom just sit and talk with elderly people about their problems or go into a house in New Hampshire in the middle of the winter, as I did, and listen to a young family talking about the high cost of fuel and what it meant to their budget. I talked with women about their problems, visited day care centers, and met with children in New York's inner-city schools. From these and many similar experiences, I could give Jimmy a firsthand report of the attitudes and needs of people in our country.

A President, no matter who he is, can become very isolated if he's not careful. Maybe something I reported to him would have an impact as he struggled with a problem; maybe not. If I disagreed with him about something, I told him. For the most part, however, Jimmy and I agreed on issues. We did find ourselves on the opposite sides of a few, such as capital punishment. (Jimmy was for it; I was against it.) He was also more conservative about the abortion issue. (I oppose it for myself, but I have a hard time with deciding for other women what is right or wrong or best for them.) I wanted Jimmy to fire Joe Califano long before he ever did, and my reasons were purely political. Joe was hurting him politically and unnecessarily, I thought, and I felt Jimmy could find someone who would do the job just as well and keep a lower profile. I was never able to budge him on these particular issues—but neither did he budge me.

Our most common argument centered on political timing, a question of strategy more than substance. The best things to do are not always the most popular things, and on more than one occasion I pleaded with Jimmy to postpone certain controversies, such as the Panama Canal treaties or some of the Mideast decisions, until his second term. My pleas always fell on deaf ears. "If securing a second term was more important to me than doing what needs to be done, than I'd wait," he would snap at me. But I didn't always give up. Instead of announcing federal budget cuts that directly affected the Democratic constituency in New York City the week before the New York primary, for example, couldn't he wait until the following week? The answer was no. "The psychology of inflation demands that something be done now, and I'm not going to wait." His standard answer when I talked about political expediency was a seemingly pompous: "I'll never do anything to hurt my country." But he meant it, and I meant it too when I appealed to him, loudly sometimes when I was very concerned: "The thing you can do to hurt your country most is not get re-elected." I believed it then. I believe it now.

Though I could seldom sway him when his mind was made up, he always listened. I am much more political than Jimmy and was more concerned about popularity and winning re-election, but I have to say that he had the courage to tackle the important issues, no matter how controversial — or politically damaging — they might be. And I admired him for it. (Often during his term, we used to sit around and try to think of something he was doing that was popular!)

He certainly wasted no time plunging into unpopular waters. As chairman of the Energy Committee for the National Governors Conference, Jimmy knew well how self-defeating and dangerous our dependency on foreign oil was. He decided to go on national television our second week in the White House to explain the seriousness of the problem and the necessity of beginning to conserve energy immediately. The difficulty lay in convincing the public that though the long gas lines of 1973 were gone, the problem had not gone away. Many people still believed there was no energy problem at all, and with good reason. President Richard Nixon, after the '73 oil embargo was lifted and oil became plentiful again, had declared that the crisis was over.

Jimmy knew that that was not true, that the oil supplies in the world were exhaustible, and we had to develop an energy program for the United States to ensure against a disastrous future. We had done our best to set an example in the Governor's Mansion. We had turned off lights, decorated at Christmas with natural, old-fashioned decorations — ribbons, pine cones, and strings of popcorn—and very few lights compared to the years before. We switched from big, gas-guzzling state cars to smaller ones. It seemed more hilarious than conserving when Hedley Donovan, then of Time Inc. and a very tall man, came to see us. On the way to a reception, he, Jimmy, and I all squeezed into the back seat of our compact car. Hedley's head and my teased, bouffant hairdo both touched the top, and traveling at the newly reduced speed limit of 55 miles per hour, we had a very uncomfortable but exemplary ride.

When we arrived at the White House, Jimmy informed me that we were going to set an example again. He said that in his first address on national television, which would be a fireside chat, he was going to ask the American people to turn down their thermostats to 65 degrees during the day, 55 at night. He had already ordered all the thermostats in the White House turned down, including those in our living quarters. I couldn't believe it; I had been freezing ever since we moved in. My offices were so cold I couldn't concentrate, and my staff was typing with gloves on. Even upstairs we were only comfortable if we were all wrapped up. Every time I had turned on the news since we moved to Washington, there were stories about its being one of the coldest winters on record, and I believed it. Now it was going to be colder.

I pleaded with Jimmy to set the thermostats at 68 degrees, but it didn't do any good. The next morning the thermostats, and the temperature, went down. I got out my long underwear, put on slacks, and began to get used to living and working in the cold. A few days later, one of the upstairs maids came in with four pairs of knee-length cotton underwear for me. She had been shopping for warm underwear for herself, and knowing how cold I was, bought some for me as well. And for the rest of the winter I wore them to stay warm in the White House!

In Jimmy's first address to the people as President, he wore a sweater and sat in front of a real fire in the Library on the ground floor. He wanted it to be an informal talk, but his message on energy was sobering when he pointed out that "the United States is the only major industrial country [in the world] without a comprehensive, long-range energy policy."

Two months later, in April 1977, he submitted his energy program to Congress, calling the effort to make the United States energy-independent "the moral equivalent of war."

We knew from the beginning that Jimmy's energy campaign

was politically risky. People want to believe that everything is going to be fine, that they are not going to have to make any sacrifices, that the future is always going to be better than the present. They don't want to hear about crises or problems, but without an aroused public, Jimmy knew he would never be able to prevail over the powerful oil companies and other lobbyists to develop an effective energy policy. There was no natural constituency for his program, parts of which were unpopular with everyone. He had to fight the oil companies, the automobile industry, the power companies—even consumers—when he decontrolled oil and natural gas. It was very difficult. When we'd ask him how his energy program was progressing, his standard reply became: "It's a bitch! I know why no other President was willing to tackle it."

By the end of Jimmy's term, the energy program he put into effect had already begun to reduce our overdependence on foreign oil supplies and to stop the upward spiral of oil and gas prices. Pat Buchanan, a conservative columnist and commentator, said, "...history will say that Jimmy Carter of Plains, Georgia, was the fellow who busted OPEC." Strong and permanent laws had been passed to establish a new Energy Department and bring order out of bureaucratic chaos, to require increasingly efficient automobiles, to use conservation incentives in electric power rates, to improve insulation in homes, to devise energy-saving machines and home appliances, to increase production of American oil, and to develop alternate energy sources. It is clear to me that the attitude of consumers has changed permanently. All of us are now conscious of the need to stop wasting energy. During and after the campaign, candidate Reagan opposed this national energy policy, but I am thankful that he and the American people will continue to enjoy the benefits of it.

Jimmy's efforts to conserve and save the taxpayers' money affected just about every part of our lives in the White House. The most painful disagreements we had were about staff. At the Governor's Mansion I had had to rely on volunteers for many things, including handling much of the mail that poured in as a result of my projects and my travels throughout the state. At the White House, I thought, I would have all the staff I needed. I was wrong. Jimmy planned to cut, not add to, the number of people working in the White House, and all my pleas fell on deaf ears. "Everybody always wants more staff, and that's why the federal government gets so overloaded," he would say to me time and again. "Anybody you talk to in the government will say, 'I need at least one more worker.'" "But I'm not anybody you talk to in government. I'm your wife!" I insisted, not always quietly.

According to the White House personnel records, I had little reason for complaint. They showed that every First Lady in recent history had drawn from staffs of similar size, the average number form 1971 to 1976 being twenty-eight persons. Betty Ford had twenty-six; I had twenty-one. A good argument for more? It didn't work. Jimmy knew as well as I did that though my number was smaller, I probably had as much help as Betty Ford. In his reorganization of the White House, the calligraphers were moved from my staff to the residence staff, and all correspondence was funneled into one unit in the West Wing. Though my staff actually numbered fewer persons, I did receive assistance from these other White House offices.

What I soon realized was that the staffs change with each administration, depending on the needs of the First Lady. In the past, if a First Lady was very active she always needed more staff and drew from other sources: Some administrations used volunteers and part-time workers; some borrowed from other agencies. Tish Baldrige, who worked for Jackie Kennedy, wrote in *Diamonds and Diplomats* that "in all, about forty people worked for me in the First Lady's Secretariat." And Lady Bird Johnson borrowed a number of people from other agencies to help with her beautification program. I tried that, borrowing a staff person from Health, Education and Welfare (HEW) who helped with my volunteer program for three months, but Jimmy discouraged that too, and with a good argument. If HEW could spare someone, then they had too much staff. He never did give in to my pleas, and though my staff was not paid overtime, the lights burned in my offices until late every evening.

Regardless of numbers, my staff and I were supposed to plan and carry out all official and social White House functions, even those involving only the President. We were responsible for all details of entertaining at teas, receptions, coffees, luncheons, dinners, and state dinners; arrangements for arrival ceremonies on the South Lawn; any lectures and briefings by the President, Vice President, Cabinet members, and senior staff; and for press coverage of most of these events. We were also responsible for sending out information about all First Family activities and about the White House, its grounds, and its history. We also had my work to do, which included the research, coordination, and implementation of all my projects. And we were already working on the details of setting up the President's Commission on Mental Health, putting together a task force to inventory federal programs for the elderly, helping make a list of qualified women for possible presidential appointments, and handling the mail addressed to the family, which averaged almost eleven thousand pieces a month!

Madeline MacBean supervised all of my correspondence, was responsible for guests and events in the family living quarters, and handled all of my personal appointments and mundane affairs, such as fittings for clothes, hair appointments, even my finances. We quickly learned that if I signed a check, people would keep it as a souvenir instead of cashing it. I had bought a pair of shoes for $69 in Calhoun, Georgia, after Jimmy was elected, for example, and I finally had to write the check off because it was never cashed. Occasionally even large checks wouldn't be cashed, so we had to put Madeline's name on the checking account. I continued to write the checks but she signed them.

When we moved in, there were seven calligraphers on the staff to handle the invitations, guest lists, menus, and place cards. Previously they had also personalized the photographs of the First Family that were requested by thousands of people, writing on each one the name of the person who had asked for it and a brief message, usually "Best Wishes." We cut the number of calligraphers to three, which meant it was my job to personalize my photographs in addition to autographing them. The job was endless. I always had a stack of photos in front of me on my desk in the bedroom or in my office. It's hard to imagine how much time a First Lady spends autographing photographs—and newspaper articles and books and signature cards and paper napkins and programs of events she attends—even quilt squares!

Many of the requests for autographs came from classes of schoolchildren, bearing each student's signature. The number was prohibitive; I couldn't send back a personal autograph to each child. Instead we had a small card printed that showed the White House, with my signature written across it with an autopen. With help from Nan Powell and Nancy Moore, the wives of two of Jimmy's senior staff members, we soon put together a small booklet to answer the thousand of requests from children for information about the White House and the First Family. Entitled "The White House . . . It's Your House Too," it included a "tour in pictures as seen through Amy's eyes," a brief history of the White House, and photographs and information about our family. It also had a question-and-answer section with the questions most often asked by children, such as, "Where does the First Family eat and sleep?" "Have any babies been born in the White House?" "How many pets are living in the White House?" The booklet proved to be a treasure. Children loved it, and it saved us much time and work.

To sort out our personal mail from the volume we received— invitations, requests for photographs and signatures, requests for assistance, letters of advice, and fan mail to all members of the family—we devised a private code. Choosing the three numbers that had been my telephone number when Jimmy and I were courting, we told our family and a few close friends to write those numbers on the outside of their letters so the mailroom would know to send them through to us.

We quickly had to develop a policy for handling gifts, too, because hundreds of them poured into the White House each week. The number and variety of gifts sent to the President and his family are astonishing. Some, like those from older people in convalescent homes who spend hours weaving potholders, crocheting little doilies for tabletops, or making fancy boxes to hold Kleenex, are from the heart. Others are more commercial and from people who want the President's name or endorsement for their products. And we learned never to mention anything we wanted. One little girl from California came to spend the night with Amy, and when she went home, she told the press that Amy wanted a chain saw for Christmas. I don't know how she confused a chain saw with an electric train, which is what Amy really wanted, but the story spread, and chain saws began arriving at the White House, even one that was red, white, and blue with stars on it. We sent them all back except one that came with a card signed by everyone in the factory where it had been made. We kept that one for the Carter presidential library!

The easiest policy was not to accept any gifts at all. That was fine until I learned that everything that came into the gift unit was being returned to the sender, unopened, and we had unintentionally hurt a lot of feelings. One group of first-graders had all written letters to the President, for instance, which were mailed in a large package that the gift unit automatically returned. The children were crushed, naturally; I heard about it only because the teacher called our Comments Office, staffed by volunteers, which handled calls from the general public trying to reach the President with problems or complaints. The point of returning the gifts had not been to hurt anyone's feelings but to make sure we were not put in the embarrassing position of having to explain why we had accepted a valuable gift and because we did not want to give one product free publicity over another. The legacy of Watergate was still very recent.

But the policy of returning every package unopened was obviously too rigid. It was much more expensive to open the packages, inspect the contents, rewrap them, and mail them back, and we were all trying to comply with Jimmy's request to be as economical as possible, but a better system had to be devised in spite of the expense. When I explained the problem to Jimmy, he agreed to change the rules, and henceforth the correspondence unit opened all the packages. They returned any that were commercial and sent solely for the purpose of advertising, donated others to various charities in the Washington area, and stored the balance in the Archives for future display in a Carter presidential library.

From the very beginning, my support as First Lady was enlisted. Betty Bumpers, the wife of the former governor of Arkansas, Senator Dale Bumpers, and an old friend of mine, had been working on a childhood immunization program to eradicate measles. She had been unable to get anyone in the Ford White House to focus on her project, with which I was familiar from my days in Atlanta. She came to me, not only as a friend, but because she knew I would bring it to the attention of Joe Califano, the secretary of the Department of Health, Education and Welfare (since 1979 the Department of Health and Human Services). I called him the same day and asked if he would talk with Betty, and Jimmy sent a note telling him to move forward on the program. During the next two years I helped them when called upon to generate publicity, or to get a wayward state in line, and the results were astounding. We reached our short-term goal of immunizing 90 percent of the nation's children by October 1979 and have now, for all practical purposes, eliminated measles in the United States. A side effect of this effort, federal health officials say, has been a decline in other serious childhood diseases, including mumps, rubella, diphtheria, and tetanus. The key was getting parents to take their children to a clinic or a doctor for their measles vaccinations, for once they were there, they got other immunizations as well.

The First Lady, no matter who she is, can be invaluable to almost any project. I got thousands of requests from individuals, from organizations, from corporations, from special interest groups, to help with their projects. It was difficult to turn down some of these worthy causes, knowing that, sometimes with little effort on my part, I could be very helpful. Tickets for fundraisers, for example, are quickly bought when an organization announces that the First Lady will be there. Making television spots or radio announcements for any cause almost guarantees that they will be put on the air. Local press coverage is always good for the First Lady no matter what she is doing, and by extension, her projects are covered. Unfortunately, at the national level, I was sometimes disappointed by the lack of coverage for what I thought was important.

One frustrating problem for Jimmy and me was letting people know what we were trying to do. Less than a month after the inauguration, I held my first press conference in the East Room and announced the President's Commission on Mental Health. A study had not been done in more than fifteen years, and we sorely needed to know whether or not we were reaching those who needed help. I had invited professionals, scientists, parents of the mentally afflicted, and volunteers to the ceremony; Jimmy appeared briefly and signed an Executive Order setting up the commission. I spoke about our plans and answered questions. The next morning when I picked up the *Washington Post* to read about it I found not one word about the commission or the press conference. Nothing! I was crushed. The *New York Times* had a good, substantive article, but the *Post*—Washington's own newspaper—had not one word.

But they carried the so-called wine story. As had been the tradition in the Governor's Mansion in Georgia—and indeed, the tradition in the White House until Kennedy was President—we had decided not to serve hard liquor on the State Floor. I had been informed that we might even save a million dollars by serving only wine and ending our state dinners before midnight so we wouldn't have to pay overtime to the staff. How many more people we could have to the White House and how many different functions, not just state dinners. And I wanted everyone to come—all those people I had met all over the country who had never had the opportunity to visit. The decision was made: We would serve wine.

The wine story created a major flap, much to our chagrin. Mary Hoyt, my press secretary, spent hours on the phone telling people that we were not trying to re-enact Prohibition. But the story continued to be covered again and again. It was frustrating. Our mental health commission was not news—I was told by the press it was not a "sexy" issue—but "no booze in the White House" obviously was. I can understand that it is much more entertaining for people to read about the glamour and excitement of beautiful clothes and celebrities and personal problems and "no booze" than it is to read about the number of people in the country who need help with mental health problems, but it didn't seem right.

It was important to me to have my mental health work covered, not so much because of my "image," although I did want people to know I was doing more than just being a hostess, but because one of the greatest problems about mental illness is that too often it is kept a dark secret. I wanted to get it out in the open.

Image, however, did become an annoyance that just wouldn't go away. I thought that if I were working productively and accomplishing something worthwhile, the image would take care of itself. Wrong. I learned that labels are easy to come by and hard to overcome. I had been called a "steel magnolia" in the campaign, to which I didn't object, and it was just as well. Once something is printed, it repeats and repeats. I learned that when reporters write new stories, they research them by reading all the old news clips, and there you are—misperceptions, false stories, and all. I had the reputation of being frugal, for example, because someone wrote while Jimmy was governor that I was so stingy I wouldn't hire anyone to cut the grass at the Governor's Mansion and I put cows on the lawn to graze instead. I hope I am frugal, but I never thought of putting cows on the lawn! Another time it was written that I was the oldest of four sisters, and ever since, reporters have asked me about my three sisters. I have one sister and two brothers.

On one occasion, John Osborne of the *New Republic*, one of the best White House reporters of our time, apologized to my press secretary for an erroneous news story that appeared after I had been to Latin America with Jimmy. On the trip I was purposely not scheduled to be at any meetings with the heads of state. The President was meeting with them, and I had already been to these countries twice and wanted to do some sightseeing. Osborne wrote that the West Wing had had a terrible time trying to keep me from joining in the meetings with Jimmy, that they practically had to muzzle me to keep a low profile because my trip before had caused troubles with the "macho Latinos." When Mary Hoyt called him in a rage to ask where he'd gained this misinformation, he said it was the sloppiest reporting he could remember and was contrite about his error. As he hung up the telephone that day, he said, "It's really too bad. I'm awfully sorry. After these things are in print... well, you know... they're in print forever."

The "steel magnolia" is in print forever. And by the end of our first year in Washington I found myself described as being "fuzzy"— which is better than having a bad image, but not as good as a good one! And it wouldn't be long before Mary was worrying about my "most powerful" image. I remember sitting on the plane, returning home after a long and exhausting three-day campaign trip, and musing that it didn't matter what I did; by virtue of a piece of gossip here or there I had gone from having a "fuzzy" image to being "most powerful."

The criticism had begun to mount when, in the second year of Jimmy's presidency, I started attending Cabinet meetings. In retrospect, I can understand why, but at the time I couldn't. Jimmy and I had always worked side by side; it's a tradition in southern families, and one that is not seen as in any way demeaning to the man. Once the press and our persistent opponents heard about my attendance at the meetings, very soon it was rumored that I was "telling" Jimmy what to do! They obviously didn't know Jimmy! But I also think there was a not very subtle implication that Cabinet meetings were no place for a wife. I was supposed to take care of the house—period.

Regardless of the "most powerful" rhetoric, which had taken on a life of its own, the Cabinet meetings were a great help to me, and I never considered not attending them because of the criticism. I had already learned from more than a decade of political life that I was going to be criticized no matter what I did, so I might as well be criticized for something I wanted to do. (If I had spent all day "pouring tea," I would have been criticized for that too.) Besides, it had been Jimmy's idea, not mine, for me to sit in on the meetings. It developed from my frustration at trying to sift through the news reports, the commentary, and the criticism, and know what Jimmy was doing. I couldn't sit in front of the television every day and wonder and worry about what I was hearing. I wanted to know the truth. One day when I was questioning Jimmy about yet another news story, he said, "Why don't you sit in on the Cabinet meetings and then you'll know what's going on and why we make the decisions."

The first Cabinet meeting I attended was on February 28, 1978. I felt quite comfortable, as there were many other people present who were not Cabinet officials: secretaries and other aides taking notes pertinent to their specific departments. I took notes myself, occasionally, if there was something I wanted to ask Jimmy about later. I would slip in and out of the meeting as my schedule allowed, sitting quietly in the background with the other non-Cabinet members. Usually I sat next to Max Cleland, the head of the Veterans' Administration, whose wheelchair was always near the door. I never participated in the discussions. I was there to be informed so that when I traveled around the country, which I did a great deal, and was questioned by the press and other individuals about all areas of government, I'd know what was going on. Or at least I'd know the general thrust of what the Carter administration was trying to do and could answer the questions with some competence and assurance.

On the days the Cabinet met, my schedule would read, as it did on Monday, November 20, 1978: "9:00 A.M. . . . FYI . . . Cabinet Meeting, the Cabinet Room . . . 2 hours." Jane Fenderson, my appointments secretary, always noted it for me and I went as often as I could, trying to keep my schedule clear if I knew something was being discussed that I needed or wanted to know about.

It was not long after Jimmy became President that he decided to test part of our national security system. The Defense Department has a specially outfitted Boeing 747 airplane, which, in the event of a nuclear attack, is available to become the temporary headquarters for the President or his surviving successor in the chain of command. Jimmy knew that this plane was supposed to be kept on alert and ready to go twenty-four hours a day so that the President and specially trained technicians could be evacuated in minutes. As far as he knew, no President had ever actually gone through the emergency procedure to be sure it would work. So on a scheduled trip home to Plains on *Air Force One*, Jimmy decided at the last minute to test the system and shifted to the airborne command airplane.

Within minutes we were in the air, a sobering experience when you considered the purpose of the plane. It is huge and has no windows; instead of rows of seats, the interior is divided into compartments containing communications equipment so the President can be in direct contact with our various missile-launching sites, our allies, and even with the leaders of the Soviet Union. Once in the air, Jimmy had an intensive instruction period with the crew and other personnel to learn the plane's capabilities. When we landed, I was greatly comforted to return to safe, peaceful, and familiar ground.

Another kind of protection was one we had with us all the time, the Secret Service.

We first had Secret Service agents assigned to us during the '76 campaign. Meeting with us in Plains, they said that from that moment on they would be with us all of the time and they explained what they would do to protect us and what we would learn to expect. They suggested, among other things, that when we were shaking hands in a crowd, we should just touch the hands and not clasp them, not only to avoid having someone's hand freeze around ours, but also to minimize the danger of being pulled into a crowd or jerked off a platform by a heavy hand. And it was easier for them, they explained, if we would move through a crowd as fast as possible and never accept anything handed to us, because there was no way to know what it really was. They still thought it would be best for Jimmy not to sign autographs in a crowd. Everything a President or family member under their protection received, including every piece of mail, would be checked first by the Secret Service.

I felt bad about disappointing people when they asked for autographs, and sometimes I would stop to sign the books or scraps of paper handed to me anyway. It was very hard to keep saying, "I'm sorry, I can't." Sometimes people would try to hand us gifts, but they were always intercepted by the Secret Service before they got to us. One day at a rally in a town in Texas, an elderly woman tried to give me a teddy bear for Amy. I was making my way through a crowd of people who were all reaching for me, and she couldn't get close enough to hand the teddy bear to me, so the crowd passed it over their heads and thrust it into my hands, only to have an agent grab it and throw it as far from me as he could. He was just doing his duty; he didn't know who offered it, and it could have exploded. But the truth is that the woman may have spent hours making the toy herself or it might have belonged to her granddaughter, who wanted Amy to have it. I felt terrible, but there was nothing I could do about it. The Secret Service agents cannot take chances.

At the White House, the agents "picked us up" from the moment we stepped off the elevator coming from our quarters, even if we were only going to be on the State Floor or the ground floor. They went with Jimmy when he went to his office, with me to mine. And they followed us at a distance as inconspicuously as possible when we walked around the grounds there or at Camp David. After a while I didn't even notice them; they were just there. But it was hard for other people to get used to them. Once when we were at Camp David I was walking with my mother, and she asked, "Who else is here this weekend?" I assured her that there were no other guests, that we were the only ones there. After a while she said, "I know there's somebody else here because someone is following us." It was the agent, but I had considered myself alone. "Just don't look back, Mother, and you'll forget they're there!"

I often had to say the same thing to Jimmy, not in the woods of Camp David, but in the motorcades that always follow a President and, to a lesser extent, a First Lady. Wherever Jimmy traveled, there was a long, long line of cars behind him carrying the press, security agents, dignitaries, and staff members and often the mayor and officials of whatever city he was in as well as friends. Sometimes there would be as many as thirty or forty cars behind him, and Jimmy didn't like that at all. Neither did he like the motorcycle escort nor the lead police car with the siren blowing. He wanted to drive casually into a community without all the fanfare, but that's not possible when you're President. When I was with him I used to say "Just don't look back, Jimmy. Don't look back!" but he usually did.

I don't ever remember being frightened about my safety when I was First Lady, but there were a few incidents that did give me cause for thought. I learned that in large crowds or complicated situations, I should do exactly what the Secret Service told me— no questions asked. If I were leaving a political rally or a meeting and one of the agents said, "Mrs. Carter, duck down and go as fast as you can to the car," I would duck and go as fast as I could to the car. Or, "Take an extra change of clothes for Charlotte [North Carolina]. You might get hit with a raw egg." I didn't know why or by whom I might get hit, but I took an extra change of clothes.

Sometimes, too, our plans and routes would be changed at the last minute to avoid threatening demonstrations. The Secret Service was very protective, and if there were even the possibility of trouble, they would get me away from the situation or stand very close to me in a crowd, ready to whisk me away if necessary. That happened in St. Louis, when Communist party members began heckling me at a rally, but I kept on shaking hands, encircled by the agents, and no danger materialized. I had one experience in the campaign, before Jimmy was President, that showed me how effective the agents could be in "whisking" me away. I was outdoors in Baltimore and about to walk down some steps into a small park when the horse of a mounted policeman nearby suddenly shied and began moving directly into my path. Immediately one of the agents picked me up, passed me to another and another, and before I knew what had happened I was standing at the bottom of the steps, well out of the way of the horse. The same thing happened to Amy, only this time it was not a horse. She had gone to a pet show at Ethel Kennedy's home when a circus elephant named Suzie broke loose and started rampaging straight toward her. The Secret Service agents picked her up and passed her over a fence just as they had passed me along. But the elephant went through the fence and they passed her back again . . . and everyone ran to the house for safety.

Apparently, the most danger the Secret Service ever thought we were in was on a trip to Venice, Italy, for an economic summit. The assassination of Aldo Moro by the Red Brigade was still uppermost in everyone's thoughts, and for the first time, Amy and I were asked to wear bulletproof outfits. I protested, but finally gave in when I realized I was creating a problem for the agents. I had a vest and raincoat, and Amy had a little blue windbreaker. They were heavy and bulky, and when I wore the vest, which fit under my clothes, I had to pin my skirt because it wouldn't meet at the waist, and I always wear a blazer or jacket of some kind to hide it. It probably felt a lot bulkier than it looked, and it was hot. Our very first outing was to a glass-blowing factory, and I had to sit in front of the red-hot kiln to watch a demonstration— I nearly suffocated from the heat. But no one ever knew except Madeline, who had to help me get in and out of it.

"Rosalynn, aren't you hot in that blazer?" or "Aren't you hot with that raincoat on?" or "Amy, do you really need a jacket?" Everyone kept asking us why we kept our coats on, but since we were traveling everywhere in Venice by boat, we could say, "We thought we might get splashed!" The raincoat was stiff and heavy, but I'm sure my posture improved during those few days—I couldn't slump. Amy took it in stride, without a complaint.

Security sometimes caused a problem for our hosts, and I tried very hard not to get involved in the details or even know about the circumstances. Once, sitting at a table in a large banquet room in Hawaii, someone told me that they had had to remove all the heavy glass ashtrays that were usually on the tables because Jimmy was going to make an appearance. On another occasion when I was campaigning, in a farmhouse in Iowa in 1980, my host was asked to move all of the furniture from one side of the room to the other. I never understood that and wouldn't have known about it if one of my press advance persons hadn't mentioned it on the plane on the way home.

I also never knew exactly how many Secret Service agents there were at the White House. The agents kept a distance, were pleasant and never answered questions from the press or volunteered any information. They were quite different from the state patrolmen at the Governor's Mansion, who opened doors for me and carried my purse, my coat, and my packages. I was very spoiled when I left the Governor's Mansion, leaving my raincoat or my purse wherever I went, depending on someone else to look after them. The Secret Service agents do none of these things; they keep their hands free at all times to protect you, and often when I am struggling with heavy packages or luggage, they are very apologetic about not being more helpful.

One of the greatest benefits of the Secret Service is that it provides privacy for those being protected. We still have agents in Plains, which, besides the protection, enables us to have a semblance of normalcy in our lives.

At the White House I soon learned that it was easier to live under the watchful eyes of the Secret Service than under the scrutiny of the press.

A few weeks after the inauguration, we decided on the way home from church to go to the Kennedy Center for the matinee of *Madame Butterfly*. We told the Secret Service agents in the car, and after lunch we just got ready and left. We didn't notify the press and we didn't notify either of our press secretaries, Mary

Rosalynn's father, Edgar Smith

Rosalynn's mother, Allie Murray Smith

Plains in 1925, with Jimmy's father's store on the corner. Rosalynn's father's garage was just to the left, out of the photograph.

Rosalynn, age 6

In the seventh grade, age 12

Rosalynn's childhood home

Jimmy as a college student, 1942

Jimmy and Rosalynn on their wedding day, July 7, 1946

Rosalynn with her family in 1951: sister Allethea, brothers Murray and Jerry, mother Allie, grandfather Captain Murray, and sons Jack and Chip

Jeff, Jack, and Rosalynn in Jimmy's 1966 campaign for governor

Victory! Jimmy is elected governor, 1970. Pictured with Chip, Rosalynn, Ruth, Jimmy, Miss Lillian

Dressed for the Governor's Inaugural Ball, January 1971: Jeff, Jack, Rosalynn, Jimmy, and Chip

Fourth of July parade on Peachtree Street in Atlanta, 1971

Jimmy taking the inaugural oath, January 20, 1977

The Carters walk down Pennsylvania Avenue, Inauguration Day, 1977.

The Inaugural Ball, January 20, 1977

In the family dining room with Miss Lillian, Judy, Chip, Sarah, Amy and her friend Kara Foster

A public meeting with members of the President's Commission on Mental Health. Dr. Tom Bryant, executive director, is seated at Rosalynn's right.

Rosalynn welcoming a guest at a White House reception for retarded citizens

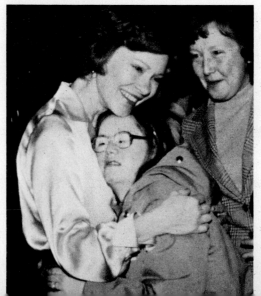

Liz Carpenter, Rosalynn, and Betty Ford at the National Women's Conference in Houston, Texas, November 1977

A working lunch in the Oval Office

Planning Rosalynn's trip to Latin America with Secretary of State Vance, the President, National Security Adviser Brzezinski, and Vice President Mondale

Being greeted at the airport in Jamaica by Prime Minister Manley on the first stop of her trip to Latin America, 1977

A lighter moment during the Camp David negotiations with President Sadat and Prime Minister Begin, September 1978

A reception for Rostropovich after his White House concert, the day the Camp David peace agreement was signed

Rosalynn dancing with the mayor of Linz, Austria, July 1978

Rosalynn and Amy with Pope John Paul II at the Vatican, May 1979

Rosalynn with Latin American leaders at the inauguration of President Bélaunde of Peru, July 1980. Left to right: a member of the Nicaraguan junta; Galo Plaza, past president of Ecuador and ambassador to the UN; President Herrera, Venezuela; President Bélaunde, Peru; President Turbay, Colombia; President Corazo, Costa Rica; a member of the Nicaraguan junta; Prime Minister Suarez, Spain

Rosalynn and Dr. Julius Richmond, the U.S. surgeon general, in a Cambodian refugee camp in Thailand, November 1979

With Soviet President Leonid Brezhnev after the signing of the SALT II Treaty in Vienna, Austria, June 1979

Viewing a gift from Vice Chairman Deng Xiaoping during a state visit following the announcement of the normalization of relations with China

Rosalynn takes a quick moment during the 1980 presidential campaign to talk with Jimmy, as her personal assistant, Madeline MacBean, stands guard.

Rosalynn and Jimmy in the Cross Hall of the White House with their grandchildren, James, Jason, and Sarah

Saying good-bye to the Mondales in the Oval Office, January 1981

At home in Plains

Hoyt or Jody Powell; as a matter of fact, we didn't even think about it. When we arrived innocently enough for the performance, a newspaper reporter who just happened to be in the audience saw us and dashed to the telephone, and the whole White House press corps descended upon us. It was then that we really understood that our private lives no longer belonged to ourselves but to the press.

Not altogether.

We did learn that we could slip away on occasion and do a few things privately. We often jogged along the C&O Canal, fished at Spruce Creek, Pennsylvania, walked in the fields on our farms at home, and vacationed on an island off the coast of Georgia out of view of the television cameras and reporters.

You would have thought I'd have learned my lesson after the *Madame Butterfly* incident, but a few weeks later, Madeline and I slipped out of the White House without telling Mary and flew to New York on a commercial airline to buy clothes on Seventh Avenue. I thought an unobtrusive shopping expedition would fill my needs without focusing attention on "the First Lady's wardrobe," something I wanted to avoid. Madeline and I spent the whole afternoon looking at the clothes of Kasper and Jerry Silverman and other designers in the building, and when we finished it was very late. Just as we walked out the front door flashbulbs blinded us—it seemed that the whole New York press corps was waiting for me. There was such a mob that the Secret Service had to be very rough in clearing a path to the car. It didn't help that on the way back to Washington, one of the other passengers on the plane heard that I was aboard and jokingly referred to a bomb in his package—and was arrested. It was only a vase, but later we had to help get him out of jail.

My quiet little shopping trip had turned into a fiasco, and when I got back to the White House, Mary was furious with me—well, chagrined. She of course knew where I had been: Her telephone had been ringing off the hook. At first she told everybody I was in the mansion, which she thought was true until word came over the wires that I was in New York City. Helen Thomas, from the White House press corps, said to her, "If you don't even know where the First Lady is, you're not going to be much good around here," which didn't smooth her ruffled feelings very much. And in spite of my trying to downplay my wardrobe, all my new clothes made the news. The next morning there was a list in the newspaper of every article I had bought—and a few I hadn't!

Our family had always been closely knit and had worked together in the past, and our years in the White House were no different. Chip, besides working for the Democratic National Committee, ran errands for his father and carried messages. During the blizzards of 1977, Jimmy sent him to snowbound Buffalo, New York, to assure the people there of his concern for their plight. Jeff and Annette represented the United States at the funeral of President Jomo Kenyatta of Kenya, and the Africans were overwhelmed. In Africa the son of a family is revered, and the fact that the President of the United States would send his own son to the funeral said words to them that we could not have expressed in any other way. The countries of the Third World yearn for some contact with the United States, and we learned early how much it meant to them to have personal contact with the President through a member of his family.

Selecting the delegation to attend the funeral of a foreign leader or world statesman in an important function of the State Department and the President's office. The group usually includes several congressmen and other well-known or distinguished Americans. Jimmy's office always suggested names and tried to make the delegation one that would have significance for the country and its people, and as often as possible he sent a member of our family as well.

Shortly after Jimmy took office, Ali Ahmed Fakhruddin, the president of India, died, and Jimmy thought it would show great respect if his mother attended the funeral. Because of her work there in the Peace Corps, Miss Lillian was very popular in India. Jimmy called her in Plains and said, "Mama, how would you like to go to India?" "I'd love to," she replied. "When?" "This afternoon," Jimmy said. Miss Lillian didn't hesitate. "This afternoon? I'll be ready!" She immediately flew from Plains to Washington. The protocol for funerals in many countries requires that women be completely covered in black: a long black dress with high neck and long sleeves, a head covering, black shoes and stockings, and no jewelry or makeup. We sent a selection of dresses to the airport, and after choosing one, Miss Lillian was on her way to India. Jimmy was right. She was the perfect choice. After the funeral she went back to Vikhroli, the village, close to Bombay, where she had lived for two years, and people turned out by the thousands to greet her. When she got back home, the State Department said she had contributed more toward good relations with India than anyone since 1960.

Even Amy joined in the activities, being a good sport when the situation demanded it. We had a White House reception to highlight a Department of Energy conservation program for children, the Captain America/Youth Conservation campaign. Hundreds of children came, and the Campbell Soup Kids, the Incredible Hulk, Spider Woman, and other Marvel comic characters were on hand. Any, who had been looking forward to it, had had her braces tightened that morning, and when she got home from school her teeth hurt so much she was crying. She was supposed to go out on the lawn, and all of the children were waiting to see her. We stopped by Dr. Lukash's office on the way out and washed her face and dried her tears. She thought she was all right so we started out, but she began to cry again. We went back into the doctor's office, took out her contacts, and put some drops in her eyes, and she bravely walked out onto the lawn for her appearance. Once outside, she saw some of her friends and she was all right. I was proud of her. She never considered not joining the crowd, even when I suggested that she go upstairs and lie down for a while.

Another time, when Amy was supposed to be on the South Grounds to unveil a poster for the new Department of Education with Secretary Shirley Hufstedler, we waited and waited. She had gone to her room to get ready, and when she didn't come out, I finally went to see what was keeping her. I found her—sound asleep in the bathtub! She did make it downstairs, albeit a little late!

It seems incredible now, looking back at my schedule, how hard we all worked at the White House right from the beginning. Reviewing my first fourteen months as First lady, the *Washington Star* added up the number of public appearances I had made, in addition to the work I was doing in my office or at night. According to the *Star*, I visited 18 nations and 27 U.S. cities, held 259 private meetings and 50 public meetings, made 15 major speeches, held 22 press conferences, gave 32 interviews with individual journalists, had 77 hours of briefings, attended 83 official receptions and social functions, held 26 special-interest and group meetings at the White House, spent more than 300 hours working in mental health, received 152,000 letters and 7939 invitations, signed 150 photographs a week, and made 16 public appearances around Washington, D.C.! It makes me tired to think of it all.

Early on I was presented with a new challenge.

~❦~ 7 ~❦~

Envoy to Latin America

When Jimmy was running for President, he said over and over again, "We have neglected our friends among the community of nations, and if I am elected President, I will do my best to reach out to these friends once again."

A few months later after the inauguration, Jimmy came home one night and asked if I would go on a special mission for him. He was so busy setting in motion a host of domestic and foreign policy initiatives, including the national energy program, the Panama Canal treaties, the Middle East peace effort, and the SALT II negotiations, that he had time only for one major trip at the beginning—an economic summit in London. The Vice President was helping him on everything and also undertook, on the President's behalf, an important trip to consult with our NATO allies. In the meantime, the Latin American countries had some real problems we needed to acknowledge, and it was necessary for us to show in a dramatic way our commitment to human rights and democracy in our own hemisphere. Jimmy and his security advisers agreed that more than an official State Department visit was necessary; someone close to him should make this carefully structured trip. Would I be willing to go?

I would have to study the many complicated issues of concern to the Latin leaders; I would be in the spotlight, with everyone watching to see how I performed, because this was not a conventional thing to do; and I might be put in a difficult and embarrassing position. But, he said, it could help him tremendously in letting the people of Latin America and the Caribbean countries know that he was genuinely interested in them.

I didn't have to think twice: "Yes, I'll go!"

Jimmy and I had long had an interest in Latin America. We had traveled in Central and South America and had many friends there, and we had studied Spanish for as long as I could remember. Jimmy spoke it well, but I had never been fluent. I planned to be, though: Several weeks earlier I had begun taking lessons three mornings a week with Gay Vance, the wife of the secretary of state, Evan Dobelle, the chief of protocol, and his wife, Kit, and my daughters-in-law Caron and Annette.

The whole field of foreign relations was new and exciting for me. Less than a month after we moved into the White House, I had attended a briefing on foreign affairs that Jimmy had arranged for his senior staff members and their spouses so they could understand the basic foreign policy issues he would be facing. The briefing was conducted by the National Security Council adviser, Zbigniew Brzezinski, who gave us an overall assessment of world politics and also discussed some of the objectives the Carter administration would pursue. Even before the inauguration, Jimmy, together with his top advisers and the congressional leaders of both parties, had made a list of the things he wanted to accomplish, which included completing the Panama Canal treaties, normalizing relations with China, developing closer rapport with Latin America, working toward peace in the Middle East, establishing a stronger and more credible U.S. presence in Africa, and negotiating a SALT II treaty. And the cornerstone of his foreign policy would be a deep regard for the human rights of all peoples.

Going through a long, question-filled campaign, living in the White House where decisions were made almost every hour, and traveling with Jimmy throughout the world, talking with people, I had come to understand how world events could affect us and to realize as never before the impact on other nations of the actions of our country . . . sometimes even those things that happen around Plains, Georgia. I realized for the first time that when we have a crop failure at home, our farmers are not the only ones affected. The Israelis tell a story about Levi Eshkol, shortly after he became prime minister. One of his aides came in with bad news: He had just become aware of a serious drought. Eshkol's face became clouded, and he asked where it was. "In the Negev" came the reply. Eshkol smiled with relief. "For a moment I thought you meant in Kansas!"

Our crop failures, other misfortunes and fortunes, and the policy decisions of our country have far-reaching consequences for others.

I had come to realize more clearly, also, as I made new friends around the world, the extent to which our basic concerns for food, health, a better life for our children, human dignity, and peace are shared the world over.

During the campaign I used to say, when asked about foreign affairs, "The best thing we can do about foreign affairs is to get our house in order at home." The strength of our country abroad *is* greatest when we are unified and politically healthy at home. Conversely, our influence is reduced because of Watergate or any scandal that soils the world's image of the United States and our sense of ourselves. Now for the first time I would have a personal responsibility to try to comprehend the complexities of specific and sometimes controversial international issues.

My visit was scheduled for the first two weeks of June 1977, two months away, and I began to prepare. I had hours of briefings by scholars from all over the country and by officials from the State and Treasury departments, the National Security Council, and the Organization of American States. I learned the history of our relations with each country I was to visit as well as the current issues we had to face. I studied the speeches Jimmy had made on foreign affairs, especially as they applied to the Latin American countries.

While I wasn't in these briefing sessions or at my Spanish lessons, I was reading everything I could about Latin America, including novels and poetry. I was to be what the State Department called a "portavoz," or spokesperson for the government, and almost everyone seemed nervous about it...except Jimmy and me.

Officials at the State Department thought I might inadvertently make promises or commitments during the trip that our government would not be able to honor. Various members of Congress were opposed because I was a woman going into very male territory. Dante Fascell, a congressman from Florida, walked into one of my briefing sessions and said bluntly, "The Latins are macho and they hate gringos and women. What else do you want to know?"

Some diplomats in Latin America were just as doubtful, saying, in effect: "In some nations you will visit, women are still treated as they were in the nineteenth century in Europe and the United States . . . decorative, useful in the home, but that's all." And one European diplomat was quoted in *U.S. News and World Report* as saying: "I don't think any Latin American statesman will take her seriously, even if she is the wife of the President of the United States."

Criticisms aside, I knew the issues and I had Jimmy's support. I knew some of the leaders I was going to meet would undoubtedly be hesitant about having substantive conversations with a woman. But I also knew that the critics who said I was wasting my time were wrong. Every one of the leaders wanted to talk to the President of the United States. And who is closer to the President, who better has his ear, than his wife? Moreover, as Jimmy noted when he announced my trip, I had long been his "partner." It was natural for him to turn to me to take on a challenge that was special and personal to him. Clearly, what I had to do was convince the critics, the press, and the leaders themselves that I was not only prepared but eager to discuss the issues and report what I learned directly to the President. I was *determined* to be taken seriously.

The countries I was to visit had been selected by the President and advisers from the State Department and the National Security Council. They chose those countries that were either already democracies or leaning toward democracy: Jamaica, Costa Rica, Ecuador, Peru, Brazil, Colombia, and Venezuela. My visit to Brazil was especially important, as relations had become strained since Jimmy's election because of their apparent move toward nuclear capability and some human rights abuses. A good relationship with the largest of the Latin American countries was a high priority, particularly as we hoped that would reinforce trends toward democratization in Brazil.

Bob Pastor, our national security adviser for Latin American affairs, was young and articulate, had studied Latin America for years, and was enormously helpful to me; he seemed to know all the answers. Terry Todman, assistant secretary of state for Latin American affairs, was also to travel with us. He had been our ambassador to Costa Rica and knew the Latin American scene. When I met with the foreign heads of state, Bob and Terry were always there, as was our ambassador to that nation. They were a wonderful backup for me, occasionally passing me a slip of paper with a comment or a suggestion for another question or point to convey to the head of state, and their copious notes were relayed back to the appropriate officials in Washington.

Before I left home, I made a brief summary of the administrations's foreign policy approach, particularly as it applied to Latin America and the Caribbean, and each time I met with a head of state I would briefly go over the summary. This would take me five or ten minutes, and provided an overview of Jimmy's approach to the region and let the leader know I was informed and could enter into a productive conversation. We would then move on to a discussion of his country's particular problems as well as regional and global issues.

In my preliminary remarks, I tried to convey the emphasis Jimmy intended to place on human rights and the enhancement of democracy in our hemisphere, the reduction of arms sales and the nonproliferation of nuclear weapons, economic progress and a commitment to narrow the gap between developed and developing countries, and a respect for the sovereignty and recognition of the individuality of each Latin American government.

Jimmy wanted the leaders to know that his definition of human rights meant not only freedom from political oppression, but also social and economic progress: that all people should have a right to the basic needs of life—food, clothing, education, shelter— as well as a voice in their own future. To downplay any sense of paternalism toward these countries and to avoid sounding moralistic, I was to point out that the United States did not have a perfect human rights record in terms of our own minorities and our attitudes toward women. But I would add, "We're working on our shortcomings." To emphasize his commitment to human rights, Jimmy signed the American Convention on Human Rights while I was in Costa Rica, the country in which it had been negotiated in 1969. The convention is an agreement among the countries of the Americas that human rights will be respected and guaranteed. With the exception of Costa Rica and Colombia, which had already taken the action, I was to urge the leaders of the other countries to sign and ratify the convention. For some, this was a difficult issue, but I had partial success. (Jimmy stressed this concern also, and by the end of his term, thirteen countries had ratified the convention, bringing it into effect.)

The Carter position on nuclear arsenals was clear: We needed to halt the proliferation of nuclear explosives, reduce nuclear arsenals, and eventually eliminate nuclear weapons from the face of the earth. Jimmy's hope was to make Central and South America a "nuclear-free" zone, and there was a treaty named after a suburb in Mexico City, Tlatelolco, where it was signed in 1967, which when ratified would be just that. (It prohibited the placement of nuclear weapons in Latin America and the Caribbean.) It was another of the OAS treaties that had not been signed by previous U.S. presidents and Jimmy signed it in the presence of a very pleased Mexican foreign minister before I left on my trip, and then asked that I encourage everyone that I visited to bring the treaty into force. The prospects for the success of this treaty, however, were being battered by Brazil's recent purchase of a nuclear reprocessing plant from West Germany, which could give Brazil the capability to produce atomic weapons.

In the area of arms sales to the emerging nations, the administration's policy was controversial. It meant reducing sales; not introducing new, sophisticated weapons into a region that had never had them; and seeking an agreement among arms suppliers and purchasers alike to limit arms transfers. The armaments race among some of the Latin countries was not only dangerous, but the huge expense was crippling economies that could ill afford it, threatening the stability of these countries and our hemisphere.

What we hoped would please the leaders I talked with was the acknowledgment that for too long we had lumped the countries together under one umbrella policy for all of Latin America and the Caribbean. We had not recognized that each country was unique, with its own issues, problems, and strengths. I was to emphasize that from now on, each country would be approached as an individual entity.

Besides these major issues, the problems of the individual countries were many and varied, including trade and commodities issues, energy resources, and the difficulties of obtaining loans from international institutions. I was not to defend any policy errors of the past, I was told, but to listen to the problems of the present. Neither was I to promise anything or give the impression that the United States was trying to tell a country what to do. Repairing our reputation of paternalism was a high priority during this trip. (I made one gaffe in Venezuela, saying I valued our "special relationship," which in diplomatic parlance, I discovered, directly denotes paternalism.) And I was to emphasize that I was not there to give aid but to address their needs in a much broader and more helpful way.

On May 30, we were off!

There were nineteen in my party, including Bob Pastor and Terry Todman, several other state department officials, Gay Vance, Kit Dobelle, a nurse, the Secret Service agents, and my secretary and press secretary. Accompanying us on an Air Force Boeing 707 were twenty-seven members of the press. To make sure nobody's baggage was overlooked during our many stops, the State Department had designed an identification tag for the luggage bearing my initials, RSC, in script. When the President traveled, his entourage was always identified by tags bearing the presidential seal, and similarly appropriate symbols were used for groups traveling with the Vice President or the secretary of state. Since the First Lady has no identifying seal, her symbol is designed personally for her, and I liked mine.

Our first stop was Jamaica, and, though it was raining, we were warmly received by Prime Minister Michael Manley and his wife. Mrs. Manley was a radio personality in her own right and had visited us in Atlanta while Jimmy was governor. We had exchanged gifts, and a painting she had given me was still hanging in our home in Plains. But I was curious to meet the prime minister. My State Department briefing book had described Manley as a leader "as magnetic as any that exists," a fiery orator, suave and sophisticated. And he was all those things: Tall, with graying, curly hair, Michael Manley was both handsome and charming.

The purpose of my trip to Jamaica was to demonstrate our interest in the country and in the Caribbean as a whole. Jamaica's problems were typical of those of the new and developing Caribbean countries. The visit was to be seen as an indication of friendship, not as an endorsement of the prime minister's policies, which he termed democratic socialist.

Manley seemed especially pleased by my visit. He had correctly judged that I would convey to my husband the substance of our discussions, and he was eager for Jimmy to know and understand his situation. Jamaica was in the throes of political and economic crises; in fact, its economy was on the verge of collapse. The high cost of oil was hurting the developing countries most, Manley told me, because there was no way these countries could manage their internal economies while spending so much on energy. Jamaica was the perfect case in point, he said, because 97 percent of the energy of the island was derived from oil that they had to purchase. His nation was further strained by an official 25 percent unemployment rate (which privately was said to be closer to 40 percent). Jamaica's position was now desperate and they needed massive economic assistance, to the tune of $200 million, at a time that Congress was debating whether or not to give them $10 million.

But while Manley was actively courting the United States, he was also an avid supporter of Fidel Castro and Cuba, an attitude that was not advancing his cause in Congress or with the President. We spent a good deal of time talking about his policies of "democratic socialism" and his close association with Castro. His skill at oratory became quickly apparent as he defended Cuba's policies, in spite of the facts. Insisting that Cuba was not the country of fifteen years earlier, when it was exporting revolution, the prime minister said Cuba's relationship with Jamaica had been absolutely principled. Cuba had assisted them in building dams, schools, and fisheries and in providing medical care while never asking for anything in return, not even to vote a certain way in the United Nations.

I was prepared for the private debate. When Manley claimed that the Jamaican government had endorsed Cuban intervention in Angola because they went in only after South Africa had also intervened, I pointed out that the Cuban troops had set sail for Angola well before the South Africans arrived. And when Manley insisted that the Russians were unhappy about the Cuban involvement in Angola, he was quickly reminded that Cuba could not have mounted a military offensive without Soviet assistance. In spite of Manley's desire for the United States to normalize relations with Cuba, I told him we could not if the Cubans continued to have military forces in Africa, to foment revolution in the Caribbean, and to violate the most rudimentary concepts of human rights. I was authorized, however, to tell the prime minister about our nation's intention to open a diplomatic interest section in Cuba, technically in the Swiss embassy, and for the Cubans to do the same in Washington under the auspices of the Czech embassy. It was a first and important step in repairing some of the broken diplomatic ties with Cuba, and Manley seemed encouraged by my news.

Manley was widely recognized as a leader and effective spokesman for the poorer countries in the Third World, and many of his concerns would be echoed by the other leaders I met. Oil-poor countries like Jamaica needed not only relief from their energy dependence, but a more realistic definition of "poverty" in order to secure loans from international financial institutions, which he said required a more balanced budget in the countries in order to qualify. This requirement, Manley warned, would force his government to cancel work programs, thereby increasing unemployment and setting off sociopolitical repercussions that could threaten Jamaica's stability.

I felt that Manley was holding up his relationship with Cuba as a threat to us—"If you don't come through with the money, I'm going to Cuba for help"—but his problems were very real and the timing critical.

I listened carefully to his thoughts on trade and the need for a new structure for the developing countries. He likened Jamaica's trade deficit and financial dependencies to the subsidizing of American farmers by the U.S. government. "The Third World are those farmers at large," Manley said. He was in favor of "indexing," adjusting the prices paid to poorer countries for basic materials to the prices paid for finished goods. Without such indexing, he said, the developing countries would continue to fall further and further behind, although he acknowledged that indexing might tend to set off an inflationary spiral.

Jamaica had been badly treated and misunderstood by Secretary of State Henry Kissinger during the Ford administration, the prime minister continued, and he had been pushed into a closer relationship with Cuba. He had not received the assistance he needed from us, and for a time he even suspected that the CIA was planning the overthrow of his government. Now he knew that things were going to be better. I realized that he was wooing me so I would put in a good word for him when I got back to Washington.

Throughout these discussions I took notes (as I would with other leaders as well), adding points I wanted to take up with Manley during subsequent meetings. Afterward I would write down these "talking points" on a card and keep it in my purse, where it would be a handy reminder during the official banquets or as I rode to a reception. At the end of each session with a leader, I would write a long memorandum to be wired back to the President and the State Department. I included virtually everything that had happened and been said, leaving it to the experts in Washington to interpret the information.

I even wrote notes to the staff members who were with me. We had been so thoroughly warned about our rooms and even our embassies being bugged that we were afraid to say anything of substance to each other. I believed the warnings. Chip had told me that on one foreign trip, he had remarked in his hotel room that he had run out of cigarettes. Within minutes there was a knock on the door, and a young man said, "Mr. Carter, I have some cigarettes for you."

During a break in the morning session in Jamaica, I went to the ladies' room with Madeline MacBean and Mary Hoyt, neither of whom had attended the meeting. This was my first "leader" and my first discussion, but I couldn't tell them anything about it. Instead, we purposefully made small talk while we wrote messages back and forth on a book of matches: "His economy is crumbling." "He wants $ from the U.S," and "He says he wants to break away from Cuba."

All in all, the trip to Jamaica was considered a success. After the chill in relations under the previous Republican administrations, my very presence signaled a renewed American interest. I spent seven hours in substantive talks with Prime Minister Manley, which I hoped would be helpful to the administration in understanding his situation. After some initial hesitation, he promised to sign the American Convention on Human Rights, and by the time I left, he had even pledged to lobby for its ratification at an upcoming Caribbean Community meeting. And our government eventually approved a reasonable aid package for Jamaicans and contacted the International Monetary Fund, the World Bank, and the Inter-American Development Bank on their behalf.

I was very pleased by the wire an embassy offical sent to the White House Situation Room as we left Jamaica: "In so far as the ordinary Jamaican was concerned, as it was very much a visit by a kind of queen, and thus a matter of great pleasure and satisfaction." And on we went to Costa Rica.

I learned a lot from my first stop, and I gained confidence as we progressed from one country to another. I had similar discussions with all the leaders, invariably spending hours more than the scheduled time with each one. I came to like the difficult talks more than the easy ones. It was a challenge to confront an argumentative leader in a friendly way about a controversial issue.

And I realized I had worried in vain about how I would be received. All of the leaders were as anxious to know about Jimmy as he was to know about them, and they all knew I would carry their concerns directly back to him rather than to a desk at the State Department. I did both.

Our reception in Costa Rica was just as warm as it had been in Jamaica, with thousands of people waiting along the highways to greet me. Costa Rica, long a friend of the United States, historically has remained the purest democracy in Central America. One reason for its success is that Costa Rica has no army, permitting the government to spend much of its money on social development. They had achieved a 96 percent literacy rate, a vivid lesson for other peoples who squander so much of their wealth on preparations for war. At a school for mentally retarded and deaf children, I was told by a teacher that there was a place in school for all children, including the physically and mentally handicapped. There is also great interest in the arts in Costa Rica, and we heard a wonderful performance by some members of their National Youth Symphony, in which six thousand children take part. They played so beautifully that I invited them to come to the White House; the next year they performed in an open-air concert on the South Lawn.

Daniel Oduber, the president of Costa Rica, was a stocky, attractive man who spoke excellent English and was a very popular democratic leader not only in his country but throughout Latin America and much of Europe. Nevertheless, it was not easy for me to carry on a conversation with him during my twenty-four-hour visit. Like many of the other leaders, Oduber didn't know how to treat me, and when I saw that he had invited his wife to join us at our first meeting, I realized that he expected my visit to be a social one. No matter what I asked him, he would answer to the men in our party. I was determined to get his attention and to have my say, and finally, when I opened my notebook and continued to address questions directly to him, he began to respond to me.

Although Oduber said he was reluctant to "bother" me on the subject of trade, I encouraged him to do so. Costa Rica was the number one Latin American supplier of bananas, coffee, chayote (Indian squash), and beef to the United States, but because we limited imports, the economy of Costa Rica was suffering. Since it was such a small country, Oduber pointed out, even the smallest increase in U.S. imports would make a big difference to them. Developing countries should be given preferential treatment in trade agreements, Oduber argued, but in fact, Australia and New Zealand appeared to get preferential treatment in the U.S. market. We talked more about trade issues and the need for developing new markets for Latin American products.

Costa Rica has been an important leader in human rights, and Oduber was very interesting on the subject. Some Central American countries had moved backward in this area, he said, while most English-speaking countries in the Caribbean had moved forward. But, Oduber said, U.S. policy should be more one of reward than punishment: Countries that were defenders of human rights deserved special treatment, not only in trade agreements, but in loans and assistance as well. This was especially important because of the inherent difficulties in democratic countries. Dictators sometimes got loans more easily, Oduber pointed out, because they appeared to do things more quickly and efficiently.

When I asked Oduber what message he wanted me to take back to the President, he said to tell him that Costa Rica was firmly behind him on the issue of human rights, demilitarization, and the need to reduce arms spending across the board. But he also told me to warn President Carter that if the high price of coffee (then $3 a pound), which had raised the standard of living of the Costa Ricans, were to drop precipitously, the government might have to purchase weapons to "combat the social chaos" that would follow.

Before I left, President Oduber pledged to increase his country's contribution to the Inter-American Commission on Human Rights, a commission of the Organization of American States that investigates human rights violations among the member countries. And I said I would talk to Jimmy about increasing Costa Rica's beef exports to the United States, though I could not promise anything specifically. I was delighted by the thawing of Oduber's stiffness toward me, but was quickly deflated when I was questioned by the press, who were far more interested in asking me about Robert Vesco, the American financier who had been accused of a multimillion-dollar fraud in the United States and who had sought refuge in Costa Rica five years earlier. At every press conference, the Vesco questions outnumbered all the others. I had anticipated this before leaving Washington and had refrained from being briefed about him so I could legitimately claim ignorance of the situation.

I wanted to leave that question to the courts and the Justice Department. The subject never came up in any of my discussions with the leaders of Costa Rica, and my truthful answer to all the questions was: "I know nothing about the Vesco situation."

Our arrival in Quito, Ecuador, was both welcoming and chilly at the same time. The weather was cold and windy, the altitude of 9300 feet enervating, and the military presence everywhere. This was the first country of my trip under military rule, a junta made up of an Army and an Air Force general and an admiral. In contrast to the schoolchildren who welcomed us at the airport in San Jose, helmeted soldiers dressed in olive drab rimmed the airport; the band was made up of gray-clad military men; and the presidential guard in blue and white colonial uniforms all stood at attention during our arrival. I reviewed the troops and then was greeted by the wives of the three leaders. They were friendly, but not totally at ease with me. To break the ice, I spontaneously decided to shake the hands of some of the hundreds of people who had come to the airport to greet me. The response was immediate, and when I left Ecuador, it had become one of my favorite countries.

After the first few days of my trip, news swept ahead that I was talking about substantive issues, and in each of the remaining countries the leaders were more prepared for my visit.

As such, my first meeting with the military regime of Ecuador was formal and stiff. The Carter adminstration had stopped their purchase of sophisticated airplanes from Israel, and several years before Jimmy became President, their trade advantages as a Third World country had been taken away because of their membership in OPEC. They were determined to give me their side of the story to take back home.

There were five in my group on one side of a long table and more than twenty on the other side, including the three military leaders, known as the Supreme Council, the head of the Joint Chiefs of Staff, and the secretaries for Foreign Affairs, Domestic Affairs, and the other government departments. They were all in uniform, and the atmosphere was hardly welcoming. I had come to express our country's admiration for the junta's policy of *retorno*, a commitment to return the government to civilian democratic rule, and to dismiss our controversial trade policies. After the OPEC embargo of oil shipments to the United States in 1973, Congress had voted to eliminate U.S. preferential trade benefits (or GSP, Generalized System of Trade Preferences, which consisted of duty-free treatment to the developing countries on certain products) to all OPEC countries. Mistakenly, both Ecuador and Venezuela, also a member of OPEC, had been included in this category, although neither country had participated in the oil embargo. The government of Ecuador was naturally angry, so much so that the government had canceled its invitation to Henry Kissinger in 1976. I was the first high-ranking U.S. representative to visit Ecuador in nearly twenty years; the last time, the country had played host to Vice President Richard Nixon and pummeled him with eggs.

But the big issue now was Ecuador's resentment over the U.S. interference into their negotiations with Israel for twenty-four Kfir fighter planes. Because these planes used American-made parts, our government had to approve their sale to Third World countries. When we did not approve the proposed sale to Ecuador, they felt we left them threatened and defenseless. I explained that our government's actions were not directed solely at Ecuador but were part of the Carter policy not to introduce new sophisticated weapons into any region. Admiral Alfredo Poveda, the president of the Supreme Council, argued that Peru had already purchased tanks and fighter bombers from the Soviets, so we would not be introducing new weapons into their region. The Ecuadorian officials were fearful that Peru was planning to attack. Not only was the hundredth anniversary of the War of the Pacific coming up the next year, a war in which Ecuador had been forced to cede almost one-third of its territory to Peru, but oil fields had been discovered in Ecuador close to the Peruvian border. To the Ecuadorian government the handwriting was on the wall, and they needed American help.

Our first meeting, scheduled to last ninety minutes, went on for over three hours. Since the members of the junta could not speak English and I was not completely at ease in Spanish, the translation took some of the time. I addressed my remarks mostly to Admiral Poveda, who became friendlier as the hours of discussion wore on. General Luis Guillermo Duran of the Army and General Luis Anibal Leoro of the Air Force each joined in occasionally, asking for special help for their services: radar and antitank missiles, technical training for pilots and other personnel, and a standing request for two destroyers and other auxiliary ships. As an alternative to offensive weapons, we discussed the possibility of our helping them to establish an effective air surveillance system.

Ecuador's concern over the arms buildup in Peru was shared by the United States, and I promised the junta that I would relay their concern not only to Jimmy but to the leaders of Peru, the next country on my itinerary. Finally we adjourned, to take up the remaining points of discussion over dinner that evening, which by then had become the general pattern.

We spent two nights in Quito, where the schedule, though planned to be light because of the effects of the high altitude, became very full due to the extended discussions and last-minute changes (the father of our ambassador to Ecuador, Richard Bloomfield, had died the day before our arrival). As it turned out, my duties throughout the trip were heavier than the President's on his own official visits: I assumed the official responsibilities *plus* the chores of a First Lady!

There were receptions to attend, informal luncheons with wives, side strips to show my interest in health and education projects, and the inevitable formal banquet held by the government. One of the visits in Quito was to the Supreme Electoral Tribunal, where I talked with the members about their plans to complete the return to democracy; another was to the Working Boys' Center, which took homeless boys from the street, educated them, and taught them to be self-sufficient. The boys, who worked when they weren't in school, gave me a carved wooden statue of a young shoeshine boy, which I kept on the mantelpiece in our bedroom at the White House and have now in Plains. The center was run by American Jesuit priests, nuns, and Peace Corps volunteers and had been constructed with U.S. AID funds. It is sustained by private contributions from the United States and is a wonderful example of what people in our country can do to help those in need in the Third World.

During all these activities we were watched closely, for fear the altitude would take its toll, and on occasion we were offered pure oxygen to breathe. We needed it to keep going, and it worked.

By dinnertime, I was well acquainted with the leaders of the country and looked forward to our conversation. After discussing again briefly the controversial issue of their exclusion from trade preferences, the conversation took a lighter turn. We talked and joked freely about families, different lifestyles, internal politics, religion, and plans for the future. I praised Admiral Poveda and the generals for their willingness to establish a democratic government. I told them that I knew it was hard for them to give up their power, but that the whole world admired them for it. Admiral Poveda said, "When we first announced it, the other military governments in South America thought we were loco, but we were very serious."

Proof of their seriousness was evident. Galo Plaza Lasso, a past president of Ecuador and former secretary-general of the OAS, was chairman of the tribunal to oversee voter registration and the writing and adoption of a constitution. He was one of the most distinguished men in the country and a good friend. (While with OAS, he had come to Atlanta for a visit and spent three nights in the Governor's Mansion.) He told me that they had already registered everyone up to those whose names started with S. And though many people in Ecuador were illiterate, they all had transistor radios, which kept them up to date about politics and other events in the country. It was through the radio announcements that they knew about the voter registration drive as well as about my visit. The day before I arrived, an American tourist buying fruit from a roadside stand was approached by a shepherd from the hills. "You are an American, and I know that you will see Mrs. Carter while she is here," he said. "Please tell her for me that all the shepherds in Ecuador are praying for her and her husband."

Our visit to Ecuador was helpful. Not only did Admiral Poveda pledge to sign and ratify the American Convention on Human Rights, but our support for their move toward democracy was very important. I was beginning to believe that being a woman in Latin America was more an asset than a liability. I could get away with a lot of things another representative of our government could never do. Unlike official visitors from the State Department, who said the expected things, I could say the unexpected. After having been through formal meetings, at dinner I would sit on the leader's right and the mood would be very relaxed and informal. Admiral Poveda was no exception. Laughingly, I said to him that evening, having talked all morning about the need to arm his country, "See what you could do for your people if you just didn't spend all your money on so many weapons. You could educate them all as Costa Rica does. Then you could be a real hero!" I wasn't really teasing, and he knew it.

Though by now the leaders of the countries were taking me

seriously and the questions about my credentials were diminishing, one critical U.S. reporter persisted as I was leaving Ecuador, "You have neither been elected by the American people nor confirmed by the Senate to discuss foreign policy with foreign heads of state," he said. "Do you consider this trip an appropriate exercise of your position?" I tried to have patience, but considering the many important issues he should have addressed, this time I'm afraid I snapped at him, "I am the person closest to the President of the United States, and if I can explain his policies and let the people of Latin America know of his great interest and friendship, I intend to do so!"

Peru was the fourth country on our itinerary, a visit I had long anticipated. We had old friends there from Navy submarine days, and I was going to have a chance to see them again after twenty-five years. I was excited but exhausted. I had been getting up before daybreak to study for my meetings and continuing again into the nights, with papers spread around me in bed. And though it was an exhilarating experience, it was also taxing. Besides the meetings with the leaders, I was holding news conferences and dealing with some very delicate subjects before the international press, and I had to be constantly on guard against making a mistake that would embarrass our country and hurt our relationship with the host country. We also planned a few days of rest at a small resort, La Granja Azul, just outside Lima. I would be ready for it.

The trip was getting tougher. Like Ecuador, Peru was governed by the military and led by General Francisco Morales Bermúdez of the Army, who preferred the title "president." Though he seemed pleased at the attention from the United States that my visit indicated, he was not waiting breathlessly to pour out his concerns to me.

Morales Bermúdez was tall, slender, erect, and serious in his uniform. But after a pleasant beginning, it soon became obvious that he did not relish the idea of being confronted with his well-known arms buildup, a subject I tried to address from the beginning of our private talks. There were very few people at our first meeting—only six or seven, including Bob Pastor and Terry Todman, and our ambassador, Harry Shlaudeman.

The president listened politely enough as I proceeded with my introductory remarks on the Carter policy, but when I started talking about our concern with the arms buildup in Peru and the millions of dollars spent on arms from Russia, he began to shift in his seat. I continued, telling him that I had just been to Ecuador and that the Ecuadorians were concerned that Peru might attack them. When he saw that I intended to pursue this sticky subject, his attitude changed abruptly. He rose to his feet and walked to a desk to get his notes. He said he was prepared to discuss these issues, but frankly wasn't certain that I was. Now that he had heard me, he felt he would need to review his notes.

Just as Ecuador was worried about Peru, Peru was worried about the intentions of Chile and other neighboring countries. Peru is bordered by five other countries that have historically been adversaries, and Morales Bermúdez was passionate in his goal to build up a strong national defense system. Over and over again he stressed the word "defense" in describing Peru's military position. He downplayed our concern, referring to Peru's "supposed, and I stress the word 'supposed,' arms buildup." The press, he said, had exploited Peru's "supposed" arms purchases when all his government had done was to buy material from the USSR, a situation they were forced into because "we were refused access to the U.S. arms market."

If that were true, I suggested, it was important for Peru to "send a clear signal, a demonstration that your intentions are defensive and not aggressive." Morales Bermúdez countered by saying that he had recently sent a signal by having a series of friendly meetings with officials from Chile and Ecuador, but, he warned, he had no intention of de-escalating Peru's arms purchases. "History has played some nasty tricks on us, causing us to lose much territory," he said. "We will not commit aggression, but we will not yield a single centimeter of our territory."

I argued with him, going several hours over our allotted time. Our meeting adjourned, on a pleasant note, however, and I looked forward to the dinner that evening so we could continue our conversation. Over dinner, Morales Bermúdez said that he planned to prove to the world that he had the good of his people at heart. He told me that night, in confidence, that he was going to establish a democracy in Peru and give up his power. And I promised that I would come back for the inauguration of the newly *elected* president (which I did in the summer of 1980).

Of all the leaders I met on the trip, I liked Morales Bermúdez the best. Before our long conversations were over, we understood each other very well and also, in a strange way, had developed a genuine friendship, out of mutual respect, I think. I called him "my favorite dictator"! After starting off so stiffly and even suspiciously toward me, Morales Bermúdez became very warm and candid. At the banquet that night, he told me how much my visit meant to him. Henry Kissinger, he said, used to talk with him, but it was only talk and nothing else. There was no satisfaction because he felt Kissinger was not interested in them at all. So my visit with Peru's president ended on a high note, and I felt invigorated as we set off for our planned weekend of rest.

What a beautiful and welcome spot La Granja Azul was, an oasis after so much work. I had a small cottage on a mountainside, with a swimming pool outside my door. The Peruvians put on a grand fiesta for us, cooking pigs and chickens in big pits covered with leaves. Our Navy friends, Maria and Manolo Piqueras, joined us. The foreign minister, Pepe de la Puente, brought his horses to perform for us, and he looked dashing in his riding outfit, a flowing cape and sombrero. After our long conversations, we all felt like old friends, and when it was my turn to address the gathering, I threw away my notes and instead sang "Happy Birthday" to Pepe—in Spanish, of course!

Our three-day visit to Brazil was the most difficult of all. We were quite concerned because the military regime was not happy with my husband. Historically, Brazil and the United States have always been friends. Brazil sent troops to fight side by side with ours during World War II, and there has long been a reserve of good will toward us. But that store of good will was being used up. As required by U.S. law, the State Department had recently made public the record, gathering during the Ford administration, of the government's human rights violations against Brazilian citizens and its mistreatment of political prisoners. There was also the issue of the nuclear reprocessing plant that Brazil was purchasing from West Germany. Jimmy had already had words with Chancellor Helmut Schmidt about it and was putting pressure on Brazil to cancel or revise the deal. I knew all of this before I arrived in Brazil, of course, where my mission was to try to ease the tensions between our countries by explaining the Carter policies on human rights, nuclear nonproliferation, and the arms race. I was not frightened. I knew the government would be courteous to me, but

I also suspected that little understanding would develop between us.

The Brazilians indeed were gracious, and their president, Ernesto Geisel, was a pleasant man. He was older, a grandfatherly type. He spoke Portuguese, of course, and I had to have an interpreter to understand him, but I always thought he understood my English before it was translated. Our official meeting was all too brief, being interrupted by the funeral of one of his close friends, and I had to save most of my "talking points" for the evening meal. President Geisel seemed more liberal on the issue of human rights than his military government wanted him to be, and I thought he seemed to be more in agreement with our interest in human rights and democracy than with his general staff.

His problems were many, including an enormous foreign debt and persistent high inflation. Brazil is a newly industrialized nation, with many natural resources, but the one thing it does not have is oil. As a result, billions of dollars a year were spent on imported oil. One solution, Geisel and his government thought, was to purchase a nuclear fuel recycling plant that would produce its own nuclear energy. Brazil, understandably, was resisting all efforts to revise the contract. Our opposition was not to the nuclear power plant, but to the reprocessing facility that could turn the spent fuel from the plant into nuclear explosives.

I discussed this in detail with Geisel, and I could never get him to acknowledge that he could have nuclear power without the reprocessing facility. Surely he knew it. I insisted, but in his mind they were one and the same. "We need the reprocessing capability with the nuclear plant for energy only," he claimed throughout our long discussion. I reminded him also of the enormous unnecessary cost of such a plant, but my arguments were fruitless. Ultimate power rested with the military in Brazil, and Geisel had recently suffered political setbacks that had diminished his authority. He probably couldn't have stopped or revised the purchase even if he had wanted to, but he certainly could have made his reservations known. (Later, primarily because of economic considerations, Brazil canceled plans for the nuclear reprocessing facility.)

The Brazilians were just as stubborn about other Carter policies. They had just signed the Tlatelolco Treaty, but only with certain conditions. We hoped they would waive the conditions and I spoke to the president about it, but without success. He was afraid of

Argentina. He said he would waive the conditions if Argentina, who had signed the treaty, would ratify it. (The Argentines never did, and in the spring of 1982, it became known that they have reprocessing capability.) Nor would the Brazilians sign the American Convention on Human Rights, fearing that "it might breed an interventionist policy in internal affairs" by other countries in Latin America. In other words, they feared inspection of their human rights abuses.

Since 1964, the military had governed Brazil with a president elected by a handful of military leaders. "If you open up the system even a little bit, they will want more, and before you know it, the people will even want to elect a president!" one of the officials said to me.

But President Geisel was gradually opening up Brazil to free speech and democracy. This was called *abertura*—literally "opening"—and it was already evident to me in my conversations with political leaders of the opposition and, most of all, with the persistent Brazilian press. Brazilian correspondents are among the most talented and energetic in the world, and they were quite interested in asking me the most delicate questions in order to use me to help the political process open further. I left Brazil with the distinct feeling that even though our relations with the military government had been strained, they were never better with the Brazilian people. Brazilians seemed eager to return to democracy, and saw Jimmy's human rights policy as a way to help them do so.

Perhaps most important, the human rights policy seemed to have recaptured the youth, who had been so angry with the United States. When Henry Kissinger visited Brazil in 1976, (and again in 1981), he was met with student demonstrations. During my visit to Brasilia, student leaders from around the country gave me a petition asking for our continued support in their efforts to return to democracy.

My conversations with President Geisel were interesting and intense—too intense, it seemed, for our ambassador to Brazil, John Crimmins. At dinner that evening, Madeline motioned for me to go with her to the ladies' room, and when we got there she whispered that the ambassador had said I was pressing the president too hard. Couldn't I just make light dinner conversation with him instead? I supposed I could, that maybe I was being too persistent. I went back to the table prepared to discuss family.

But President Geisel had other plans and continued on the same subject. The evening ended cordially, but with the clear understanding that we agreed to disagree.

From Brasilia we went on to Recife for a change of pace, to stay in a home I had visited during an exchange program when Jimmy was governor. But the interlude proved more controversial than we had planned. Two U.S. missionaries claiming human rights violations had come to the consulate the day before I arrived and asked to see me. They said they had been arrested by the police and detained for three days without being allowed to contact our diplomatic officials. I called Jimmy to see if he thought I should meet with them. These were our people being mistreated, I told him, and I thought I should see them even though such a meeting might be unpopular with the Brazilian government. He agreed.

The meeting with the missionaries caught everyone by surprise, including the governor of the state, with whom I met later in the day to make clear our dissatisfaction with the way the Americans had been treated. The incident created a small flurry of excitement among the government officials in Brasilia. However, it was not significant enough to be mentioned in the State Department cables back to Washington except to say that the governor expressed regrets and said he wanted everyone who visited his state to have proper treatment. Our point about human rights had been made.

With the several strains in our relationship with Brazil, the message I tried to leave was that the United States and Brazil had real differences, but the relationship was important to us both; we had to continue our efforts to find workable accommodations.

The other two countries I visited, Colombia and Venezuela, are both democracies and both our good friends.

My arrival in Colombia coincided with an anniversary of rioting in which a student had been killed. Large demonstrations were planned, and the government was concerned about my safety. A van of armed soldiers followed me all day. Having never worried about my security and never asked questions about the arrangements the Secret Service made, at least I was conscious of my protection here. I felt very safe.

Colombia had a good record on human rights. They were as concerned about the arms buildup in Peru as we were and worried as well about Brazil's acquisition of nuclear reprocessing capability. Since we agreed almost unanimously on these major issues, the bulk of my conversations with the president, Alfonso López Michelson, were concerned with other issues between our two countries.

Our main concern was the problem of drug trafficking. Colombia was a major supplier of cocaine for U.S. markets as well as a source of marijuana and possibly opium. U.S. intelligence had determined that a high government official was helping and profiteering from the drug trade. What was not known was whether the president was aware of it. Peter Bourne, from Jimmy's office, and Mathea Falco, a special narcotics adviser from the State Department, were due to visit López Michelson soon and inform him about the corruption in his Cabinet. It would be helpful to them if I could find out how much he knew. I tried.

To see if I could get any response, I told the president about the impending visit of the U.S. narcotics officials. Rather than asking why they were coming, he seemed pleased that we were finally going to help him with the drug problem. We should, he said, because the real issue was who was responsible for it in the first place. Was Colombia corrupting American society by supplying the drugs or was the United States corrupting Colombia by creating the demand? It was, after all, American money, American channels, and American aircraft that were making the narcotics trade possible. It had been three years, López Michelson pointed out, since he had asked President Ford and Secretary of State Kissinger for help in combating the problem. They had promised communications equipment and helicopters, but our two countries were still debating the terms of an agreement to supply just three helicopters. (I was sure that past administration officials felt it would be senseless to give help if people high in the Colombian government could subvert the efforts.) I probed a bit further, saying that the big business of narcotics could have a corrupting influence on government and that we should work together to solve the problem. But the president said we should have started three years earlier. Just recently his government had discovered marijuana plantations in northeastern Colombia using advanced agricultural technology financed by Americans!

I was getting nowhere, and I had been told that López Michelson was easily offended, so I had to be very careful. And since Colombia was our good friend, I didn't want to be the one to harm that relationship. I decided to leave the issue of corruption to Peter and Mathea.

Without further questioning on the subject, I described the collaboration between Mexico and the United States in curtailing the drug traffic across our borders. The situation in Mexico had greatly improved since Jimmy had been in office, and "President Carter," I told President Michelson, "would like to work together with Colombia in the same spirit of cooperation."

How much did López Michelson know? Maybe nothing, but I was never sure. He was interested that we wanted to help and didn't seem evasive. He didn't seem to be trying to hide anything from me or covering up for anyone, but in all our conversations I never quite knew whether he was being frank. At least we agreed that the problem was serious and of mutual concern.

Other points of contention were the sixty-odd Americans in jail in Colombia on drug charges, some of whom had gone for two years without a trial, and the status of Richard Starr, a young Peace Corps volunteer who had been kidnaped earlier in the year by leftist guerrillas and hadn't been heard from since. López Michelson was reluctant to assume responsibility for the jailed Americans, though I told him I thought surely they should have the right to a fair and speedy trial. The country's judicial burden, he said, was as heavy as that in the United States. He had urged the attorney general to try and speed up the trial process, but presently there were eight thousand cases pending, with the Americans' among them. And he was wary of government involvement in the search for Richard Starr. He said if the military were forced to try to find and rescue Starr, it would be even more dangerous for him. (It would take another three years before Starr would be released. At the request of his mother, early in 1980 I interceded again with a personal request to the new Colombian president. Three months later Starr was released, and he came to see me at the White House. He was very appreciative and said that my help had been significant.)

My conversation with the president ended on a pleasant note. He was happy about the easing of certain trade import limits on Colombia by the United States and hoped that their cut flowers, especially carnations, would be included. Also, López Michelson was a friend of General Torrijos of Panama, and he promised to urge him to speed up the pending Panama Canal Treaty negotiations.

At a champagne reception at López Michelson's Palacio San Carlos before I left the country, the guest list had been expanded from "wives only" to include the Colombian government ministers and U.S. government officials. This change, the State Department wired home, "reflected the growing Colombian realization that Mrs. Carter's tour is substantive and serious and not a flying coffee klatsch."

Seven countries are almost too many for one trip, and everyone in our party was exhausted when we landed in Caracas, Venezuela. This was our last stop, and because President Carlos Andrés Pérez was due to make an official visit to the United States in a few weeks, my conversations with him were relatively brief, for they were designed to set the stage for his later discussions with Jimmy.

The president was jovial, with a hearty laugh, and he liked to talk. He had a reputation for being shrewd, energetic, tough, and honest. He was known as "a man in a hurry" who, I was told, kept such a grueling schedule that it was hard for others to keep up with him. I found him delightful and could easily understand why he had evolved into a leader with great influence in the Caribbean and throughout the developing world. He was direct in his conversation, down to earth, and sure of himself. I trusted him immediately.

Pérez, one of Jimmy's avid supporters abroad, had good things to say about my tour. He described it as a wonderful demonstration of good will and respect by the Carter administration, which had been lacking in past U.S. policies. No wonder I liked him.

Venezuela's record on human rights was unexcelled in the hemisphere, and the Carter administration's initiatives on human rights and nuclear nonproliferation had struck responsive chords. Pérez thought that Jimmy's human rights policy, which, he said, indicated a deep concern for all the people of the world, was encouraging democracy in all of Latin America. And he said that Carter's willingness to negotiate the Panama Canal treaties had added a new dimension to U.S.–Latin American relations: a spirit of equality, mutual respect, partnership, and an end to the damaging image of colonialism and intervention.

After our mutual pats on the back, we got down to the everyday issues. Venezuela had a plentiful oil supply, and the country's economy was booming. But, like Ecuador, Venezuela had been denied its trade preference with the United States because of its membership in OPEC. Pérez thought his country's exclusion was discriminatory, especially since it had not supported the oil embargo in 1973 and had actually increased their oil shipments to the United States during the embargo. I told him that we had greatly appreciated Venezuela's help during the oil crisis and that my husband agreed that the trade restraints should not apply to Venezuela and Ecuador, but that because of deep feelings against OPEC in Congress, the President couldn't promise him an early reversal of the exclusionary provision. He was close enough to the political scene in our country to understand this, but that did not make it easier to accept.

Pérez, I was not surprised to learn, had protested to Germany its sale of the reprocessing plant to Brazil and to the Soviets their sale of planes and weapons to Peru. He said he didn't expect it to make a difference, but he could not refrain from expressing his opposition to these disturbing developments.

I spoke to him about the status of William Neihous, the manager of Owens-Illinois in Venezuela, who was kidnapped in Caracas more than a year before my visit. Like Richard Starr's mother, Mrs. Neihous had written to me, pleading for help for her husband. President Pérez assured me he was doing all he could. The major suspects in the case had been arrested, he told me, but hadn't told the police anything about Neihous. "Unfortunately, the practice of democratic human rights makes the suspects brave in their refusal to talk," Pérez said. And the suspects never did talk or release Neihous. Instead, he finally managed to escape and return home to the United States after we had left the White House.

Though we had been exhausted upon our arrival, Venezuela was a wonderful last stop for our trip except that I became ill. Looking back, it seems incredible that with all the traveling we had done and all of the luncheons, receptions, and dinners we had attended, we had not been ill before. And even when it finally happened to me in Caracas, it was quickly over. I was in a briefing with members of a Children's Foundation Scholarship Fund, who were telling me about their program for needy children, when suddenly I was too hot, and I knew I had to get to a restroom in a hurry. I excused myself, but returned to deliver my remarks and finish the meeting. I did cancel the next evening on the schedule, though, took a Dramamine, and went to bed; but on the entire 12,000-mile journey, that was the only event I missed.

I left Latin America with an overwhelming sense of kinship

with the people I had met and with friendships that would prove to be lasting. I also had sensed a feeling of great willingness, even eagerness, on the part of the leaders with whom I had met to cooperate with us in solving the problems that confronted all our people.

It was good to get home to Jimmy and my family, and although I was very tired, I felt buoyed by the trip. I had been just like a campaign: tense at times, with much preparation necessary, selling yourself—or in this instance my country, and a feeling of satisfaction when it was over. As I was flying over the ocean, heading north, I received a message from Jimmy: "The President of the United States requests the honor of your presence for dinner tonight at 8:30 at Aspen Lodge." To which I replied: "The First Lady accepts with pleasure."

I learned from my own experiences in Latin America how very important were our human rights efforts. The people in those countries and others in the world were beginning to look to us, during Jimmy's administration and under his leadership, as people who genuinely cared about them. National leaders realized that in order to gain aid from the United States or to associate with our great nation in achieving their most vital goals, they must respect the human rights of their people. It was no accident that when I went to Latin America, I visited only the countries that were leaning toward democracy so as not to put a stamp of approval on regressive regimes.

I continued my interest in the Latin American and Caribbean countries throughout my time in the White House and stayed in touch with the friends I had made. The leaders of Peru and Ecuador kept me posted on their progress toward democracy. With each step they were very proud and I was proud with them. And finally, when they had gone through the entire process—adopted a constitution, registered their people to vote, and elected a new president—I went back to join in the celebration of the inaugurations.

One of my friends was Osvaldo Hurtado Larrea, who was elected vice president of Ecuador. At the inauguration in 1979, he promised to send me the English translation of his new book about the political processes in his country. In it he wrote: "The battle for democracy fought by the Ecuadorians would have had to run even greater risks if not for the fact that the government of the United States was in the hands of President Jimmy Carter, whose forthright stance on human rights in the hemisphere and throughout the world served on more than one occasion to reinforce Ecuador's commitment to the plan to return the country to civilian rule." That made it all worthwhile. (Hurtado is now the president of Ecuador, having assumed this position in 1981, when President Roldós and his wife were both killed in an airplane crash.)

Even in countries as repressive as Argentina, where thousands were taken away from their homes, never to be seen again, even there some progress was made because of our public condemnation of these savage brutalities. Jacobo Timerman, the former Argentine editor who was imprisoned and tortured by the government, has said that he knows "positively that many lives were saved" because Patricia Derian, Jimmy's assistant secretary for human rights, went to Buenos Aires and made a great public scandal about human rights violations.

Now, because of irresistible demands from a persecuted people, there is a new president of Argentina, Raul Alfonsín, whose remarkable election has brought democracy back to that tortured nation. According to an article in the *New York Times* by Robert Cox, who lived in Argentina for twenty years and was the editor of the *Buenos Aires Herald*, "Mr. Alfonsín believes that Jimmy Carter's human rights policy saved thousands of lives in Argentina. It is even possible that he himself owes his life to the unsilent diplomacy of Mr. Carter's human rights team in the State Department during the three years after the Argentine military coup of March 1976 . . . years in which at least 6,000 people were abducted, routinely tortured and secretly murdered by the military." When Alfonsín met for the first time with the U.S. ambassador who served at the end of the Carter administration and the beginning of the Reagan administration, he openly introduced himself as a "Carterite."

That courageous and invaluable stand for human rights has been changed by the new administration in Washington. There is no longer a clear signal around the world that America stands for freedom and democracy, for an end to torture and murder by any government, and that our country will be a strong voice for the oppressed. Instead, our own leaders have expressed their quick and public approval of oppressive regimes, by reciprocal visits, attempts through presidential appointment to subvert the role of our State Department in protecting human rights, and by the use of armed force and interventionist tactics in the smaller countries in our hemisphere. These policies have been almost universally bemoaned by those who spend their lives in service to suffering people in other countries, and within the United States our abandonment of the long-standing bipartisan commitment to civil rights has incurred the condemnation of almost every existing organization devoted to this worthy cause.

As a southern woman, I have seen the beneficial transformation of our lives that came with the end of the discrimination and oppression of black citizens in our region. The flaming desires of the 1950s and 1960s in our nation are now mirrored in other countries of the world, and nowhere more vividly than in Central and South America. I learned on my trip to Latin America that *Derechos Humanos!* is a cry that cannot be stilled. For our own government to stand silent and even to align itself with torturers and murderers such as those in El Salvador is a disgrace to us all and a shameful violation of the principles espoused by the American heroes who have offered their lives for the cause of freedom and human rights.

❧ 8 ❧
People, Parties, and Protocol

Social affairs filled the calendar at the White House during Jimmy's term, not only for foreign heads of state, but for congressional groups, women's organizations, senior citizens, mental health workers, and even poets. I wanted the White House to be accessible for everyone to share its history and graciousness, whether as a tourist or as a visiting dignitary. There were few days when some event wasn't scheduled, from the very formal state dinners and other ceremonial events to casual picnics and special events on the South Lawn. Everywhere I had been in the campaign I had said, "When we get to the White House, we want you to come to see us." Not everyone believed me, but thousands were able to accept our invitation.

Before Jimmy's inauguration, the press had painted us as country farm people who would bring gingham and square dances to the White House. We did. Sometimes. But we also brought a parade of America's greatest classical talent and some of the most elegant events ever held at the White House.

My apprenticeship in the Governor's Mansion was a valuable asset as I approached the White House entertaining. This time I was not intimidated by the prospect of hundreds of different events each year. The White House had a competent staff of waiters, butlers, florists, chefs, and calligraphers for rendering formal invitations and place cards, programs, menus, and other official inscriptions. And my own staff for entertaining, headed by my social secretary, Gretchen Poston, was experienced and hardworking.

The State Floor of the White House was well laid out for parties and receptions. Occasionally we took our guests onto the lawn for a ballet or a concert, but most of the entertaining centered in the East Room, the large, normally empty room that stretches across one whole end of the White House. Originally intended to be the most elegant reception room in the house, the East Room remained unfinished for years. After Abigail Adams had hung her laundry in it, Thomas Jefferson divided it into two offices for his secretary; then it was once more a huge barn of a room. Now it is beautiful, with crystal chandeliers, gold damask draperies, fulllength portraits of Martha and George Washington, new parquet floors, and a Steinway grand piano from Franklin D. Roosevelt's presidency. The piano, large and ornate, with gilt American eagle supports, was badly in need of restoration and about to be replaced. I strongly objected, believing that it had historical value and should be kept, so rather than relegate it to the warehouse, we had it restored.

The smaller Red, Blue, and Green rooms are lovely for more intimate receptions and meetings. The Green Room, so named during the administration of John Quincy Adams, was my favorite. It is a cozy room where, during state visits, I often entertained the wives of the visiting dignitaries, such as Mrs. Menachem Begin of Israel, Mrs. Deng Xiaoping, wife of the vice chairman of China, and Margaret Trudeau, the wife of the Canadian prime minister, Pierre Trudeau. Margaret's quip to the press when they kept pestering her about her clothes, "When you are interviewing my husband, do you ask him who made his suit?", still delights me.

The Blue Room, in the center of the house, is directly under the Yellow Oval Room and has the same graceful shape. Redecorated by James Monroe, the first President to live in the White House after it was burned by the British in 1814, the Blue Room contains seven of the original gilded Bellangé chairs Monroe ordered from France. While we were in the White House, we acquired one of the original settees Monroe had purchased to match the chairs.

There are no government funds for purchasing furnishings or works of art for the White House. All of them have to be donated.

Working with the Committee for the Preservation of the White House, we set up a White House Trust Fund so that money would be on hand when special items became available. Among the objects we were able to obtain were a bronze bust of Benjamin Franklin by Jean Antoine Houdon, a necklace and brooch that had belonged to Mrs. John Quincy Adams, and frescos painted by Constantino Brumidi that had been in the ceiling of the Cross Hall and dated from the time of Andrew Johnson. I also worked to acquire paintings by American artists. There was a splendid art collection on loan in the White House, but I felt there was a need to develop a good, permanent collection of American paintings. Once a George Caleb Bingham became available unexpectedly, but we couldn't raise the money for it in time. (It brought $900,000 at auction, so we probably could never have afforded it anyway.) We were, however, able to acquire many good paintings, including a different George Caleb Bingham, *Cincinnati Enquirer, 1888* by William Michael Harnett, a Charles Willson Peale portrait of George Washington, a portrait of Andrew Jackson by Ralph E. W. Earle, a beautiful landscape by Thomas Moran, *Sailing Off the Coast* by Martin Johnson Heade, and paintings by George Henry Durrie, Ernest Lawson, John Henry Twachtman, and Lilla Cabot Perry. The Trust Fund was one of the things I discussed with Nancy Reagan when she came to the White House for our first meeting.

The Red Room always made me feel at home, for it was decorated with the same red Scalamandré silk used in the Governor's Mansion in Atlanta. Once known as the Yellow Room, this was one of Dolley Madison's favorites. It was here that she held her famous "fashionable Wednesday night soirees" and her portrait still keeps a watchful eye over the room's proceedings. Like the other smaller rooms on the State Floor, we used the Red Room for receptions. After the tourists left each day at noon, all the ropes that had blocked off the rooms were taken down, the carpets that had been rolled up were set back in place, and our guests could move freely from room to room.

The State Dining Room, where we held formal banquets and other large luncheons and dinners, was enlarged during the administration of Theodore Roosevelt to seat 140. At Roosevelt's request, bison heads were carved on the new stone mantel, the head of a large moose was hung above the fireplace, and other big-game trophies were scattered around the walls. Mercifully, the trophies are long since gone, but Jackie Kennedy had the bison-head mantel reproduced and put back. It is on this mantel that John Adams's prayer to heaven to bestow blessings on the White House and to guarantee that only "honest and wise men ever rule here" is inscribed. To make sure no one forgets, the Healy portrait of a seated Abraham Lincoln, his chin in his hand, looks down on the room from over the mantel.

The last public room on the State Floor, the Family Dining Room, has been "replaced" in its original purpose by the dining room upstairs in the living quarters. Now it is used for official functions with small numbers of guests, who would be lost in the State Dining Room. Jimmy regularly held his foreign policy and congressional leadership breakfasts in this room and I used it for luncheons with the Mental Health Commission and other groups. This room also doubles as a serving kitchen when there are large affairs in the State Dining Room.

I found the china in the White House fascinating. Upstairs we used the Woodrow Wilson china, which is plain with a small gold border and the presidential seal in gold. Downstairs we used the Truman china, with a wide green border rimmed in gold, and the Johnson china, trimmed with wildflowers. Truman had wanted enough china to serve a hundred guests. Lyndon Johnson purchased more because he wanted to be able to serve two hundred people. So even for our largest seated dinners, there was plenty of china.

We were lucky to have any of the older pieces at all. For the first hundred years, presidents had often auctioned off or given away the old china, replacing it with new selections they liked better. Mrs. Benjamin Harrison was the first to realize the importance of preserving the china from past administrations and to start collecting it. Mrs. Theodore Roosevelt went a step further and refused to let any be sold, even the pieces that were cracked or damaged. Instead, she had the useless items broken and scattered into the Potomac River, a practice that continued for many years.

Every night at our family meal upstairs, the table was set with service plates from one of the past presidents. Then they were taken away, and dinner was served on the Woodrow Wilson china. One of our favorites was the china of Rutherford B. Hayes; each plate was painted with realistic American flora and fauna, including a wild boar. Amy didn't like the boar plate, so every time the table was set with the Hayes service, Jimmy and the boys made sure she got the wild boar. And no matter how many times it happened, when she looked down and saw it she always had the same startled look on her face: "Not again!"

Knowing how much we enjoyed thinking about other presidents each evening, I would have loved to have left some Carter china behind, at least a collection of service plates. But I didn't know I was going to leave so soon!

State dinners were always the most glittering events, and over the years we gave many of them. In our first twenty months in the White House, we welcomed nearly a hundred heads of state—prime ministers, presidents, and kings. The details involved in planning were myriad. I was responsible for the arrival ceremony on the South Lawn, the guest list for the dinner, the seating, the menu, the table decorations, and the entertainment. I was also responsible for planning an interesting schedule for the visiting dignitary's spouse.

Because I wanted to impress our foreign guests with the best America had to offer in a way that would have particular meaning to them, Gretchen Poston and I often met with State Department officials to get background information, and with members of the National Security Council and the protocol office as well. Gretchen then went to the embassy of the visiting country, along with our chief of protocol, to discuss the habits, likes, and dislikes of our guests. Weeks before the visit, she prepared a booklet for me with all the pertinent information and her suggestions for the state dinner. Then we would meet to make the final decisions. It was a good system and resulted in some beautiful evenings with no subtle detail and no guest's preference overlooked.

We knew from the State Department briefing book, for example, that Chancellor Helmut Schmidt's wife, Hannelore (or "Loki," the book told us she was called), had taught mathematics and biology for years and had become a self-educated botanist. On a trip for the U.S. Bicentennial celebration, Loki had been smitten by a small purple flower she had seen. Gretchen discovered that the flower was crepe myrtle, so we filled the White House with large, informal arrangements of it for the Schmidts' state visit and put small plantings of it on the tables for the guests, including Loki, to take home.

We chose the entertainment just as carefully to suit the tastes of the honored guests. We knew that President Anwar Sadat was an avid devotee of the American West and watched two Westerns a day. ("I'm hooked," he had told me.) For his visit we chose the country singers the Statler Brothers to perform—Sadat was delighted. The taste of President Pérez of Venezuela was more erudite and centered on the ballet, so we invited Cynthia Gregory and Ted Kivitt from the American Ballet to dance in the bandshell on the South Lawn. They danced Variations from the second act of *Giselle*. When we asked the daughter of Prime Minister Ohira of Japan what her father liked, she replied that he loved informal American cooking and popular music. "Please don't have anything classical or my father will go to sleep," she told us. The solution: an open air barbecue on the roof of the West Wing corridor, which overlooks the Rose Garden and is reached through French doors opening from the State Dining Room, and entertainment by Bobby Short.

King Baudouin and Queen Fabiola of Belgium could only come for lunch, and it was one of the most beautiful events in all our four years. We used an E-shaped table in the East Room, rather than the usual round tables in the State Dining Room, and decorated it with the first dogwood blossoms of spring and the famous gilt service brought from France by President James Monroe. For the luncheon, perfect little whole lobsters followed by medallions of veal were served on the Johnson china. And for dessert, coconut ice cream was served in pink hibiscus shells of spun sugar made by our talented new pastry chef. The New York Harp Ensemble played throughout the meal, followed by a short performance of a children's Suzuki violin group, which included Amy. Six young musicians, one only seven and far more advanced than Amy, not only charmed the king and queen with their talent but took on the Marine String Band as well. On their way out, as the children passed the Marine Band, which was playing a Beethoven piece, they stopped, tucked violins under chins, and joined in without missing a note.

Both Jimmy and I were concerned that our first state visit be exactly as we wanted it, and we did a lot of homework in advance. We watched a film of President Ford receiving Chancellor Schmidt of Germany to see how the previous administration had handled the arrival ceremony. It was very elaborate, but we decided to make only a few changes in the pomp and ceremony because we learned how important it was to the visitors. They enjoyed the spotlight and wanted a big "show" that would be seen on television and read about back home. We simply removed some of the trumpeters and their banners, but for the first time we included women in the honor guard that stands in front of the platform, holding the flags of each branch of the military service. And rather than have the wives stand to one side, as Betty Ford had done, Jimmy wanted us to stand next to our husbands on the platform. I was happy about that but disappointed when he insisted that "Hail to the Chief" not be played when he walked out on the lawn to await the arrival of the visiting head of state. The honors should go to the visitor, he said firmly, not to himself.

On the afternoon before the arrival of the Mexican delegation, Jimmy and I met in the Diplomatic Reception Room with Gretchen, Evan Dobelle, and a military aide to "walk through" the arrival ceremony. It was planned down to the very second. We were to walk from the Diplomatic Reception Room when the signal came that the limousine bringing the visitors had left Blair House—a journey of less than two minutes—to be waiting outside when they arrived. As the visitors stepped from the car, we were to greet them and proceed along a red carpet to a platform set on the south grounds. Our places on the platform would be marked by toe cards and, once there, we were to stand at attention while the national anthems of both countries were played and the cannons boomed their salute.

The two leaders then would review the troops standing at attention on the lawn; Jimmy would make welcoming remarks, followed by our visitor's response. We would proceed up the curved stairway to the porch leading into the Blue Room and pause, with the honorees always to our right, to wave to the crowd and pose for photographers. Then we were to go into the Blue Room and position ourselves at the proper toe cards to be ready for the receiving line and small reception. When the official party walked over to the Oval Office and Cabinet Room to begin their work, I was free to resume my normal duties.

Upstairs in our living quarters, just inside the hall by the elevator, was a table where the daily newspapers, schedules, and messages were left for Jimmy and me. Those needing immediate attention had a red tag clipped to them. After our rehearsal of the arrival ceremony, I picked up from the table the red-tagged briefing book with the last-minute details of the pending visit. The book, prepared by the State Department, contained the schedule of events, an analysis of the issues that would be discussed by the two leaders, background material on Mexico, and biographical sketches of the president and his wife and the other members of their party. I read through the briefing book so I would know which subjects to choose for conversation as well as which issues were sensitive and to be avoided.

Our first arrival ceremony went like clockwork. The López Portillos arrives on the dot, as we did. *"Buenos dias, Señor y Señora. Como estan?"* Jimmy said, welcoming them in Spanish. All went perfectly until we got to the Blue Room. I was standing in the correct toe card, but Mrs. López Portillo was on my left instead of my right. We couldn't have planned it that way. What had happened? I motioned to the military aide across the room until I got his attention. "Something's wrong," I said to him. "She's on my left." "No, it's all right . . . and very proper," he who had been there longer than I said. But of course; the guests were coming from the right and I had to greet them first and introduce them to her. Earlier, I had been nervous about the protocol and fearful that I might do something unintentionally to cause embarrassment. At that instant I relaxed and decided never to worry again. It is proper to keep the honoree on the right when possible to show respect. Sometimes, as in this instance, that rule has to be suspended; I learned that real protocol is warmth and putting your guests at ease, an important part of traditional southern hospitality, not just rules.

It was lucky I realized that in the morning, or I would have been very upset by what happened that evening.

Everything was in place: The round tables were set for eight and decorated, as was the rest of the White House, with red tulips and white candles to honor Valentine's Day. We were using the green and gold Truman china with the vermeil flatware, and engraved menus and place cards were at every setting. Pots of tulips were banked around the platform set up in the East Room for the entertainment, and on the platform, just arrived, was the piano of Rudolf Serkin.

I counted my blessings as I went upstairs to get dressed in my evening clothes. How different it was from the Governor's Mansion in Atlanta, where I had had to worry about every detail of the entertaining. Here, once the plans were made, almost everything was done for me. At daybreak this morning the florist had sent his people to the market to obtain the baskets of tulips while someone else picked up the plants and trees at the Botanical Gardens. Volunteers in the flower room were just finishing arrangements for the tables. The chief usher was keeping a watchful eye on all the proceedings; the chef, the maître d'hôtel, the waiters and butlers, would prepare and serve the food with ultimate professionalism, and social aides, young military men and women in their dress uniforms, would be on the State Floor to assist the guests. And upstairs the valet had even laid out Jimmy's tuxedo! Entertaining in the White House, I decided, was going to be fun.

"Rosalynn, *todos quedan para ti!*" Jimmy was calling, using one of his favorite expressions. "Everybody's waiting for you!" It wasn't true, or maybe it was. But I was ready, and on time. The military aide had notified him that President and Mrs. López Portillo were leaving Blair House and were due to arrive in two minutes. That was our clue to go downstairs, and Jimmy and I reached the steps of the North Portico just as the big limousine rolled under the large white columns. The timing was perfect. And so was the pleasant chat we had upstairs with the López Portillos, our children, and a handful of guests in the Yellow Oval Room.

"President Carter, it's time to go downstairs," the military aide said. Drawing a deep breath, I moved with Jimmy to the top of the grand stairway.

The Marine Band announcing us blared forth, the military aides snapped to attention, and at the foot of the stairs the guests and a battery of press waited expectantly in this very formal atmosphere. First down the stairs in the spotlight the whole way padded Misty Malarky, Amy's Siamese cat! I don't know who was more surprised, the guests, the press, me, or Misty. But immediately there was laughter in the great hallway, and a relaxed and comfortable, warm, elegant, and thrilling evening had begun.

That night we had very special entertainment. We knew that Mrs. López Portillo had been a concert pianist and especially admired Rudolf Serkin. I had sent Gretchen to see Serkin with a handwritten note from me, asking him to be our first performing artist at the White House. He had accepted. And so did Carmen López Portillo! After Serkin played his most deserved encore, Mrs. López Portillo played two Chopin pieces—and brought the house down.

As we welcomed more and more foreign leaders to the White

House, I was glad that we had made one change in the ceremonial demands of the state visit. Previously, the foreign guest had entertained the President the succeeding evening at another full-scale dinner. Jimmy decided to forgo this precedent. He felt that two days of meetings and one dinner was sufficient time for him to spend with the visitor, and while we were in Washington, the Vice President represented him at further functions—which also gave the Vice President a better chance to know the world's leaders.

Of course, even with all our planning, not all the White House functions went off without a hitch. At our very first governor's dinner, James Rhodes of Ohio appeared with two of his grandchildren. An aide told him there was no place for the children and the governor left. When Jimmy and I heard about it we immediately told the staff to "find him" and arrange to have the children play upstairs with Amy, but he was gone. In another mixup, the wrong national anthem was played for the arrival ceremony of President Nicolae Ceausescu of Rumania in April of 1978. The anthem had been recently changed, but we were not aware of it. We should have been.

Another consideration in a state visit was the matter of giving and receiving gifts. Traditionally the President and visiting leaders exchanged gifts, and the guests often came laden with overwhelming and expensive items, although they all knew that an American President could not accept anything valued at more than $100 from an official of a foreign government. That was the law. Anything more valuable goes to the Archives and becomes government property. All of these items, however, are available for display in the presidential library.

No matter what the gift or how valuable, the visitors would always try to get around the limit by insisting that their gift was only worth $99, but each item went to the Gift Unit to be appraised at its true retail value. If it was too valuable, we could keep it while we lived in the White House, but when the time came to leave it had to be turned in. Sometimes I thought the policy was excessively restrictive.

Although we kept few of the gifts for any length of time, some things were sentimental and hard to part with. I had a beautiful necklace with a hammered silver pendant that President and Mrs. Sadat had given me, and of course I wanted to keep it, but the law applied to members of the family too. Amy tearfully had to give up the coral head of Christ that Pope John Paul II had given her when we visited him at the Vatican and the small gold bracelet inscribed with her name (and valued at $150) given to her by President Pertini of Italy. There was no provision for us to purchase any of the items, even at the full retail price.

Sometimes the generosity of our foreign leaders was almost embarrassing. When I attended the inauguration of President Ló-pez Portillo in Mexico, I admired a ring his wife was wearing, an intricate design of silver circles and diamonds. Immediately she commissioned a jeweler to make one for me. And when I admired a beautiful carved table in the museum in Mexico City, she instructed the museum to pack it up for me. Obviously I couldn't take the table out of the museum, and I had trouble convincing her I couldn't accept it. I learned not to comment on things I liked.

Among the hundreds of gifts, many of them treasures, that will be displayed in the Carter presidential library in Atlanta is a "$99" antique urn given to Jimmy by an archbishop of Greece—and valued at $250,000.

We had to decide what to give in return to foreign leaders. It was a constant consideration, not only for state visits, but also when we traveled to other countries. There were only a few items in the State Department storeroom that were appropriate for gifts: a number of Mickey Mouse clocks, which we gave to the children on our travels in India, Africa, and Latin America, and thirty-seven sets of china plates decorated with paintings by Winslow Homer and mounted in velvet-lined mahogany display boxes. There was only one problem with the plates: Richard Nixon's name was embossed in gold on the back! We simply had Nixon's name removed and replaced with a gold seal—and Jimmy Carter's name! But we needed many more appropriate gifts. The ones that remained in the storeroom, like the huge crouched Cybis bull, were those that had been passed over by other presidents and officials who gave gifts on behalf of our government.

We decided to ask all the governors to contribute an item native to their states that could be a special gift for a foreign leader. We received some wonderful items: a Williamsburg silver dish from Virginia, which we liked so much that we purchased more in various shapes and sizes and used frequently as gifts, with the presidential seal engraved on them; beautiful hand-woven woolen shawls from Kentucky, which made lovely gifts for wives when I needed something casual; and a hand-crafted ukulele from Hawaii, which was perfect when we visited Portugal. We learned that early Portuguese sailors had stopped in Hawaii and introduced the musical instrument that later became known as the ukulele.

Since Jimmy is a great book enthusiast, we often tried to find an outstanding book to satisfy a visitor's special interest. I took a book of NASA photographs showing Costa Rica from space to the president when I visited, and he liked it so much that it became a standard gift for others whose countries were viewed in the photographs. We also gave the usual gifts of Steuben crystal and Boehm pieces, but the favorite White House souvenir turned out to be the handsome leatherbound albums we gave each foreign leader, filled with photographs documenting his visit from the arrival ceremony to his departure.

Selecting the entertainment for state occasions or for any of our other functions was always a thrill and a job I enjoyed doing myself. Our most talented artists willingly donated their time and art for the White House. Beverly Sills came to perform, as did Isaac Stern, André Previn, Sarah Vaughan and Dizzy Gillespie, George Shearing, Shirley Verrett, Itzhak Perlman, Pinchas Zuckerman, Leontyne Price, Tom T. Hall, Sarah Caldwell and the Opera Company of Boston, the Romeros, André Watts, the Guarnieri String Quartet, the Alvin Ailey Dance Theater, Andres Segovia, and many, many others.

One evening we heard the soprano Clamma Dale twice. As Jimmy stood to make his toast at a state dinner, suddenly the room was filled with a beautiful voice singing trills up and down the scale. Jimmy stopped, then started again, only to have more trills fill the air: It was Clamma, warming up in a small room downstairs, and the sound was being carried into the dining room by the airshaft in the fireplace. An aide had to ask her to practice in another room, even though our guests probably would have preferred listening to her rather than to the toasts.

Watching the performers rehearse the afternoon before their performance became one of our family's favorite times in the White House. Everyone gathered in a relaxed and informal way, even sitting on the floor, while we listened to Willie Nelson or John Denver sing, or to Vladimir Horowitz play the piano and Mstislav Rostropovich, the cello, or to watch Mikhail Baryshnikov dance. Baryshnikov was Amy's favorite performer, and during that rehearsal she watched in fascination as the ballet company carefully planned their routines and marked the stage in the East Room so they wouldn't leap into the low-hanging chandelier.

Some of the functions we held at the White House were specifically for working purposes. Whenever there was an important issue that Jimmy wanted passed through Congress, we invited influential people from around the country for a luncheon, tea, reception, or dinner and a briefing on the issue. In urging the Senate to ratify the Panama Canal treaties, for example, we welcomed several thousand influential citizens to the White House in order to build a constituency for it. We were more than willing to let senators give us the names of a hundred or more leaders from their states, whom we would then invite to join us: editors, college presidents, political party leaders, elected officials, and campaign contributors as well as representatives of organizations like the Jaycees, garden clubs, senior citizens, schoolteachers, and religious and women's groups, most of whom had never been to the White House before. Jimmy and other members of the administration would then brief them, in this case on the background and purpose of the Panama Canal treaties. So effective was this "guest" policy with the Panama Canal issue that it became a pattern over the next years to garner support for all important legislation.

For one Senate wives' annual luncheon we had a party "for women about women," presenting the play *Out of Our Father's House*, performed by Geraldine Fitzgerald, Carol Kane, and Maureen Anderman. Each guest was given a copy of the book on which the play was based, *Growing Up Female in America: Ten Lives*, autographed on the spot by the author, Eve Merriman. And to go along with the program, my remarks that day, of course, stressed the importance of the Equal Rights Amendment. We had other political events that were simply fun, like the Congressional Ball at Christmastime and the Diplomatic Children's Party, at which Walter Cronkite once read "The Night Before Christmas."

Jimmy and I always looked forward to the annual dinner for the governors and their wives, since many of them were old friends. One year the invitations read: "to a Ball to be held at the White House." And what a ball it was! We reversed the order of the evening and started with dancing. As the guests arrived, they were ushered into the candlelit East Room to waltz to the strains of the Marine Band. Then they sat at small candlelit tables around the room as Beverly Sills and Alan Titus sang selections from Franz Lehár's Viennese operetta *The Merry Widow*. Just before the last chorus of "The Merry Widow Waltz," the performers stepped down from the stage, and while they were still singing, Alan waltzed me around the room while Jimmy danced with Beverly. Soon everyone was on their feet and we danced until a late buffet was served, dining in the Red, Green, and Blue rooms. In each one the tablecloths matched the color of the walls, and the rooms were lit mainly with the glow of firelight and candles. It was a wonderfully romantic and old-fashioned evening, and the music played on and on.

We also honored groups of all kinds at the White House and held the first reception ever for American poets. One of the poets told me that John Kennedy had once invited them, but had to cancel the invitation because of the Bay of Pigs invasion. Twenty-one poets read from their works in seven different rooms, including James Dickey, Gwendolyn Brooks, John Ciardi, Lucille Clifton, Stanley Kunitz, and David Ignatow. The house was full, and I told our guests before the readings that it was an experiment, but it worked wonderfully.

We also welcomed ethnic groups, including the Armenian Americans, another first. The Armenians were great supporters of Jimmy's human rights policy, having suffered a holocaust themselves. We enjoyed the day they were there, eating Armenian food in the East Room and singing Armenian songs.

Each year, as soon as the weather warmed up, we entertained outdoors. We could only seat 140 in the State Dining Room, but outdoors we could serve many more people. With the bandshell we set up on the South Lawn for entertainment, we gave as many summer picnics as we could arrange. A group of congressional wives had visited me soon after we arrived in Washington to say that since we had Amy, we could probably understand how much they would like their children to come to the White House. Many had lived in Washington for years, and their children had never been invited to the White House nor seen a President. So we began a series of family picnics that were fun. One year we gave an evening picnic-concert for seven hundred members of congressional families, complete with pony rides, magicians, clowns, volleyball, and horseshoes, followed by André Kostelanetz leading a full symphony orchestra in Tchaikovsky's *1812 Overture*, with its grand finale of cannons and fireworks. It was so beautiful as the skies suddenly erupted with sparkling fireworks accompanied by the moving music that many, I included, had tears in their eyes.

A particularly outstanding event on the South Lawn was our Jazz Festival, which drew dozens of leading jazz musicians such as Eubie Blake, who at ninety-five pounded out his own compositions on the piano, and Kathryn Handy Lewis, who sang her father's "St. Louis Blues." But it was the President who, with Dizzy Gillespie, won rave reviews in the *New Yorker* for their rendition of "Salt Peanuts!" In contrast, we held an elegant and formal dinner in the Rose Garden for the leaders of NATO, after which we strolled across the lawn to watch the New York City Ballet perform in the bandshell against a wooden background. We even erected a small ice rink on the South Lawn one snowy winter evening and Peggy Fleming skated for our guests, who stayed outdoors just long enough to watch her performance before hurrying back into the warmth of the White House.

The greatest logistical challenge of all was the banquet on March 26, 1979, the night the Middle East peace treaty was signed. We had been planning quietly for the occasion and assembling guest lists, but there was nothing we could do publicly because no one was certain there would even be a treaty. However, within one week after we knew it would be signed, we entertained eighteen hundred people at a seated dinner under chandeliers in a striped tent on the South Lawn!

We installed a telephone bank in my offices with two shifts of volunteers to receive the responses to our invitations, which had to be sent as mailgrams because of the last-minute timing. Six support tents, one of which served as a kosher kitchen, were erected on the lawn. We brought in army trucks with refrigerated trailers to cool the salads and desserts and rowboats filled with ice to chill the wine. Special tablecloths and napkins were made by Carleton Varney, our reliable designer for many events, and the guests were equally divided among Israelis, Egyptians, and Americans, with each of the 180 tables seating persons of all three nationalities. Each country furnished entertainment: we invited Leontyne Price, the Israelis selected Itzak Perlman and Pinchas Zukerman, and the Egyptians brought a popular rock band!

When the evening arrived, everyone who came could feel an electric charge of peace, good will, and hope as ancient enemies embraced each other and thanked their American friends for making this wonderful evening possible. At least for once, a circus tent looked like the most beautiful ballroom I had ever seen.

I will always be proud that we initiated the series of Sunday afternoon performances in the East Room by our most prestigious national artists. We knew that no matter how many events we had or how many people we invited, only a small portion of the millions in our country would ever be able to enjoy the extraordinary music we were privileged to hear in the White House.

And thus an idea began to take shape. We would televise these special performances for everyone. Public television officials were intrigued with the idea. Together we made great preparations, compiling a list of artists we would like to have perform and working out suitable dates for them, consulting music critics and others for suggestions, and trying to choose the few lucky guests interested in music and the arts who would be invited for the performances. We worked out every little detail of the program with the television producers: the lighting, the seating arrangements, and the right narrators.

Our first performer was Vladimir Horowitz. On the afternoon before the performance, Horowitz arrived for the rehearsals with his wife, Wanda, the daughter of the conductor Arturo Toscanini. He had made few appearances in the past several years, and had even turned us down the year before, saying that he wanted to wait to celebrate the fiftieth anniversary of his debut in the United States by performing at the White House the next year. Now that moment had arrived, and it would be the maestro's second performance in the White House—forty-seven years after he had first performed for Herbert Hoover!

Listening to Horowitz rehearse was unforgettable. His piano arrived in the morning in time to "warm up" to the temperature in the East Room, which we learned was important. In the early afternoon a small group gathered to listen to him play, including Amy, who sat quietly in Jimmy's lap, and grandbaby Jason, who sat in mine. But after a while Horowitz stopped playing and said something was wrong. The sound in the room was too harsh, he said, and asked if we had a carpet we could put on the floor. Jack and Jeff brought one of the Oriental carpets down from the third-floor hallway; Horowitz stepped down from the platform, and he and Jimmy got down on their hands and knees together and unrolled the carpet. (The White House photographer missed a priceless and historic photograph.) Then Jimmy sat down on the piano bench and Horowitz began to play again, but it wasn't until they rolled out two other Oriental rugs from upstairs on the East Room floor that the sound was finally perfect.

And so was Horowitz's performance the next day. We invited his friend "Slava" Rostropovich and his wife, Galina Vishnevskaya, Andres Segovia, Isaac Stern, William Warfield and Todd Duncan, Dave Brubeck and Billy Taylor, our friend Robert Shaw, and an array of others.

The most excited guests, though, must have been the four students who had stood in line for tickets the month before to hear Horowitz's first concert at Carnegie Hall in twenty-five years only to have the line cut off just as they reached the window. I had clipped the story in the newspaper and sent it to Gretchen, asking her to try to locate the students and invite them to the White House, only to discover that Jimmy had clipped the same article to send to me, and Gretchen had clipped it herself. Miraculously, we found all four students, though when they received their White House invitations they didn't believe they were authentic. One, Bruce Josephy from West Haven, Connecticut, wrote to ask if his admission through the Southwest Gate would be "guaranteed." It was. And the concert itself, like the others that followed, was magic.

We continued the concerts with a roster of world-renowned artists: Maestro Mstislav Rostropovich, who I think is the greatest cellist in the world, with his daughter accompanying him on the piano; Leontyne Price, Jimmy's favorite of all sopranos; Mikhail Baryshnikov dancing with Patricia McBride and Heather Watts; and Andres Segovia playing his classical guitar. Every three or four months, the performances were carried live into the homes of millions of people.

Unfortunately, in the fall of 1979 PBS decided they could no longer televise the series for political reasons. The time for the presidential campaign was approaching, and the public broadcasting officials must have been worried that they would have to give equal time to other presidential candidates if they continued to carry the program. It seemed sad that even culture was considered political. Isaac Stern had already agreed to be our next performer, and millions of people lost an opportunity to see and hear him play because of this decision.

Some events seemed to sail beyond the meticulous planning

and the White House pomp and glitter. They took on a special significance as they unfolded, and made me feel that history was being made right before my eyes. The visit of Pope John Paul II was such an occasion. Amy and I had visited the Pope in Rome early in 1979, and I was delighted that he accepted our invitation to come to the White House when he toured the United States later that year.

I was the privileged person to go to Boston to greet him upon his arrival in our country. The weather was damp and windy the day he was to arrive. I had struggled with my welcoming remarks the night before at Camp David and had gotten up at 5:30 A.M. to drive into Washington for the flight to Boston, since the weather was too bad for a helicopter. I was worried about the hat I planned to wear at the arrival ceremony. Would it blow away in the wind? Would it cover my face too much? I wanted everything to be perfect for this visit—the first state visit of a Pope to Washington. A large crowd of dignitaries waited quietly in the mist at the Boston airport. The Pope's plane landed and there he was, standing in the doorway in his crimson robe, lifting his arms in greeting. The group cheered as he came down the steps, knelt down, and kissed the ground. His special blessing of that ground and of our country seemed to wash over me as well. I was thrilled to welcome him to the United States and to hear him recall our first meeting and my invitation for him to be with us in Washington.

At the end of his tour, five days later, Jimmy welcomed him to the White House among one of the largest crowds ever assembled there. Thousands of dignitaries and officials from all over the country had asked for months in every possible way for themselves or their constituents to be included at this reception. Even with strict control, the invitation list grew and grew until we decided to hold the reception outdoors, with the Pope to appear first on the north side of the White House and then on the South Lawn, to accommodate as many people as we could. The weather had continued to be rainy and cold throughout the Pope's visit, and I couldn't imagine how miserable an outdoor reception at the White House was going to be for the thousands of people crowded onto the wet lawns. As the Pope arrived, however, the clouds lifted and sun poured onto the lawns and crowds. Leontyne Price sang "The Lord's Prayer" to open the ceremonies. Jimmy made his remarks, and when the Pope began to reply, a sudden breeze lifted his cape up around his face. Jimmy reached over and gently held it down while we listened intently to the Pope's clear, slow English, challenging us to be the kinds of leaders the world needs to stand for peace and human rights. It was a moment when time seemed to stop, when I was full of the promise of what could be possible, in this house, from this place. Then Maestro Rostropovich and the National Symphony began to play, and the Pope moved slowly through the crowds, touching, blessing, as many as he could reach. Leontyne Price's "America the Beautiful" captured the moment as the Pope prepared to go, leaving behind him a feeling of fresh new hope that peace among all people is really possible.

❦ 9 ❧

Summit at Camp David

September of 1978 found us at Camp David. We hadn't come to "get away from it all." This time was different. We were anxiously awaiting the arrival of Prime Minister Menachem Begin of Israel and President Anwar Sadat of Egypt. Jimmy had invited them to our beautiful, secluded place in hopes of furthering the stalled peace efforts in the Middle East. They had both accepted, and their arrivals were imminent.

Everything was ready. There was added security, which was to be expected with three heads of state present. Working with Kit Dobelle, the chief of protocol, we had made great preparations to assure the convenience and comfort of everyone.

We would stay in our regular cabin, Aspen. The Sadats would be in Dogwood, the same one they enjoyed on an earlier visit, and the Begins would be in Birch, the other prominent cabin on the grounds. Both Dogwood and Birch were just across the winding driveway and through some trees from our cabin. We were all less than a hundred yards apart.

The other guests, officials and support staff, would double up in the smaller cabins on the grounds. There were really not enough houses to go around. When we first presented the plan for rooms to the advance team of Israelis and Egyptians, each said they needed more space. We kept taking away from the space of our American team until finally most of them were assigned to the military barracks on the base.

223

Large vans had been moved into the camp and converted into communications centers, one for the Israelis and one for the Egyptians, with direct telephone lines to their respective countries so the absent leaders could continue to manage the affairs of their governments.

Several dozen Navy stewards were on board and ready to help, though we worried that they might need more arms and legs! We were expecting more than a hundred people when everyone was counted, since each leader would be bringing his major advisers and a secretarial staff. Each would also bring his personal physician and Sadat, his own chef; because of his health, Sadat's diet was severely restricted, consisting primarily of boiled meats and vegetables and honey-flavored mint tea.

The food arrangements had been complicated. President Sadat's chef would be preparing all his meals. We would need to prepare kosher food for Prime Minister Begin and any other Israelis who preferred it. Our meals would be prepared in the kitchen in our cabin; and then, of course, we would have to feed all the other participants.

After much discussion, we decided that all the food for the three principals would be cooked in our kitchen at Aspen, including all the kosher food. We set a section of the kitchen aside for the pots, pans, and dishes used in preparing the kosher food. Later we marveled at the ease with which Sadat's chef, our regular stewards, and the kosher cooks shared the same kitchen. And we had a lot of laughs about the food.

Jimmy and I were planning to eat in our cabin and thought that the Begins and Sadats would eat in theirs. Everyone else would have meals at Laurel, the staff dining hall, which had a large kitchen and dining room that could accommodate everyone as well as a comfortable sitting area, large fireplace, and television sets. But instead of eating in their cabin, the Begins often ate at Laurel with their staff, causing a crisis in our kitchen. When the cooks saw them walk by on the way to Laurel at mealtime, they would have to put together more kosher food quickly, load up the golf cart with it, and hurry down to the big dining hall. Everybody who ate with the Begins ordered kosher food. But when the prime minister ate in his cabin, there were few requests for it.

The food was always delicious at Camp David, and at the summit everyone ate and ate. Originally, the members of the delegations thought everyone would be involved in all the talks, but it didn't happen that way, and many were left with much spare time. They watched movies, played tennis, rode bikes, did some background work for the talks and . . . ate. At first they worried about eating the delicious cakes, pies, and mousses and gaining too much weight. But the desserts were too good to pass up, and for months afterward the participants complained about the ten extra pounds they'd put on at Camp David.

Other special arrangements also had to be made. Sadat had requested a private place for his prayers, so the movie theater, which doubled as a chapel for us on weekends, became a temporary mosque.

We chose Holly, the cabin that ordinarily served as a recreation center for the Camp David personnel, as the meeting place for the peace talks. Ideally located between Laurel and the cabins of the three principals, it had a small, cozy reading room that made an ideal conference room and was far better suited for the mood we wanted to create than the formal, cold conference room at Laurel. Holly also had a pool table and movie screen in another room, and we ordered some good movies to provide diversion from the very serious and tense negotiations. The projector ended up running almost twenty-four hours a day, and the projectionist later reported that fifty-eight movies were seen during the thirteen-day period we were there.

The tennis courts were freshly groomed; bicycles were in the racks; there were chess and other games such as Ping-Pong and bowling; and, of course, the wooded trails were beautiful and peaceful, and almost always one could see squirrels and woodchucks and deer. This was surely the ideal place for the peace talks, with a chance for easy informality for the participants.

Even before his inauguration, Jimmy had decided that working for peace in the Middle East would be one of his most important responsibilities. He was convinced that an end to war in that region was vital to the peace of the world and, morever, he believed the time had come when Israel and the key Arab countries might be ready to negotiate.

Before Jimmy began his concerted effort toward this goal, no Arab leader had even been willing to recognize the right of Israel to exist, and the new Israeli prime minister, Menachem Begin, seemed completely rigid in his views. But Jimmy continued to work with the leaders of all the countries involved, and a breakthrough finally came when President Anwar Sadat of Egypt made his dramatic visit to Jerusalem in November 1977. This proved both a joy and a terror for the Israelis. They yearned for peace but they were afraid to trust their ancient enemy. Other Arab nations bitterly opposed the Egyptian initiative, and after a few weeks all momentum toward peace was lost again and the issues seemed irreconcilable.

Jimmy had pondered the developments, and on a July afternoon as we were walking through the woods at Camp David he told me of an idea: "It's so beautiful here. I don't believe anybody could stay in this place, close to nature, peaceful and isolated from the world, and still carry a grudge. I believe if I could get Sadat and Begin both here together, we could work out some of the problems between them, or at least we could learn to understand each other better and maybe make some progress. Everything's going backward now." I agreed with him, and encouraged him to pursue the idea.

After thinking and talking about it all weekend, Jimmy had decided it was worth a try. It would probably not be pleasant, and such an effort was full of serious political risks, but it was obvious that there would never be an agreement between the two antagonists without the help of the United States. There had been too many harsh public statements on both sides over the past years and too many rigid positions taken that made it impossible for either leader to change his mind or his position without a third party to act as a scapegoat.

"Are you willing to be the scapegoat?" I asked.

"What else is new?" he replied.

And what if they came and it was a colossal failure? "You've never been afraid of failure before," I reminded him. He had always told me that "you can guarantee that you won't fail if you don't try anything. You can also guarantee that you won't succeed."

Summits between leaders are usually held after all disagreements have been worked out, and they gather to make minor last-minute decisions and announce the good news to the press. Jimmy intended to meet with hostile parties to get talks started with no guarantee of positive results. Furthermore, as an impartial mediator, he would have to bear the brunt of each leader's animosity toward the other.

I had confidence in him, though. I believed that if anybody

could make it work, he could. His advisors, however, were not so sure. After our conversation that weekend, he had asked Fritz Mondale, Cy Vance, Harold Brown, Zbig Brzezinski, Jody Powell, and Hamilton Jordan to join him for a special meeting, and when he told them what he had in mind, none of them thought he had much chance of success. Yet no one had a better idea.

In June Jimmy had discussed the idea of a deeper personal participation with a small group of political advisers including Charlie Kirbo, the distinguished Washington leaders Clark Clifford and Sol Linowitz, and one of our nation's top businessmen, Irving Shapiro. Most of them tried to talk him out of it, citing the political liability: "Stay as aloof as possible from direct involvement in the Middle East negotiations; it's a losing proposition." There was little chance for success, they said, and he needed a success. Also, they pointed out, there hadn't been peace between the Arabs and the Jews for hundreds of years. Why did he think it was possible now?

Jimmy listened to all their arguments, but as he later wrote: "No one, including me, could think of a specific route to success, but everyone could describe a dozen logical scenarios for failure— and all were eager to do so. I slowly became hardened against them, and as stubborn as at any other time I can remember."

Early in August of 1978, Secretary of State Vance flew to Israel and Egypt to personally deliver invitations to the two leaders. Both accepted enthusiastically.

The wives of both leaders had been included in the invitation. "There are going to be a lot of hard feelings and tough fights," Jimmy told me. "The atmosphere will be more congenial if all of you are there."

We knew that Prime Minister Begin, especially, was much more relaxed and willing to talk openly when his wife, Aliza, was with him. During a private dinner with them one night in our dining room in the White House, the prime minister had been remarkably frank and open and charming. But after dinner, when we went with Jimmy to the Oval Office for discussions, he had withdrawn and become very formal again, hesitant to discuss any alternatives to his rigid positions on the controversial issues. The presence of Aliza, then, seemed essential.

And I was pleased that Sadat's wife, Jehan, was coming. We had become friends during a state visit our first year in the White House. I had learned that she was an early riser, up at four-thirty every morning to study for her degree in Arabic literature. I told her she was like Jimmy, who also woke up alert and ready to go to work, and that I was just the opposite. She said that Sadat was too, never having an appointment until ten o'clock in the morning and never going to bed before midnight.

Jimmy and Sadat had also liked each other immediately, and after this initial state visit, the two began to telephone each other regularly and to exchange correspondence, often handwritten notes. President Sadat had promised Jimmy that evening in April when they first met that "at a crucial moment you can count on my support when obstacles arise in our common search for peace." Months passed, with no progress toward peace in spite of all efforts, and on October 21, 1977, Jimmy wrote to him: "The moment has arrived."

Sadat's reply was immediate, and within days they were on the telephone to discuss several proposals. Then a final plan was decided upon—and Sadat stunned the world with the announcement that he was going to Jerusalem!

Afterward, the reaction to the trip from Sadat's Arab friends was almost totally negative, and the talks that followed between him and Prime Minister Begin were fruitless. Sadat had become very bitter, and everyone was worried about what he would do. That's when Jimmy decided to invite him to Camp David for the first visit—to reassure him in order to keep the peace effort alive.

He had accepted the invitation eagerly and arrived with Jehan on February 3, 1978, seven months before the Camp David negotiations began, as it turned out.

It started out as a cold weekend in more ways than one. In conversations even before we got to Camp David, Jimmy realized that Sadat had come to tell him that he was going to condemn Begin and break off all efforts to reach a settlement. It was only after hours of intense personal discussion that Jimmy was able to get him to agree to continue his efforts.

The thaw came in the personal and political relationships, but not in the weather. When we got to Camp David, the temperature was well below freezing and the snow was knee deep, a sight the Sadats had seldom seen, and they hoped to see snow falling before they left. We made the mistake of suggesting that we walk the quarter mile from the helipad to the cabins to enjoy the new snow, but President Sadat, who refused to wear a hat, got bitterly cold on the way and was shaking when we reached our cabin. Thanks to the Navy stewards, there was a roaring fire in the fireplace to greet us, and Sadat was soon warm. But we were worried about him, and he about himself, since he had had a heart attack and was always very careful about his health. After that we stayed inside most of the weekend, going from cabin to cabin only for meetings and meals, except once, when we took a brief ride in the snowmobiles, making sure Sadat was bundled up against the cold. I wish we had taken a photograph of him with my white wool scarf tied around his head! I rode with Anwar and Jehan rode with Jimmy, and we raced each other around the snow-covered field where the helicopters land. The Sadats loved it, and afterward they had an argument about whether or not snowmobiles could be used on the sand in Egypt. He said yes; she, no. I wonder if they ever tried.

I learned to make hot mint tea that weekend for Sadat. Though he didn't eat much, he loved tea, made by boiling fresh mint leaves in water and adding honey—that's all. It was good but very sweet, and I decided that was how Sadat got his energy. Jehan said it was also very soothing and calming, and a cup at bedtime helped one sleep.

A very religious person, President Sadat prayed five times a day. Most of the time he stopped wherever he was to say his prayers, but he also believed that work was sacred, and he told me that he would occasionally put off a prayer until later if he was working. He said that many Moslems do not have this same belief and will interrupt their work to pray.

While we were getting acquainted, the Sadats described to us their first meeting, at the home of Jehan's cousin, whose husband was one of President Sadat's best friends. Sadat was well known in Egypt, having joined with a small group of other revolutionaries to overthrow an oppressive government, and he had been thrown into prison for his activities. He was something of a folk hero to the people, and Jehan had fallen in love with him, sight unseen. She said she longed to meet him and visited her cousin's home often, hoping to get a glimpse of him. One day at her cousin's, she was eating mangos and had gotten juice all over her face. Going to the bathroom to wash up, she walked into the hall and there he was, just sitting there. She said that after dreaming for so long of a romantic meeting with him, she was mortified that he would first see her with mango juice all over her face. He laughed at her—and she cried. And the romance began.

After their marriage, they were very poor. Sadat had been a lieutenant in the Army before going to prison and had applied to get back in, but they hadn't heard whether he would be accepted or not. One evening when they were despondent, waiting to hear from the army and without enough money to pay the rent, they decided to go out for some tea. A fortuneteller came by their table and wanted to tell Jehan's fortune, a common practice in Egypt. At first Sadat refused, then decided it was all right. The man looked at her tea leaves and told her two things she still remembered: She was going to have four children, three girls and one boy, and she was going to be the First Lady of Egypt. "The First Lady of Egypt! What does that mean?" she asked the fortuneteller, but he said he didn't know. She said she remembered their walking back home hand in hand, happy and singing, with her teasing Sadat that maybe she would marry a king someday since she was going to be First Lady. The same day they learned that he had been accepted back into the Army.

She would never have her fortune told again: She indeed had three girls and one boy and became the First Lady of Egypt.

That February weekend had gone well, and Jimmy was able to convince Sadat not to denounce Begin and terminate the peace negotiations. And when we left the camp on Sunday afternoon, it had begun to snow softly.

In the months that followed, however, there had been rounds of verbal attacks and increasing tension between Sadat and Begin, and despite Sadat's expressed desire for an agreement and an end to the war (Israel and Egypt were still legally at war), there were a few conditions upon which Sadat insisted, and on these he was extremely rigid.

In our experiences with the Begins and the Sadats, we had found the two men to be very different. President Sadat would speak at length about peace and how to achieve it. Prime Minister Begin liked small talk, especially about his grandchildren, and he yearned for a peaceful life with them. But when serious discussion about peace efforts arose, he would change the subject and talk for hours about his past experiences and the Holocaust—the death of his family at the hands of the Nazis, the time he had spent in a Russian prison, and his years as a leader in the underground. Listening to him made it easier to understand how his strict beliefs and positions had developed. Jimmy knew that because of these beliefs and positions he would be very suspicious of any bold peace effort, and it was going to be hard for him to make the compromises necessary to reach a final agreement.

Tuesday, September 5, 1978. The long-awaited day was here. Early in the afternoon, Jimmy had briefed me on the points of the "talks," which he had summarized on a lined pad. He planned to have me and Mrs. Begin present during his initial meeting with the prime minister in hopes of a casual and easy conversation. And he wanted me to understand the issues as well as the nuances of certain words and phrases. What we called the West Bank, for example, was Judea and Samaria to Begin. The Palestinians to us were Palestinian Arabs to Begin. And so on.

We watched on network television as each delegation arrived at Andrews Air Force Base; from there they were to come by helicopter to Camp David.

Sadat arrived first and emerged from the helicopter with his arms opened in embrace. He clasped Jimmy to his chest, then kissed me on both cheeks. But Jehan had not come with him. She was with their grandson, who was ill in a hospital in Paris. I was disappointed.

Two hours later Prime Minister Begin also arrived. As we watched on television, we saw that Mrs. Begin was not with him, either. We later learned, however, that she was simply delayed and would arrive the next day. But my chance to sit in on the first meeting was gone. When we met Begin at the helipad he and Jimmy embraced exactly as Sadat and Jimmy had done, and he kissed me on each cheek. So far, all was fine. The good will lasted only a few hours.

Despite all the anticipation and preparation, the first negotiations with the two principals were very discouraging. After meeting with Begin the first evening in the small study in our cabin, Jimmy felt the whole plan was probably futile. Instead of looking to the future, Begin remained entrenched in the past, talking about his by now familiar experiences with Jimmy. He was exactly as we had expected, hesitant about any bold peace effort. "I believe Begin will consider the summit a success if anything happens, even a very small thing, so that he can say we 'started something' . . . but I don't believe he has any intention of going through with a peace treaty," Jimmy told me that night.

* * *

Wednesday, September 6. The next morning was even worse. Jimmy emerged from his first meeting with Sadat visibly shaken. Not only had the leader whom Jimmy had counted on to be flexible presented a plan that was rigid and uncompromising, he had insisted upon showing it to Begin. "Begin will blow up," Jimmy said to Sadat after hearing the harsh Arab rhetoric blaming all previous wars on Israel and demanding that the Israelis offer indemnities for their use of occupied Egyptian land, pay for all the oil they had pumped out of wells in the Sinai, withdraw all their forces entirely to the original pre-1967 boundaries, allow the Palestinians to form their own nation, and relinquish control over East Jerusalem. Such a plan would obviously be totally unacceptable to the Israelis, but Sadat was adamant.

Reluctantly, Jimmy arranged a meeting of the two men in the afternoon for the presentation of the Egyptian document. Again, they would meet in the study in our cabin, but this time there would be ground rules. Knowing that Begin would completely reject Sadat's harsh document, it was decided that the Egyptian plan would be presented, the leaders would immediately disperse, and all comments would come later. Begin and Sadat, after all, had not been on good terms before they arrived. Now, Jimmy thought, things were going to be worse, and he was right. After Sadat read the plan aloud with much feeling, at times gripping the arms of the chair, only a few harsh words were exchanged, but more were to come.

Aliza Begin had arrived earlier in the day, and the Begins went for a walk with us after the meeting was over. (Sadat declined to join us, saying he had already had his exercise for the day). Begin, understandably, was shocked by Sadat's proposal and said he didn't know what to make of it. Was Sadat just being dramatic in laying out the maximum Arab positions without intending to pursue all of them, he mused as we strolled around the camp, or was there really no chance for any negotiating? Aliza and I listened as Jimmy tried to assure the prime minister that his first answer was right, that Sadat would be flexible as the negotiations progressed. But I don't think Begin was convinced.

I had decided to keep notes during the Camp David summit, since this was an extraordinary moment in history. Little did I know at the beginning that I would have almost two hundred typed pages by the end.

After only one evening and one full day, the situation seemed deadlocked already, and I asked Jimmy if he were sorry he had brought the two leaders together. "You know me better than that," he chided, but I sensed that some of his original optimism was gone.

The international "call to prayer" for the success of the Camp David meetings, which I had worked on with Jimmy's Prayer Breakfast group and Jody Powell, now seemed more important than ever. Since the major parties in these negotiations were deeply religious men, we had thought it appropriate to ask everyone in churches all over the world to share a special prayer for peace. The wording was delicate, but after much thought we were successful in drafting a statement that was approved by Christian, Moslem, and Jew: "After four wars, despite vast human efforts, the Holy Land does not yet enjoy the blessings of peace. Conscious of the grave issues which face us, we place our trust in the God of our fathers, from whom we seek wisdom and guidance. As we meet here at Camp David, we ask people of all faith to pray with us that peace and justice may result from these deliberations."

This was the press release and the only statement that was issued the first night of the talks. And for a long time it was the only issue everybody agreed on.

Thursday, September 7. It was a beautiful fall day, just the sort of day at Camp David that Jimmy had hoped would inspire peace and cooperation. But the foreign delegations were unmoved by the serenity. Jimmy had met informally with Begin and the Israelis at Holly early in the morning to discuss in general terms what he hoped to accomplish in the next few days, but all they could talk about was the unreasonable tone of Sadat's plan. The mood was pessimistic, and when the time came for Sadat and Begin to meet again, Jimmy was braced for the worst.

Since Begin liked the little study in our cabin, Jimmy decided that the three leaders would meet there for the remainder of the talks. When Prime Minister Begin arrived, followed shortly by President Sadat, Jimmy and I both walked out to greet them. The first problem of the day arose when we invited them into the cabin. Neither Begin nor Sadat would make the first move, each one hesitating over who should enter first. Then they laughed and Begin insisted that Sadat go ahead. As we watched, Jimmy said to me that Begin would never go ahead of Sadat, being perfectly proper according to protocol—president above prime minister—and that was true all during the summit.

Issues inside the study were not so easily settled. I sat down at my desk in my bedroom to work on some correspondence and almost immediately began to hear raised voices in the study. I was so nervous about what was happening that I couldn't concentrate and decided to go out of the house for a while. I called Aliza Begin and invited her to ride around the grounds with me in a golf cart. When we got back, the men were still meeting, so I asked her to have lunch with me. We ate on the back patio and spoke only of general things, including her interest in promoting volunteerism in Israel. She never mentioned the mission our husbands were involved in except to say that they were working hard and she hoped things would turn out well. I was just as glad not to talk about what was going on in the study. I didn't want her to know how worried I was.

When the men finally broke for lunch after three hours, Cy, Zbig, Ham, and Jody rushed to our cabin. "What happened?"

Jimmy answered, "It was mean. They were brutal with each other, personal." He said he made notes, looking down at his pad so they would have to talk with each other instead of through him. Sometimes when their words became too heated he had to break in. But at least they were still talking.

After the grueling session in the morning, the men went back for two more hours at five o'clock. And once more, the voice level rose. Jimmy told me later that Sadat kept referring to Begin as "Premier Begin," and Begin persistently derided Sadat on every issue in his position paper.

It was a relief for me to hear Amy's voice on the telephone. It was her first day at a new school in Washington, and I called to make sure she had gotten along all right. I wanted to stay in touch with her, too, so she wouldn't worry about us, because there was not much news from Camp David, only speculation and tension about what was happening. She was fine, excited about her teachers and her new schoolwork. Talking with Amy made my life seem normal again for the moment. It didn't last.

Jimmy had had such high hopes, and now he didn't know what to expect. He would only say after this last two-hour "confrontation" that they had reached a stalemate, and unless he could think of something, the talks for all practical purposes had failed. "There must be a way," he kept saying. "We all three want peace.

The people of Israel and Egypt want peace. We haven't found it yet, but there must be a way." When Jimmy's pondering, he gets quiet, and there's a vein in his temple that I can see pounding. Tonight it was pounding, and neither of us could eat much as the sun set on our third day.

At least there was something different on the agenda after dinner. We had invited the Marine Corps Silent Drill Team to perform for the foreign delegations, the families of the base personnel, and the press. This was the only time the press was admitted to the camp during the talks and more than 120 came—to observe only. When we planned the performance, we thought everyone would be hammering out the details of a negotiating document and it would be a pleasant break. Little did we know how despondent everyone would be.

The Marines were spectacular, marching silently without commands or music in close-order drill, doing intricate maneuvers with rifles and bayonets. A light mist of rain in the air made it even more breathtaking to see, with everyone anticipating rifles that had to be handled in perfect coordination slipping in hands, but it went off without mishap. After the performance, the Marine Band struck up a medley of patriotic songs from the three countries. And though the music was moving, it was also sad, since many of us in the audience suspected that the countries were no closer to peace than they had been before, and prospects for a breakthrough seemed gone. Sadat, especially, looked forlorn as the music swept over the crowd.

He was still very quiet and obviously depressed at the reception following the drill. I sat with him for a while on the low brick wall around the patio at Laurel and told him that I was sorry to see him so sad. "I have given so much and 'that man' [Prime Minister Begin] acts as though I have done nothing," Sadat told me. "I have given up all the past to start anew, but 'that man' will not let go of the past." I tried to reassure him, knowing he was going to meet with Jimmy after the reception, but he seemed inconsolable. Though I praised him for his patience and courage, as the world viewed it, for what he was trying to do, Sadat hardly seemed to hear me. "I would do anything to bring peace to our countries," he said. "But I feel it is no use."

After Jimmy and Sadat left the reception for the meeting with the Egyptian delegation, I stayed on. We had made a great effort that night to encourage the Israelis and Egyptians to mingle. We had put food on different tables around the room and on the patio, for example, hoping people would circulate instead of staying in small cliques. And our plan seemed to be working. Everybody was moving from table to table, sampling the fondue at one, dipping strawberries into chocolate at another, in a warm and sociable atmosphere. They were talking peacefully. Why couldn't their leaders?

When Jimmy got back to our cabin it was almost 1:00 A.M. He said Sadat had been cooperative and might make modifications. He also would accept a strong American role. Jimmy felt better but was still not very hopeful. It wasn't that the talks had broken down. They had just not had a chance to get started.

Friday, September 8. After a discouraging early morning strategy session with our people while Begin and Sadat met with their own advisers, Jimmy wanted a change of pace and we tried to play tennis, but we soon gave up. The telephone at the tennis court kept ringing: Senators were calling about legislation, and Harold Brown about a new defense bill. Working with Jimmy's outline of a comprehensive proposal, our own delegation at Camp David had begun to draw up an American plan to present to Israel and Egypt to keep the talks going. But when we got back to the cabin from the tennis court, we learned that Sadat was ready to go home, and the Israelis were already saying that Begin was preparing his reasons for not accomplishing anything.

"Get Phil Wise for me," Jimmy said. I called Phil, one of Jimmy's staff assistants, who came immediately, to be dispatched just as quickly to Begin's cabin. "Tell Begin I want to meet with him after lunch, then tell Sadat I want to see him an hour and a half later," Jimmy told Phil. "That will keep Sadat here for a while."

"Rosalynn, get Cy Vance on the telephone." When I did, Jimmy told Cy that it was time to get tough with Sadat, whose plan he never took seriously, and with the Israelis, whose positions he could not accept. "Proceed with the American plan. It must be fair to both sides," Jimmy said. "I know of no other possibility for progress." He had hoped that this could be avoided. An American plan gave both countries the chance to say that the President of the United States had tried to force an agreement on them. Worse still, each country could later claim that had it not been for American interference, Israel and Egypt might have worked out their own agreement. But now there was no other way.

Even though Jimmy had sent word to Begin that he would come to his cabin, Begin, following protocol, said this would not be possible, so they met in the little back room again. Predictably, the prime minister protested the drafting of an American plan. Jimmy believed Begin feared that if an American plan was basically fair, he might be forced into compromising on some difficult issues, although no one thought he wanted to face that. Jimmy insisted, telling him that our plan would contain no surprises and that he would present it to him first, before the Egyptians saw it.

The meeting with Sadat was scheduled for four o'clock, and at three fifty-five Jimmy and Begin were still in the study. I sent a note in to Jimmy, telling him what time it was, and immediately the two men emerged from the room. Prime Minister Begin left after inviting us to join them in the evening for their Sabbath dinner.

Jimmy hurried to Sadat's cabin to tell him he couldn't afford to leave with a stalemate. "You promised me," Jimmy said, reminding Sadat of his pledge to pursue peace. At least, Jimmy told him, the Egyptians and Americans could agree on a proposal even if the Israelis never accepted it. Sadat agreed. "You write it. You know the issues that are important to me. I will support any reasonable document you put forth."

So there it was. The Israelis, albeit reluctantly, had accepted the possibility of an American plan. And Sadat had handed the drafting of a plan over to the Americans. The summit, for the moment anyway, had been saved. Everyone was relieved.

I noted in my diary after these meetings that "when Sadat trusts someone, and he trusts Jimmy and Weizman, he will work with them and go all out with them. When he doesn't, and he doesn't trust Begin at all, he can be quite abusive.

"Begin, on the other hand, doesn't harbor such hard feelings. He is locked into positions by his past and is absolutely rigid about them. He does not want to be faced with having to negotiate on these positions. And he does not want to become emotionally involved. Zbig told me that at an earlier meeting, when Jimmy made an emotional plea to Begin and the Israelis for the chance to bring peace to the Mideast, Jimmy said, 'This Arab, who, after years of wars and distrusts and hatreds, is willing to negotiate . . . the whole world watching . . . you can do down in history as the great leader who brought peace,' Begin just looked down and began to recite paragraph and page numbers of the document, determined not to become emotionally involved or face the difficult decision."

The movie theater had become a banquet hall for the Jewish Sabbath dinner in the evening. Jimmy and I joined the prime minister and the Israeli delegation, and the mood was one of joy and friendship. There was no sign of the tension of the moment. I sat between Begin and Moshe Dayan, and Begin told me that they always put aside their concerns and observed the Sabbath with rejoicing and singing because the Bible says that you cannot serve God with sadness. Everyone sang and we tried to join in: There was laughter. It was a good evening.

The prime minister, helping me with the words of the songs, began to explain the meaning of one of the words. He was speaking of the Latin derivative, and I asked him how many languages he could speak. I am fascinated by languages and admire and envy anyone who is bilingual or, as in Prime Minister Begin's case, multilingual. He said he used to teach Latin and that he could speak Russian, German, the Slavic languages, English, Hebrew, and French fluently and could read Italian easily. He considers himself to be, and I think he is, a master of words. He will stop in the middle of a conversation when he uses a word and tell you how that word was formed and what it means. Jimmy says he does the same thing in discussing the peace proposals. Every word has to be labored over and considered in the context of its meaning in any prior agreement or settlement. It was very frustrating in the drafting of the peace proposal.

Begin also told me that he found Sadat to be a very bitter man at times, but, he said with amazement, "on several occasions since we have been here he has called me 'your kind sir,' and one time he even said, 'My dear Mr. Begin, Mr. Begin, Mr. Begin'!"

I found my other dinner partner, Moshe Dayan, to be charming. I also liked what he said (or maybe that's why I found him charming). He told me, and I quote from my diary, "that he had been preparing for this meeting for the last thirty years . . . that there had not been one instance when the Middle East countries were negotiating for peace. He had negotiated for other things, but never for peace, and he said this could not happen, this meeting and the possibility for negotiating for peace, if it had not been for President Carter. There had never been a President in the past willing to devote as much time to an all-out effort as President Carter. He said Nixon wanted to help but he was not willing to put his personal prestige on the line, and without this, the meeting would not have been possible."

Dayan pointed out that he had been involved in every single negotiation since Israel was founded. He had seen the birth of the country, and with this summit, he might finally see peace brought to the region. He said that if for some reason Sadat could not be reasoned with and left, he did not see any opportunity for peace anytime in the foreseeable future. It would only mean more hostilities and more bad feelings. This conversation made me even more aware of the stakes involved in the talks.

Thus, at the end of the fourth day of the summit, Jimmy and I returned to our cabin with our spirits buoyed. There was no special reason for optimism, but at least, as Jimmy said, "we have bought some time with our American plan." And we had bought ourselves some relaxation: We watched the movie *Sleuth*, with Michael Caine and Laurence Olivier, before going to bed.

The weekend, September 9 and 10. All efforts on Saturday went toward drafting the American plan. Jimmy spent most of the day on it, consulting closely with our American team to put together a fresh and comprehensive proposal. From sunup they worked through sundown, and shortly after midnight the document was ready to be put in final form. Everyone was exhausted but pleased. Jimmy said, "Now all we have to do is get both sides to agree to sign it!" Everyone laughed.

The prediction of our team was that when the plan was presented, Sadat would sign it and Begin probably would not. But if it was obviously fair, Begin would take it back and maybe his Cabinet or the Knesset would overrule him and accept it. I hoped I was not being too optimistic.

It had been a long day but the most pleasant day of the summit for me. There was at least a glimmer of hope again, and late Saturday afternoon I had gone out to ride a bike with Amy, her friend Elizabeth Moore, and Jeff and Annette, who had all come for the weekend. Jimmy joined us briefly, saying he had to get out of the back room for a while and get some fresh air. There was also the satisfaction of having the U.S. plan completed. I would wait until tomorrow to begin worrying about how Prime Minister Begin would react to it. When we finally went to bed that night, it was long after midnight, and there were not many sleeping hours left before dawn.

The next day was Sunday, the sixth day, and we had thought we would only be here for three or four days. Yet the new U.S. plan had not even been seen by the Israelis or Egyptians. How long was it going to take for everyone to see it, discuss it, dissect it, agree to any of it? One thing I think everyone agreed on was that if the summit could end in success, the time involved didn't matter.

But now everyone was exhausted and it was time to take a break, so on Sunday morning after church Jimmy decided to take Sadat and Begin to nearby Gettysburg. It would be good to get them together again, away from the tense atmosphere of the peace talks. They all agreed not to discuss any political issues. The two leaders had not seen each other since the Marine drill on Thursday evening, when they had not spoken to each other.

Aliza Begin and I rode together with the three men in a limousine, with Jimmy sitting between the other two leaders. On the way to Gettysburg, Begin and Sadat, who had both been in prison for their political actions, talked about their experience as prisoners. Sadat said that for more than a year he had no reading material and did nothing but meditate. Once he was given access to books, he became a voracious reader. Begin had no reading materials either, but, he said, "the prison was a university." He had spent most of his time teaching history and languages to his cellmates, who were generals and high-ranking Polish officials. I'm sure he was a good teacher, being knowledgeable about both subjects.

No one mentioned the negotiations. Sadat, not surprisingly, was very interested in our Civil War. He knew much of the history of the area we were going to visit and recalled the details of the battle. Begin, an admirer of Abraham Lincoln, recited the Gettysburg address to us as we neared the famous battle site.

Everyone seemed to enjoy the morning, but the task for the afternoon was to present the U.S. proposal to Begin, and our team was on edge. They knew that all the serious issues would be addressed in the document and that the prime minister had yet to acknowledge that they would even be considered during the summit.

When the men returned to Camp David for their meeting, Aliza and I continued on to a Folk Craft Show in the national park close to Camp David. It was a nice diversion, but after Aliza was presented with a ceramic bowl by the park ranger and had bought two cornshuck dolls for Amy, we left. We were both nervous and anxious to get back to see what was happening at the negotiating table, though we never mentioned it.

When we arrived there was no news. Jimmy, Mondale, Vance, and Brzezinski had met with the Israeli team and given them copies of the plan. Each had read it silently. Afterward, without commenting on it, Begin had insisted that they adjourn to study the proposal and meet again in four hours. Our team returned to our cabin to compare impressions of the meeting. Everyone agreed that Dayan, Weizman, and Barak, the attorney general of Israel and a trusted adviser to Begin, had been sympathetic. After reading the proposal, in fact, Weizman had looked up at Cy and nodded his head. But everyone also knew that even if Begin's aides might support the plan, it was no guarantee that Begin would. His aides couldn't disagree with him publicly, but surely they could privately, and we all wished we could hear the discussions among the Israelis now.

The evening was long and suspenseful. After Jimmy left at nine-thirty for the meeting in Holly with Begin and his people, I watched a movie in our cabin, then walked to Holly and sat on the steps, talking with some of the assistants who were also nervously waiting. Around midnight, when the meeting still hadn't broken up, I went to the Israeli communications trailer and had a cup of coffee with one of the secretaries there. When there was still no sign of the men, I walked back to Aspen and went to bed, but I couldn't sleep. Jimmy finally came in at 3:45 A.M. "What happened?" Always my first words. He said, "We had to do a song and dance with Begin over every word. I'll tell you about it in the morning."

He was obviously exhausted and didn't want to talk, and if things had really blown up he would have told me so, so I reconciled myself and tried to go to sleep.

Monday, September 11. A bittersweet day. Begin had not rejected the U.S. proposal outright the night before, but he had been very difficult during the meeting. Entrenched in the past, he had started by refusing to accept the language in the new proposal that had even been used, and accepted by Israel, in United Nations Resolution 242. Understandably, Jimmy was furious. "If you won't accept past agreements, then we're wasting our time here," Zbig told me that Jimmy said. "It's time to go home. It was a mistake to have called you here in the first place." Jimmy admitted to me that he had gotten really mad. He seldom did that, but he said, "Begin was completely unreasonable. If we accomplish anything, it will be a miracle."

After arguing over the language in UN Resolution 242 for the major part of an hour, they had finally gotten down to discussing the specifics of the new proposal. Begin disagreed on almost every major issue and with the wording on everything. Frequently, the Israelis had long discussions with each other in Hebrew. Jimmy said it irritated him until he decided that it saved time. They could have a private discussion at the table, with no need to go into another room for a conference. "But," he said, "it was so tedious, so time-consuming, so discouraging, so frustrating." Once more Jimmy had difficulty keeping his patience. "I finally said, 'Listen, we're trying to help you bring peace to your land. You would have us feel that we are going out of our way deliberately to be as unfair to Israel as possible. That's not true. We want to help, but you make it very hard for us. We need some degree of co-operation and trust.'"

From all reports, Jimmy was superb that night. Cy Vance told me afterward that Weizman said to him, "I have not known your President before, but I am really impressed with him. . . . He was totally in command." Cy told him that he had known and served with four presidents and that President Carter was the most intelligent and able, to which Weizman replied, "I can already see that."

At least Jimmy now had something to show Sadat, and after a new draft was typed, incorporating some small changes the Israelis had made and with which Jimmy agreed, the two men met alone in our cabin. Jimmy was pessimistic about the Israelis' signing any agreement at all, and he told Sadat that he wanted a document that the Americans and Egyptians could accept and one that under close scrutiny by everyone—Israelis, American Jews, Arabs, Congress—would be considered completely fair. But Sadat also had changes to make: some minor, some that were going to be problems.

With the first reactions to the new proposal, the two sides were still poles apart on most of the controversial issues, including the dismantling of all Israeli settlements on Egyptian soil. Begin claimed that the settlements in the Egyptian-owned Sinai were a necessary buffer between Gaza and Egypt while Sadat would never yield on the question of leaving Israeli settlements anywhere in the Sinai region. The Arab role in Jerusalem was also highly controversial, along with the free participation of the Palestinians in all future negotiations and the definition of the permanent status of the West Bank. There was also talk brewing in each camp about the compromises that would or would not be made before any agreement could be reached. Any little spark of hope or cloud of pessimism always took over the scene, and now it was pessimism. Everyone was downcast.

It was generally accepted at Camp David that Begin's team was more flexible than he was. On the other hand, Sadat seemed more flexible than the other Egyptians, who acted as a restraining force on him. Osama El Baz, for example, had been a member of Palestinian organizations as a student and was the real hard-liner of the Egyptian delegation. Jimmy knew that if El Baz approved something, all the other Egyptians could accept it. As each delegation had great influence on its respective leader and represented the varying interests of the Egyptian parliament and the Israeli Knesset, both of which would be voting on the results of the summit, the teams now took on vital roles in the negotiations.

While the Egyptians were studying the U.S. plan, Jimmy met with Dayan, Weizman, and Barak and was heartened by the discussion. They spoke frankly about their positions on sensitive issues, positions they had not been willing to state aloud before. And Dayan gave him the best news. Begin, he said, was not going to reject the U.S. proposal outright. Instead, he was working on the politics of the proposal. He had three alternatives: (1) accept parts of the plan; (2) recommend that parts be accepted but let the Cabinet and the Knesset make the final decision; or (3) recommend that parts be rejected but still leave the final decision to the Cabinet and the Knesset. Begin may understandably have been covering himself, but even so, there was now a possibility that something might be accomplished.

The day ended late, but with Jimmy feeling more positive in spite of his exhaustion. No one had slept more than a few hours in the last forty-eight, and since Saturday Jimmy had been in continuous meetings. The other leaders were tired, too, having worked well into the nights, but at least they could rest between meetings. When Jimmy got through working with one leader, he went right on to meet with the other. I kept urging him to rest, but he said he couldn't. There was so much tension, and every minute was valuable in keeping feelings assuaged and the Egyptians and Israelis assured that they were not wasting their time, that there was progress and the possibility of accomplishment. In between, he devised strategy and drafted texts with his own team. Then he dictated his notes, as he did after every meeting, and went to bed. I didn't know how long any of them could keep up this pace.

Aliza Begin was just as worried about her husband. Unlike Sadat, who was extremely careful about his health and rigid in his diet and exercise (he walked exactly four kilometers every morning at eight o'clock), Begin seemed unconcerned for his health. But Aliza was attentive to his every action, while Begin, in turn, worried about Aliza's health. He told us that she was not well, and it was evident that she had a breathing problem. She used an inhaler often, but also smoked cigarettes continuously. I was worried about her too. The Begins were very close and caring about each other, and I don't think the prime minister ever would have stayed as long if Aliza had not been there.

Tuesday, September 12, day number eight. "We were both up early. Jimmy said he was still going to try to get a document that everyone could sign. He has developed a friendly, close feeling with some of the Israelis. Today he plans to have a tough session with Sadat. He says Sadat has five of his army divisions deployed along the Suez Canal facing Israel, and it's time for him to realize that his greatest threat is from his African neighbors. His troops should be free to fend off Communist-inspired attacks from Africa. He thinks Sadat's main worry of the moment is what the Saudis and other Arabs will think of him and any agreement that he accepts."

I had to go into Washington that morning for a reception for the American Newspaper Women's Organization. It was good to get away for a while, especially when I thought things were looking up. I was determined to be optimistic. I thought Sadat and the Egyptians would be amenable to Jimmy's tough session, but I have to admit that there was a bit of nagging fear behind my optimism all afternoon and I was anxious to get back.

When I returned to Camp David, Jimmy and I went for a walk. It was a beautiful evening, the night air damp and cool. Jimmy was beginning to hope for a proposal both men could sign. He said it would be unfair and unprofitable to make Begin look bad by having the United States sign a separate agreement with Egypt. After all, Begin was being very courageous. He was having to compromise long-held positions, and when he got back home, those opposing him would be his own party people, the ones who had hidden him when he was in the underground and with whom he had worked during all these years.

The next day Jimmy planned to start drafting the final document, with one writer from Begin and one from Sadat to help. He believed this would expedite the process by allowing disagreements and the need for certain language to be dealt with at the beginning.

This process would dominate the talks for the remainder of the time, the drafting and redrafting, with Aharon Barak from the Israelis and Osama El Baz from the Egyptians and with Cy Vance, who stayed with them to take notes during the long sessions. They spent hours and hours drafting a proposal, going over it continually with each side, making subtle and delicate changes to incorporate each one's wishes. Israeli language, Egyptian language, decision. For example: "Jerusalem shall be an undivided city" instead of "It shall be undivided." El Baz said it would please the Arabs; Barak, the Israelis would probably accept it. (In the end, any reference to Jerusalem was taken out.) After the changes were made, a new draft would be typed, the Israeli and Egyptian teams would study it, and the process would begin all over again, slowly and steadily narrowing the differences.

Meanwhile, Zbig and the other members of our team met with the foreign ministers and advisers of both delegations, building on the proposals advanced and feeding ideas for resolving the differences.

Wednesday, September 13, the ninth day of the summit. Another day of drafting, another day of slowly and steadily making progress. After having tea with Aliza Begin in the afternoon, I had to go back to Washington. No one had ever dreamed that we would be locked into the peace talks this long, and events had been scheduled at the White House every day for the rest of the week except Saturday. On Sunday morning there would be a reception for four hundred members of the Hispanic community followed by a long-awaited cello concert in the afternoon by Mstislav Rostropovich. Some of these events were my commitments, others

were Jimmy's; some, especially the concert, were ours together.
I would have to fulfill them all because Jimmy could not leave
the camp. Tonight we were having the race car drivers, the bal-
loonists who had just flown across the Atlantic, and Willie Nelson
to entertain. And Jimmy would miss it.

While we had been at Camp David, the helicopters ran regular
schedules to and from Washington. Staff members—including
Chip, who was running errands for Jimmy and me; Cabinet members, if they needed to talk with Jimmy personally or have him
sign some official document; and Fritz Mondale, who was handling
everything possible at the White House—flew back and forth for
meetings. And there were always staff reports and papers to read
and sign. The affairs of government did not stand still while the
future of the Middle East was being debated on the mountaintop.
Jimmy continued to deal with these matters and with the members
of Congress, having remarkable success on Capitol Hill during
this interval. I had my work to do also and I stayed in constant
touch with my staff; I also missed Amy. But I wanted to be near
Jimmy, to help him as much as I could. And I had become so
caught up in the drama of the peace negotiations that as much as
I wanted to get away from the tension, when I did I couldn't wait
to get back.

And the drama was growing. Though the differences between
the two leaders were being narrowed, there were serious disagreements that had not been resolved. Furthermore, the Egyptians were
getting more and more resistant to some of Sadat's concessions.

When I returned from the White House in the evening, I found
Jimmy in bed reading. He said things had gone well with the
Israelis during the day, terrible with the Egyptians. In the nego-
tiating session, El Baz had insisted that Egypt would not allow
Israel to have a say in the fate of the West Bank refugees, which
Jimmy knew to be contrary to Sadat's views. When questioned,
El Baz finally admitted that he had not even discussed the issue
with Sadat. Jimmy became angry and ended the meeting, telling
the Egyptian that he wanted to see Sadat immediately. But word
came back that Sadat had gone to bed and asked not to be disturbed.
Jimmy then made arrangements to walk with him the next morning
at eight o'clock.

I woke up suddenly at 4:00 A.M. and realized that Jimmy was
awake too. He was worried about Sadat: "I don't know exactly
why, but I have an uneasy feeling about Sadat's safety." Despite

the hour, he called the Secret Service agents and Zbig and asked them to come to our cabin. He told them about the concessions made by Sadat that were not well accepted by others in the Egyptian delegation and about a heated discussion he had seen on Sadat's porch late the previous afternoon among some of his more militant advisers; he also told them about the message he had received early in the evening that Sadat had retired when it was common knowledge that he stayed up late every night. Jimmy directed the agents and Zbig to check on Sadat quietly and to increase the security around his cabin. That was all he could do and we went back to bed.

Thursday, September 14. At eight o'clock we looked out the window and there was Sadat, hale and hearty, ready for his daily walk. Relieved, Jimmy immediately joined him, and our fears of the night dissipated in the morning sun.

When he returned, Jimmy went straight back to his study to work on the proposal before the other "drafters" arrived. When I looked into the room to see what his mood was, he pushed back his chair and said, "Come here." I went in and sat on his lap. He was obviously pleased and hopeful for a change, and I was happy for him. "I think it's all coming together now," he said.

I tried hard to contain my optimism on another trip to the White House. I held a luncheon for officials of Washington's Community Foundation and other leaders in the city in an effort to encourage greater participation and encouragement for the foundation. It was essential not to show any emotions, good or bad, about the progress of the peace talks, which could only create speculation, but with things so positive it was hard.

When I returned to Camp David that afternoon, I rushed to find Jimmy, Ham, and Zbig in the swimming pool behind our cabin. One look and I immediately knew that something was wrong. The talks had collapsed completely, they told me. "You're teasing. I know you're teasing me," I said desperately. "No," Jimmy said quietly, "we've failed. We're trying now to think of the best way to present the failure to the public." And all day while I was gone I had felt so good. I wished I had just stayed away.

Through all the drafting and redrafting of the treaty, Jimmy told me, they had made a lot of small, substantive agreements, but now they had reached an impasse. Begin would not give in on withdrawing the Israeli settlements from the Sinai, and he did not stand alone among his delegation on this point. And Sadat said he would negotiate only on *when*, not *if*, the settlement would be withdrawn. Jimmy could think of no way to resolve this fundamental difference. "The Egyptians are adamant on their conditions, and Begin has not moved on a single major issue since we've been here," Jimmy said. "All our people have decided we're wasting our time." The only avenue left, he concluded, was an American-Egyptian agreement, "if the Egyptians don't get disgusted and leave first."

I was crushed, not only for Jimmy, but also for the people in both countries who so desperately wanted peace. Only Cy Vance, who stopped by our cabin for a few minutes, made us feel better. Cy had experienced ups and downs of negotiations for years, and he said that he really thought Jimmy had accomplished all that he could have been expected to accomplish. The feelings ran too deeply on both sides, and the stakes were too high for any major compromises. By the time Cy left, Jimmy felt more resigned to the fact that writing an agreement both Israel and Egypt would sign was impossible. Still, we were both dejected during dinner and afterward tried to distract ourselves by watching a movie.

Friday, September 15, day eleven. It was as hard to hide my dejection today, at a reception for five hundred members of the Italian-American community, as it had been to control my optimism the day before. Hamilton Jordan and I flew to Washington together, and we could think of little to say to cheer each other. Hamilton had been at breakfast earlier with Weizman, Barak, and Dayan, and they were all frustrated that this longed-for chance for peace now seemed beyond grasp. Weizman had confessed to me that he was so nervous he had watched one movie after another for the last twenty-four hours.

All day long I could hardly concentrate on what I was doing or saying. Though I dreaded returning to more bad news, I ran to our cabin as soon as the helicopter landed to see what had happened.

And it was wonderful! In the seesawing of emotions that marked the Camp David summit, the news from Cy and Zbig returned me to highest optimism. "We're closer than we've ever been," Cy said. "The chances are better than we ever dreamed possible."

The Israelis had been suddenly and unexpectedly flexible. "I think each decided it could happen," Cy said. "The Israelis, that we might sign a fair agreement with Sadat alone, making them look bad, and Sadat, that it just might be possible to negotiate with Israel." Already Cy and Zbig had drafted new language for the proposal that they wanted Jimmy to see.

What a difference from the night before.

I rushed to Sadat's cabin where Jimmy was waiting for me and found them and Fritz laughing and talking and watching the Ali-Spinks fight on television. I happily accepted a cup of sweet mint tea from Sadat and joined them to watch the fight. Sadat, we learned, was a great fan of Muhammad Ali, and when the fight was over and Ali had won, they all decided to call and congratulate him. The only disappointment of the day was when Ali didn't return Jimmy's call until the wee hours of the morning and Sadat was already asleep.

At least I thought that was the only disappointment until Jimmy and I were alone and he said, "I want to tell you something that I don't want you ever to tell anybody—don't even put it in your diary." Once again Sadat had decided to leave. And once again Jimmy had stopped him.

After the summit, Sadat was the first to tell the story. He said that he had planned to leave but changed his mind when President Carter came to talk with him, but "I will never tell what was said at that meeting. Never!"

It had happened just after I left for Washington. Jimmy had been meeting in his study with Defense Secretary Harold Brown when suddenly the door burst open and there stood Cy Vance, his face as white as a ghost's. "Mr. President, President Sadat is leaving," he blurted out. "He already has his things packed. All the Egyptians are packed, and they have ordered the helicopter." Immediately, Jimmy told me, he sent Cy to tell Sadat that he wanted to see him before he left, and a few minutes later he hurried over to Sadat's cabin himself.

It was true. Sadat was leaving. He'd had a conversation with Dayan the evening before in which Dayan had said that the Israelis were not going to sign any agreement now. Instead, they planned to meet with the Egyptians at a later date and begin negotiations again. Sadat had been awake all night thinking about the implications. If he stayed and agreed to the U.S. proposals, all the other Arab countries would continue to condemn him. And if later he did join into new negotiations with the Israelis, he would be forced to start with the compromises already made in the agreement signed with the United States. Sadat said he just couldn't do that; he was going home.

Jimmy said he was thinking hard and praying at the same time. He finally said, "Well, Mr. President, if we come to that point, and if we do decide that the only thing is for the United Sates and Egypt to sign some kind of agreement here, I will write you a letter saying that if the Israelis don't sign, or when the negotiations start again, this treaty will be null and void and neither the Egyptians nor the Americans will be held to it." Jimmy said he had never talked with anyone else in his life the way he talked with Sadat, except maybe with his children. He reminded Sadat that he had come to Camp David in good faith, that he had given his word as a friend that he was going to try to make a success of the summit, and that he couldn't leave now and let the world know he hadn't kept his word. And, Egypt's responsibility for breaking off the peace talks might damage U.S.-Egyptian relations.

Mostly, though, Jimmy emphasized their personal relationship. After a moment, as they stood looking at each other, Sadat responded, "All right." And the summit, once more, was saved.

In gratitude, Jimmy asked if there were anything he could do for Sadat. "Yes," he said. "I want you and Rosalynn to come to Egypt for a visit." Jimmy said we would be delighted to, but asked if there were anything special he could do for the Egyptian people. After some hesitation, Sadat told him they could use a little more wheat and corn. A little more wheat and corn! That was up to Congress, Jimmy said, but he certainly could ask them for it on Sadat's behalf. Not many months later, Congress approved this request.

Saturday, September 16. The end was in sight. Jimmy had set Sunday, the seventeenth, as the deadline for the talks whether there was to be an agreement or not. If the principals were serious in seeking peace, they had had ample time to work out most of the issues. If they were not serious, then enough time had been wasted. Still, even at this eleventh hour, we did not know which way it would go.

After joining Sadat on his morning walk, Jimmy was optimistic. "We're going to get it," he said, and for the first time he really thought so. All along, Jimmy felt Sadat had been thinking that Begin wouldn't sign a treaty under any circumstances. But this morning, Jimmy said, he felt Sadat had changed his mind about Begin. "'That man' might just sign an agreement," Sadat had confessed.

While Jimmy spent the day drafting the final proposals, I went for a long bicycle ride to try to relax. Amy and Zbig's daughter, Mika Brzezinski, who had come for the weekend, joined me. But there was really no getting away from the tension. After lunch Fritz stopped in for a moment to see Jimmy, who was still working with Cy on the Sinai settlements. "How does the President feel?" he asked. I told him I thought everything was going all right for the moment but couldn't be counted on to last. "Good heavens, this is nerve-racking," said Fritz, whose comings and goings hadn't given him a chance to get a sense of the tension. "You keep going from one extreme to the other."

The next extreme came late in the afternoon. After finishing the new draft of the Sinai proposal, Jimmy and Cy were again skeptical about its acceptance by both countries. From optimism to despair once more was just too much for me, and I thought I was going to be sick. Sadat was on his way to our cabin to read the proposal and I just had to get out. I called Susan Clough, Jimmy's personal secretary, and asked her to play tennis with me.

By the time I came back, Sadat was gone and Jimmy was writing a clean draft, as he had done so many times before, in preparation for his meeting with the Israelis momentarily. Our American team, after the meeting with Sadat, had decided that they were not going to get a Sinai agreement, Jimmy told me. I tried not to show my disappointment but decided we would just have to reconcile ourselves to "half a loaf"—but could we be sure of that?

Begin arrived with Barak and went into the study with Jimmy. They stayed and stayed. At eight-thirty I sent cheese and crackers in to them. At ten minutes before twelve I went to bed, but I couldn't sleep. A few minutes later I heard the men come out of the study, and I got up to learn what had happened. Begin left, but Cy and Barak stayed to eat the pepper steak that had been ready since dinnertime. The news was good. Begin had been more flexible than Jimmy had ever anticipated concerning dismantling the Israeli settlements in the Sinai and freezing further settlements in the West Bank and Gaza. But still, nothing was signed, and the end of the summit was only hours away.

* * *

Sunday, September 17, 1978. I packed my bags to leave for a full day's schedule at the White House, not knowing if I would have time to return to Camp David before the summit ended. I didn't want to leave with the proposals still uncertain and the clock ticking, but the reception for the Hispanic community and the Rostropovich concert had been scheduled for months. One of us had to be there, and it was obviously going to be me. Once more, however, my anticipation was high. Jimmy came into the bathroom while I was dressing to say that some of the Sinai problems had been worked out. "I think we've gotten everything we wanted," he said. "I'm going to try to get Begin and Sadat together today. They haven't seen each other since we went to Gettysburg."

At the White House, it was all I could do to concentrate as I spoke to my guests and shook hands with all of them, and I must admit that my mind wandered during the beautiful concert. I was anxious to call Jimmy and see what was happening at Camp David, and during the applause at the concert's end, I slipped away long enough to run to the telephone. "Are you going to be successful? Should I come back?" I was full of questions and I told him, "I want to be there when anything happens. If you sign the agreement, I want to be there." There was no assurance yet that there would be an agreement, he told me. A few "obstacles" remained, but if an agreement was signed it would be done at the White House.

I panicked at the thought of delaying the signing. "Don't wait," I said to Jimmy. "I think if they agree, you ought to get their names on the line immediately and not take a chance on having them change their minds between Camp David and the White House!" I relaxed when he said, "Don't worry, we'll have the agreements initialed before we leave Camp David, and don't worry about a celebration, or anything, until after it's over." Nobody was going to start a celebration until "the names were on the line"!

All I could do was wait. Kit Dobelle, the chief of protocol, and I were the only ones at the White House who had any idea that the possibility of an agreement was at hand. I couldn't even tell my social secretary, Gretchen Poston, or the household staff, already working overtime with the reception and concert, that they might have to prepare for another big event. We also had Aliza Begin with us. She had flown in from Camp David for the concert and was ready to go back from the moment it was over. I didn't tell Aliza what was happening either. "Don't come back yet," Jimmy had said. "Just stall, but don't let anybody know why."

After a while, Kit took Aliza to the Israeli Embassy to wait with the explanation that no helicopter was available, which was true. All the helicopters were standing by at Camp David to bring back the negotiating teams when and if the word was given.

They were gone only a short time when the telephone rang. It was Jimmy: "We're coming home! The agreements are initialed and we'll sign them in the East Room tonight!" I was so happy, I cried.

It was done. The impossible had been made possible. Through all the hard work and despite all the worry, the misery and the ups and downs, it was done. A miracle? Yes, for anyone who had been there and seen the obstacles and the hard feelings and adamant positions—it was a miracle.

Now we had to get ready to share it with the public. And fast.

Kit, Gretchen, and I called the Cabinet members and the White House staff to come and bring their families. We got in touch with the Israeli and Egyptian embassies and members of Congress while the press secretaries, Mary Hoyt and Jody Powell, alerted the news media. Chairs were set up in the East Room in no time, and the flags of the three countries were rushed over from the State Department.

The kitchen staff outdid itself. They had already served seven hundred people that day; suddenly, another two hundred were about to appear. Gretchen told me later that she almost had to send someone to the all-night Safeway in Georgetown, but the chefs managed instead to put together leftover cheese from the morning brunch, strawberry and pecan tarts from the concert, and some hastily defrosted cheese rings and carrot cakes. Happily, there was orange juice on hand for the Arabs, who didn't drink, and plenty of white wine and champagne for others who did.

The first helicopters started landing at 8:00 P.M., some at the Mall, which required a limousine shuttle service to the White House. Still other delegation members arrived from Camp David by car. Against all security precautions, Jimmy, Begin, and Sadat rode together in one helicopter. Luckily, there wasn't time to ponder the international repercussions had there been engine failure. And how quickly the word spread! When the three leaders stepped out onto the South Lawn, they were greeted by cheering, flag-waving crowds and the bright lights of the waiting television cameras. The only confusion occurred in the arrangement of the flags in the East Room. The flag of the United States customarily hung farthest to the right, but in this instance it had been put in the middle, as the television crews wanted each leader pictured in front of his own country's flag. Although we moved it before the ceremony, at a moment like this, when emotions were running higher than any flag, protocol could have been temporarily suspended.

And emotional it was, with tears of joy streaming down even the most formal of cheeks. "Even Mr. Dayan, who is a very cold fish, has tears in his eyes tonight," Prime Minister Begin told me. Overwhelmed by the enthusiastic reception, Begin turned to his wife and said, "Mama, we'll go down in the history books!"

History was indeed made that night. Though it would take Jimmy many more months and two trips to Egypt and one to Israel to cement the treaty, peace finally became a reality between these two long-standing enemies. Begin and Sadat shared the Nobel Peace Prize that year, but it was Jimmy who had made it possible.

Both men knew it. In their remarks before the television cameras that Sunday evening, each leader recognized the role Jimmy had played and the risks he had taken. "Dear President Carter," Sadat said, ". . . you have been most courageous when you took the gigantic step of convening this meeting. The challenge was great, and the risks were high, but so was your determination. . . . Dear friend, we came to Camp David with all the good will and faith we possessed, and we left Camp David a few minutes ago with a renewed sense of hope and inspiration. We are looking forward to the days ahead with an added determination to pursue the noble goal of peace."

Prime Minister Begin was no less aware of Jimmy's accomplishment. "The President took a great risk for himself and did it with great civil courage," Begin said. ". . . It was a famous French field commander who said that it is much more difficult to show civil courage than military courage. And the President worked. As far as my historic experience is concerned, I think that he worked harder than our forefathers did in Egypt, building the pyramids. . . . Today, I visited President Sadat in his cabin, because in Camp David you don't have houses, you only have cabins. And he then came to visit me. We shook hands. And thank God, we again could have said to each other, 'You are my friend.' . . . The Camp David conference should be renamed. It was the Jimmy Carter conference."

There was hardly a dry eye in the room or in the countless living rooms around the world when Jimmy then presented the documents for all three men to sign. And sign they did.

For the Government of the Arab Republic of Egypt: A. Sadat.

For the Government of Israel: M. Begin.

Witnessed by: Jimmy Carter, President of the United States of America.

❧ 10 ❧
The Office of the First Lady

Before going to the White House, I knew that some First Ladies had had special areas of interest and, because of their influence, had been able to accomplish worthy goals. Eleanor Roosevelt worked for social change; Jackie Kennedy restored the White House to an American showcase in which we all could take pride; and Lady Bird Johnson renewed our interest in beautifying the country's highways and parks. And although I wanted to work with the elderly and issues of concern to women, my main project as First Lady would be to develop a strategy for helping the mentally ill.

I had begun this work in Georgia and wanted to expand it to the national level. Mental illnesses or serious emotional problems affect one in every four families in the United States; it could happen to any of us. Each of us at one time or another will be affected by marital problems, delinquent children, drug- or alcohol-related stress, the inability to deal with death or a serious accident or illness, or simply by low self-esteem. Many will also experience the tragedy of a severe mental illness, in ourselves or in our families. Perhaps we will be able to cope. Perhaps not. Then what will we do? To whom will we turn? The thought of mental illness often strikes chords of dread and fear. These fears and suspicions, many based on myths, are as old as mankind, and they are deeply ingrained.

When I was a child growing up in Plains, there was a young man in our community, a distant cousin, who was in and out of the state mental institution. When he was at home I was afraid of him, and when I heard him singing loudly as he came down the street I would run and hide. I don't know why I had to get away— he was never violent, just very nervous and very loud. He probably wanted nothing more than friendship and recognition, yet he was "different," and when I heard him, my impulse was to flee. Today he could be treated and could lead a more normal life.

Although most people who suffer can lead more normal lives, there is such a stigma about mental illness that many who could be successfully treated still hide their problems. Admitting to a mental health problem can be not only socially embarrassing, but also threatening to one's family and livelihood. While in the White House, I received a letter from a Culver City, California, housewife whose medical record of mental illness had prevented her from adopting children. She wrote: "I don't blame anyone for not wanting to seek help if it's going to be held against them for the rest of their lives. Solving mental problems should be like mending a broken leg, and no one carries the stigma of a broken leg around with them for the rest of their lives. Once the leg is mended, no one asks why it was broken."

I wanted to take mental illnesses and emotional disorders out of the closet, to let people know it is all right to admit having a problem without the fear of being called crazy. If only we could consider mental illnesses as straightforwardly as we do physical illnesses, those affected could seek help and be treated in an open and effective way.

There hadn't been an assessment of how we were meeting the mental health needs in our country since the Final Report of the Joint Commission on Mental Illness and Health given to President Kennedy in 1961. Indeed, the whole subject of mental health as a national priority was a relatively new one, stemming from World War II, when psychiatric screening of those drafted into the service revealed a startlingly high incidence of rejection for psychiatric disabilities.

Since then, our knowledge of the causes and treatment of mental illness has steadily increased, and we have come to realize that mental health is much more than just the absence of mental illness. It is the very quality of the life we lead. Until recently, most communities or states provided services chiefly for those who were severely disturbed. Mental sickness meant schizophrenia and manic-depressive disease, or other debilitating psychoses. Mental illness just meant "crazy people"—until we began to take a broader, more enlightened approach.

Yet the benefits of our increased knowledge have been applied to few of those affected, and we still do not understand what causes most major mental disabilities. Why? I wanted to find out. Politically, the issue had always been shuffled to the back burner, but fortunately, we were now in a position to make mental health a top national priority.

In a speech in Bakersfield, California, during the campaign I had made my one and only campaign promise: to study the mental health needs of our nation. Jimmy fulfilled that promise when he signed the Executive Order creating the President's Commission on Mental Health. Because of federal nepotism laws, I could not be appointed the formal chairperson of the commission but had to settle for "honorary" instead. Physician-attorney Tom Bryant, the former health director of the Office of Economic Opportunity, was named chairman and executive director, and Peter Bourne, a psychiatrist who was also a close friend and associate in my mental health work in Georgia and who became Jimmy's special assistant for health issues, was assigned primary responsibility for coordinating and following up on the commission's report. Our task would not be easy. Not only was the subject of mental health not politically appealing, but in order to accomplish anything we had to establish it as one of Jimmy's major domestic priorities instead of having it dismissed as a First Lady's "pet project."

With the Executive Order signed, we went right to work. We chose twenty commissioners from more than one thousand people suggested, among them Florence Mahoney, for many years a health research supporter who had become a Washington legend in the art of lobbying Congress to increase funding for science and mental health; Mildred Mitchell Bateman, the outstanding black psychiatrist and former mental health commissioner for West Virginia; Julius Richmond, a pediatrician and the surgeon general of the Public Health Service who had been the first director of the Head Start Program; and George Tarjan of UCLA, a world-renowned child psychiatrist, who was later elected president of the American Psychiatric Association. The others, whom I had not known personally but who each became a close friend as we worked together, were equally well qualified. Some were mental health professionals, but the majority were not. We all felt a deep commitment to helping those suffering from mental and emotional disabilities, and we saw the commission as an opportunity to act on our concerns. Others active in the mental health field shared our sense of excitement and purpose. For example, Mary Lasker, a prominent philanthropist affectionately—and justifiably—regarded as the grande dame of medical research, promptly sent a check for $10,000 to be used in our work. Additional individuals as well as several private foundations soon followed suit, providing assistance for which I shall always be grateful.

Our first action was to hold public hearings across the country. We listened for hours to advice and suggestions from hundreds of professionals, laypersons, former mental patients, community leaders, and legislators. At the same time, more than four hundred and fifty volunteers on thirty task panels developed comprehensive statements in special areas of concern such as research, prevention, and the needs of special populations.

What we learned was sobering. Federal and state programs were fragmented and fraught with bureaucratic problems. One woman told us that her family was visited weekly by three different social workers, all from separate agencies. Another pinpointed the terrible consequences of cultural misunderstandings and the lack of bilingual therapists: A Haitian woman had gone in fear to a therapist because her husband's ex-wife had put a hex on her. She was diagnosed as paranoid and treated with a powerful sedative. Further investigation by a bicultural therapist revealed that her dilemma was quite common in her particular culture—she was not paranoid at all. What she needed was understanding and guidance. Blacks, Hispanics, Asians, and American Indians often felt intimidated and harassed by white mental health personnel (fewer than 2 percent of the psychiatrists in our country were black, fewer still Hispanic, and there were only thirteen American Indian psychiatrists). Women, too, many of whom feel powerless and alienated by their rapidly changing roles in society, also needed specialized attention. And over and over again at every stop we heard of the plight of the chronically mentally ill who were returned to their communities as a result of court orders, the 1963 Community Mental Health Centers Act, and advanced treatments, only to live marginal existences. Often these people remained jobless, homeless, feared by society, and even hungry because no adequate community services were available to them.

We sifted through thousands and thousands of pages of data in order to prepare a final set of recommendations, which we presented to the President at a ceremony in the Oval Office: 117 in all; 8 major ones. Jimmy had given us only a year and an operating budget of $100,000 to produce the report. With assistance from the Department of Health, Education and Welfare (later to become the Department of Health and Human Services, or HHS), through private funds, and through the contribution of many hundreds of hours of time by the commission members and volunteers, we managed to meet our deadline.

Our commission was convinced by the one-year study that many Americans were either "unserved" or "underserved," not having access to adequate mental health care at reasonable cost because of where they lived or who they were—their race, age, sex, or economic circumstances. A much larger number did not receive care because they feared the consequences of seeking treatment. The recommendations we made were designed to correct these conditions and bring us closer to quality care for everyone.

We had learned that when people have mental problems, they don't go to a mental health professional first. They go to their families and friends, to priests or to nurses and doctors who may have no specific connection with the local mental health worker. Each could benefit the other by sharing information about their troubled community members and by working together to help them. Also, there are always volunteers eager to help, people with both expertise and time to give.

While Jimmy was governor, I learned at first hand how important a volunteer can be. One of the most important things mentally ill people need is a friend, someone who is genuinely interested in them. This is one reason the 1963 Community Mental Health Centers Act was so important. It began making it possible to bring many of the afflicted back from the institution to the community, where those who had families could even stay at night with loved ones but still have a place to go during the day to be cared for. But over time, the act had been amended to the point that it was virtually impossible for communities with no services to get federal aid to start any kind of program at all. Our commission recommended changing the act so a community would no longer have to provide all twelve separate services required by law to be eligible for funding. We wanted those communities that couldn't afford to provide the complete program to be able to begin a center with one service, and at least provide the one most needed, as they moved to develop a comprehensive program.

Often the chronically mentally ill wander from one temporary shelter to another, in and out of institutions, with no one who really wants them or who can provide long-term care. We recommended changes in housing programs and in the Medicare and Medicaid laws to help correct this. We also recommended "performance contracts" to help the states take care of their chronically mentally ill. The states would decide what kind of programs they needed and then sign contracts with the federal government for funding. This was very important to state officials, who complained that the federal government didn't always know what was best for their people.

Our commission found that existing health insurance programs did not include mental illnesses, and we recommended such coverage. We recognized that people avoid psychiatric help because of the stigma, and insurance coverage would not only be an incentive to seek necessary treatment, but would also help reduce the stigma.

Another major problem was the lack of adequate personnel in some parts of the country. This was brought home to me one day when a woman called to say that her child was the only one in her county who needed speech therapy. The little girl had gradually lost her voice and could only mutter, but no treatment center was available to her. We finally arranged for the mother and child to spend two weeks at one of Georgia's regional centers, where both had professional counseling and the mother had instruction in speech therapy so she could help her child at home. To bring about a better distribution of mental health personnel, we recommended grants and loans for students who would in turn repay them by working in rural areas and in the inner cities where such personnel shortages are acute. We also recommended incentives to train more personnel in the special needs of minorities, as shown by the Haitian woman, as well as of children, adolescents faced with drugs and other problems, the elderly, and women.

Years ago, when my cousin was home from the institution, everyone in our small community knew when it was time for him to go back. He would get more nervous and excited, and louder and louder when he walked down the streets, and soon the sheriff would come and take him away. Though it is not that simple now to "commit" a person to an institution, in all too many states it is relatively easy. We recommended an advocacy program and a bill of rights for the mentally ill that would remind us that civil commitment is an intrusion on personal liberty and autonomy, a step not to be taken without adequate legal safeguards, and that guardianship laws can lead to a deprivation of legal rights.

We gave special emphasis to research and programs for prevention. I learned one day on a visit to the National Institute of Mental Health (NIMH) how inadequate our research programs often are. Federal grants are given for short periods of time, while research sometimes takes many years. The time and funds for programs often run out, and projects are suspended before results are determined. I was told that just as we are on the threshold of new discoveries about the brain, our scientists are discouraged. How will we ever make the necessary breakthroughs with all the stops and starts of our research projects? It was a discouraging picture that day of what should be one of the most important emphases of our mental health work. We had a substantial increase in funds for this research during the Carter administration, although still not enough, but with the cutback in funds for domestic programs by the Reagan administration, these gains were short-lived. This is a pity—shameful and so wasteful. How many lives could be saved, and how much expense to the taxpayers saved, with new knowledge and new "cures"? There shouldn't be even a flicker of indecision about moving forward with our research programs. The same holds true for programs of prevention. Some argue that the complex causes of mental illnesses make it difficult to develop effective prevention programs, but we already know that proper prenatal and perinatal infant care, periodic checkups, and the immunization of young children can prevent serious mental disability. Our commission urged the establishment of an Office of Prevention within the NIMH.

Our commissioners believed that the associated stigma is *a* primary if not *the* primary obstacle to better mental health care. I went to Hollywood and spoke to producers, directors, and television and movie stars to encourage them to portray the mentally ill with accuracy and sensitivity rather than as "mad bombers" or "insane murderers." And we proposed the development of effective public education programs. Now we don't even know how to present mental illness so that people will understand it better. In one community that wanted to enlighten its citizens, a series of advertisements was launched; afterward, polls showed more people reacting negatively to the problem than before it began. It's not easy to deal with fear and prejudice. I know—but I wouldn't try to run away from my cousin now, I would try to run toward him. But I had to learn that.

Once the commission's report was completed, the next step was to make sure the recommendations would be implemented. At Jimmy's direction, every affected department in the government drew up timetables and plans for acting on the recommendations that did not require congressional action. And since the major work of the commission was over, Tom Bryant began putting together a group of prominent citizens to form a Public Committee on Mental Health to continue the momentum.

But the legislative process to implement the portion that did require congressional action became maddeningly slow. We had a setback when Dr. Peter Bourne wrote a required prescription for an assistant, using a pseudonym to protect her from the public scrutiny that affects all White House employees. Because of the attendant publicity, he resigned, and without Peter there was no senior-level advocate on the White House staff to guide the report through the day-to-day work necessary in translating a national commission report into policy. Instead, the major responsibility fell to HHS Secretary Joe Califano. Much valuable time was lost in too many meetings with him and his staff, and it was finally necessary for me to go directly to the President and to Jim McIntyre at the Office of Management and Budget to get things moving. I told Kathy Cade, my projects director, to keep Tom Bryant and the other members of the commission in touch with the White House staff and the people at HHS to be certain that our commission's fresh look at the problems didn't get watered down to "business as usual." We hadn't put in all of those long hours and hard work just to see yet another national commission report gather dust on some busy Cabinet officer's bookshelf. I knew Califano had his priorities, but I also had mine—and I saw the President more often than he did!

Despite the delays, in May of 1979 Jimmy submitted the Mental Health Systems Act to Congress.

The response to our work was overwhelmingly favorable. The American Medical Association and the American Bar Association both adopted resolutions at their annual meetings commending the report. Conferences were planned in a number of states to focus on mental health issues and needs. We invited hundreds of people, including special interest groups (the elderly, women's groups, children's advocates), to the White House to advise them of the report and encourage them to lobby for its passage, and we invited members of the congressional committees who would be responsible for the legislation. When the time was right, I went to Capitol Hill myself to testify before the Senate committee, for which there wasn't much precedent. We could find a record of only one other First Lady who had testified before Congress—Eleanor Roosevelt on behalf of the coal miners.

While the legislation was making its way through Congress, I was speaking everywhere I had a chance: to the World Federation for Mental Health in Vancouver, British Columbia; to the World Health Organization in Geneva, Switzerland, which invites only one outside speaker each year; in Manitoba, Canada, where the St. Boniface General Hospital Research Foundation in Winnipeg offered me a $20,000 honorarium to speak at their annual fundraising dinner (they agreed to donate the money to our Public Committee on Mental Health). Though the committee needed the money to help inform the public about our report, I almost had to renege on this invitation. The Canadian government refused to let the Secret Service agents carry guns into the country, but finally I reached a secret compromise with the agents. I would go to Canada and make the speech, but I wouldn't spend the night. They agreed and I was "protected" by the Royal Canadian Police that day—though my hosts and the press couldn't understand my promptness in getting away.

In the meantime, I remained in constant touch with the chairmen of the House and Senate committees handling the legislation, Congressman Henry Waxman and Senator Ted Kennedy. I had to swallow some pride—for the cause—during the campaign of 1980, when Senator Kennedy one day would be on the stump making one of his statements, such as, "President Carter is making the poor eat cat food," and the next day would be saying to me, "Mrs. Carter, the committee is completing work on the Mental Health Systems Act."

"Thank you, Senator."

We continued these courtesy calls even during the worst part of the campaign.

In September of 1980, the Mental Health Systems Act was passed by Congress and funded—the first major reform of federal, publicly funded mental health programs since the Community Mental Health Centers Act of 1963. In spite of delays, to have investigated, recommended, and legislated a comprehensive mental health program in a four-year period was a great accomplishment, and we celebrated.

Our celebration was brief. Within a month Ronald Reagan was elected President, and with the change of administration, many of our dreams and the bulk of the funding for our program were gone. I felt betrayed. After four years of hard work and efforts by thousands of people, carefully studying an existing system of care and making changes so it would be responsive and cost-efficient, community-controlled, and accessible to those who so desperately needed it, and after having had the benefit of eighteen months of public scrutiny and careful adjustment—after all this, the funding for our legislation was killed by the philosophy of a new President. It was a bitter loss.

Fortunately, we had taken some important steps that did not require congressional action, steps that could not be instantly undone:

1. Financial support for mental health efforts was increased, especially funds for community-based services, because Jimmy had included those increases in his last budget; but the increases only remained in effect for one year.

2. The same was true with the 65 percent increase in funding for research (which had steadily declined since 1969) to study childhood and adolescent psychopathology, hyperkinetic and learning disability syndromes, the effects on children and families of marital disruption, the correlation between alcohol and mental disorders among parents, as well as drug abuse. Again, these increases lasted only one year; then President Reagan began proposing budget cuts.

3. An Office of Prevention was established within the NIMH for the first time in history; it remains today and is a major contribution. However, the NIMH, which had become in the Carter administration the badly needed coordinator of many of the mental health programs in other federal agencies, has had its responsibilities for services severely curtailed.

4. The entire training program at the NIMH was reorganized to address the attention of our report. More psychiatrists were recruited for the National Health Service Corps. Sti-

pends for summer fellowships in psychiatry for medical students were increased and offered also to premedical students to encourage them to consider careers in psychiatry. The broad clinical training program was redirected to encourage larger numbers of minorities to pursue mental health careers and to increase the numbers of people trained to deal with the special problems of children, adolescents, and the elderly. This has remained in effect, yet even these gains are now under review.

5. The NIMH also collaborated with the Office of Housing and Urban Development (HUD) in a housing program for the chronically mentally ill, working together for the first time at the state level to improve services for the mentally disabled, but this valuable initiative has also been cut back.

6. Perhaps most important, the amount of attention we gave the issue changed the way some people regarded mental illness, which is the first step in successful treatment.

There was more, so much more, that could have been done if the laws had been implemented. Instead, the Mental Health Systems Act is gathering dust on a government shelf, and sick people and their families continue to suffer needlessly. That's the real shame.

While working on the mental health commission, I was shocked to find that not only is there a need for mental health personnel for the elderly, but that there are relatively few physicians trained in the special health needs of our older citizens. This will be increasingly important in the coming years.

We're living longer and longer. The statistics are eye-opening: Today some 27.4 million Americans are over sixty-five and another 33 million are between fifty and sixty-five. This "graying of America" is expected to continue so that by the year 2030, one out of every four of us will be sixty or older.

The problems of the elderly became another area of my interest as First Lady, and Dr. Robert Butler, who was director of the National Institute on Aging while we were in Washington, sent me a copy of a speech he made one day summing up the needs: "The challenge confronting our nation today is to assure that our swelling number of older citizens do more than simply survive. Our challenge is not to replicate years in which huge numbers of us live on, dependent, frail, ridden with disease, unproductive, unhappy and lonely, in fear of crime, dissatisfied with ourselves, falsely regarded as sexless, and tempted to suicide. Our challenge is to extend the fruitful middle years, healthy and vigorous years in which we can live creatively, to the best of our ability, carrying our own weight and paying our own way as productive contributors to our society."

As a result of visiting such places as convalescent homes, nursing homes, and other senior centers every day during the campaign, certain images stuck in my mind: a group of older citizens in Boston seated on the lawn in front of a convalescent home, listening to me tell them of the needs of the elderly I had seen every day, when someone from the audience interrupted with, "What about those you don't see? There are a lot of them in this city at home alone, with no way to get about and no one to care for them." In another instance, three elderly men were playing cards at a convalescent home, and I asked them what they had done before retiring. One had been a college president, another, an English professor, the third, a doctor, and they said they did the same thing over and over every day—play cards and feel useless.

When my mother was forced to retire from her job as postmistress on her seventieth birthday, in 1975, I came back home from a campaign trip and my brother told me that she had cried all week. "Mother," I said jokingly to her, "I can't understand why anyone who has had to get up and be at the post office at seven o'clock every morning for as long as I can remember wouldn't love to stay home and sleep late and be leisurely for a change." She shook her head. "It's not that," she said. "It's just that no one thinks I can do good work anymore."

She was devastated, as were the three men who had nothing to do but play cards all day. I couldn't help but think of my grandfather, who had come to live with us and helped Mother with the farm, the household, and the children almost until the day he died, and of Miss Lillian, who joined the Peace Corps at sixty-eight because for the first and only time she had seen the words "Age no barrier" in an advertisement. Neither one of them had to retire—and neither, it turned out, did my mother. Soon after she left the post office, she started working afternoons in a flower shop and has been happy and "contributing" ever since.

Once we were in the White House, I began to meet regularly with Nelson Cruikshank, the counselor to the President on Aging, who kept me informed of legislation before Congress that concerned the elderly. I invited representatives of all the elderly advocacy groups to a roundtable discussion on aging. Included were Congressman Claude Pepper, chairman of the House Select Committee on Aging, affectionately called "Senator" and a champion for the elderly, Maggie Kuhn of the Gray Panthers, Bert Seidman of the AFL–CIO, and Peter Hughes of the American Association of Retired Persons. We put together a brochure with fifteen recommendations of things people could do in their communities to help the elderly. We distributed these to states and organizations, and I visited some of the programs as they were carried out.

As Nelson kept me informed, I lobbied for the Age Discrimination Act, which eliminated mandatory retirement at any age in the federal government and raised the age limit from sixty-five to seventy in the private sector; the Older Americans Act, which coordinated existing legislation and authorized substantial increases in appropriations for the various social services and health and nutrition programs for the elderly; the Rural Clinics Act, which expanded medical services to underserved rural areas; and Social Security Reform, which strengthened the short-term and long-range status of the funds.

One important thing I learned in my work with the mentally ill and with the elderly was that when people in communities across our country are aware of problems, they will respond in very helpful and ingenious ways. This was vividly demonstrated in Washington, D.C., at what is known as the Green Door. Two young women became concerned about the chronically mentally ill in a large city institution, St. Elizabeths Hospital, and developed a model community-based program for them. The men and women who came to the center were capable of learning and working and shouldn't have been in an institution, but they had nowhere else to go, no home and no family to care for them. They came from St. Elizabeths every day to keep house and to cook, and they even learned to print a small bulletin about their thoughts and activities. They learned also to take the buses to reach the Green Door and had opened a storefront Thrift Shop, selling donated items for expense money for their "home." The community had joined in to help, but it had all been made possible because two young women cared about them and their poor living situation and recognized that their talents could be developed if given a chance.

There are people in every community who need help and understanding, and programs like the Green Door can be replicated in other cities. I participated in a special segment of *Good Morning America* about the Green Door, and soon afterward in Texas I was thrilled to have a man say to me, "Mrs. Carter, I saw the program on television about the Green Door, and I want you to know that we're forming a center just like it in our community."

Schools and libraries and hospitals also need help, as do beautification programs and housing programs. As I traveled around the country, visiting mental health centers and homes for the elderly, I began to try to point out other needs where community participation could play a role.

In Washington, D.C., General Hospital was in dire need of help; it had even lost its accreditation. The hospital commissioners came to see me to discuss how I might help encourage local voluntary efforts to improve the hospital. We enlisted the aid of a radio announcer and, with a little publicity and a few telephone calls, a host of organizations and individuals soon joined the project. A decorating company offered to donate fabric and make drapes for the hospital, a hardware store offered paint, and the Singer Sewing Machine Company donated fifteen sewing machines for use in the utility room, among other contributions. The Jaycees took on the hospital as a project, and the D.C. Police, a local garden club, the mayor's wife, the Young Women's League and other civic organizations, members of the business community, and numerous individuals became involved. Furniture and plants for the landscaping were donated, and on some days everyone pitched in, painting and cleaning and planting. I painted a wall in the reception room myself. We learned from the nurses that there was also a lack of ongoing educational programs for the staff. In particular, the nurses felt a need for special training to help them serve the large number of elderly patients. With the help of the American Nurses Association, a nursing education program for geriatric patients was launched and filmed at D.C. General. I introduced each segment of *The Rosalynn Carter Nurse Training Program*, which was later made available to all veterans' hospitals in the country. Our volunteer team celebrated when the hospital received its accreditation again, and D.C. General is now a much-improved hospital.

There were other projects in our nation's capital. At the beginning of the Carter administration, Washington was one of the only major cities in the country without a viable community foundation to encourage private contributions to meet local needs. Although the Community Foundation of Greater Washington had been established several years earlier, it had never really gotten off the ground. At the request of the chairman of the Board, I met with representatives of some of the major philanthropic organizations in the country, such as the Ford Foundation, to encourage their support for the Washington effort. One of the events for which I left Camp David during the thirteen-day peace summit was a luncheon at the White House for business leaders in the District to ask for their support. The community rallied around the foundation, which is fully operational now, focusing many of its grants in the areas of family aid, mental health, the neighborhoods, aging, and youth.

Most of the people I worked with on these projects were people outside the government, who lived in the city but had never been inside the White House. They were pleased to accept my invitations to teas, receptions, picnics on the South Lawn, and other events. I in turn was pleased to accept in December of 1980 a special commendation from the D.C. City Council for my efforts among Washingtonians on the other side of the fence from 1600 Pennsylvania Avenue, whom I had come to love.

I regularly visited similar programs across the country, usually going on tours of three or four days, stopping in several states to visit centers for the mentally ill and the elderly as well as other community projects. One that I particularly enjoyed was the grand opening of the Palace Theatre in Lorain, Ohio. A group of housewives had restored the decaying shell of an old theater to its original beauty, and I brought Chet Atkins with me to perform on their opening night. Another favorite was a program called Cities In Schools, in which social workers, policemen, recreation and other government officials, teachers, scout leaders, and private citizens worked together in the schools to keep the most disadvantaged children from dropping out.

Whether it was working on a comprehensive mental health plan, working for legislation to help the elderly, providing a "home" for the chronically mentally ill, or restoring the accreditation of a public hospital, I found men and women, old and young, volunteering their services. Someone said to me one day in Massachusetts when I was commending a group of elderly volunteers for helping in the public school, "When you're all wrapped up in yourself, you're a very small package."

My greatest disappointment in all the projects I worked on during the White House years was the failure of the Equal Rights Amendment to be ratified. Jimmy and I made dozens of calls to state legislators as individual states considered the issue, and it was very close at one time, so close that if only thirteen legislators—two in Florida, two in North Carolina, and nine in Nevada—had voted yea instead of nay we would have made it. The ERA would have been over the top . . . but it was not to be.

My files are full of speeches about the ERA; they are full of the phone calls I made to legislators in various states. They are full of letters written and invitations to fund-raisers and other meetings I attended, including the Houston Conference celebrating the International Women's Year in the fall of 1977, where Lady Bird Johnson, Betty Ford, and I appeared together. I held many events and meetings at the White House and did just about anything I could think of for the cause. I remember when my staff was wondering if it would be appropriate for a First Lady to be auctioned off at a dance for the ERA. Jimmy said, "Well, it's better than being a wallflower!" And so I danced for the ERA.

Our one victory came during the fall of 1978, when Jimmy and Fritz Mondale worked to turn seven congressional no votes into yes votes to pass legislation extending the ratification deadline. It was even more disappointing to see the deadline for the extension go by in 1982 with the ERA still not ratified.

Why have we had such a hard time trying to get the amendment ratified? After all, it is a simple twenty-four-word declaration: "Equality of rights under the law shall not be denied or abridged by the United States or by any state on account of sex."

Most people think it says much more than this. I have had women tell me that if I would send them a copy they would pay the postage, as though it were volumes. And Erma Bombeck has described it as the most misunderstood few words since "one size fits all."

The Equal Rights Amendment says nothing about men having to give up their places as head of the household or about women being drafted or forced to go to work, leaving their children at home. It says nothing about unisex bathrooms, homosexual marriages, or about personal family relationships, and it would not force any changes in them. What it would do is guarantee women the legal protection that should be rightfully theirs under the Constitution.

The U.S. Constitution is the most basic concept of what this nation stands for: freedom and equality for all. Yet today the only right the Constitution guarantees women is the right to vote. It contains no clause granting women legal status as persons or guaranteeing equal protection for them. Some argue that women's rights are guaranteed under the Fourteenth Amendment, passed to protect slaves. However, the Supreme Court in case after case has not extended this amendment to include women, although it has repeatedly been urged to do so.

One of the problems is the fervor and organization of the opposition. It is so vocal and so powerful at the polls that local legislators, who are the ones who must vote for ratification, are reluctant to do so. I have talked with many who have told me that they couldn't afford to go against this opposition. Also, due to the many erroneous and often wild contentions by the opposition, people are confused by what the ERA really is and what it would do to their lives.

The image of the ERA has been a serious problem. Attention has often centered on those supporters who have appeared to be demanding and strident man haters—mostly urban, professional women. "Nice" women, as my daughter-in-law Judy says, have been reluctant to be identified with such a group, though they support the ERA itself. In fact, I learned that a majority of people do support the ERA when they know the facts.

During the campaign for the ratification of the ERA, I talked with one state senator who had always been opposed to the amendment until he had gone with his wife to make a will. He told me he had found out that under the laws of their state, his wife would have no control over what he owned. If he died without a will, the business that he and his wife had developed together would go to his blood relatives, not to his wife. Furthermore, if he changed the ownership of his property and put half in his wife's name, they would have to pay a gift tax on the half he gave her. He told me he had changed his mind and was going to support the ERA. I wish a few more legislators had confronted the issue in such a personal way.

In years past, many laws were written with different provisions for men and women. In some states, women could marry at an earlier age than men. Men could drink at an earlier age than women. In Alabama, girls had to be seventeen before they could be newspaper carriers; boys only had to be ten! In some instances, women were required to have their husbands' consent to sell property. Everyone agrees that today these laws are outdated. But society at the time thought that women were different and should be protected; staying at home with the family, teaching school and working with children, or being a secretary helping a man were the kinds of things that women really wanted to do and could do well.

The movement for equal rights for women began with the simple reasoning that while women are biologically different from men, they have the same ability to serve as doctors or lawyers or do other things that had traditionally been viewed as men's jobs, and that society should take advantage of these talents.

I am grateful that because of the women's movement, there are not as many discriminatory laws as there once were. The lieutenant governor of Louisiana, Bobby Freeman, told me of one celebrated case in his state where a woman worked and bought her home. Her husband was disabled and did not contribute to the purchase, but later he placed a second mortgage on the house without her knowledge. The lender foreclosed and took the home. Under Louisiana's law at the time, the wife had no right to protect her house from her husband's mortgage or even to know about it, even though she had paid for it. Since then, the law has been changed.

An Equal Rights Amendment to the Constitution would protect women's gains and ensure that future laws would not discriminate against them. But great progress comes slowly, and someday, a day I hope to see in my lifetime, we will look back on this struggle as we look back now on the long but successful struggle for women's suffrage and wonder why. Why all the controversy and why such difficulty in giving women the protection of the Constitution that should have been theirs long ago?

While Jimmy was President, I understood clearly that times were changing in our country and that women everywhere were undergoing a period of adjustment. Many were forced to work outside the home to help supplement the family income or to support a family as a single parent; many were pursuing careers for their own fulfillment; and many others chose to remain at home and care for their families.

I felt very fortunate to identify with women in all these categories. I am a relatively traditional person and enjoy my roles as wife and mother, but it has also been natural and essential for me to expand my life and to participate outside the home as a partner and businesswoman and in public service as First Lady.

Jimmy has always supported women's causes, but he didn't have much choice, surrounded by active women as he was: his mother, me, and Amy. It was interesting how the pattern in our family reversed. I had been surrounded by men, Jimmy and the three boys, for years. Then, after our sons were grown, Amy came along, Miss Lillian moved back home to Plains, and Jimmy was surrounded by women.

Before his inauguration, Jimmy asked me to work with his staff and our women's campaign committee to develop a list of women who would be likely prospects for available positions in the federal government. Keeping an up-to-date list of qualified women in every job category, ready to submit for consideration as appointments became available, was very helpful. Some statistics:

Only six women had ever been appointed Cabinet secretaries in the history of our country; Jimmy appointed three of them.

Only five women had ever been appointed as undersecretaries in the history of our country; Jimmy appointed three of them.

He appointed 80 percent of all women ever to hold the post of assistant secretary.

He was the first President to name women as general counsels and inspectors general.

Of the forty-six women serving as federal judges at the end of his term, forty-one had been appointed by Jimmy. We knew a number of women who would have been good Supreme Court justices, and it was always understood between us that a woman would be appointed if a vacancy occurred. That didn't happen, but the appointment of many women judges helped to compensate for their not having a voice on the Supreme Court and ensured a permanent and powerful voice for women in interpreting the laws of our land.

In previous administrations, a total of twenty-five women had held ambassadorial posts. Jimmy appointed sixteen women as ambassadors.

And more women were serving on federal boards and commissions and on delegations representing the United States at conferences throughout the world.

In addition to receiving presidential appointments, women need to be elected to positions at all levels of government. When we were in Washington, there had been only fourteen women senators and ninety women in the House of Representatives in our history. I agree wholeheartedly with the well-known slogan: "A woman's place is in the house . . . and the Senate."

We also included women in all activities at the White House, taking care to invite representatives from women's groups to participate in all events—government consultations and briefings on such issues as SALT II, inflation and energy, education, Middle East peace, and on the progress of women's issues. Every year we held receptions and briefings for congressional wives, women in business, women legislators, rural women, Jewish women, black women, Mexican-American women, Democratic women, educators, and many more, and I learned a lot from these discussions.

From my own experience, I remembered how the long hours at Carter's Warehouse had to be coordinated with my duties as a mother and housewife, and supported flexitime schedules for working mothers in the federal government, our nation's largest employer. And I was pleased when expanded day care centers became one of Jimmy's priorities. When my mother had to work full-time while we were children, she was lucky to have friends and relatives in Plains who could care for us. Most working women today are not so fortunate.

I had learned about small business management also by working alongside Jimmy at the warehouse, and now I wondered what I would have done if it had been necessary to organize my own business. Women were given some help in the Carter years: The Small Business Administration offered entrepreneurial training workshops for them and significantly increased loans available to businesses owned by women; the Farm Home Administration sponsored workshops and made it a priority to inform rural women of loans available for their businesses; HUD had seminars to teach women about housing finances and their rights to mortgage credit, removing barriers to women who wanted to own homes.

The President's Advisory Committee for Women came to realize that women nominees for federal judgeships were being penalized because they had had relatively little experience as judges in the lower courts or because they had taken several years away from their careers to have children. We discussed this with Jimmy and the attorney general, and they both agreed to be careful not to discriminate against women in the appointment process because they were mothers or because they had not been treated fairly when previous appointments had been made.

Other steps were taken to tackle the issues of discrimination, including: the amendment of the Civil Rights Act of 1964 to protect working women from occupational discrimination based on pregnancy; the consolidation of nineteen separate enforcement units in the federal government under one agency to handle discrimination complaints more efficiently; and the development of an interagency task force to eliminate sex discrimination from laws and policies and to focus government resources on increasing opportunities for women.

In most cases, the executives responsible for carrying out these decisions were women, often the "first" in their positions, which further strengthened the effectiveness of the programs.

The need for advice about the special concerns and problems of women in our country has been recognized by every President from John Kennedy through Jimmy Carter, all of whom appointed a women's advisory group. My daughter-in-law Judy served as honorary chair of this group, working closely with Kathy Cade in my office and Sarah Weddington in Jimmy's and with Chairpersons Bella Abzug, Carmen Delgado Votaw, and Lynda Robb. Unfortunately, there has been no such opportunity for American women to present their views to President Reagan, perhaps another cause of the highly publicized "gender gap" that affects his administration.

The political victories for women were important ones, and being a woman who mattered pleased me very much during my time as First Lady. But I never forgot that I was there because my husband held his high office, not because I had been elected. I had helped him get there, and I liked to think he couldn't have done it without me, but the situation was clearly the same one women have faced for centuries. First Ladies throughout our history have been expected to be adoring wives and perfect mothers, to manage the public and social aspects of the White House to the satisfaction of all critics, and to participate in "appropriate public service." The role of First Lady is a difficult—and sometimes nearly impossible—one to fill, and each one of us has dealt with this challenge in her own way.

The role has changed dramatically along with the expanded opportunities of other women in America. This was brought home quite vividly to me and Jimmy during our first visit to Gettysburg from nearby Camp David. After studying the battlegrounds of the

War Between the States, we went by the beautiful farm of the Eisenhowers to pay our respects to Mamie Eisenhower, whom we had long admired. We spent several hours with her, listening to her description of life in the Army, in the White House, and during their retirement. She was also eager to hear about my own experiences, but was somewhat taken aback by the variety and extent of my projects. She finally said, "I stayed busy all the time and loved being in the White House, but I was never expected to do all the things you have to do."

Until quite recently, First Ladies were expected to limit themselves to the duties of official hostess and private helpmate, and most of them never varied from this narrowly restricted role. Eleanor Roosevelt was the notable exception, and she was severely criticized for her personal involvement in public affairs. Nowadays, the public expectation is just the opposite, and there is a general presumption that the projects of a First Lady will be substantive, highly publicized, and closely scrutinized. I am thankful for the change.

I remember one special evening at the White House, a reception for the President's advisory committee, women appointees and officials, activists, and legislators from all over the country who were working for the ERA. Some of our special guests gathered upstairs before the reception. Joan Mondale was there; she had become a valuable asset to the nation through her knowledge and promotion of the arts and was a wonderful example of what women can accomplish through public service. Three generations of Johnsons were there too: Lady Bird, her daughter Lynda Robb, and Lynda's three small daughters; and three generations of my family: me, Judy and Amy, and my tiny granddaughter, Sarah. I was struck with the picture we made: grandmothers, mothers, daughters, all of us playing out very traditional public roles—but this night we were all there to celebrate and to stand for and to work on some very nontraditional choices and opportunities for women.

We went down the elevator together and made slow progress through the huge crowd of women into the East Room, finally reaching a small platform. And with the little girls wiggling behind me, I was ready to welcome the guests. "Welcome to your house," I found myself saying. "This house belongs to all Americans— and that means more than half of it belongs to women." The crowd roared its approval, and I couldn't have been more proud to have been a part of it.

* * *

In the mid-seventies, there were several million homeless refugees
in Southeast Asia, Indochina, and Africa. The problem became
so urgent that the United Nations convened a special conference
in Geneva, to which Jimmy sent Vice President Mondale. The
United States was working with international relief agencies such
as ICRC (International Committee of the Red Cross), UNICEF,
the World Food Program, Catholic Relief, CARE, and others that
were trying to provide food, clothing, medical care, and shelter.
We doubled the quota of refugees we could accept, and Jimmy
was already working to convince other countries to share the responsibility.

But in the fall of 1979 a new wave of refugees, the Cambodians,
flashed on our television screens every day and every night. There
was talk of another holocaust and, indeed, it was becoming evident
by the numbers and condition of the refugees reaching Thailand
that a whole race of people was facing extinction.

As Jimmy and I discussed the situation, we realized that governments alone could never do enough to ease the problem. Help
was needed from people all over the country, and judging from
my mail and the telephone calls coming into the White House, I
knew people were eager to help. But they didn't know how.

On Sunday, November 4, at Camp David, the same day we
learned that Iranian terrorists had taken over our embassy in Tehran, Henry Owen and some other members of the National Security
staff suggested that I go to the refugee camps in Thailand myself
to call attention to the need for help.

From intensive briefings by officials at the State Department
and the White House and a meeting with representatives of the
international relief agencies, I learned the dimensions of the tragedy. Almost half the total population of Cambodia, now called
Kampuchea, had died. A corrupt and vicious government, headed
by Pol Pot, had exterminated more than one million of its own
people in an attempt to create a "new society"; it had collapsed
when the country was invaded by the Vietnamese earlier in the
year. As the fighting continued, with the forces of Pol Pot still
holding out, hundreds of thousands of Cambodians had been driven
or had fled into the countryside, transportation systems had been
destroyed, and hunger and starvation had become widespread. For
two years the rice crop had not even been planted.

Now these hordes of Cambodians were massed in their own

country along the border of Thailand. But the Thais, overrun already with refugees, were reluctant to let them enter their country. Until recently their professed policy had been to admit women and children, but in reality Thai soldiers were driving all the Cambodians back by the thousands as they attempted to cross into Thailand. It was only after Prime Minister Kriangsak of Thailand had gone to the border area one day and watched a refugee die before his eyes that he altered Thai policy to admit all refugees. Now they were coming in by the thousands and Kriangsak was becoming increasingly unpopular.

On November 9, 1979, accompanied by a group of highly qualified advisers, I left for Thailand. On the twenty-two-hour flight I reviewed all I had learned about the current situation in Southeast Asia and listened to the members of our delegation discuss their special areas of concern.

Nothing, however, had prepared me for the human suffering I saw in the refugee camps when I arrived.

The Sakeo Camp had sprung up on the border of Thailand only a few days before our visit, and already there were acres and acres of blue plastic held up by sticks sheltering thousands of emaciated human beings of all ages, sick and dying from malnutrition and disease. The odor of human waste was everywhere, and a few large tents set up in the mud by relief agencies provided little shelter from the blistering sun, flies, and mosquitoes. Members of the U.S. and international press gathered around to see our reaction, but I felt momentarily paralyzed by the magnitude of the suffering. "Just brace yourself," Morton Abramowitz, our ambassador to Thailand, had told me in the plane. "You're helping us by coming here. Remember that your visit is worthwhile and you'll be all right."

Swallowing hard and blinking back my tears, my reaction was to move, not just stand there—to do something, to talk to someone. I leaned down to touch the brow of one of the refugees and spoke quietly, "Hello," but there was no reaction. I kept moving, kept speaking to them, but most just stared into space with blank looks on their faces. Some were frightened. Occasionally one would respond. They were lying on the ground, on mats or dirty blankets or rags. All were ill and in various stages of starvation— some all bones and no flesh, others with stomachs swollen as though to burst and with cracked feet. All had malaria, dysentery, or tuberculosis, and were retching, feverish, and silent.

One woman, shivering in her blanket even though the temperature was over 90 degrees, was crying softly. Dr. Julius Richmond, the U.S. surgeon general, who had come with me, was pleased that she was at least showing emotion, but there were no words to comfort her. Her husband and all seven of her children, she was able to tell me, had been killed.

Another woman had arrived just the night before with her husband and three small children, one a baby twelve days old that had been born on the way out of Cambodia. The family had lived on the bark from trees while they wandered, searching for the border, and had brought the baby to the camp to give away, though all had stayed.

Seeing the children was the most heartrending part of all. Hundreds of them rested under one tent, with emaciated bodies and limbs so thin and fragile, and they were eerily quiet. There were no sounds of childhood here, not even any crying, only an occasional whimper.

I picked up a baby boy four months old, who weighed only four pounds and looked like a tiny monkey, and a little girl whose limbs fell limp. Standing in the middle of the tent, cuddling a baby girl who hadn't the strength even to hold up her little arms, I felt like a new mother again with my own baby Amy in my arms. How I loved her and what a joy she was, and what opportunities she had ahead of her! And what about this baby girl? What was ahead for her; what would her future be? Clutching her to me and looking at the poverty and disease and suffering around me, tears welled up in my eyes again. I thought about our country and how little we realize of the suffering and distress and grief in the world.

I had been thinking to myself, as the television cameras followed me through the camp, that if Americans could see and understand this unbelievable suffering they would surely respond. I gently put the baby girl down on her mat, and we continued through the rest of the camp.

We came to the hospital, a shack made of waist-high woven palm fronds for walls, open at the top, with a thatched roof and mats on the floor. The people here were supposed to be the ones in the worst condition, but to me they looked the same as all the others. In a corner, marked off by more palm fronds, a French doctor had set up a delivery room, and thirteen or fourteen babies had already been born.

Under the low shelters made from the blue plastic that stretched far and wide, the rest of the people huddled together, without enough room even to stand. Every inch of ground was covered with people, and every time more ground was cleared, more people appeared to cover it.

As we were leaving the camp, walking to the cars, I heard a commotion behind me; someone had come to say that the baby girl I had been holding had just died.

With a great sense of sorrow we moved through the rest of the day's schedule, visiting a camp for Laotians. The conditions there were much better than at the new Sakeo Camp, but many of these refugees had already been here for three or four years, waiting to resettle abroad. Back in Bangkok, we visited the Lumpini Transit Center, a filthy but hopeful compound where those fortunate enough to have been selected for emigration awaited final processing.

My next mission was to ask the king of Thailand to cooperate with the relief effort. He had been reluctant to let the large number of refugees come into the country in this latest surge and was very displeased that his own prime minister had opened the borders. He remained convinced that Thailand was doing too much to help with not enough assistance from others.

When I tried to talk to him about the need for additional sites, he told the story of a "little policeman" whom he could trust and his "superiors" whom he could not. "If you give the superiors $120 million for food, medicine, and supplies, they spend $100 million and pocket the rest," he told me. "But if you give $20 million to the little policeman, he will make a list and justify every expense." Ambassador Abramowitz later interpreted this story as meaning the king didn't trust Prime Minister Kriangsak and was about to replace him.

A subsequent meeting with officials from the international relief agencies and voluntary organizations was more effective. Prior to the prime minister's decision to open the borders, the agencies had been working separately on trying to get supplies into Cambodia, but with little contact among themselves. When the refugees had begun to pour into Thailand, the agencies were forced to work together. Our meeting focused on their problems and possible solutions. The group agreed that the greatest need was for one overall coordinator, someone who could bring order to all the disparate efforts. This agreement in itself was a tremendous step forward for the very independent, self-motivated groups present, indicating the urgency of the situation and the determination of the organizations to meet the ever more pressing needs.

General Joseph Heiser of our delegation, a retired Army logistics expert, reported a serious lack of coordination in logistics. Water-hauling trucks and sanitation provisions were nonexistent. One group would request trucks for carrying supplies while another reported that they had 370 trucks en route to the camps and didn't know how they would use them all. In addition, the general learned that inside Cambodia, even if there were trucks, there were no bridges, no barges for use on the rivers, and no unloading equipment. And if ships got into the port in Cambodia, most people were so weak from starvation that they couldn't unload them.

Dr. William Foege, the director of the Centers for Disease Control in Atlanta and another member of my group, had discovered that there were few children in the camps between the ages of one and five, an indication that a whole generation of children was in danger of being lost to malnutrition and disease. He told us further that the emergency treatment for malnutrition, malaria, and dysentery had to be followed up with specialized treatment and preventive measures, which would require many more doctors and nurses than were currently available.

Upon returning home, armed with all this information, I tried to do everything at once. I called Kurt Waldheim, the secretary-general of the United Nations, to urge him to name an overall coordinator for the relief effort. I learned on the trip that if a UN initiative came from the United States it would never be accepted by certain other countries, so I told Waldheim I would not mention our conversation. Later in the day he called to say that he was going to appoint Sir Robert Jackson, who had been the relief coordinator for the tragedy in Bangladesh, as the coordinator in Thailand and that he would announce it in a day or two.

Almost immediately an airlift of special foods for infants and children was sent by our government to the refugee camps as well as desperately needed communications and water supply equipment. Father Theodore Hesburgh, the president of Notre Dame, and representatives of more than forty U.S. voluntary agencies met at the White House and formed the National Cambodia Crisis Committee. Composed of more than a hundred prominent individuals representing business, labor, the media, entertainment, and the religious and voluntary communities, it assumed responsibility for mobilizing support in the private sector. Logistical support was provided by the Cambodia Crisis Center, which acted as a clearinghouse for everyone who wanted to contribute to saving the Cambodian people; the committee set a fund-raising goal of $70 million.

In the meantime I made public service spots for television, appealing to people for help and showing footage of the camps from my trip; I also made speeches, including a major one to the Council on Foreign Relations in New York, appeared on the *Today* show and others, traveled to promote fund-raising programs, and held luncheons and receptions at the White House.

The United States government granted UNICEF an additional $2 million for the immediate purchase of rice, and the UN high commissioner for refugees was authorized to use $4 million of U.S.-allocated funds for the immediate support of refugee programs in Thailand. Jimmy directed the State Department to work with the Thai government and the international agencies in Thailand to prepare for the new refugees expected on the border and to continue its efforts to move food directly into Cambodia. U.S. refugee quotas from Thailand were increased, and the Peace Corps was directed to accelerate its support of the UN efforts on behalf of refugees. The surgeon general, Dr. Julius Richmond, who had accompanied me on the trip, established a clearinghouse for volunteers in the health field who were willing to lend a hand in Indochina.

The immediate response of our government to the crisis was tremendous, but even more so was the response of the American people. Major corporations, small family businesses, labor unions, governors, professionals, and laypeople alike rallied to help. There were extraordinary grass-roots campaigns, such as in one county in Maryland, where nearly two thousand volunteers trudged from door to door and raised $50,000 in one weekend. Every day my mail brought hundreds of wonderful examples of Americans pitching in to help. In grade schools and high schools, students sold candy, washed cars, and sold breakfasts to each other to raise money. One small boy offered his tennis shoes for a child in Cambodia, and another sent his allowance—15 cents.

The response was overwhelming, with contributions far exceeding what we had ever anticipated. The horror I had witnessed in the refugee camps was far removed from the lives of most Americans, but the concern and caring they poured out was proof of how our people can respond to human suffering, which touches us all.

A year later, the National Cambodia Crisis Committee ran full-page ads in all the major newspapers to report that while work still remained to be done, the crisis was over: "Famine conditions no longer exist. Refugees who fled to the border areas are returning to their villages. Health facilities are being restored. Children are back in school."

When I talked with Ambassador Abramowitz later, he told me that while the statement was somewhat optimistic, the Cambodian people are surviving—under tenuous circumstances, and with the essential support that the international organizations continue to give.

Prime Minister Kriangsak had been replaced within months of his opening the Thai borders. Lumpini was cleaned up as the result of the efforts of many people. China still supplies the Pol Pot forces (about 25,000 to 30,000, the same number that was still holding out when I was there). The Vietnamese-controlled Cambodian government is very weak and could not exist without Vietnam. There are, at this writing, about 90,000 refugees in Thailand waiting to be resettled and an additional 150,000 in camps along the border, who we hope will eventually drift back into the countryside. This number is half what it once was.

❧ 11 ❧
Iran and the Beginning of the End

Iran...*I-R-A-N*. These four letters had become a curse to me. There was a time when the name brought to mind stories of ancient Persia, Ali Baba and thieves and magic lamps and genies, flying carpets, beautiful women in veils and belly dancers, camels and deserts.

But no more. My memories now are of terrorists in the streets, anti–American and anti–Jimmy Carter slogans, and hostages held and held and held. My memories are of families at home, hoping and praying for loved ones behind embassy walls, and of the weight of responsibility on the shoulders of the one I love for the lives of those our nation came to love.

The summer of 1979, a full four months before the hostages were taken, our country was already in a bad mood. Gas lines were long and tempers were short. Farmers in the South and Midwest faced a severe drought, accompanied by escalating expenses. And for the first time in the history of our country, a national poll found that the majority of Americans believed that the next five years would be worse than the past five. Part of the American dream was being shattered by a cartel of oil-rich Arabs and the shortsightedness of our own oil industry. And Jimmy Carter was President.

During an economic summit in Japan in June 1979, when Jimmy helped convince the European countries to join in con-

demning OPEC for the skyrocketing costs of energy and adopting
stronger policies of conservation and energy independence, OPEC
announced an additional price increase. As gas lines lengthened
in our country, we canceled a planned stopover in Hawaii to rush
home. Jimmy's closest advisers—Hamilton, Jody, Jerry Rafshoon, Stu Eizenstat, the director of the domestic policy staff—
and members of the Energy Department had already prepared the
first draft of a speech for him to give to the nation a few days
later. Congress had been dragging its feet for almost two and a
half years instead of enacting the comprehensive energy legislation
first proposed in April 1977. The powerful groups opposing the
legislation made it easy for Congress to stall. Jimmy didn't want
simply to bemoan the problem again without saying what could
be done about it. But his advisers insisted, and he finally agreed
to schedule the speech, believing he could work out a good text.

Over the weekend at Camp David we both changed our minds.
Neither one of us could sleep well because of the time change
from Japan, and I was up at 4:00 A.M. Jimmy had been reading
the speech the night before and had left it on the coffee table. I
picked it up, but only read a page or two. When Jimmy got up a
little later, he asked me what I thought of it. "Nobody wants to
hear it," I told him. "They've heard about new energy programs
ever since you've been in office, and prices are still going up.
They don't want to hear about a new program that will allocate
energy to the elderly at a lower cost. They just want to be told
that everything is going to be all right and that somebody under-
stands the situation and has it under control." He was glad I agreed
because he said, "I decided last night to cancel it."

His advisers were taken aback, especially Fritz Mondale. Can-
celing at the last minute, they pointed out, would be seen as a
sign of confusion and lack of leadership. But Jimmy was firm.
He was going to invite leaders from every segment of American
life to Camp David that week for a "domestic summit" to talk
about the bigger problem facing America, how to convince the
public that the energy crisis was real, how it tied in to unemployment and inflation, and, most important, how our nation could
rally to resolve the oil crisis and renew our confidence in the
social, political, and economic future of the country. He needed
the support of the American people to get the remaining parts of
his energy legislation passed, and he wanted to motivate them to

go over the heads of the oil company lobbyists and other special interest groups to reach their congressmen. The competition for public support was intense. Among other things, every day people were watching television commercials by the oil companies, one starring Bob Hope, implying that no action was needed, that everything was just fine. No wonder people were confused.

For ten days Jimmy brought groups to Camp David: governors, labor and business leaders, members of Congress, local officials, oil industry executives, economists, energy experts, even religious leaders and philosophers. Intense interest was generated in what he was going to say to the nation, and when these meetings were over, on July 15, he delivered his speech to a tremendous audience. My heart was in my throat all the way through, pulling for him to do a good job. He reminded the people that our country was good and that it was strong, and though we had come through some crises that had shaken our confidence—a President who had to leave office under a cloud, a war in Vietnam we couldn't win, and now an energy shortage that was forcing us to realize for the first time that our resources were limited—we could heal these wounds of the past and regain our confidence, and a good way to demonstrate that was by joining together to solve the energy problem. It was a profound and effective speech, and I was delighted when the public opinion polls indicated that people had responded to Jimmy's words just as we had hoped. (This good speech later was labeled the "malaise" speech by Ted Kennedy.)

Some of Jimmy's advisers thought he had to go still further to establish a firm sense of authority over the government and that this was a good time to make the first changes in his Cabinet. A fresh start, everyone decided, would signal to the public that there would be a new opportunity to turn around the pessimism in the country. The concept was right, but its execution was wrong, and the momentum of his speech was lost.

I never really knew what happened when Jimmy called the Cabinet members together to discuss the desired changes with them, but what should have been a private and very frank discussion turned very public when it was leaked to the *Washington Post*. He had explained to his Cabinet that he was going to make a few changes among them and wanted their advice. One suggestion was that everyone might give him a written resignation, but Jimmy didn't want to do that. Then it was suggested that they could all offer to resign verbally, allowing him to refuse to accept resignations from those he wanted to keep.

Two of the Cabinet members had long wanted to return to private life, and Jimmy complied with their requests. He also requested and accepted the resignations of the secretaries of HEW, Transportation, and the Treasury, and then immediately announced that the Cabinet changes had been completed. We thought what he had done was positive until we read the newspapers the next morning. Blowing the Cabinet reshuffle out of all proportion, the headlines compared it to Nixon's Saturday Night Massacre, during the Watergate crisis.

Our challenges were just beginning, but I had become more philosophical about crises by this time. They never stopped coming, big ones and small ones, potential disasters and mere annoyances. I worried over each one in passing and celebrated our victories as they came, then went on to the next one.

In the next twelve months, Afghanistan would be invaded by the Russians, forcing Jimmy to impose a grain embargo and to cancel the U.S. participation in the 1980 Olympic Games; Billy would be investigated for allegedly representing Libyan interests without registering as a "foreign agent"; boatloads of Cubans, among them "undesirables," would arrive on our shores; and the Democratic party would be torn apart by Ted Kennedy's primary and convention presidential challenges. And then there was Iran. Iran.

In the midst of all these crises, we were having some successes in spite of the bad press. Congress was finally working to complete action on the energy bills. The last of the legislation was passed to complete deregulation of the airlines, railroads, trucking, finance and banking, and communications. A "superfund" was being established to deal with the growing problem of toxic waste. The final touches were put on laws to implement the Panama Canal treaties and the normalization of diplomatic relations with China. In addition, the Alaska Land Act was moving toward passage: A landmark act, it would designate more than ninety-seven million acres for new parks and refuges and classify fifty-six million acres as wilderness areas under federal protection. This legislation would double the size of our National Park and Wildlife Refuge System and the Wild and Scenic River System and triple the size of our Wilderness System. The signing ceremony for this bill in the East Room was one of my most satisfying moments.

But for now it was the bad news that the press heralded. The Iranian situation, which was the worst news, did not develop overnight. It began for me early in 1977, with just another demonstration; I heard some noise outside and walked over to the window to see what was happening. There was a small group of demonstrators in front of the White House carrying placards denouncing the shah and shouting anti-American slogans; they all wore hoods. One of the butlers told me that they were students from Iran—students in *our* country on programs paid for by *their* government, the government they were denouncing. No wonder they were wearing hoods. But I didn't worry about them. We had been in Washington for only a few months and had already become accustomed to some kind of demonstration in front of the White House almost every day.

Nevertheless, it was embarrassing when Empress Farah came to have lunch early in July of that first year. She was beautiful, with her hair pulled tightly back in a bun. Composed and sure of herself, she seemed to me to be a real force in her husband's life. She was deeply involved in preserving the culture of Iran by establishing museums, sponsoring programs to develop the arts, and working to provide schools. When she arrived at the White House, at least a thousand demonstrators showed up, shouting "Death to the shah!" and "The shah kills people!" For her protection we increased security, and I brought her in on the south side of the house, away from the demonstrators. I was going to ignore the subject, but she immediately brought it up and reassured me that demonstrations had become a part of her life wherever she went outside her own country. As we ate lunch that day, we listened to the muffled voices of the Iranian "students" in the distance.

The demonstrations during the shah's state visit a few months later, in November, were far worse; the press described them as "the worst violence in Washington since the Vietnam era." Anti- and pro-shah demonstrators clashed south of the White House with such fury that the police had to break up the melee. They chose to protest loudest just as Jimmy was delivering his welcoming remarks on the South Lawn. Suddenly my eyes started burning and stinging. I looked at Farah, who was trying to blink back tears, and Jimmy, gulping, had to cut his speech short. It was tear gas! Tear gas was wafting right across the White House lawn to the platform where we were standing. At first I couldn't believe it; then I tried to ignore the pain in my eyes and stood perfectly still on the platform, chin up, appearing, I hoped, absorbed in the ceremony as though nothing was happening. As Jimmy stepped back so the shah could respond to his remarks, he turned to see if I was all right and slipped me his handkerchief. I dabbed my eyes just as the shah finished his brief speech.

It was an unforgettable experience. Though the rest of the state visit went peacefully, Jimmy knew from intelligence briefings that there was much more to these demonstrations than the shah would admit. He took the shah to his small study near the Oval Office and questioned him about the consequences of suppressing his people and his reported violations of human rights—probably the first time an American official had ever addressed the issue with him. The shah replied that his opposition was just a few communists and there was no reason for concern. At the state dinner that night he was charming as he joked with me about having attended more official dinners at the White House than I had. Like Farah, he was embarrassed by the demonstrations and the image it projected of his country, but he dismissed them as "little more than a nuisance."

Seven months later, the anti-shah demonstrators had become a nuisance for us as well. In June 1978, Jimmy and I were in Atlanta, where he was speaking at a Baptist Brotherhood meeting, when suddenly a group of Iranian demonstrators unfurled a large banner from the balcony denouncing the shah. They shouted their familiar epithets—"Death to the shah" and "Down with the shah"—so loudly that Jimmy had to stop speaking until they were ushered out. Then, in October, a gang of Iranian students attacked Chip on a Texas campus. Secret Service agents and members of the college football team managed to drive the students off, so Chip was not injured, but clearly the situation was getting worse.

By January 1979, the shah was in serious trouble. Jimmy was getting regular briefings on the Iranian situation, and at a Cabinet meeting that I attended, he reported that Iran was in a state of revolution. There were forty thousand Americans in the country, and he had begun quietly to move them out.

I had paid little attention to Iran until the rioting broke out in Tehran and other cities and our people had to be evacuated. I was working on my own projects, and there always seemed to be crises in some part of the world. This was just another one. I knew that Jimmy and the State Department were helping the shah as he tried to stabilize the country, to initiate reforms to better his relationship with the Iranian people, even to establish a temporary government to serve while he went on a brief vacation outside Iran. It didn't occur to me for a long time that his government might collapse or that our people might be harmed. All I knew was that the situation was deteriorating and that Jimmy was becoming more and more preoccupied with it.

The troubles in Iran followed us to Guadeloupe a few days after the Cabinet meeting. Jimmy, Prime Minister Jim Callaghan of Great Britain, President Valéry Giscard d'Estaing of France, and Chancellor Helmut Schmidt of Germany had planned to discuss mutual problems in a relaxed, informal setting, and wives had been invited along. Our bungalow was on a white sand beach, the water a stone's throw away; a score of sailboats bobbed at anchor, and the scent of hibiscus and bougainvillea filled the air.

But no sooner had we arrived than the telephone rang; it was Fritz Mondale reporting on Iran. For more than an hour Jimmy sat on a washing machine in the corner of the kitchen, talking on a secure telephone; then he spoke with Cy Vance, who had come to our bungalow. We were going to support the shah and the military, Jimmy said, because we didn't know what form the government might take without military support, and the military leaders were loyal to the shah.

At a candlelit dinner the first evening in a small thatched hut with the sound of waves in the background, the subject of conversation was—Iran. In my diary I noted the following exchange: Schmidt: "We all knew how weak he was, but I'm surprised that he's going under before the Saudis." Callaghan: "Everybody is of the same opinion . . . very weak. Nobody has been willing to tell the shah the truth. We haven't told him the truth about the disintegrating situation in ten years." Schmidt: "There was absolutely no dissent around him. The only one ever to disagree with him was his wife." It was interesting to me that "after the fact" everyone claimed to have known what was going to happen.

Jimmy continued to evacuate the thousands of Americans from Iran, as the crisis dominated the daily news on television. Every night we watched as hundreds of thousands of Iranians marched in the streets of Tehran, calling for the return of the Ayatollah Khomeini, a Moslem mullah living in exile in France. The Iranians had overwhelmingly rejected their leader, and the shah decided to leave Iran while there was still a chance for a new prime minister with strong military support to take over and stabilize the country. Walter Annenberg, the well-known American publisher, had offered his California estate to the shah, but at the last minute the shah chose to go to Morocco instead, presumably to stay close to his country in case the turmoil died down and he could return. We were surprised but relieved.

The turmoil didn't die down, and the pressure on Jimmy to bring the shah to our country mounted, mostly from people who were trying to protect financial investments or who felt indebted to him for being such a good friend of the United States. But Jimmy resisted. On April 19, 1979, I wrote in my diary: "We can't get away from Iran. Many people—Kissinger, David Rockefeller, Howard Baker, John McCloy, Gerald Ford—all are after Jimmy to bring the shah to the United States, but Jimmy says it's been so long, and anti-American and anti-shah sentiments have escalated so that he doesn't want to. Jimmy said he explained to all of them that the Iranians might kidnap our Americans who are still there and also destroy our satellite observation stations in northern Iran."

There it was, without the comforting luxury of hindsight, seven months before the Iranians made good Jimmy's fears. In the meantime the shah had moved from Morocco to the Bahamas, then on to Mexico.

That was in April. There followed months of quiet and improving relations with Iran. Khomeini even sent an emissary to meet with our State Department people to discuss how relations between our two countries could be improved. One day we were at Camp David, having just returned from Boston and the dedication of the Kennedy Library. Jimmy had made a superb speech, and I was pleased and feeling very smug about the whole event. The date was October 20, 1979. We had just changed into comfortable clothes when the telephone rang. It was a long call and to my astonishment, I heard Jimmy say, "Let him come on in, and instruct our embassy in Tehran to notify the Iranian prime minister."

"Who? Let who come in?" I asked.

"The shah," Jimmy said. "He's got cancer and the State Department says he requires treatment that he can only get in our country. I just can't keep him out and let him die. He's been our friend too long to turn our backs on him now."

The shah, it turned out, had been sick for a long time, but our government had only recently found out how critically ill he really was. Jimmy had been the last holdout, but when the message about the shah's need for special medical attention came, he had finally given in. It was the only humanitarian thing to do. And he didn't think the shah would be here very long.

Also, Jimmy felt better about the arrangements at our embassy in Iran. As the violence had increased in Iran, he told me, the State Department had improved the security system. Security personnel had been added, the embassy buildings had been strengthened structurally, and of more than eleven hundred staff members who had been stationed there, only about seventy remained. Thirteen were Marine guards; the others were primarily engaged in closing out our relationship with the shah's regime, helping straighten out hundreds of disrupted commercial contracts, disposing of sensitive government documents, and packing and shipping household goods.

Most important, he said, was the firm assurances from top Iranian officials that our embassy would be protected, as it already had been once before. Earlier in the year a group of militants had entered the embassy grounds and Iranian officials had moved promptly to expel them.

Despite Jimmy's unease about admitting the shah to the United States, he told me, "We've taken every precaution I know."

Two relatively uneventful weeks passed, and we were at Camp David again. Early on Sunday morning, November 4, Zbig called. "Mr. President, our embassy in Iran has been overrun by militants and they're holding fifty to sixty of our people." Jimmy immediately set the government's wheels in motion, calling in Cy Vance, talking with other State Department officials, and convening the National Security Council to size up the exact situation and prepare our reaction—thus beginning a series of emergency meetings that were to continue daily for 444 days, until the end of his term of office. Everyone was disturbed, but at the time it seemed to be just another burdensome event in Iran that had to be resolved. There was no panic. We assumed the takeover would be temporary and that the Iranian government would step in to remove the radicals from our embassy and release our people, just as all other governments in history had done.

It was a tense day, and as the hours passed it became clearer that the Iranian government was not able to respond. With the country in such turmoil, there was no one person or faction with enough authority to make decisions. And our people were still being held. We began to believe that Jimmy's worst fears had been realized.

Three days later, as I was leaving on my mission to the refugee camps in Thailand, Iran dominated everyone's thoughts. Only the return of the shah, the militants said, would make them release the hostages. We were more concerned then about what needed to be done to get them out rather than whether or not they would ever get out.

When I returned from Thailand, Jimmy and Cy Vance had already met with the families of the hostages, having called them all to Washington. The families were still stunned by the news and very emotional, but I think they were reassured. Jimmy told them all that was being done, and when the meeting was over they issued a statement of support for his actions. An Iran Working Group had been set up at the State Department to monitor the situation around the clock. Jimmy had put the military on alert to take action if the hostages were harmed in any way; and plans were already under way for a military presence in the area. He had been poring over maps and charts to locate oil refineries and other strategic targets and had ordered the secretary of defense to develop a hostage rescue plan. Though Jimmy was calm, he was becoming increasingly angry, as was the rest of the country.

"Are we still using their oil?" I asked Jimmy. "I don't know anybody in the United States that wants to use Iranian oil." A few days later our country stopped buying oil from Iran, and at the same time, plans were made to seize all Iranian assets in the United States, amounting to about $12 billion.

I have to admit to some wishful thinking in the back of my mind that we send the shah back home, but that was never a serious consideration. It would be a cowardly thing to do, and I knew if we sent him back to Iran he would be killed. But I never stopped wishing we hadn't let him come into the country in the first place. I wished Jimmy had followed his first instincts. But when the shah became ill, it was the right thing to do, and I suppose we always have to do "the right thing."

I became fiercely defensive toward those who criticized Jimmy for not closing the embassy and evacuating everyone when the troubles began. You don't let a group of militants drive you out of a country. Were we supposed to run away just because some radical students were marching with anti-American posters in the streets? Jimmy was not about to give the impression that the United States was afraid and had to leave. No, he left enough people there to carry out the functions of the embassy while the almost forty thousand American civilians were evacuated. And it was a miracle that while thousands were killed in all the turmoil, rioting, and trouble, only one American lost his life, a reporter who was shot while covering a revolutionary skirmish before the major crisis erupted. What Jimmy had done was exactly correct. No embassy can be completely impregnable; diplomats can't work in an isolated fort. They have extensive duties to perform in any foreign country and at the same time must depend on the foreign government for their ultimate protection. The government had not lived up to its obligation. And the clock began to tick!

Immediately, Jimmy had sent a clear message to the Iranians: If a hostage were put on trial, all Iranian commerce would be interrupted; if a hostage were injured or killed, the United States would attack Iran militarily. But as the days passed, I became very impatient and began to say to him, "Do something! Do something!" and very quietly he would explain the unacceptable repercussions of any drastic action he might take.

Of course he was doing everything possible to resolve the crisis, exploring every diplomatic channel and planning military actions as well. Even the bombing of Tehran was assessed as an option. But to sacrifice the hostages just to demonstrate our nation's strength could not be seriously considered by the President. He reminded the public frequently that we had two ultimate goals: to guard the interests and integrity of our nation, and to return all the American hostages to their homes, safe and free.

At first, the public supported Jimmy all the way. During any crisis, the incumbent President can almost count on a surge of approval, and the Iranian crisis was no exception. Within the first few weeks of the embassy takeover, the country was caught up in an outpouring of patriotism and support for the President, just as the 1980 campaign was beginning. Unfortunately for Ted Kennedy and Jerry Brown, both announced their candidacy the same week the hostages were captured; they were then in a predicament, trying to decide how to attack Jimmy in the midst of the general approbation. And from that time on, our fortunes and theirs would be strongly affected by the hostage situation.

* * *

On a long-planned campaign trip to New Hampshire, Miss Lillian, my daughter-in-law Judy, Joan Mondale, and I flew into the state together, then went our separate ways.

I loved being back in New Hampshire. It brought back memories of four years earlier and wonderful people and hard work, and snow and cold weather and tensions and not knowing, and finally a victory—a victory that had sent us on our way to the White House. I loved every minute of being back, seeing my friends and reminiscing. All day I was asked about the hostages, and everyone said, "Tell the President we're behind him and praying for him."

We had fun exchanging stories on the way home. Miss Lillian was feeling good and entertained the press accompanying us on the plane. Judy had a live lobster in a bag for Jimmy, and Joan was pleased with her crowds. The headline story of the day came from a visit Miss Lillian had made to the Bow Men's Club, which had never before had a woman in attendance, not even to cook, and which she had enjoyed immensely. Speaking in her usual off-the-cuff way, she said, "If I had a million dollars, I would hire someone to shoot the ayatollah!"

The shah's presence in the United States soon became a political football. In December, Ted Kennedy denounced the shah and in turn was criticized from all sides. I watched him on the evening news, defending himself to the press with great irritation. And candidate Reagan was going to the other extreme, saying that the shah should get permanent asylum in the United States.

But the shah and his advisers had decided that he wanted to leave, and the hospital was ready for him to go, but no other country wanted him. The president of Mexico reneged on his earlier promise that he could return to Mexico. The shah's second choice was Austria, but that country said no. None of the large nations such as Great Britain or France would take him, but tiny Panama decided to offer him asylum. We were standing in a receiving line in the Cross Hall of the White House, shaking hands with members of Congress who had come for the annual Christmas ball, when Jimmy got the telephone call saying that Torrijos had consented to take the shah. I could hardly conceal my happiness. I felt sorry for the shah, who had truly become a man without a country, but I hoped his leaving the United States would mean the end of the hostage crisis.

In December, Jimmy announced his candidacy for a second

term as President, and I was really looking forward to his campaigning again. He had been working on the crisis day and night, and I thought it would be a good change for him to get out in the countryside and feel the approval in the air for what he was doing. We had a big announcement party planned in Washington, with simultaneous ones to be held all over the country, followed by a week of travel and much-needed fund-raising. But once more, Iran changed our plans.

Jimmy decided he couldn't leave the White House to barnstorm around the country as a candidate. He needed to stay near the Situation Room to respond instantly to any message from Iran. He also thought it important with the crisis at hand to continue in the role of a President representing all Americans and not move into a highly partisan political campaign just representing Democrats.

Christmas came, and for the first time in twenty-six years we didn't go home to Plains. Instead, when the Christmas parties at the White House were over, we went to Camp David for the remainder of the holidays. It was quiet—only Jimmy, Amy, and me. We invited the senior staff at Camp David and the Filipino stewards to bring their families and join us for Christmas dinner, and all day I had my fingers crossed. With negotiations for the release of the hostages going on around the clock and the shah in Panama, I thought we might just have the most wonderful Christmas present in the world—I thought the hostages might come home. I had begun to have feelings of hope in Washington the night of the tree-lighting ceremony on the Ellipse. After Jimmy delivered a somber Christmas message to the nation, Amy pulled the switch to turn on the Christmas lights. The crowds gasped as the tree remained dark, lit only by a large star on top. "On top of the great Christmas tree is a star of hope," Jimmy's voice rang out. "We will turn on the other lights when our hostages come home, safe and free." All night and Christmas Day I was just sure we would hear good news. But the day came and went and the good news never came. Instead, two days after Christmas, there was more bad news. The Soviets had invaded Afghanistan.

One more crisis. Our government had been watching the Russians amass their troops on the Afghan border, but no one had expected them actually to invade. Usually the Soviets use surrogates like the Cubans or Vietnamese to do their dirty work, but this time they had gone into Afghanistan themselves. And the stakes were high.

"There goes SALT II," Jimmy said.

He had worked hard for this treaty and had been sure it was gaining support in the Senate. Now the chance for ratifying it would be gone. Of all the goals Jimmy had as President, reducing the threat of nuclear war and preventing an expensive and dangerous nuclear arms race was the most important of all to him, and he had the sentiment of the people with him in his efforts for peace. There were no anti-nuclear demonstrators when Jimmy Carter was President.

I've never seen Jimmy more upset than he was the afternoon the Russian invasion was confirmed. "We will help to make sure that Afghanistan will be their Vietnam," he said, and Soviet troops are still bogged down in a very resistant Afghanistan. The invasion meant more than losing an opportunity for progress toward peace. It meant making some sacrifices and controversial decisions that were very difficult. It meant withdrawing from the 1980 Olympics in Moscow, registering our young people for the draft, reducing exports to the Soviet Union, and imposing a grain embargo just before the Iowa caucuses.

Because of the hostages, Jimmy was staying close to the White House, but I was facing the farmers—and Ted Kennedy—in Iowa. I was already nervous about the Kennedy challenge before Jimmy announced the grain embargo. We had beaten him in an earlier straw vote in Florida, but he had discounted that victory, claiming that he hadn't been able to spend enough time in the state. The real test, Kennedy predicted, would be in Iowa, where he was making an all-out effort. Much of his entire national organization moved into the state, with hundreds of people working telephone banks to get voters to the caucuses, and he was campaigning two or three days a week in the state himself.

It was important to beat Kennedy early in the election year. Not only did we need the public's endorsement for Jimmy's policies, but we needed a strong Democratic party, with everybody working together, to meet the challenge of the Republicans in the fall. If Kennedy lost in Iowa, I reasoned, he would withdraw from the primary race for the sake of the party and our country. I had hoped he wouldn't run, but I never denied that he had a legitimate right to challenge Jimmy if he didn't agree with his policies. With a second loss, however, it would be counterproductive for Kennedy to stay in the race. So the political stakes were high in Iowa.

And the odds for winning suddenly seemed low. The grain embargo was obviously an unpopular decision with the Iowa farmers and a good political issue for Kennedy. I was impatient with Jimmy for having made the embargo decision when he did, but he insisted the issue went beyond politics. "It's the *only* effective economic action we can take against the Soviets," he told me. And off I went to face the anti-Carter, pro-Kennedy demonstrators and an antagonistic press corps. The farmers, though, were far more supportive than I had anticipated, and I called home to report this to Jimmy.

With the help of Fritz Mondale, Secretary of Agriculture Bob Bergland, our children, and other surrogates who came into the state, we reassured the farmers that Jimmy would make good on his promise to keep the price of grain up by developing new markets (which he did, resulting in the highest export of grain that year in history). Our son Jack, who ran a grain elevator himself, went from elevator to elevator in Iowa, listening to concerns and putting in a good word for Jimmy.

It was a tense time for us all, not really knowing how people would react to the Kennedy challenge, and I knew we could be wrong about the farmers' acceptance of the embargo. "Hold your breath and watch the grain prices. They could kill us," Jack said.

But life went on at the White House. Jimmy was absorbed with the hostages and the Afghan situation and with the everyday workings and responsibilities of the presidency—and not nearly as concerned as I about the campaign.

I was also tending to my duties as First Lady as well as spending two days a week traveling to Iowa, Maine, New Hampshire, and other states. When I was traveling I felt cut off, just as Jimmy could not afford to be, from the rapidly changing crises around the world. I called Jimmy at night and at different times during the day, if I had a major speech or press conference scheduled, to see if anything new had happened. If I couldn't get through to him I would talk to Jody or Hamilton or Zbig. I had developed a standard campaign speech by then, changing the first paragraph every day to bring it up to date with the latest news.

As the campaign and the situation in Iran wore on, I also had to counter accusations from our political opponents and the press that Jimmy was "hiding in the Rose Garden" or even, as one ludicrous rumor had it, having a nervous breakdown. Jimmy wasn't hiding; he was giving his complete attention to the crises involving our nation. In addition, everything was so sensitive in the hostage negotiations that any public statement he might make could be misinterpreted by the irrational kidnappers in Iran. He couldn't negotiate through the press, and he couldn't go around the country without answering innumerable questions about the hostages.

The nervous breakdown rumor bothered me the least. I knew Jimmy was doing exactly what he thought was right, and he was doing it, as I said in my speeches, "courageously and calmly." I still believe his decision not to campaign at that point was the right one. If he'd gone out on the campaign trail, the same critics who were saying, "What is the President doing in the Rose Garden?" would have been saying, "Why isn't the President in the Rose Garden taking care of the emergencies?" It was a no-win situation during a critical election time.

At the beginning of the year, all our political efforts were centered in Iowa. The price of grain held, and on January 21, we nervously waited out the election returns. And the news was wonderful! The farmers had stuck by us and we won overwhelmingly. We defeated Kennedy in ninety-nine out of a hundred counties, a margin for which we hadn't dared to hope. I waited for Ted Kennedy to withdraw, but he didn't. Despite repeated defeats, even beyond the point where he could possibly have any hope of being nominated, Kennedy stayed in the race, much to my chagrin.

I continued to campaign several days a week. No matter what issues I studied, all the questions were about the opinion polls, which were up for us; the hostages, who were still being held; and Ted Kennedy, who was becoming more and more strident. But after we won so overwhelmingly in Iowa, it was even easier to bear Kennedy's continuous attacks. I wrote in my diary on February 15, 1980: "I . . . can't believe how EMK distorts the facts, as with registration . . . telling young people that they are on their way to the Persian Gulf and talking about 'daily body counts' on television. I had expected better of him."

Early in the year, I went to the State Department to meet with the families of the hostages. It was a tearful experience, but I was reassured because they were still supportive of Jimmy, who had seen them earlier in the day. The families were brave and patient throughout the ordeal in Iran, setting an example for the rest of the country. The State Department stayed in touch with them daily and brought them all to Washington regularly, where they were kept up to date on what was happening. They formed their own organization, Family Liaison Action Group (FLAG), which arranged meetings with experts on terrorism and with former Vietnam POWs. Founded by Penne Laingen, the wife of the chief of mission in Iran, Bruce Laingen, who was being held in the Iranian Foreign Ministry. FLAG also pushed the State Department to answer questions concerning legal, medical, psychological, financial, and repatriational matters. It opened up new mail routes to the hostages. Penne edited a bulletin to the families, keeping them posted with any news and helping to serve as a conduit for their ideas and concerns. And it was Penne's idea for Americans to tie yellow ribbons around the trees in their yards.

She said she had always been big on symbols, and one day a reporter called and asked how she was coping with her husband's being held hostage. She said they talked about religion, the dignity of the Foreign Service, and her feelings of honor for our country. When the reporter asked what she would suggest rather than the demonstrations and egg throwing that had recently occurred at the Iranian Embassy in Washington, she said, "Be constructive instead. Tie a yellow ribbon around an oak tree!" The reporter asked, "Have you done that?" "As a matter of fact, yes, as a family gesture."

The story was printed in the *Washington Post. Newsweek* picked it up, and from there it grew—from one person's attempt to do something constructive in a situation that didn't allow for much activity to a symbol none of us will ever forget.

With Penne Laingen and other family members, I tied a yellow ribbon on a tree in the front yard of the White House, just as other Americans tied them on trees, car antennas, mailboxes, light posts, and front doors. I visited a mental health center and was presented with a quilt that the students had made, with a green background, a giant brown tree—and yellow ribbons tacked all over the tree! The yellow ribbon had become the symbol of remembering, and by the time the hostages came home, it had become the symbol of freedom.

There were other symbols and signs of remembering. A candlelight vigil was held every Sunday evening at sundown across the street from the Iranian Embassy in Washington. A group gathered there no matter what the weather—in the bitterest cold, rain, wind, and in the heat of summer. Similar activities were held across the nation. And when Bruce Laingen wrote home to "ring out the bells" when thirteen of the hostages were released—most of the women and the blacks—the bells continued to ring across the country for the hostages still being held.

So much depended on Jimmy's bringing the hostages home. But as time wore on, the continuous news coverage made a bad situation worse. Night after night, the television news dramatized the number of days the hostages had been held. I tried to turn off the television quickly if we were watching CBS, before Walter Cronkite could sign off with his daily count. A special nightly program was born just to cover Iran. All of the networks ran footage of the terrorists humiliating our people and shouting anti-American and anti-Carter slogans, which was exactly what the terrorists wanted. I thought the American press was giving Khomeini and the kidnappers the worldwide recognition they craved, the image of being powerful just because they were keeping a few innocent victims. And I often thought that if the press had not made such a continuing furor over it, we might have gotten the hostages home sooner, but on the other hand, I also knew the enormous coverage could have prevented further abuse or even the execution of our hostages.

Though some people thought the hostage crisis made our country seem weak in the eyes of the world, it took great strength on our part to be able to wait out this group of terrorists and eventually to bring every hostage home safely. A weaker or less caring country would have had to go into Iran militarily to prove its strength to the world, probably sacrificing the lives of those it wanted to save in the process.

Our lives became a seesaw of emotions as scheme after scheme fell apart. In one episode, known only to a tiny group working in the White House, Hamilton Jordan was negotiating through intermediaries with Iran's President Bani-Sadr and Foreign Minister Ghotbzadeh. Hector Villalon, an Argentine businessman living in France, and Christian Bourguet, a French lawyer, had approached Hamilton through Panamanian contacts. They wanted to deal with him because they knew he reported directly to Jimmy and not to the State Department, which they believed to be controlled by David Rockefeller. At the climax of these negotiations, Hamilton, equipped with a red wig, flew to Paris to meet personally with Ghotbzadeh.

The message from Paris came during a family dinner on March 31. Jimmy answered the telephone, and I could tell that something important was going on. "What's happened?" I asked him, though I thought it had to be Hamilton. "It will soon be over," he said quietly, "one way or the other. We'll know early in the morning." I couldn't eat any more. Ever since Christmas I had thought there was a chance to bring them home. Carefully I put my knife and fork down on my plate and left the table. I went into my bathroom and cried because I thought this would be the answer to so many things. Lately, sensing some movement, the news media had been filled with rumors that something positive might happen, and once more, everyone's hopes were high. I didn't want our people to be disappointed again, and I wanted them to realize that what Jimmy was doing had been right. I prayed that the news would be good the next morning and that the hostages could come home.

The next day the deal fell through, and I was sick. Bani-Sadr had weakened. If Ghotbzadeh had been president instead, history might read differently. He saw the enormous economic and political damage that was being done to his country by their holding our people, and he worked in every way with us to release them. But in the end, he didn't have the power or the backing of the Revolutionary Council to overcome Bani-Sadr—or even to save himself. In large part for his efforts on our behalf, Ghotbzadeh was executed by a government firing squad in 1982.

Over the next weeks, the questions on the campaign trail changed from "What's the President doing about the hostage situation?" to "Why doesn't he do something?" The mood was beginning to turn from one of interest and support to one of questioning, and each week I rushed home after my last appearance, praying that a miracle had happened and that there would be some word of encouragement—invariably to be disappointed.

There were always negotiations, always plans that "just might work," and constant pressure upon Jimmy to take drastic action, and instead of giving moral support to him in a difficult situation, I'm afraid I was sometimes guilty of adding to the pressure. Each time I wanted him to "do something—anything," he usually would calmly say, "Like what? What else do you want me to do?"

"Couldn't you mine the harbors?" I would ask.

"Our threats against them are effective" was his reply. "Khomeini knows we'll mine the harbors and strike militarily if any of our people are hurt. But if I act now and mine the harbors and close off all the oil going to our allies, and the mines stay there for a while and they still don't release the hostages, then what? Or rather, suppose that after a week or so with all of their shipping cut off, the Iranians decide to take the hostages out one at a time— one every morning at daybreak—and stand each one up before a firing squad, then what? Then we would be at war, and all our Americans in Iran would be dead. I have to be patient until we can be sure the hostages will be safe and free."

I was glad he was the one in charge.

By spring the campaign was in full swing. Even though some disenchantment with the hostage situation had set in, we were still winning two-thirds of all the delegates. Once more we won in Illinois, even though at the last minute Jane Byrne, who had given us a firm commitment, threw her support to Kennedy. That made our 2 to 1 victory over both of them doubly sweet, but our triumph was short-lived. A week later, "the right thing to do" got in the way of politics again in the New York primary, and we lost dramatically to Kennedy for the first time.

Just before the primary, Jimmy, over all my objections, announced anti-inflation steps that included budget cuts in a number of social programs which were dear to the Democratic constituency in New York. The voters did not think this was "the right thing to do"!

An old mistake in the United Nations Security Council hadn't helped, either. One day when I was campaigning in New York, I picked up the newspaper in my hotel room to discover that Secretary of State Vance had created new headlines by making a major statement about a controversial vote the United States had made in the United Nations Security Council regarding Jerusalem that had angered our Jewish constituency. Overnight the UN flap had been refreshed in people's minds, and I was angry. Heaven knows, Cy Vance doesn't have a political bone in his body. His concern for his country is his total commitment, but I went straight to the telephone to call Jimmy. "Doesn't Cy know we're in a campaign?" I asked. "It was bad enough in New York already, but I may as well come home now. We're finished, and I've got to go out and smile at people all day."

"If you can't stand the heat, get out of the kitchen," Jimmy would say on such occasions. But he knew I wouldn't have been anywhere else. Earlier in the administration, he had told me one day when I was complaining about all of the controversial problems we had to face, "If you think we have problems, I'm going to send you something when I get back to my office and you'll see we have a gravy train!" He sent me Robert Donovan's book about Harry Truman, *Conflict and Crisis*, and he was right. Truman's problems seemed insurmountable in the last days of the war and the time immediately following. He said that all the time he was in the White House, he looked forward to one week without a crisis—and it never came. To paraphrase Harry Truman: "The heat comes with the kitchen." It always has; it always will. And I enjoy the battle and the confrontations, but I also like to win.

The New York primary gave new life to Kennedy's lingering candidacy which would in the long run cause us and the Democratic party to suffer interminably.

Campaigning wasn't always easy with the crises, the "Rose Garden," Ted Kennedy, the UN vote. My diary notes reflected my mood: ". . . a tough day . . . UN snafu unsettling . . . I got hives during the day. At last event in Illinois I had a big welt under my left eye, and I could feel it getting bigger and bigger all the time the cameras and photographers were focused on me. I just kept saying my speech and answering the questions like it wasn't there. When I got back to the White House, Dr. Lukash said it was something I ate. I think he's wrong. I've decided I'm allergic to campaigning!"

Some problems were physical: "My mouth got sore . . . from talking so much. The harsh TV lights shining on me all the time didn't help much." Again: "In the middle of the night in Wichita, Kansas, I heard someone at the door say quietly, 'Mrs. Carter, get up and get dressed. There's a fire in the hotel and we might have to evacuate.' I was standing in the middle of the floor, nonchalantly trying to decide whether or not to dress or put on my robe . . . the message had been so calm. Then Madeline opened the other door and smoke poured in. No more hesitation! I put on my robe and we dashed from the room. Following the agents and with Mary Hoyt trailing, we went down eight flights of stairs . . . and to safety."

Before too many months passed, the hostages seemed like family to us as Jimmy schemed and plotted to bring them home. And every time we saw them on television, I counted quickly to see how many there were. Even when they had bandannas over their eyes and I was furious to see them humiliated that way, I was still glad to know they were alive. Once when someone asked Jimmy how he felt watching the hostages being paraded on television, I heard him reply, "How would you feel if one of them was your son and you were watching him, not knowing whether the terrorists were going to kill him or not?" We were usually quiet watching the news from Iran, but I could always tell by the grim set in his chin and the vein that throbbed in his temple that Jimmy was filled with anger and revulsion as he watched the terrorists.

Soon after the New York primary, Hamilton Jordan called to ask me how a campaign trip had gone. We were both worried about the next primaries, coming on the heels of Kennedy's victory in New York, but I said I thought it was going well and he felt encouraged. Hamilton and I usually agreed on the assessment of our political fortunes. If I were discouraged, it seemed that he was discouraged. One day in April when I was feeling blue, Jimmy came home and told me that if he could survive Hamilton and me, he would be all right.

He was right. We continued to defeat Kennedy and Jerry Brown in almost every primary.

But there was much more at stake than the primaries. On April 12, not two weeks after the Ghotbzadeh plan had fallen through, Jimmy told me about a "special mission" that was being planned. We were sitting on the Truman Balcony after lunch, and he told me that they had been planning a rescue ever since the hostages were captured and had decided now to go through with it. He said it was the hardest decision he had ever made in his life, but "if they come out at all, we are going to have to go in and get them."

There was still some risk involved with the plan, he said, but he was convinced it could succeed. I was glad to hear about it. I had wanted him to do something for a long time, and I was pleased that he thought this would work. He had watched over the months as the plans had been developed and perfected, and although he did not reveal them to me that afternoon, he had examined the meticulous details and preparations with those involved.

More important, Jimmy's decision to mount a rescue mission had the backing, he thought, of all his advisers. They had been working together on various plans for five months, finally accepting this one as the best. As secretary of state, Cy Vance had been an important voice in planning the rescue operation, including a secret reconnaissance flight to the desert in Iran. And though he hadn't been at the meeting this morning, he had been represented by Deputy Secretary of State Warren Christopher. It was assumed that Cy still supported the plan. The only question remaining was the timing of the attempt, which would be soon but depended on many factors: the readiness of our secret forces in Iran, the final briefing of our rescue team on U.S. Navy ships near the mouth of the Persian Gulf, the weather, and even the proper phase of the moon. Absolute secrecy was necessary. "If anyone—anyone—finds out about the plan, it will never work," Jimmy said. And no one did.

I tried not to be too optimistic and felt some trepidation as the day for the mission approached. Everyone in the White House who knew about it—and there were very few—had to maintain regular schedules and not indicate that anything was afoot. I wanted to be there on the day itself so I could follow what was happening, but my schedule was already set, and instead I was off on a campaign trip to Michigan, Texas, and Tennessee.

All of the questions that day were, as usual, about the hostages, Afghanistan, and Ted Kennedy. Typically, in an interview for an Italian television reporter, the first question was: "The Pre-see-dent, when come he out of the Rose Gar-deen?!" I wanted to tell her that he was very busy that day in the Rose Gar-deen, thank you!

I was tense and nervous as I traveled, but with feelings of hope and expectation. Again and again my thoughts went back to my conversation with Jimmy on the Truman Balcony. Our undercover people in Tehran had reported that the guards had become lax around the embassy, laying their guns down on the ground and lounging against the gates to laugh and talk with the passing crowds. I learned later that one of the employees in the embassy had pinpointed the room of every single hostage. The rescue team members would wear special glasses so they could identify our hostages in the dark. They had practiced scaling walls, working in similar desert conditions in Arizona, and had even secretly landed a small plane in Iran to test and photograph the landing site. A warehouse had been rented on the outskirts of Tehran to house the trucks that would take the rescue crew to the embassy. Overseeing all of this was Colonel Charlie Beckwith, a good and tough man who would lead the Special Forces team and who assured Jimmy and his advisers that the mission would be a success. No detail had been overlooked.

When I set out on my campaign trip, I hoped and prayed and honestly thought that when I got home it would be all over and the hostages would be free. Instead, when I called Jimmy on April 24 from a hotel suite in Detroit to see if anything had happened, the dream began to turn into a nightmare.

As soon as he answered the telephone I knew something was wrong. "The news is bad," he said in a voice that sounded as sad as I had ever heard it, "but I can't talk to you about it now. This is an open telephone line." While my heart went out to him, my mind raced. "Have the children moved?" I asked, quickly inventing a code. "No, they haven't moved," Jimmy replied. "But I can't talk about it on the telephone." Numbly I hung up, not knowing what had gone wrong.

Suddenly I knew I was going to be sick. "Are you all right, Rosalynn?" Madeline called anxiously through the bathroom door. I couldn't afford to let her know what was happening at the White House, so I told her that I just didn't feel well but would be all right. All I wanted to do was to go home and be with Jimmy, but I couldn't. Instead I went downstairs to deliver the most difficult speech of my life. While I smiled outwardly and tried to act happy and glad to see everybody, I was miserable inside—and afraid.

Had our planes been shot down over Iran, or by some other country? Were we on the brink of war? Were all the hostages dead?

I had to speak to Jimmy again.

I called as soon as we got to the plane, but he still couldn't tell me anything. Open radiophones can be monitored by the press, the Russians, and anyone else. He told me to call him from Texas, even though he still might not be able to tell me anything.

It was close to midnight when I arrived in Austin, but there was still no definitive news from Jimmy. "Everything is going to be all right," he told me quietly. "Go to bed and get some sleep, and I'll call you as soon as I can tell you anything. But I want you to come home. You won't be able to campaign tomorrow, but don't say anything about leaving until I call you back."

Go to sleep? How could I sleep with news so bad that I had to go home? I paced nervously, waiting for him to call again, and finally went into Madeline's room and talked to her. I had to confide in someone. Don't go to bed, I said, because we have to go home. Then I told her about the rescue mission and that something had gone wrong. We called for coffee and sat there, wondering what terrible thing had happened. After waiting and waiting and still no call, I took a bath and dressed again. Then the telephone rang, and the whole story unfolded. The open line made no difference anymore because the press was being informed at the same time Jimmy was talking to me. I still have the note I wrote that night as he talked. It reads: "U.S. aircraft preparing for a possible rescue mission accident on ground in a remote desert area of Iran . . . 8 casualties no hostile action no Iranian casualties."

"I'm sorry" was all I could think of to say to Jimmy as I listened to the suffering in his voice. "I'll fly home as soon as I can."

When we got back to the White House at 8:00 A.M., I went directly to the Cabinet Room where Jimmy was meeting with members of his staff, going over questions and answers with Secretary Harold Brown for an upcoming press conference at the Pentagon. When I entered, Jimmy looked at me from his place at the head of the table, despair in his eyes. I went to his side and stood by him until someone pulled up a chair for me, and I sat down for a while. I was exhausted from being up all night, and soon left to go upstairs to bed. It was not long before Jimmy followed. He was devastated. He had so counted on the mission to be successful. Just the week before he had had a session with the military involved, and there wasn't a question about any part of the rescue that they couldn't answer. "We won't let you down, Mr. President," Colonel Beckwith had said, and they had done their best.

The next few days were grim. Like the night my father died, every time I woke up I wanted to go back to sleep, hoping it would all go away. I hurt for Jimmy, who had to suffer the bitter disappointment as well as the responsibility for the failure *and* for the hostages, whose safety was now of even greater concern, and for the men who died in the desert and for their families. There was an outpouring of support for him as all the world mourned with us, and roses, yellow roses, poured into the White House.

Then, at the end of the week, it was announced that Secretary Vance had resigned. He had told Jimmy a few days before the rescue mission that he did not support it, but he agreed not to announce his resignation until after it was completed.

I was sorry Cy was leaving. He and Gay had become close friends. I had studied Spanish with Gay, and we had skied together at Camp David. But Jimmy made the decisions, and Cy had differed with him before and threatened to resign on several occasions. He would just have to go, but I wished it could have been at a different time, when Jimmy was not so vulnerable from the failure of the rescue attempt.

Cy had been a good counterbalance to Zbig Brzezinski, the national security adviser. Zbig was aggressive, with innovative ideas—maybe too innovative sometimes. Jimmy had to sift through them, but they were always refreshing approaches to the complicated problems. Cy, in contrast, mirrored the State Department— sound in judgment, cautious, reluctant to "rock the boat," jealous of bureaucratic prerogatives. He leaned to the dovish side of any argument, while Zbig was more hawkish. The two provided a good range of opinions from which Jimmy could make the final decisions, and he liked it that way.

Somehow it was time to move forward again, to stop reliving the tragedy and wishing it had never happened. There were too many other things to do. Not surprisingly, I guess, after the mission failure Jimmy went up dramatically in the polls. According to the May 6 notes in my diary, Pat Caddell had said, "Dissatisfaction with the President over hostages had been festering and rescue mission had effect of lancing the boil." Even though the mission had failed, the people realized that Jimmy had been doing something, that our country had taken action, and they approved.

We learned that Bruce Laingen, the senior hostage, approved too. On May 14, I noted in my diary: "Penne Laingen gave me a letter from her husband received since rescue attempt. Wanted Jimmy to have letter. He says he is still at Foreign Ministry . . . security tighter . . . can't leave room except to go upstairs to bathroom . . . never outside . . . watches TV and gets news. Very supportive of President and rescue attempt. Wonders where other hostages are and worries about hostage families. Said over and over that he feels a deep sense of sadness for President because of failure and knows he was trying to do what was best. Says he is sure timetable is not changed because of rescue effort. Release depends on Majlis [the Iranian Parliament]."

With sanctions imposed against the Soviets, the Iranian negotiations a moot issue, and the failed rescue mission behind us, there was no longer any need for Jimmy to remain in the White House, and he and I both turned back to the campaign while carrying out our respective duties each day.

One day soon thereafter, we sat on the Truman Balcony and talked about the issues and "the duties of the President" behind the scenes on that particular day: Sadat wanted to break off all peace talks; Lloyd Cutler, the White House counsel, said he might have to resign; and Trudeau might sell two million tons of Canadian grain to the Soviet Union. After much effort, by the end of the day Sadat was going to continue, Lloyd was going to stay, and Trudeau was not going to sell grain to Russia. And another bright spot: Argentina had decided to boycott the Olympics—the first South American country to join us.

May brought a new crisis. Castro opened the doors for Cubans who wanted to leave their native land, and they started coming into Florida by the thousands. Despite the most strenuous efforts by our Coast Guard and Navy ships, many of them managed to reach the numerous coves and inlets along the coast of Florida in makeshift boats or boats chartered by their families in America. Once they arrived, our immigration statutes prevented the return of refugees to the oppression of a Communist regime. All our officials could do was confiscate the boats—whenever they could catch them.

Jimmy tried to make the best of a bad situation. "We ought to be thankful we have a country that people want to come to. You don't see thousands of Americans lined up to get into Cuba . . . or Russia!" he said in a speech in Iowa. The Cuban exodus was a serious political setback for us, but the end of the campaign was in sight. Eight primaries were scheduled at the end of May and the beginning of June, and our polls indicated we would win only three of them, but we weren't concerned. Three states were all we needed, and when all the primaries were over, we actually had seven hundred more delegates than we needed to win the Democrat nomination.

On the last campaign day, I realized that it would be my last primary ever. Jimmy wouldn't be eligible to run again, and though it was a relief to have it all over, I felt a sense of sadness too. But this campaign had been successful, with all our ups and downs and crises, and we celebrated on the plane on the way home. When we got back to the White House, Gretchen Poston had a table and chairs set up in the yard by the entrance to the Dip Room—and a bottle of chilled wine waiting for us. Jimmy had gotten home before I did, and even though it was midnight, he came down and we had a celebration.

What should have been happiness during the next few weeks became discouragement. The Cubans were still coming into Florida, the hostages were still in Iran, the Russians remained in Afghanistan—and Ted Kennedy would neither quit nor pledge his support to the Carter-Mondale ticket. Even after Jimmy invited him to the White House and told him he had fought a good fight and that it was time to join together for a strong Democratic party to defeat Ronald Reagan in the fall, he said there were still unresolved differences between them.

In the meantime, we were off to Venice for an economic summit. Amy and I accompanied Jimmy, and we visited Yugoslavia on the same trip and enjoyed a lovely formal state dinner. Served on silver trays, the meal was beautiful—veal surrounded by vegetables, served on a bed of grits! I didn't have my glasses with me and took carrots, peas, and a nice big piece of braised celery. I missed the veal—and learned not to be so vain and always to wear my glasses or contacts.

The summer of '80 was going as well as could be expected. Jimmy had a good summit meeting in Italy, and our delegates were sticking with us in spite of the "unresolved differences" with Kennedy. These differences came to a head a few weeks before the delegates were to assemble in New York City for the convention, when Kennedy tried to change the rules to make it an "open" convention. Instead of the delegates honoring their pledges to the voters who elected them, Kennedy wanted them released so they could be free to vote for him.

But Kennedy was not the only cloud on the political horizon as the time for the Democratic Convention neared. There was also Billy.

Jimmy and I finally got away in July for a week's vacation on Sapelo Island. We read, fished, and enjoyed the beach, and I slept late while Jimmy got up early every morning to run. Off and on we watched the Republican Convention on television, though sometimes the demagoguery toward Jimmy was so negative I would have to leave the room. I was glad that Ronald Reagan was nominated, and I didn't have the slightest sense of foreboding. His politics were so bad, I wrote in my diary, that I thought we could beat him with no trouble. I didn't know of a single issue on which I agreed with him. We continued to enjoy our vacation.

Our enjoyment came to an abrupt halt on Wednesday, July 17, when the morning paper arrived with breakfast. Along with the news of the convention, there was Billy all over the front page, accused of being an unregistered foreign agent for Libya, of having taken $220,000 from them, and of having improperly used his influence with our government to further his own business dealings. I couldn't believe it, and neither could Jimmy, whose telltale vein started throbbing in his temple while he read the stories. We knew that Billy had been a host at a reception in Georgia along with the governor, the president of Georgia Tech, and others to a Libyan delegation on a trade mission, and earlier he had made a highly publicized trip to Libya with a group of legislators and businessmen from Georgia. But unknown to us, through intermediaries the Libyans had arranged for Billy to represent them in the sale of their high-quality oil, and they had advanced him some money on future earnings. When the stories broke, before he had done any business for Libya, there was a flood of accusations based primarily on his failure to register at the outset as an agent of a foreign country. This was a legal requirement, and Billy and his attorneys had been negotiating the issue with the federal agencies for several months.

The press loved what they hoped would be a real scandal, and for weeks there was story after story about the "Billy affair" or "Billygate." A congressional investigation was launched into all sorts of allegations. At the time Jimmy should have been working on his acceptance speech for the approaching Democratic Convention, our lawyers had us both searching through our diaries and files for any mention of Billy or Libya. Jimmy had a press conference in the East Room to answer any and all questions, and he compiled a report for Congress certifying that no one in the entire government had done anything that was illegal or improper. The only reference I had made to Billy or Libya had occurred months before, when I had called him from Camp David to see if he knew anyone in Libya who might help us get the hostages out of Iran.

But everyone, it seemed, was after Billy, making him an object of ridicule in the process. The Internal Revenue Service was already investigating the false allegation that he had "laundered" $1,285,000 in 1976 campaign funds through Carter's Warehouse, and Billy had been subpoenaed in an investigation of the former budget director, Bert Lance. After it was all over he was found

innocent of all the charges against him. The worst thing the Justice
Department, the IRS, Congress, or anyone was ever able to say
about Billy was that he had "used bad judgment." Though I was
upset about the timing of the Libyan allegations, my heart went
out to him, to Sybil, and to their six children. His income from
public appearances and talk shows dropped to zero, and he was
also trying to overcome a bout with alcoholism. His life and his
family's were laid bare in the press, and the trumped-up stories
made invaluable weapons for the Republicans to use against us.

After the presidential press conference, the charges disappeared
from the front pages, and by the time the Democratic Convention
convened in August, most of the wild stories about Billy had been
replaced with Kennedy's last-minute maneuvers for an open convention. Predictably, with all the problems we had had in the last
few months, we were now very low in the polls, and I was very
nervous.

The convention opened on Monday, August 11, and we weren't
scheduled to arrive in New York until the third day, so we sat in
the den at Camp David with two telephones and systematically
went down the lists of our delegates, calling them all to be sure
they were not shifting to Kennedy. Everyone we talked with had
already been called by our people and by Kennedy's people, and
most of them by the news media. They were tired of being pres-
sured and wanted us to know that they were still with us. After a
few hours, Jimmy and I began to relax.

When the open convention effort failed, the Kennedy challenge
was over, this time for good. For the first time in months I breathed
a sigh of relief. It had been long and hard and unpleasant, and in
the end we had been scarred, though how much we were yet to
know. But for now, with all the crises, I was taking one day at a
time, and these were successful and relatively happy days.

The convention went well, at least as far as I was concerned.
Kennedy's speech was stirring and emotional, and his call for
massive government spending programs roused a spirit that appealed to the more liberal delegates.

Jimmy's acceptance speech the next night was also effective,
and at the end of it the delegates were on their feet, applauding
and cheering. There was bedlam on the convention floor, with
horns blowing and music. Only a few of us noticed that the balloons clustered in the ceiling didn't release from their net at the
first tug and were late falling. Everyone noticed that Ted Kennedy

was even later. There were waves of applause on the floor as our family and the Mondales stood on the platform waving to our friends, and one party dignitary after another was called up on the platform—but still no Kennedy. I soon realized we were biding our time, waiting for him, as more party officials were called up to take their turn with the swelling ranks.

What I didn't know was that the television press kept taking note of the Kennedy absence while we joined the celebration on the podium. Instead of the evening belonging to Jimmy, Kennedy became the focus in the eyes of the press and the television audience. When the senator finally did arrive, there was a great round of applause, and after shaking hands with Jimmy and me and others on the platform, he stood awkwardly to one side. At that moment I felt truly sorry for him. He had waged a vigorous campaign and had been defeated by an incumbent President at the lowest ebb of his popularity. It must have been a terrible blow to him, and it was obviously very difficult to take. At this point my southern hospitality got us into more trouble. I walked over to Jimmy and asked him to speak to Ted again to put him more at ease. Jimmy did, taking a few steps over to shake his hand again, which the press misinterpreted the next day as "chasing him around on the platform" to get his attention and support. Jimmy's speech, too, was criticized as being lackluster compared to Kennedy's. What we and the delegates thought had been a great convention for Jimmy turned out to be a terrible one to the press and, therefore, to much of the viewing public.

Once more Hamilton saw the dark side. It was the balloons not falling on cue that signaled trouble ahead, he said later; the balloons were an omen of the campaign yet to come. I knew the race against Reagan would not be easy—with a divided party, with the hostages, the economy, the grain embargo, and everything else. But for once I disagreed with Hamilton. I was sure that Jimmy Carter was going to be re-elected President of the United States.

❧ 12 ❧
The Last Six Months

I was so sure we could beat Ronald Reagan in the general election. I couldn't believe the people would fall for his rhetoric or support the platform laid out at the Republican Convention. Reagan was on record as being against SALT II and all the other nuclear arms agreements negotiated by both Democratic and Republican presidents, against the Panama Canal treaties, against President Nixon's overtures and Jimmy's normalization of relations with China. He was against the ERA, the Department of Education, and the Department of Energy, against our human rights policy, against environmental protection laws—against virtually everything we were for. And the news from voters was heartening. On my birthday, a few days after the Democratic Convention, the polls showed that we had come from 25 points behind Reagan to 7 points. It was a lovely present, and a needed one. The press may have panned everything we had done at the convention, but the public hadn't. And they weren't being taken in by Ronald Reagan.

The press, however, seemed to be. As the campaign continued through the fall, the news media assumed that Reagan was a good guy who was careless with his comments but didn't really mean what he was saying. Jimmy was portrayed as a mean person who criticized Reagan for his positions and refused to debate John Anderson, an Independent candidate.

At the same time, Jimmy was having a great deal of success with his legislative programs. Congress, as he said, "kept cranking out good legislation" in 1980, but when he did something, the press was not very good. I couldn't help but remember when Jimmy ran against Gerald Ford in 1976, and it seemed that almost every day the President was shown on television proudly signing some piece of legislation in the Rose Garden, some of which he had even tried to defeat. Now it seemed that the television networks had declared a moratorium on any reporting that showed legislative achievements, giving the impression that under Jimmy's leadership, the government had ground to a halt. It was frustrating.

Congressman John Anderson seemed to be a special favorite of the press. In his party's primary election, the formerly conservative, now liberal Republican hadn't won a single primary or caucus, had run third in liberal Connecticut and Wisconsin, and had even lost his home state of Illinois. With no wins as a Republican, Anderson decided to abandon his own party and run as an Independent, launching his "National Unity Campaign" in the spring of 1980. With no party backing but with continuous coverage by the news media, Anderson made inroads in the liberal Democratic constituency whose support otherwise would have gone to Jimmy against Reagan.

A little-known politically conservative organization, the Moral Majority, headed by the TV evangelist Jerry Falwell, was also suddenly big news. Falwell opposed Jimmy in 1976 and again in 1980, but during the interim he had gained influence through his daily television programs and had become an important political force. In the South and West, his supporters were always evident during my campaign tours. At every stop, their "religious" condemnations centered on abortion, busing, SALT II, the Panama Canal treaties, the Department of Education, and the ERA. Making my way through the crowd after a speech in a Texas shopping center, I realized how organized the Moral Majority had become. All along the path the police had cleared for me were women holding their hands up with printed cards pasted in their palms that read: YOU DON'T LOVE JESUS. "I do love Jesus," I said to some of them. "If you loved Jesus, you wouldn't support the ERA" came their replies.

Campaigning wasn't all frustration, of course. With few exceptions, people were approving and excited to see me, but I had to keep reminding myself that it was the position, not me. Nevertheless, I enjoyed it and always felt "cheered on." And some of the remarks were fun: "You're more beautiful than in person!"

"Me and my husband have your full support!" One young man said, "The President has aged so much . . . his hair has turned gray; his face looks so wrinkled; the four years as President have taken such a toll—and I'm too kind to say what has happened to you!"

Sometimes Jimmy did look tired, and the presidency had aged him—by at least four years! But he didn't look as bad in the 1980 campaign as he had earlier in his administration, when he and Dr. Lukash had suddenly doubled the distance they ran to about thirty miles each week. Jimmy lost almost ten pounds, and until his face filled out and his weight stabilized, he looked drawn and exhausted. Whenever anybody said he looked tired or old, I would usually tell him to get a haircut. It was amazing how much difference it made in his looks. After a haircut he could always depend on people telling him, "Oh, Mr. President, you look so rested. You must be feeling good!"

But in the campaign two problems continued to plague us. The OPEC price increase was having an effect on consumer prices, whereas most of the conservation benefits from the new energy laws would not be evident until the next presidential term. And the hostages remained captive in Iran. Any reports, even good news, about the hostages became bad news politically for us, reminders of our inability to set them free.

By October 24, a week and a half before the election, the hostage situation was once again almost totally dominating the news. NBC was even claiming that they would be released in two shifts, starting the following weekend. Naturally I was deluged with questions, but I had no answers. I called Jimmy, who was campaigning in Grand Rapids, Michigan, but he told me to downplay the stories, that nothing was ever definite in dealing with the Iranians. They were probably playing with us to some degree, he thought, in order to get the media attention they relished. Jimmy had hoped that public expectations wouldn't get so high and that people would concentrate on the real differences between him and Reagan, but when the weekend passed without the hostages being released, Jimmy was blamed. Short of their actual release, we were in a political no-win situation.

Timing was an important factor, too, in the presidential candidates' debate, scheduled just one week before the election. Jimmy had been urging Reagan to agree to a two-man debate throughout the campaign, but he had refused. When he finally consented, the timing was good for him and bad for us.

We were sure Jimmy would do well, but not sure we would still have time before the election to correct any misunderstandings or false allegations that might arise. Although none of us knew it then, we had far more serious reasons for concern than just the timing. Much later it was discovered that Jimmy's secret briefing books had been stolen and delivered to the Reagan camp, and they were apparently used to prepare Reagan's rejoinders to Jimmy's debating points.

Jimmy also made some mistakes in the debate, which we didn't realize at the time. We proudly listened to him discuss the issues in a serious and presidential way while Reagan, with his professional acting ability, gave relatively superficial answers accompanied by an "aw, shucks" attitude and simplistic quips, such as "There you go again." When it was over, all of our team thought Jimmy had won the debate hands down, and so did the Reagan people when we went backstage immediately afterward. It was not until the next day that we realized how important the general demeanor of the candidates had been. Also, Jimmy's remark quoting Amy about nuclear weapons had been totally misconstrued by the press and the Republicans, who alleged that Army might be the one who was running the country. It was a mistake for Jimmy to bring it up in the debate. It would be different today with the change in attitude after three years with no progress on nuclear arms control, and seeing teenagers often on television talking about it. People didn't think of Amy, though, as a knowledgeable young teenager, whose class discussed the anxieties of nuclear war; they remembered her as the child who walked down Pennsylvania Avenue on inauguration day almost four years earlier. Lost in the clamor that followed was Jimmy's point in bringing it up: that everybody was concerned about the issue, even the children, and the reason for emphasizing it was his opponent's bellicose statements against both the Russians and the SALT II treaty.

As the last weekend before the election approached, we were still a little behind in the polls, but holding our own. I believed that a growing concern about Reagan's positions would turn people away from him when they actually went to vote. That would be a miracle, to be sure, but we had seen miracles happen. Later in the week our polling began to show us moving up, and by Saturday night we were practically even with Reagan. The election was still three days away, and I was sure we would be in better shape by Tuesday. I couldn't wait to win in order to justify what Jimmy had done and to give him a chance to complete the major tasks ahead.

At daybreak on Sunday morning, Jimmy called from Chicago, saying he was going to have to cancel his schedule and fly home. Word had just come from Warren Christopher at the State Department that the Iranian parliament had accepted four of our critical points in the ongoing negotiations and that Prime Minister Rajai and President Bani-Sadr had been authorized to implement the agreement with us. There were still some differences to iron out, but for the first time in many months, an offer from the Iranians seemed acceptable. Jimmy needed to study the proposals and respond, which he obviously couldn't do in Chicago. I was to take Mondale's campaign schedule for the day and Fritz would fill in for Jimmy.

I felt a surge of hope, a feeling I hadn't allowed myself since the failure of our rescue mission. But Jimmy quickly tempered it. "I want you to be prepared," he said over the phone. "This means it could go either way."

"What could? The release of the hostages or the election?"

"Both," he said quietly.

If this Iranian proposal seemed acceptable, the Republicans could blame him for using it as a last-minute political ploy. If it were unacceptable, he would have to bear the stigma of another failure to win the hostages' release. For a moment, neither one of us spoke. It was the first inkling I'd had that Jimmy thought he might lose—and the first time I had considered the possibility either. "Don't worry," Jimmy finally said. "We've done our best. Go on out and campaign, and I'll handle this as well as I can."

As luck or fate would have it, election day was the anniversary of the embassy takeover, and the newspapers, *Time* and *Newsweek*, and all the television networks were recounting the humiliating and tragic events. At the same time, the public was in a fever pitch of expectation about the parliamentary debates going on in Iran. After Jimmy canceled his campaign trip and came home, the press and the people were waiting to hear from him, hoping that the hostages were being released.

Jimmy's statement to the public on Saturday night, November 2, was honest, moving, and firm, but he could not tell the people what they wanted to hear. After reading the new proposal from Iran, he had found that too many significant differences still remained to treat it as any more than a constructive move in the negotiations. To downplay any political motives in the heated political atmosphere, Jimmy cautioned that his actions would not be influenced by the impending election but would, instead, guard the honor and integrity of our country. I was riding through Ohio on a bus at the time of his statement and didn't hear it. But when I called Jimmy that night from my next stop, Eau Claire, Wisconsin, he and I both thought that he had handled the hostage statement correctly and that the people might respond favorably. In retrospect, we should have known differently.

The Monday morning news shows I watched in my hotel room in Eau Claire all said that a Reagan victory was almost assured, though no one knew how to read the hostage issue. Instead of the terrible sinking feeling that I should have had, I felt very calm—and very strong. This was the last day of campaigning before the election, and all day long as I moved through press conferences and airport rallies in Wisconsin, Illinois, Missouri, and Alabama, I kept saying to myself, "We'll show them. We'll just show them like we have so many times before."

What I didn't know was that we had fallen dramatically in the polls. There were only hours before the election, hours before the anniversary of the hostage crisis, and the public knew that the hostages were not going to be released. There was simply no time left for them to be free on the fourth of November, and that meant there was no timetable now for their release at all. Damn, damn Khomeini! All the understandable disillusionment of the American people fell on us.

I got the final bad news from Pat Caddell. After my last stop in Huntsville, Alabama, before heading home to Plains to vote the next day, I called Pat from the airport. The early figures had slipped, he told me in a discouraged tone of voice, but he wouldn't know how serious it was until he got more figures later in the evening. He asked me to call him when I got home. Our friend Tom T. Hall, the country and western singer who had performed for the rally, was waiting for me when I finished the telephone call. "Well, we did the best we could," he said uneasily. "Chin up."

Our chins were certainly high on the flight home. Several members of my staff had flown to Huntsville for the rally, to be part of an actual event rather than just part of the planning, as they had been for months. We toasted each other with wine and fruit punch and ate the cake the Secret Service agents presented to me, which had "First Lady: Four More Years" inscribed on the icing. Mary Hoyt gave a very funny speech about our campaign days together, and she and Madeline and one of my press aides presented me with a huge gift certificate made from campaign posters for a much-needed new briefcase. Our spirits were determinedly high, but when the plane dropped me off in Plains before taking the others on to Washington, I could feel the love—and anxiety and the worry.

It was 2:00 A.M. when I got home. Jimmy was moving from California to the State of Washington on a last-minute campaign swing, since the earlier polls had shown there was a chance of his carrying the West Coast. To my surprise and delight, I found Jack at the house waiting for me, but I just said hello and went straight to the telephone and tried to call Pat. When his line was busy, all of a sudden I decided not to try again. I knew what he would say and I didn't want to hear it.

And at that moment, just five hours before the voting booths opened, I faced the truth. "We're going to lose," I said to Jack. "I know, Mom. I came back home tonight so you wouldn't be all by yourself."

It was the first time I had really admitted it to myself. And immediately my thoughts turned to the family. Did Jimmy know? Did Judy and Chip and Jeff and Annette, still off campaigning, know? What about Amy, at the White House? I worried about them and wished they were all with me in Plains that night. Jack and I stayed up talking until three-thirty. He said he didn't want to go to bed because he wanted to put off election day as long as possible. Amazingly, when I finally lay down for a few hours before getting up to meet Jimmy, I fell sound asleep.

Jimmy's helicopter landed in the field by our house at seven-thirty, and as soon as we looked at each other, we both realized that each understood the bad news. Jimmy smiled at me through his exhaustion, and together we composed ourselves for the television cameras and went to vote. "How bad is it?" I asked him in the car. He turned thumbs down and said, "It's gone . . . it's all over." He had heard Pat's latest figures on the plane coming home from Seattle and we were 7 points behind. But no one in Plains knew that. Even when Jimmy's voice broke as he thanked the crowd at the depot, our homefolks were optimistic. "They say you're going to lose, but we know you're going to win," people kept saying. "We're so proud of you."

When we reached Washington later that morning Amy was still at school, but Chip, Edna Langford, Judy, and the grandchildren were waiting for us at the White House. Before we left home, we had told Miss Lillian about the latest polls. Now it was time to tell the children. Jimmy had gone straight to the Oval Office, but the rest of us were sitting in the West Hall talking nervously when I broke into the conversation: "I have to tell you. It's over for us. We've lost." Everyone was stunned but brave as I told them about Pat's numbers. Only Chip's friend Heidi, who was sitting on the floor, started to cry. Seeing her, I was afraid I would give in, so I went into my dressing room to change into slacks.

When Jimmy came back from the Oval Office, we were both so exhausted we went into our bedroom to take a nap. I had had a momentary surge of hope when Tim Kraft, at the campaign headquarters, told me that our people around the country were still optimistic and that he couldn't believe Pat's figures. I ran into the bathroom to tell Jimmy, who was changing, but he just sat down on the edge of the tub and said, "Pat knows."

"I know he does," I replied, and I sat down on his lap and put my head on his shoulder and cried. We clung together as the realization sank in further.

When we gathered at six o'clock that evening in the Oval Office with Charlie Kirbo and his wife, Boo, Bob Strauss, and Jimmy's closest staff members, Pat Caddell confirmed that the exit polls showed we were losing overwhelmingly. "Mr. President, you're a great example," someone said. "You don't seem bitter at all."

"I'm bitter enough for both of us," I said. I meant it. I was bitter at what I had seen on television for weeks that I thought was so unfair to Jimmy; bitter about the hostage situation dominating the news for the last few days before the election as the media "celebrated" the anniversary of the hostage capture; bitter at the opposition for deliberately misleading the American people; bitter that they blamed Jimmy for the hostage crisis when they should have praised him for his sound judgment and patience. Jimmy could have blown up Tehran and been reelected. Yes, I was bitter. And so was everyone else in the room. But I was the only one who admitted it.

Though the butlers were gloomy during dinner, the rest of us were remarkably at ease. Our children, the Kirbos, and Edna

Langford talked about what we had done and what we could have done better. We all agreed that the people were making a terrible mistake. The election returns kept coming in. Hamilton and Jody were relaying messages to Jimmy all evening and trying to decide when we should concede. I wanted to concede right away when it was so obvious that we had lost and the television networks began announcing the results, but Jimmy said we had to wait.

It was not a pleasant evening. When we finally did go to campaign headquarters at about ten o'clock to concede, we were criticized because some polls were still open on the West Coast. We hadn't thought about it; we just assumed that anybody interested in the news already knew that we had lost and that Jimmy didn't really need to concede at all.

Standing by Jimmy's side that night, listening to his concession speech and looking out over all those people who had worked so hard and long for us, was very painful. Many were crying and my heart went out to them. But mostly I worried about our family and how the loss would affect them. I hoped they wouldn't be hurt too much. Amy was the one who was showing it most. She had cried when we left Plains to come to the White House; now her heart was broken because she had to leave her friends in Washington to go back to Plains. All of us had suffered some sort of individual loss, but the one I hurt for most was Jimmy. The most difficult concept to bear was his rejection by the American people, for whom he'd worked so hard and for whom he cared so much.

I spent the next few months saying good-bye both emotionally and practically to our years in the White House, and at times it was very difficult. Jimmy was still busy being a full-time President and continuing the negotiations with Iran, but I had a lot of time to think and sometimes brood. We went to Camp David for a long weekend to rest after the election and I read four books in two days. I didn't want to think about the defeat. I escaped by reading while Jimmy immersed himself in the carpenter shop and made four small flyline reels for his fishing friends.

Returning to the White House was not easy either. Many of the staff members were on the lawn to greet us, the ushers and doormen were gathered at the door, upstairs the maids and butlers were waiting, many of them teary. The household staff had become friends and like a family to us, and I tried to comfort them. "You'll like the Reagans," I said. "They will be different from us, there's no doubt about that. But you'll like them."

It was late in the afternoon and Jimmy went to the Oval Office, the servants back to their duties, and I was alone. I walked through the Lincoln Bedroom, where my mother had always stayed, the Queen's Bedroom, which Miss Lillian had called her own, and Amy's bedroom, my favorite. We had completely redecorated it and now everything would probably be sent to the warehouse to become just another relic from a past administration. I looked through the drawers in each room to be sure we wouldn't leave anything behind, then went upstairs and walked through that floor, absorbing it.

I felt very melancholy as I wandered around the rooms that had become so familiar to us and stayed awhile in our special place, the Truman Balcony, where Jimmy and I had sat so often discussing the events of the day. We had enjoyed living in the White House, even with the pressures that naturally come with it. That day I was trying to detach myself from a life that would soon be over, one I had thought I would enjoy for four more years.

In the days that followed, I didn't have a specific schedule to follow for the first time in four years and didn't even bother to keep my diary. I had a lot of spare time and I read and rested, ran with Jimmy in the afternoons, and saw a movie with him almost every night. I also spent a lot of time on the telephone, thanking the many people who had helped us during the four years. And though by then I was basically at peace with our circumstances, I had some weak moments. It was ten days after the election before I got out my briefcase from the night of the last campaign trip, but I finally went through it. There were all kinds of speech cards, underlined and marked all over as I always did, and I wanted to keep them. Reading them over, I found them all so convincing that I couldn't see how anybody could have looked at the facts and voted for Ronald Reagan.

Suddenly I was brought back from my reverie by the sound of voices from the loudspeaker outside. I walked to the window in my bathroom and saw Jimmy standing there on the lawn alongside Prime Minister Begin. As I stood and looked at them I began to cry—really cry, to sob—for the first time. It all seemed so unfair. Even the Middle East peace process that Jimmy so wanted to complete was ending for him, and maybe for the people in that war-torn part of the world. He should have been re-elected.

But he wasn't, and we would be leaving, and I wanted to remember the White House the way it was when it was "our" house. I asked the White House photographer to take pictures of each room for our archives, and I spent one afternoon cataloguing the paintings on the second floor that we had lived with and loved.

Even the press turned sentimental. One night on the news, the announcer described as "touching" the scene of Jimmy saying good-bye to Chancellor Helmut Schmidt, followed by the sight of Ed Muskie putting his arm around Jimmy's shoulders as they walked back to the Oval Office. What had actually happened, Jimmy told me, was that after the farewell he had turned to Muskie and said, "Sometimes Helmut Schmidt can be a pain in the ass." With that, Muskie had put his arm around Jimmy and said, "I couldn't agree with you more, Mr. President." Laughing, they walked into the Oval Office.

With Christmas coming, the defeat and the bitterness behind me, I turned my attention to entertaining our friends for the last time. Night after night we had farewell parties, and when there were not enough nights, we had luncheons, too. We also had a wonderful Christmas present from the Algerians. Their delegation came to see us at Camp David right after the holiday to report that they had seen the hostages and that all fifty-two of them were alive and in good shape. We were as thrilled as their families were at the good news.

The last weeks after Christmas were hectic. In the end, we found ourselves rushing to get everything done, packing between parties and writing thank-yous. And the house was always full of company—friends and relatives who wanted to spend just one night in the White House while we were still there. Sometimes I had to go into my room and shut the door just to be able to think and Jimmy stopped coming home for lunch. In the midst of all the hospitality on the second and third floors, the Oval Office was a haven. He needed a quiet place to work and think and to write his farewell address.

On January 14, 1981, six days before the end of his presidency, Jimmy gave his farewell address to the nation. From behind his desk in the Oval Office he spoke of three issues: the threat of nuclear destruction, our stewardship of the physical resources of our planet, and the pre-eminence of the basic rights of human beings. These issues were uppermost in his mind all the days of his presidency and had been the theme of his acceptance speech and his inaugural address four years earlier. These three issues still loom before us and all the countries of the world; they will define our future and test our country and our leaders to their utmost.

As I listened to him in the Roosevelt Room next to the Oval Office with the staff and the Cabinet members, I thought about all the dreams and all the wisdom and all the toil that had gone into the last four years. And I was thankful for Jimmy's time in history. He had served with honor and had relished every moment of it. He was leaving too soon to have accomplished all that he wanted to do, but he would leave a legacy . . . for that which is good and right and honorable, for peace and human rights and compassion.

When he was finished, no one moved for a moment. Could it be that he was really leaving? That his days as President were numbered? There were tears, yet a sense of pride overcame the sadness.

I predict that this speech will be read and studied as a guidepost for our future, a standard to be sought for our country. This time the press agreed, saying, "Though no one is much interested in what Jimmy Carter has to say anymore, his speech spelled out the issues of the future in a clear way."

Jimmy and his aides were still working day and night to gain the hostages' freedom and I hoped that Jimmy would be the one who succeeded in bringing them home. During the first two weeks of January the signals from Iran became suddenly positive, though there were the usual peaks and valleys of emotion as the news was good one day, bad the next. I wanted to get very excited, but Jimmy kept cautioning. "Our dealings with the Iranians have been so uniformly disappointing, it's still wise to doubt success," he said both to me and to his staff. "They have no responsible leaders."

By January 16, the Iranians had requested that Algeria arrange transportation for the hostages and provide a team of doctors. Jimmy had approved the refueling of the planes the Algerians would use in Crete or at one of our military bases in Greece or Turkey. But still no one knew what would happen. In the midst of this tension and muted excitement, we made our last visit to Camp David.

I was torn about going. I had loved it so and anticipated great difficulty in going through the weekend, knowing that never again would we enjoy the solitude, the beauty, the relief, it had given us for four years. But this was not to be just like any other weekend. Though we took a sentimental stroll around the grounds while Jimmy took photographs of his favorite places, he spent most of his time on the telephone with the State Department and the White House Situation Room. And the news got better and better.

By Sunday afternoon, January 18, I was on pins and needles: The Algerian planes were standing by, ready to fly into Iran to pick up the hostages. The plan was to fly them to Wiesbaden, Germany, for physical examinations and a few days of rest before bringing them home. More than anything, Jimmy wanted to be in Wiesbaden to greet them, but the timing was so tight it meant he might have to miss the Reagan inauguration. "After all, I don't have a vital role to play," he said in jest. Of course, we knew he couldn't miss the ceremonies. And besides, the negotiations were not over. An aide was even now on his way to Camp David with new proposals for Jimmy to read, proposals that could go either way. Suddenly the waiting game got to me. "Don't we need to go back to Washington?" I kept saying to Jimmy. "Don't you need to be there to see what's happening?"

But as always he was calm, not wanting to raise false expectations. "We haven't heard from the Algerians yet," he said. "Just wait. Be patient."

Later that day, the telephone rang again. "The word from Algiers is 'Go'!" Jimmy said. "That means us too. Grab your things." In a rush we bid our farewells to the Navy stewards who had made all our visits to Camp David so comfortable. How ironic it was to have the hostage crisis, which had begun at Camp David fourteen months before, end—or almost end—there. And how wonderful for us. Instead of leaving for the last time with sadness, we left with happiness and the highest hopes. My excitement was hard to contain, and in the helicopter Jimmy leaned over and kissed me.

The moment the helicopter landed on the South Lawn, Jimmy rushed off to the Oval Office. He remained there for the next forty-eight hours, resting only intermittently on the sofa, until the last minutes of his presidency. Jimmy and his negotiating team wanted to secure the release of the hostages while he was still President, and everyone in the Oval Office was conscious of the large grandfather clock by the door, ticking the minutes away. According to Lloyd Cutler, Jimmy's legal counsel, the financial and political arrangements were "the most complicated transactions in history."

There were a thousand and one details, requiring twelve banks in our country plus the Bank of England and the banks in Algeria and Iran working together in three languages and as many time zones. The Iranians would not deal directly with us, but instead asked every question about the highly technical legal documents through the Algerians. Every proposal and counterproposal required translation, first from Persian to French to English, then the reverse as our country responded. It took so much time that I began to think the unthinkable, that we might not get the hostages out after all, and they would have to remain imprisoned for many more months while all the negotiations were repeated or modified by a new President.

On Sunday night I stayed in the Oval Office with Jimmy and some members of his Cabinet and staff until past midnight. The worldwide teamwork was fascinating, all centered around Jimmy, with reports coming in from Ed Muskie at the State Department; Warren Christopher in Algiers; Harold Brown at the Pentagon, directing our armed forces around the world; William Miller in charge of the banks and financial negotiations at the Treasury Department; and Fritz Mondale, Lloyd Cutler, Ham, Jody, and others in and out of the Oval Office. At 2:00 A.M. I decided to go to bed, Jimmy having promised to call me the moment he heard anything. But I couldn't sleep. "What am I doing?" I thought. "I can sleep all I want after we're home in Plains." I got up, took a bath, and as I stepped from the tub the telephone rang. Warren Christopher had just informed Jimmy that some of the papers had actually been signed by the Iranians. I was hurriedly dressing when the telephone rang again at two-fifty. "It's done!" Jimmy said in a jubilant voice. "We've got an agreement! Come on over."

The scene in the Oval Office was joyous, the earlier weariness replaced by exhilaration. No one wanted to miss this historic moment, and whole families began to appear—Lloyd Cutler with his wife, Louise, who had been sleeping on the sofa in his office, and Jody with Nan and their daughter Emily. Lloyd uncorked a bottle of champagne, and just as we raised our glasses in a toast to "freedom," the telephone rang with the news that the Algerian planes were on their way to Tehran! The Oval Office erupted into applause. It was Day 443.

At 4:56 A.M. we all went to the news room, where Jimmy updated the White House press as much as he could about the promising situation. While I sat on the floor and listened, the reporters kept asking more and more questions, but Jimmy didn't have time to talk. I remember one question, though: "Mr. President, how does it feel to have achieved this before leaving office?" Jimmy's reply: "I'll answer that question when they're actually free." As we walked back to the Oval Office, he said, "I still have a sense of foreboding about the hostages."

Nevertheless, we made positive preparations, even though nothing could be certain. At 5:30 A.M. Jimmy asked San, the valet, to pack a bag for him so he could be prepared to go to Wiesbaden and return before the inaugural ceremonies. With the time difference, night fell in Iran at 9:30 A.M. our time, and Jimmy thought that if the planes hadn't taken off by then, the Iranians would delay the flights until the next morning. Because of Iran's war with Iraq, all airports, including the one in Tehran, were closed after dark. As we spoke, there were only three hours of daylight left in Iran. "We're running out of time," Jimmy said as he went into his back office to lie down and I went home to bed.

It was 5:45 A.M., Monday, January 19, and I only slept a few hours. I got up when Eivind Bjerke, who had come faithfully to do my hair for four years, arrived and keeping an eye on the clock, I watched the nine-thirty deadline go by with no call from Jimmy. Unless the Algerians and Iranians decided to fly the hostages out at night, there was no way Jimmy would be able to meet them while he was still President; the 2:00 P.M. deadline came and went, precluding Jimmy's going at all. Still the hours ticked by, with no confirmation of the hostages' departure.

I began to worry about Jimmy. He hadn't been to bed since Saturday night at Camp David, and though I didn't know it then, he would not sleep again until we got home to Plains on Tuesday afternoon. Meanwhile, in between writing thank-you notes and packing, I was running back and forth between the Oval Office and our living quarters to see if there was any news and to try to get Jimmy to rest. He was exhausted, but there was no time to stop. A major complication had developed with the Bank of Iran, which took hours of translation and maneuvering to work out.

It was an agonizing time, sometimes with long delays between messages while everyone stood by helplessly. Now and then I would plead, "Can't you get some rest now, Jimmy? It's been a long time since you slept, and you have to be fresh for the inauguration tomorrow. I want everybody to say you look handsome. I don't want them saying you look old and tired."

We had planned a farewell party for the Cabinet and senior staff members our last night in the White House and had invited the Kirbos and the Mondales to spend the night. At the time we had thought our last evening would be melancholy and lonesome. Instead, it was filled with expectation. Jimmy could leave the Oval Office only briefly to greet our guests, and when he returned to his second all-night vigil, Charlie Kirbo and Fritz Mondale went with him.

When the telephone rang at dawn, I sprang awake. But the Iranians were stalling. As far as he knew, Jimmy said, the planes were ready, but the hostages were not yet aboard. Our hopes had risen and fallen so many times in the last thirty-six hours that I was numb by now. "Do you think they'll leave while you're still President?" I asked. Jimmy sighed and said, "I hope so. We're counting on it. Otherwise, they may never be free."

I dressed hurriedly and went to the Oval Office. Not only was the time running out for the hostages, but the time for the inauguration ceremonies was rapidly approaching. I brought Jimmy a razor so he could shave in the little bathroom off his study, and Eivind cut his hair while he brought me up to date. The whole time, Jimmy kept answering the telephone. I was just leaving to go back upstairs when the phone rang again. Jimmy answered it and, after a few words, he shouted for all to hear: "Flight 133 is loaded and ready for takeoff!" I ran to him and he put his arms around me as he continued the conversation. There were cheers and smiles, and I cried with thanksgiving as I ran back upstairs. It was 8:00 A.M.; Jimmy would leave office in exactly four hours.

I busied myself packing the last-minute things and getting Amy dressed. But after an hour or two Jimmy still hadn't come upstairs, and the Reagans were due to arrive shortly. Finally I ran back to the Oval Office. "Jimmy," I said, "you've only got fifteen minutes to put on your morning clothes to greet the Reagans." This time he had to leave, although the latest news was disappointing. Warren Christopher had called to say that he had been assured that the planes would leave before noon, but that Iran had asked Algeria not to announce the departure until after the planes had cleared Iranian air space—and Jimmy would be out of office. "I'm sorry," I told Jimmy. "So am I," he said, "but it's all right as long as they're actually coming home."

In spite of Jimmy's calm words, I thought it was a despicable act on the part of the Iranians. They had kept the planes waiting on the runway, knowing full well the time of our inauguration. They wanted to time the release after Jimmy left office.

Suddenly, it didn't matter. As all the deadlines had slipped by—first for Jimmy to greet the hostages in Germany, then to be able to announce their release as President—the thrill now was that they were at last going to be free because his negotiations had been successful. And now that our prayers were being answered Jimmy looked just wonderful, knowing what very few people knew: that the hostages were preparing to leave Iran. They were coming home!

After saying our quick good-byes to the household staff, Jimmy and I rushed into the elevator to go downstairs to meet the Reagans. Drawing deep breaths, we smiled at each other as the elevator door opened and we stepped out calmly, as if we had had all the time in the world. "Hello, Governor and Mrs. Reagan," I said cordially at the front door. "Welcome to the White House."

After coffee with a handful of guests in the Blue Room and with one last look around, we murmured good-bye to this house and all the memories it held for us and made our way to the limousines. I felt remarkably at ease as I rode around the circular driveway with Mrs. Reagan; then, glancing out of the window, I saw one of my friends from Georgia who had come up to arrange the flowers in the White House. She was standing there on the lawn, overcome with tears. I waved to her and wanted to reach out and say "It's all right, Alice." There was a casual conversation in the car as Nancy Reagan and I rode to the Capitol, the same small talk that Betty Ford and I had made four years earlier to the minute. I had been nervous then and I thought Nancy Reagan must be now. I tried to put her at ease while at the same time feeling very smug. I knew the hostages were coming home but I couldn't say anything about it. Instead, I waved at the crowds all along the way even though I knew that they were mostly Reagan supporters.

I didn't feel very sentimental during the inauguration, even when the Marine Band played "Hail to the Chief" for Jimmy for the last time. Two and a half months had passed since the election, and I had long since accepted Jimmy's defeat—though with continuing regrets. My eyes wandered around the dais, and I couldn't help noticing how young and handsome both Jimmy and Fritz Mondale looked as they stood side by side on that beautiful morning.

The four years had had their problems, of course, but they had also been filled with triumphs. We weren't defeated. Hardly. We were leaving the fruits of our labor, and the hostages safe and free—the best presents we could give back to the country that had given us so much.

After the inauguration, a Secret Service agent pushed through the crowd as we were leaving the platform to go up the steps to the Capitol. "At twelve thirty-three, the first aircraft took off from Iran," he whispered in my ear. "Nine minutes later the other plane followed."

It was done, over, accomplished. And within the hour, Jimmy had reviewed the troops for the last time at Andrews Air Force Base, we had stood at attention for the final twenty-one-gun salute and the playing of the national anthem, and we had said good-bye to the Cabinet members gathered there. It was time to leave Washington, and we filled *Air Force One* with the people who had been with us from the beginning: Ham Jordan and Jack Watson, Jody and Nan Powell, Frank and Nancy Moore, Stu Eizenstat, Mary Hoyt and Madeline MacBean, and—spontaneously—two of Amy's heartbroken friends who were clinging to her at the airport and wouldn't let her go. The next morning Jimmy would fly to Wiesbaden to welcome the hostages back to freedom. But now we were going back to where it had all begun. We were going home to Plains.

✌ *Epilogue* ✌

The way I now feel about my hometown of Plains is something I couldn't have imagined at earlier times in my life. It was a place to get away from when I was growing up, and when Jimmy and I first came back from the Navy, I was overwhelmed by the awful thought of having to live here forever. But later, as public service and politics claimed more and more of our time, Plains became a refuge—a calm, quiet place in which to regroup my thoughts and renew our ever more exciting plans. It was always the welcome rest stop in months of campaigning, the one place I didn't have to consider every living soul as a potential vote for Jimmy, where there were no speeches I had to give, no hands I had to shake.

When Jimmy lost the election in 1980, there was no question about where we would go: We would go home. I was hesitant, not at all sure that I could be happy here after the dazzle of the White House and the years of stimulating political battles. But as we recovered from the exhaustion of our last months in Washington and settled into life at home, we slowly rediscovered the satisfaction of a life we had left long before.

I had been afraid we might be bored and restless without a major new goal in the works. What I felt instead was a growing sense of relief that there was no pressure to move on to the next big project as well as a certain satisfaction as I looked back that my childhood dreams had been fulfilled in ways beyond my wildest imagination.

Jimmy devoted the first year at home to writing his book *Keep-*

ing Faith, and we had long discussions—some hilarious and some quite painful—about our years in the White House. Together we planned his presidential library and the Carter Center of Emory University, where he and other leaders will continue to address the momentous questions that he faced as President and that still confront our nation and the world. While I was writing this book (which has taken me two and a half years), he was working to raise $25 million in private contributions to make these new plans a reality.

Besides these new duties and the pleasant realization that life in Plains is satisfying and enjoyable, we have done some things just for fun. Jimmy began working in his woodshop with an array of tools and equipment presented to him as a going-away gift by his Cabinet and staff. I've enjoyed baking bread and experimenting with a food processor, which is new since I last took cooking seriously. We planted a garden our first year at home and struggled to can or dry or freeze the almost inexhaustible supply of vegetables that we harvested ourselves. Walking through the woods and fields for miles without seeing a house, and only rarely meeting a car while bicycling along the back roads around our home, are luxuries we hadn't fully appreciated before. We've learned again to anticipate the seasons of nature and gather the wild fruits, such as plums, blackberries, mayhaws, and persimmons, that grow along or near the rural trails. And having my mother close by to call for a recipe or just enjoy seeing every day is a joy.

We haven't been isolated in Plains; visitors come from far and wide to see our community and to visit us. Our first year at home President Sadat came to see us, and Jehan has returned on several occasions. Prime Minister Begin made the journey as well as the former prime minister of Japan, Fukuda. Former President Giscard d'Estaing of France and Anne-Aymone, his wife, came to see us. Some of the hostage families also have come to discuss their experiences in Iran, and we have welcomed Cabinet members and others who worked with us in Washington. And Plains is a popular tourist spot. Though we don't have the crowds that once overran our small town, on any day one can find people from many states driving through and visiting the small "campaign headquarters" that was once the railroad station.

Along with our old friends John and Betty Pope, we built a log cabin in the north Georgia mountains on Turniptown Creek, with a beautiful waterfall and small rapids in our front yard. Jimmy designed and built most of the furniture for the cabin, and everything down to the pans in the kitchen is fresh and new and exactly what I wanted.

We have traveled in our own country as well as to China and Japan, Scandinavia and Central Europe, the Middle East, and, our latest trip, to Australia and New Zealand—often on business, but sometimes just for fun. Now we can enjoy more fully those people and places that were once obscured by the heavy schedule and full entourage of the presidency. Sometimes we've even taken along a grandchild who is old enough to enjoy the trip.

While our own lives seem to be settling down, the rest of the family seems to be doing just the opposite. Our house is especially quiet since Amy's departure last fall to a boarding school near Atlanta. We were reluctant to see her leave, but at sixteen Amy has become, among other things, a very persuasive young lady. She is thoroughly enjoying the challenge of a more demanding academic schedule and the relative freedom her new life offers.

Jack and Judy have moved from Georgia to Illinois, where Jack works at the Chicago Board of Trade and Judy works in a public relations firm. Chip, who was divorced from Caron while we were in the White House, moved back to Plains and has recently married Ginger Hodges, an accountant. Jeff and Annette remained in the Washington area, where they are partners in a very successful computer software business. Our grandchildren—Jason, eight, Sarah, five, and James, seven—are now old enough to visit without their parents, and we are expecting the arrival of our fourth grandchild later in the spring, when Jeff and Annette become parents for the first time. Jimmy has already provided a handmade cradle.

Billy overcame his problems with alcohol even before we left the White House, and he and his family are now living and prospering in Waycross, Georgia.

There have also been major unsettling changes in our family. The deaths of Jimmy's mother, Miss Lillian, and his sister Ruth within a few weeks of each other last fall brought about the abrupt passing of a long and eventful era in the Carter family. Miss Lillian was always, by sheer force of personality, the strongest link that held together her collection of strong-willed and independent children, in-laws, grandchildren, and great-grandchildren. I loved her and admired her strength. We are all diminished by her absence.

And losing Ruth, my special lifelong friend, has left a void that I don't know how to fill.

During the last few months as I finished this book I have been thinking about what I want to do next. As much as I enjoy being at home and having a "normal" life, I know there is still much that needs to be done. The Carter Center in Atlanta is already exploring ways to improve human life and to promote peace. The response to the idea both here and from other countries has been gratifying. Jimmy's commitment to human rights and his willingness to take the political risks of failure in negotiating peace are still appreciated all over the world.

I'm involved in an organization, the Friendship Force, that I helped initiate while Jimmy was President. It's an exchange program whose purpose is to further friendship and understanding among the different peoples of the world. Visitors live in foreign countries with host families with whom they have been matched by occupation and interest. More than 160,000 people have already participated in this exchange, and this number should continue to grow.

Then there are those causes I have followed for many years. The need to provide adequate services for the mentally afflicted is urgent, and I have just begun discussions with Emory University officials about ways that will allow me to continue my work from an institutional base. I will also continue my efforts on behalf of women and the elderly and poor, who today have a smaller public voice than ever. There are other concerns that all of us share. World tensions and bloodshed are increasing, and our country has become more and more dependent on armed intervention instead of peaceful negotiation to resolve disputes; and we seem to be joined in a horrifying escalation of the nuclear arms race.

When Jimmy was President and we went to Camp David for the weekend, the cares sometimes seemed far away, but the problems and the needs and the responsibilities always summoned us back. And I can't remember ever not being willing, even anxious, to assume the weight of the responsibilities again, feeling sure that the course Jimmy was taking was best for our country. I am still convinced of it today and wonder what it would be like to be in Washington with stable oil prices, grain stored by a previous administration to help over a drought year, all the hostages safely home, and Jimmy Carter's steady hand at the helm.

With his philosophy of fiscal conservatism and compassion, I

believe our country would be well on the way to curing some of
the ills that are now threatening to tear our society apart and divide
us even more than ever before into the haves and have-nots. But
that's water over the dam, and our country is still very strong.
We're strong enough to withstand personalities, parties, and policies, and though it may take a while, we will be all right again—
and maybe learn a lesson or two in the process. But one thing I
know: things would be different if we were back in the White
House.

I would be out there campaigning right now if Jimmy would
run again. I miss the world of politics. Nothing is more thrilling
than the urgency of a campaign—the planning, the strategy sessions, getting out among people you'd never otherwise meet—
and the tremendous energy it takes that makes a victory ever so
sweet and a loss so devastating. I'd like people to know that we
were right, that what Jimmy Carter was doing was best for our
country, and that people made a mistake by not voting for him.
But when all is said and done, for me, our loss at the polls is the
biggest single reason I'd like to be back in the White House. I
don't like to lose.

Plains, Georgia
February 1984

Index